Wildlife Forensics

Wildlife Forensics

Methods and Applications

Edited by

Jane E. Huffman
East Stroudsburg University, USA

John R. Wallace
Millersville University, USA

WILEY-BLACKWELL
A John Wiley & Sons, Ltd., Publication

This edition first published 2012 © 2012 by John Wiley & Sons, Ltd

Wiley-Blackwell is an imprint of John Wiley & Sons, formed by the merger of Wiley's global Scientific, Technical and Medical business with Blackwell Publishing.

Registered office: John Wiley & Sons, Ltd, The Atrium, Southern Gate, Chichester, West Sussex, PO19 8SQ, UK

Editorial offices: 9600 Garsington Road, Oxford, OX4 2DQ, UK
The Atrium, Southern Gate, Chichester, West Sussex, PO19 8SQ, UK
111 River Street, Hoboken, NJ 07030-5774, USA

For details of our global editorial offices, for customer services and for information about how to apply for permission to reuse the copyright material in this book please see our website at www.wiley.com/wiley-blackwell.

Library of Congress Cataloging-in-Publication Data

Huffman, Jane E.
Wildlife forensics : methods and applications / Jane E. Huffman, John R. Wallace.
p. cm.
Includes bibliographical references and index.
ISBN 978-0-470-66258-8 (cloth) – ISBN 978-0-470-66259-5 (pbk.)
1. Wildlife crime investigation. 2. Forensic sciences. 3. Wildlife crimes. I. Wallace, John R. (John Robert), 1960- II. Title.
HV8079.W58H84 2011
363.25′93367–dc23

2011031523

A catalogue record for this book is available from the British Library.

This book is published in the following electronic formats: ePDF 9781119953135; Wiley Online Library 9781119953142; ePub 9781119954293; Mobi 9781119954309

Set in 10/11.5 pt Sabon by Aptara Inc., New Delhi, India

First Impression 2012

Printed in Singapore

M WEP278177 160424

This book is dedicated to all wildlife agents/investigators for their outstanding service in protecting and conserving wildlife resources. We remember those wildlife conservation officers who gave the ultimate sacrifice so that others may enjoy the beauty and bounty of wildlife.

Contents

Developments in Forensic Science

The world of forensic science is changing at a very fast pace. This is in terms of the provision of forensic science services, the development of technologies and knowledge and the interpretation of analytical and other data as it is applied within forensic practice. Practicing forensic scientists are constantly striving to deliver the very best for the judicial process and as such need a reliable and robust knowledge base within their diverse disciplines. It is hoped that this book series will be a valuable resource for forensic science practitioners in the pursuit of such knowledge.

The Forensic Science Society is the professional body for forensic practitioners in the United Kingdom. The Society was founded in 1959 and gained professional body status in 2006. The Society is committed to the development of the forensic sciences in all of its many facets and in particular to the delivery of highly professional and worthwhile publications within these disciplines through ventures such as this book series.

Dr. Niamh Nic Daéid
Series editor

About the Editors

Dr. Jane Huffman, Ph.D. is the director of the Northeast Wildlife DNA Laboratory at East Stroudsburg University, where her work focuses on the application of genetic methods to wildlife law enforcement and conservation management. She runs wildlife DNA forensic training courses for conservation officers from New Jersey and Pennsylvania.

She, along with her students, has undertaken a wide range of applied research projects including the development of DNA profiling systems for game species in PA and NJ and microscopic hair characterization. The laboratory provides species identification tests for illegally sold wild meat. She provides forensic analysis and expert witness testimony in PA wildlife crime prosecutions

Dr. Huffman is also the graduate student coordinator for the Department of Biological Sciences at East Stroudsburg University.

Dr. John R. Wallace, Ph.D., D-ABFE, F-AAFS, is one of 15 board-certified forensic entomologists and a diplomate of the American Board of Forensic Entomology. Dr. Wallace is a Professor of Biology and focuses on teaching courses in Entomology, Aquatic Biology, Aquatic Entomology, Forensic Entomology, Forensic Science, and Ecology and Evolution. His research interests cover topics such as mosquito and disease ecology as well as mosquito and blackfly surveillance, and the role of aquatic organisms such as insects, algae and crayfish on decomposition within forensic science.

As a forensic entomologist, Dr. Wallace has participated in criminal investigations all over the country since 1995. He has taught forensic entomology courses at the University level and workshops at various universities to law enforcement throughout the United States, published more than 45 articles or book chapters in National/International journals. He is a Fellow of the American Academy of Forensic Science and an active member since 2002. Dr. Wallace is a co-founder and past President of the North American Forensic Entomology Association (NAFEA) in 2005 as well as the editor-elect for the NAFEA newsletter.

Contributors

Barry W. Baker, M.A.
U.S. National Fish and Wildlife Forensics Laboratory,
United States Fish & Wildlife Service,
1490 East Main Street,
Ashland, OR 97520-1310, USA

Jason H. Byrd, Ph.D., D-ABFE, F-AAFS
William R. Maples Center for Forensic Medicine,
Department of Pathology, Immunology, and Laboratory Medicine,
College of Medicine,
University of Florida,
Gainesville, FL, USA

Suchitra Changtragoon, Ph.D.
Forest Genetics and Biotechnology Division,
Forest and Plant Conservation Research Office,
Department of National Parks, Wildlife and Plant Conservation,
61 Phaholyothin, Chatuchak,
Bangkok,
Thailand 10900

Elizabeth M. Erhart, Ph.D.
Department of Anthropology,
Texas State University-San Marcos,
601 University Drive,
San Marcos, TX 78666, USA

Edgard O. Espinoza, Ph.D.
U.S. National Fish and Wildlife Forensics Laboratory,
United States Fish & Wildlife Service,
1490 East Main Street,
Ashland, OR 97520-1310, USA

Jesica L. Espinoza, J.D.
Office of Law Enforcement,
United States Fish & Wildlife Service,
16507 SW Roy Rogers Road,
Sherwood, OR 97140-9292, USA

Michelle D. Hamilton, Ph.D., D-ABFA
Department of Anthropology,
Texas State University-San Marcos,
601 University Drive,
San Marcos, TX 78666, USA

Christopher R. Hardy, Ph.D.
James C. Parks Herbarium,
Department of Biology,
Millersville University,
Millersville, PA 17551, USA

DeeDee Hawk, M.S.
Wyoming Game and Fish Wildlife Forensic Laboratory,
Department 3312,
1000 E University Avenue,
Laramie, WY 82071, USA

Jane E. Huffman, Ph.D., M.P.H.
Northeast Wildlife DNA Laboratory,
Department of Biological Sciences,
East Stroudsburg University,
East Stroudsburg, PA, 18301, USA

Rebecca N. Johnson, Ph.D.
Australian Museum, Head of Research
DNA Laboratory,
6 College Street,
Sydney, NSW 2010, Australia

Shamus P. Keeler, M.Ed., M.S.
Southeastern Cooperative Wildlife Disease Study,
Department of Population Health,
College of Veterinary Medicine,
University of Georgia, Athens, GA 30602
Department of Infectious Diseases,
College of Veterinary Medicine,
University of Georgia, Athens, GA 30602, USA

Lisa Knecht, M.S.
Northeast Wildlife DNA Laboratory,
East Stroudsburg University,
East Stroudsburg, PA 18301, USA

Irving L. Kornfield, Ph.D.
Molecular Forensics Laboratory,
University of Maine,
Orono, ME, USA

David L. Martin, Ph.D.
Canorus Ltd.,
5669 Snell Ave. #297,
San Jose, CA 95123,

David S. Martin
James C. Parks Herbarium,
Department of Biology,
Millersville University,
Millersville, PA 17551, USA

Sabrina N. McGraw, D.V.M., M.S.
Southeastern Cooperative Wildlife Disease Study,
Department of Population Health,
College of Veterinary Medicine,
University of Georgia, Athens, GA 30602
Department of Pathology,
College of Veterinary Medicine,
University of Georgia, Athens, GA 30602, USA

Michael McMaster, J.D.
20234 E Lake Cir,
Centennial, CO 80016-1281, USA

M. Katherine Moore, M.S.
Marine Forensics Program,
Center for Coastal Environmental Health and Biomolecular Research,
National Centers for Coastal Ocean Science,
National Ocean Service,
National Oceanic and Atmospheric Administration,
219 Fort Johnson Road,
Charleston, SC 29412 USA

Robert Ogden, Ph.D.
Program Director,
TRACE Wildlife Forensics Network,
c/o The Animal Conservation and Education Department,
Royal Zoological Society of Scotland,
134 Corstorphine Road,
Edinburgh EH12 6TS, UK

Douglas E. Roscoe, M.S., Ph.D.
New Jersey Division of Fish and Wildlife,
Office of Fish and Wildlife Health and Forensics,
P.O. Box 394,
Lebanon, NJ 08833, USA

Eric G. Roscoe, J.D., LL.M.
5415 Connecticut Ave. NW,
Washington, DC 20015, USA

Jill C. Ross, B.S.
Department of Biology,
Millersville University,
Millersville, PA 17551, USA

Michelle R. Sanford, Ph.D.
Department of Entomology
2475 TAMU
College Station, TX 77843-2475, USA

William Stansley, M.S.
New Jersey Division of Fish and Wildlife,
Office of Fish and Wildlife Health and Forensics,
P.O. Box 394,
Lebanon, NJ 08833, USA

Lerah K. Sutton, B.A.
William R. Maples Center for Forensic Medicine,
Department of Pathology, Immunology, and Laboratory Medicine,
College of Medicine,
University of Florida,
Gainesville, FL, USA

Jeffery K. Tomberlin, Ph.D., D-ABFE, F-AAFS
Forensic & Investigative Sciences Program,
Department of Entomology,
2475 TAMU,
College Station, TX 77843-2475, USA

Pepper W. Trail, Ph.D.
U.S. National Fish and Wildlife Forensics Laboratory,
United States Fish & Wildlife Service,
1490 East Main Street,
Ashland, OR 97520-1310, USA

John R. Wallace, Ph.D., D-ABFE, F-AAFS
Department of Biology,
Millersville University,
Millersville, PA 17551, USA

B.S. Weir, Ph.D.
Department of Biostatistics,
University of Washington,
Seattle,
WA 09195-7232, USA

Foreword

Killing wild animals is big business. While much wildlife trade is legal, a massive black market exists. The species and products involved run the gamut from tarantulas to tigers. The rarer the animal, the more people want it. As a result, wildlife trafficking targets those species already under threat and least able to withstand the losses.

Laws to protect wildlife can be found in international treaties, like the Convention on International Trade in Endangered Species (CITES), and in national legislation, such as the Lacey Act and Endangered Species Act in the United States. Yet, to be effective, those laws require enforcement.

Enforcement involves not only catching poachers and traffickers but also prosecuting and convicting them. For that, one must link a suspect to his or her crime. The problem is, when an animal is hunted down and killed, there aren't any eyewitness accounts. The victims' relatives and neighbors can't talk. And once the victim leaves the poachers hands, it's sliced and diced and processed until it's eventually transformed into a host of consumable products – from trinkets and high fashion accessories to traditional medicines. Its identity is lost. That makes the prospects for prosecution slimmer and slimmer.

Wildlife forensics changes that. By identifying the victim and allowing the evidence to speak, it connects suspects to their illegal actions.

Wildlife forensics, like human forensics, uses science to answer a legal question. For wildlife forensic scientists, however, most of the time that legal question is to identify the victim. For wildlife crimes, figuring out *what the victim is* is essential to establish that a crime even took place. That's because some species are protected and others are not. For instance, a wool shawl made from cashmere goats is legal but one from Tibetan antelopes is not. Traffickers know the differences in the laws so that, when caught, they often claim that the item they smuggled is legal because it's from an unprotected species. Unless an investigator proves otherwise, the suspect goes free. That's where wildlife forensics comes in: proving the crime.

Identification of a species from a part or product is extremely complicated. For example, take an item like a feathered headdress. Normally, ornithologists have a lot to go on when they identify a bird: its size, shape, plumage pattern, geographical location, habitat, vocalizations, flight pattern, diet and other behavior. But when a forensic ornithologist receives that item in his or her lab, (s)he has just a fragment of that information to go on – often just an isolated feather.

Most birds have about 5,000 feathers. Within the same species, those feathers will vary depending on their location on the bird and whether they are from males or females, or juveniles or adults. To complicate matters, feathers from one part of the bird – like the wing or tail – might exhibit diagnostic characteristics, meaning something unique to that species, while feathers from another part of that same bird – like the chest – might not. The same thing happens with claws or teeth. A single species can display significant variation, and there may or may not be distinguishing traits for each variation.

Now, imagine you don't even know what the part is. Imagine the evidence is a tooth or tusk that's been carved, so that you no longer have the size or shape to go on. Or a rhino horn or bear gall bladder that's been ground up into a medicine. For each species, wildlife forensic scientists must find some sort of identifying characteristic. Not only that, but they have to do it for each part of each species, and they need to account for the many different ways a part might be processed or manufactured.

The complexities don't stop there. Wildlife forensic scientists have to be ready to answer new types of legal questions as they occur. Sometimes that will still mean answering the "what is it?" question but for species that are newly protected. Other times, it will mean focusing on a different question, like "where did it come from?" When trade is permitted for distinct populations of otherwise protected species, as has happened with the recent one-off sales of elephant ivory from southern African stockpiles, the ability to tell where a sample came from is critical. The "where did it come from?" question of geographic origin is also a critical question to determine whether an exotic pet was captive-bred, which typically is legal, or wild-caught, which is not. For each part of each species, and for the legal question involved, the characteristic might be different, and the method for finding them may also vary.

In my view, *Wildlife Forensics: Methods and Applications* will go a long way toward helping share information and advancing the field of wildlife forensic science. Every step – whether it's a new case that results in uncovering an identifying characteristic for a species' part or a budding scientist exploring these issues – pushes the science forward. The end result will be more and more heroes able to link suspects to their crimes – and ultimately a slowdown in the extent of wildlife trafficking.

Rhinos can't call 911. Instead, law enforcement agents, and the wildlife forensic science that support them, give them a voice – one that grows stronger every day. This book will help in that vital mission.

Laurel A. Neme, Ph.D.
Author, *ANIMAL INVESTIGATORS: How the World's First Wildlife Forensics Lab is Solving Crimes and Saving Endangered Species*
May 2011

Acknowledgements

The editors of this work would like to extend our deepest appreciation and gratitude to the contributors of this text. This book would not have been possible without the diverse experiences, professional efforts and research endeavors of those who contributed. JH would like to thank Terri Ombrello and Kim Harle for their invaluable assistance and comments, Alan Semon and Matt Guesto for logistical assistance. JW would like to thank Susan, Harrison and Max Wallace, Peg Wallace, Ann and Bob Stackpole, Ostrowski/Sikora/Sheaffer families for logistical assistance to be able to work on this book and to Laurie Goodrich (Hawk Mountain Sanctuary) and Wallace research lab for their invaluable discussions.

1

Wildlife Ownership

How the state became responsible for management

Eric G. Roscoe and Michael McMaster

Introduction

Forensic techniques that identify wildlife, and assist in linking wildlife crimes to the responsible party are invaluable to the legal community. This book has been devoted to assisting law enforcement in the identification of individuals responsible for wildlife crimes. The identification techniques provided by forensic science are even more important in the courtroom. Oftentimes law enforcement has a good idea as to who committed a crime, and simple investigative techniques will reveal the most likely suspect. However, once that suspect is identified, focus turns to providing enough admissible proof in court so that a conviction can be obtained. DNA identification has permitted attorneys to quantify facts that in the past where left up to impressions. Proof that meat found in a suspect's freezer matches with 98% certainty a carcass found in the woods removes the factual issue from the table. The judge or jury only needs to consider whether the law, as applied to the fact that the freezer meat matched the carcass, requires that the suspect be found guilty or not. There may be due process problems inherent in jurors' willingness to accept DNA evidence as infallible without being able to properly weigh the effects of mishandled evidence or improper gathering techniques, however, that is beyond the scope this book (DeWitt, 1996).

The question of the law is separate from the factual question in the case. In criminal proceedings the prosecutor decides which law is to be applied, meaning which law has been violated. The prosecutor and, if there is a jury, the judge will

Wildlife Forensics: Methods and Applications, First Edition. Edited by Jane E. Huffman and John R. Wallace.

explain the law that the suspect is accused of breaking, and what facts the state will prove in order to find the suspect guilty.

The purpose of this section is to address the question of law. State authorities draft most laws regulating the taking of wildlife in the US. The federal government tends to regulate broader issues that concern the transportation of wildlife across state lines as well as internationally. State and federal governmental authority to regulate the taking of wildlife is derived from a legal history stretching nearly 2,700 years. The first half of this section follows the development of wildlife regulation from the property rights of ancient Rome through the royal prerogatives of King Charles' England to the unlimited resources of Colonial America. The second half focuses on present-day state, federal, and international regulations affecting the taking, transportation, and management of wildlife.

Ancient Rome and the Concept of *Res Nullius*

Ownership is a pivotal concept in understanding the Roman citizen's relationship with wildlife. Some of the earliest legal writings, dating back to the time of the Sumerians in ancient Mesopotamia, recognize the ability of humans to own or possess animals (Wise, 1996). The concept of wildlife as property allows separation between what is mine and what is yours. This is my dog, not your dog. In the legal realm, ownership is incredibly important when determining schemes of compensation. Laws based upon the economics of owning property allow compensation for damaged or stolen property (ibid.). You have killed my dog so you must give me your dog or financially compensate me. Ownership of the dog as if it were property allows the law to create a resolution to situations in which one suffers a loss. If I could not own the dog, then I would suffer a loss for which there is no compensation if the dog is killed or stolen by another.

The Romans divided property into three main categories: *res publicae*, *res communes*, and *res nullius* (Blumm and Lucus, 2005). *Res publicae* refers to things owned by the state such as roads, ports, rivers, and public buildings. *Res communes* includes things that belong to the community like air, running water, and the sea. *Res nullius* are things owned by no one such as unoccupied lands, property of the enemy captured in battle, and wildlife. Things labeled as *res nullius* only belonged to no one as long as no one had taken possession of the item through *Occupatio* (Wise, 1996). An individual could own wildlife only after physically capturing the animal (Blumm and Lucus, 2005). If the animal escaped the cage, then it became *res nullius* again, if the animal fell dead on neighboring property, the property owner maintained the right to prevent a hunter from trespassing to retrieve the game (Wise, 1996).

Roman law saw wildlife in the open as owned by no one until it was captured. English law took a different perspective. Wildlife was property under English common law, but instead of being owned by no one, it was owned by the king.

Common Law England: The King's Ownership

The English took the Roman understanding of ownership one step further, and eliminated the need for capture. In Rome, one was prevented from trespassing on someone else's property to hunt wildlife. English law concluded that if a restriction could be made on the land one owned, then it would make sense that the ability to restrict access to the wildlife on that land would imply a similar ownership in the wildlife (Blackstone, 1979).

During the time of the early Britons, England was replete with game, which they hunted for sustenance. The arrival of the Saxons brought domestication of wildlife, and the cultivation of lands. As the Saxons planted fields and staked off their own respective plots of land, they pushed wildlife off into the forested areas. The forests had never been distributed to private owners, and therefore they belonged to the Crown (ibid.). As wildlife now resided in these large forests, the king took ownership of them and reserved the right to hunt them. However, anyone owning their own land still had the right to pursue game within the confines of their privately owned property (ibid.).

With the Norman Conquest came a new view of the king and his powers. There is still debate over whether the Normans actually introduced feudalism to England. What is certain is that the Normans helped to establish a new system of property rights within England, but whether it could properly be called the traditional feudal pyramid power structure is a question best left to historians (Thomas, 2008). The right to pursue and take wildlife was vested with the king, and only those granted authority by the king. The king possessed a right known as the chase and he held the title of "lord paramount of the fee" (Blackstone, 1979). These two concepts combined to give the king the power to pursue game no matter where it might be, and these principles removed the right of anyone else, regardless of their status as landowners, to hunt wildlife. Once all the rights to pursue game and own them as property became vested in the king, the only way individuals could acquire a right to property in wildlife was through particular privileges granted directly by the king himself (ibid.).

There were four specific grants that permitted an individual to hunt game. These were: the chase, the park, the free warren, and the free fishery. The king reserved the forests for himself, and granted authority to others through chases and parks. A chase or park was a designation given to property that different individuals owned. If someone owned a chase or park, the king had granted that person the authority to hunt any game found on that land (ibid.). The park was more limited than the chase because the right to hunt extended only over one's own property, whereas the chase allowed a person to hunt on other people's property (Blumm and Lucus, 2005). Some of the more powerful lords turned their own property into parks, and hunted the grounds for leisure and sport. The lords maintained full authority to hunt their own parks as long as the land did not fall within forests that the king owned, in which case separate permission would have to be granted by the king (Green, 1997). The grant of warren was another type of property, the owner of which was allowed only to hunt "inferior species" including waterfowl and small upland game. The grant of free fishery permitted a person to take and kill fish from public streams and rivers (Blackstone, 1979). Individuals possessing a grant were the only people in England permitted to acquire a property right in wildlife.

Unlike in Rome, the right to capture wildlife was not affected by whether one owned the property upon which he or she was hunting, but rather by what type of grant the individual possessed. Determining who owned a particular animal after it was pursued and subsequently killed could result in very odd decisions, at least by today's standards. If individual A has a chase, chase in the sense that he owns property on which he is permitted to hunt and may also hunt on property owned by others, and individual B owns an adjoining chase, the wildlife on each chase belong to the chase's respective owner. If a deer walks from chase A to chase B and is killed by the owner of chase B, then owner B possesses a property right in that deer. Likewise, if A finds a deer on B's chase and kills it, the deer belongs to B due to his ownership of the chase on which it was killed. If, however, owner A is hunting on his own property and his pursuit of a deer leads him to kill it in chase B, then A would possess a property right in that deer. The effort A places in pursuing the game vests a property right in A's subsequent success even though he did not kill the game on his own property (ibid.).

If the hypothetical scenario is changed just slightly, a less familiar result can be obtained. Assume that instead of A, a property owner with the grant of chase from the king, we have C, a property owner with no particular grant. C is trespassing on A's property and begins pursuit of a deer. The deer is subsequently killed on B's chase. The result is A still possesses ownership in the deer. Since C had no right to begin pursuit of the deer, his efforts in the chase do not serve to divest A of his original right of ownership in the deer (ibid.).

The system of grants developed as a result of the natural evolution of property rights in England, and along with the grants came specific justifications for their existence and maintenance. Four reasons stood out more than most. The first reason was to encourage the improvement of land by ensuring that a landowner had exclusive ownership over everything in and on his land. The second helped to preserve certain species by preventing over-harvest. The third reason ensured that farmers and craftsmen would not take up hunting as a hobby, thus keeping them hard at work harvesting and building. The final and most important reason for grants was that they protected against insurrection from the peasant classes (Blackstone, 1979).

While hunting restrictions were in place to help preserve certain populations of wildlife, that goal was ultimately tangential to the main interest of maintaining class distinctions (Blumm and Lucus, 2005). It would be much more difficult for the peasants to revolt and overthrow the ruling class if it was illegal for them to own firearms. If peasants did not have the right to hunt, then there was no reason to legalize firearm ownership for their class. In addition, the lack of target practice ensured the ruling class that even if the revolting peasants did manage to get their hands on firearms, they would not possess the skills necessary to utilize them effectively. William Blackstone in his commentaries discusses how the conquering feudal lords benefitted by arming their militaries while at the same time ensuring that the native conquered citizens did not have the arms necessary to fight back (Blackstone, 1979, p. 413).

As any elementary school class learns, the restrictions on English people, particularly those relating to religious freedom, led to the Pilgrims landing at Plymouth Rock (Ward, 2006). What lay before them was a vast untouched wilderness. The fact that the land was unclaimed, there were vast quantities of wildlife, and the societal class structure had no place in the New World, meant the new settlers had no need for restrictions on hunting or fishing.

The New World: Hunting for the Market

Settlers in America, instead of transferring the English notion of grants, adopted a more Roman approach, utilizing the rule of capture to determine ownership in wildlife. Three major influences brought about the abandonment of the English system. The first being the reasons for settlement in America. Citizens of England fled because of oppressive English policies, one of which was the restriction of hunting only to those with sufficient wealth or status. The second and more pressing reason was the need for food and clothing. Hunting was not just a sport to be pursued in one's leisure time, but rather a means of survival. The third influence on early settlers was the genuine expanse of America. There was so much unsettled wilderness that any regulation of those areas would hinder economic growth. This need to develop the New World, commonly referred to as Manifest Destiny, led to a further development in the rule of capture known as the "free take imperative" (Blumm and Lucus, 2005).

The concept of free take stems from a mindset that is very different than that of modern-day Americans. In most modern American cities the majority of people commute in to work from the suburbs. People actually seek out areas of the country where they can escape the city and find their own little piece of wilderness (Barta, 1999). The early settlers saw the wilderness as an unclean, dangerous area, and settlers implemented policies designed to tame the wilderness and expand civilization. A good example of this drive toward expansion can be seen from the top of the Governor's Mansion in Colonial Williamsburg. During the 1700s if one were to climb into the cupola that sat atop the mansion, one could look 6 miles to the south and see the James River and if one looked 7 miles to the north, one could see the York River. What one would not see is a single tree. Every tree between both riverbanks had been cut down because people did not want to live in or near the wilderness. How these policies were applied to hunting is best exemplified by the case of *Pierson v. Post*, this case is known by law school students as the first case they ever read in Property.

Pierson v. Post involved two hunters: one hunter, Post, pursued a fox with hounds along a piece of unowned wasteland. The other hunter, Pierson, knew of the pursuit by Post. Waiting until the opportunity presented itself, Pierson shot the fox and carried it off, effectively preventing Post from capturing the animal (*Pierson v. Post* [1805] 3 Cai. R. 175, 180). The issue in the case was, who had the legal right of ownership in the fox? The Supreme Court of New York looked to ancient texts of medieval law as well as the writings of an old German jurist (*Pierson v. Post* [1805] 3 Cai. R. 175, 177). The justices could not turn to British case law to resolve the issue since most cases involving ownership in wildlife had been resolved either according to statute or according to the rights of the landowner. The court was addressing the question of pursuit without the usual guideposts provided by landownership. They had to determine whether pursuit alone was sufficient to create an ownership right in the animal being pursued (*Pierson v. Post* [1805] 3 Cai. R. 175, 178).

Regardless of the sympathy felt for Post, the individual who expended the effort in pursuing the fox, the court held that only through the killing or physical restraint of the animal could one take ownership. The animal must be deprived of its natural liberty through a mortal wounding, netting or ensnaring in order for an individual to rightly claim possession (*Pierson v. Post* [1805] 3 Cai. R. 175, 179). The dissenting justice on the Pierson Court was concerned with the chilling effect created by such a rule, and argued that the pursuer should take a right in the fox since the advancement of society would be fulfilled by the "destruction of a beast so pernicious and incorrigible" as the fox (*Pierson v. Post* [1805] 3 Cai. R. 175, 182). The viewpoint of all the justices was that the elimination of the fox was beneficial for economic expansion, they just disagreed as to which conclusion would result in the least amount of future ownership disputes in wildlife. *Pierson v. Post* set a precedent that the individuals killing the animal took possession, thus alleviating problems associated with wildlife pursued for short periods of time and then subsequently killed by another individual.

The development of a legal standard that recognized the individual mortally wounding, snaring, or netting an animal as the person with a right to possession helped to move hunting of wild animals into a marketplace pursuit. In the modern day, companies develop new innovative products because of the protection provided by patents. If a company develops a new invention and obtains a patent for it, they can enjoy exclusive distribution and use of that invention for a set period of time (Bravin, 2008). The right to possession in a mortally wounded animal or netted bird created a similar certainty to that of modern-day patent law. If a whale was killed by company X and later discovered by company Z, company X had a right of possession in that whale even though the mortal wound did not result in the whale being immediately landed (*Ghen v. Rich* [1881] 8 F. 159, 160). Unlike in *The Old Man and the Sea* (Hemingway, 1952), "I am a tired old man. But I have killed this fish," or perhaps more like in *Moby Dick* (Melville, 1949), whales often ripped the harpoon lines free of the ship and custom dictated that the first harpoon to stick and hold created a right of ownership in that whale (*Ghen v. Rich* [1881] 8 F. 159, 161).

With the certainty created by the law of property combined with incredible technological developments in firearms, whaling vessels, and rail systems, America was able to expand at a blistering pace, and the market in wild game expanded along with it. Unfortunately, wildlife were not able to keep pace with technology. The ability to kill wildlife faster than they could reproduce decimated populations. Passenger pigeons numbered in the tens of millions in the early 1800s, but due to over-harvest for market, the last passenger pigeon died in captivity on September 1, 1914 (Wilcove, 2008). By 1880, the population of buffalo in America had been reduced from tens of millions to less than a few herds (ibid.). The concept of hunting for market needed to give way to what we now call conservation.

Conservation of Wildlife Through Sport Hunting

While hunting regulations imposed by the aristocracy in England worked in an indirect way to maintain populations of wildlife, the US developed its own form of aristocracy in the captains of industry which eventually led to the conservation programs everyone knows today. Theodore Roosevelt was the biggest proponent of helping to preserve American wildlife for future generations. Much like the aristocracy of England, the wealthier individuals in America did not hunt for market or sustenance, but for sport. By the late 1880s, it had become clear that something needed to be done about the decimation of wildlife. One could not walk a few feet across the western plains without seeing buffalo bones, but could walk for hundreds of miles without seeing a single live buffalo (ibid.). Theodore Roosevelt helped to establish the first lobbying firm for conservation of big game species known as the Boone and Crockett Club (Brinkley, 2009). "If his father could found the American Museum of Natural History from a parlor in Manhattan, Theodore saw no reason why this group, meeting in the cramped uptown quarters . . . couldn't save buffalo and elk in the American West" (ibid.). A new legal doctrine had to take the place of free take, it was and still is known as "fair chase."

The notion of fair chase was not welcomed with open arms, after all there were huge industries devoted to hunting wildlife to sell at market, but one unfortunate event along with some favorable court rulings led to the ultimate success of sport hunting and sustainability-based conservation methods. The assassination of incumbent US President William McKinley thrust Theodore Roosevelt into the US presidency along with his policies and views about conservation. Theodore Roosevelt championed the idea of scientific management of resources; policies based on rational decisions made by trained experts could help to prevent scarcity of wildlife (Rothman, 2000). To implement these policies required a battle between what had been the traditional view of local control, and what was needed to help ensure conservation efforts were successful, which was centralized control. Not only would there be a question of the power of the federal government over the state, but also there would be disputes over the state's power to regulate the individual (ibid.). Free take represented zero regulation and destroyed wildlife populations. In order to restore those populations, fair chase, by its design, required regulation.

The legal concept behind fair chase is known as the public trust doctrine. Long before Theodore Roosevelt came into the public eye, in 1821 a New Jersey Supreme Court case helped lay the foundation of the public trust doctrine (Blumm and Lucus, 2005). *Arnold v. Mundy* examined the English concept of land vesting in the sovereign and turned it on its head. In England, the sovereign was the king, but in the US, the sovereign is the people. The people through an elected democratic republic run the country. Therefore, the court held that the use of navigable waterways was common to all the people. The use could only be curtailed by the sovereign to ensure the "order and protection" of the resource (*Arnold v. Mundy* [1821] 6 NJL 1, 12). The court established a notion of public trust, which permitted the states to regulate waterways for the order and protection of those waterways. Wildlife would slowly change from being *res nullius*, owned by no one until capture, into something more like *res communes or res publicae*, owned by everyone and subject to regulation by the state for the benefit of everyone.

Management: The Property Right of States

Who creates and enforces the law is oftentimes just as important as the underlying legal theories. In the United States, the power of the government is divided between the federal government and the various state governments. The United States Constitution directs the balance of power between these two sovereign bodies. The Constitution limits the power of the federal government to only those functions that are enumerated in the Constitution. State governments, however, are not similarly limited. Each state government possesses what are called "police powers." These powers are the general powers necessary to protect the safety and welfare of the citizens. Both state-level governments and the federal government participate in the creation and execution of wildlife law. But the balance of power has not always been clear.

The landmark Supreme Court case *Geer v. Connecticut* set the stage for the battle between state and federal governments over the regulation of wildlife, which lasted nearly one hundred years. The Court in *Geer* considered a Connecticut statute that prevented the transportation of game taken within Connecticut from being transported outside the state's borders. The issue was whether the Connecticut statute violated the Commerce Clause of the US Constitution. In resolving this issue, the Court relied on the public trust doctrine in stating that several states hold wildlife in trust for their citizens. By doing so, the Court recognized that the state is the owner of natural resources, such as wildlife, and can create laws and regulations which protect and secure its benefits for the citizens and future citizens.

The *Geer* case is historically important for two reasons. First, the decision's lasting impact on wildlife law was the recognition of the state ownership doctrine. But the decision is also important because the Court's rationale in *Geer* was used to suggest that the state's ownership of wildlife was to the exclusion of the federal government (Blumm and Lucus, 2005). If true, the federal government would not be able to regulate wildlife because wildlife would be under the exclusive authority of the states (Wood, 2000).

State ownership of wildlife was successively questioned in the years that followed *Geer*. Before *Geer* was overruled in 1979, the Supreme Court slowly weakened the exclusive powers of the state over wildlife. For example, the Supreme Court held the Constitution's Equal Protection Clause prevented state ownership from being used in a discriminatory manner. In *Takahashi v. Fish and Game Commissioner*, the Supreme Court held that the state of California could not withhold a commercial fishing license from a resident alien, while at the same time granting it to individuals with US citizenship. Simultaneously, the Supreme Court slowly acknowledged the expanding powers of the federal government. In *Missouri v. Holland*, the Court held that the Migratory Bird Treaty Act of 1918, an international treaty, superseded conflicting state laws pursuant to the Supremacy Clause. Thus, the attack on *Geer* came from both directions: the exclusive power of the state was limited and the power of the federal government was expanded.

In 1979, the Supreme Court overruled *Geer* in *Hughes v. Oklahoma*. The *Hughes* court applied an expanded theory of the Commerce Clause to invalidate an Oklahoma law, which prohibited the exportation of minnows from the state. The Commerce Clause is a clause in the US Constitution that empowers the federal government to regulate interstate commerce. Originally, the Supreme Court narrowly interpreted the Commerce Clause. But over time, the Supreme Court expanded its view, especially in response to the New Deal legislation during the Great Depression. In 1977, the Supreme Court held that the Commerce Clause applies to the regulation of wildlife (Blumm and Lucus, 2005). Two years later, in *Hughes*, the Supreme Court held that that federal power to regulate wildlife allowed for the Supreme Court to overrule *Geer*. But more important than what the *Hughes* case did, is what it did not do.

Under *Hughes*, the Supreme Court undermined the notion that the state ownership of wildlife made the regulation of the wildlife the exclusive domain of the state. Instead, the states would be subject to the supreme powers of the federal government and federal wildlife law would be analyzed under the federal government's power to regulate interstate commerce. However, the *Hughes* court left intact the public trust doctrine. This allowed the states to remain stewards of the land, free to regulate wildlife, but subject to the oversight of the federal government (ibid.).

Although *Hughes* expressly overruled *Geer*, the limits of the Hughes decision are important in understanding the proper scope of state wildlife regulation. First, the *Hughes* case subjects state regulation to constitutional limitations, such as the limits of the Equal Protection Clause as seen in *Takahashi*. Similarly, state law must comply with federal law. For example, a state statute cannot undermine the intent of the federal statute, or prohibit what a federal statute expressly permits (ibid.). Nevertheless, the *Hughes* case did not completely remove state stewardship of wildlife. The majority of states in the United States have statutory provisions that expressly endorse the state ownership doctrine and some have even included it in their state constitutions (ibid.). Further, each of the fifty separate legal regimes must work in conjunction with federal laws related to the regulation of the wildlife.

Federal Law and the Regulatory State

Even before the Supreme Court attempted to resolve the conflict between the federal government's constitutional powers and the state's ownership of wildlife, the federal government had undertaken efforts to regulate wildlife. The first federal statute that attempted to regulate wildlife was the Lacey Act of 1900. The Lacey Act made it illegal to transport game between two states taken in violation of state law. Although the statute benefited the nascent conservation movement, the Lacey Act was intended as a pest control measure (Kaile, 1993). By preventing interstate transportation of wildlife, the legislature sought to protect local crops and ecosystems from the potential dangers associated with the introduction of foreign species. Despite later amendments to the Lacey Act, the statute had limited impact on the actual regulation of wildlife. The importance of the Lacey Act is that it was the first step taken by the federal government to regulate the ownership rights of individuals in wildlife.

The next milestone in the expansion of federal regulation of wildlife was the passage of the Endangered Species Conservation Act in 1966. Unlike the Lacey Act, which focused on state law, the Endangered Species Act of 1966 involved the federal enforcement of exclusively federal law. As such, this act was the first comprehensive federal legislation specifically designed to protect wildlife (ibid.).

The 1966 Act was intended to reduce the risk of extinction by addressing some of the causes, specifically habitat destruction. The Act enabled the Secretary of the Interior to acquire lands as means to stop or prevent the extinction of a particular species. The Act, however, was quickly criticized as being largely ineffective. Critically, the Act's criteria were limited to the deleterious effect on habitation and did not address other reasons for extinction (ibid.).

As a result of these shortcomings, the Endangered Species Preservation Act of 1969 was passed. Importantly, the 1969 Act enhanced the provisions of both the 1966 Act and the Lacey Act. The 1969 Act required that the Secretary of the Interior develop a list of endangered species. Once on the list, the importation of the animal and its byproducts were prohibited. The 1969 Act also expanded conservation involvement, adding provisions that allow private individuals to petition for the protection of a certain species as well as calling for international participation by the United States in the protection of endangered species (ibid.).

Dissatisfaction with both the 1966 and 1969 Acts, and a growing conservation movement led to the passage of the Endangered Species Act of 1973. This Act served to replace the 1966 and 1969 Acts, and put into place the most expansive environmental protections of the time. The Act established the familiar structure of a two-part list. The Secretary of the Interior established an "Endangered" and a "Threatened" list based on separate criteria. These two lists permitted the proactive protection of species before they were on the brink of the extinction. Further, the Act expanded its scope to include plants and invertebrates (ibid.).

Arguably, the Endangered Species Act's most important provision was to require all federal agencies to use their authority to assist in the conservation of the threatened or endangered species. Moreover, the Act prevents federal agencies from acting if that action would threaten a listed species. These provisions of the Act represent the expansion of the regulatory state and its application to wildlife management. No longer is the management of wildlife left only to the states. Instead, it has become a combined effort of both the federal and state governments.

The basic structure of the Endangered Species Act has remained the same despite later amendments, including substantive amendments in 1978, 1982, 1988, and 2004. And since its passage, the federal government has continued to be an active participant in wildlife management through additional statutes and agency actions that are beyond the scope of this book. Once a theory developed about the state having some ownership interest in wildlife, the ability to protect and manage wildlife for the benefit of future generations became possible (Archer *et al.*, 1994).

Globalization: Working toward Worldwide Conservation Practices

As the human population expands and the exploitation of natural resources increases, the boundaries between nation-states become less important. This is especially true for wildlife because, by definition, wildlife does not abide by national boundaries. As a result, there has developed a growing body of international law relevant to wildlife.

While the expansion of international wildlife law in the past few decades dwarfs that of the previous two centuries, the first example of an international treaty intended to protect wildlife is the Treaty Concerning the Regulation of Salmon Fishing in the Rhine River Basin, signed in 1886 by Germany, Luxembourg, the Netherlands and Switzerland (Freyfogle and Goble, 2002). However, it has only been since the 1960s that there has been a concerted and sustained global effort to protect and manage wildlife.

International wildlife law is based largely on treaty law; the other source of public international law is what is known as "customary law." Moreover, the treaty-making process oftentimes codifies then-existing customary law. For example, during the 1973 Conference of the Law of the Sea, the generally accepted norm that coastal countries have the jurisdiction and sovereign right to protect and manage their surrounding marine environment was incorporated into the United Nations Convention on the Law of the Sea. Customary law, however, is not directed by a supreme sovereign. Instead, it originates from universally recognized practice (Lyster, 1985).

Treaties, on the other hand, are similar to contracts between individuals but are between nation-states. They can be between two nations (bilateral) or between several (multilateral). There is no standard or formalized method for the formation of a treaty because the global community is not governed by a single government. Instead, various organizations serve as the fountainhead for treaties. Important to the development of wildlife treaties has been the Organization of American States (OAS), the United Nations Educational, Scientific and Cultural Organization(UNESCO) and the International Union for Conservation of Nature (ibid.). Once a treaty is drafted, it becomes open for signatures. But a treaty is not binding as soon as a country signs it. Instead, a treaty must be ratified. The signature merely represents that that nation will make a good faith effort to ratify the treaty with its domestic government or make it known that it no longer intends to be a party to the treaty. Ratification varies by country; the United States requires the President's approval, with the advice and consent of the Senate. Only after this process will a treaty be binding between the signatory countries.

Wildlife treaties fall into three main categories. First, some treaties are limited to a specific species or related species. Second, other treaties focus on wildlife of a limited geographical area. Finally, some treaties attempt to address the regulation wildlife on a much broader scope without limitation of species or location (ibid.).

Treaties of the first type usually involve an economically valuable species that populate areas outside of the single national jurisdiction. An example of such a treaty is the 1931 International Convention for the Regulation of Whaling. The intended subjects of the treaty were without a doubt economically valuable, but were particularly vulnerable because they primarily lived beyond the reach of any one national legal system. Likewise, treaties of this kind are also relevant to migratory animals, especially birds, because the protections afforded to the species may vary between each country the animal travels through.

The second category of treaties is likewise limited in scope. In this case, the treaties are limited to a specific geographic region. An example of this type of treaty is the Convention on the Conservation of Antarctic Marine Living Resources. This treaty is an outgrowth of the Antarctic Treaty, where the signing parties agreed to several limits to the use of Antarctica. But the Antarctic Treaty did not contain provision related to the exploration or management of the wildlife located there. Instead, the Convention on the Conservation of Antarctic Marine Living Resources was intended to augment the Antarctic Treaty and preserve the living marine resources.

Finally, and perhaps most importantly, the final type of treaty are the treaties that are not limited to a specific species or geographical region. These treaties, however, are not unlimited in their scope. For example, the Convention on International Trade in Endangered Species of Wild Fauna and Flora (CITES) is limited to international trade. But its scope is so broad that it warrants distinction from the two previous categories. Other examples include the Convention concerning the Protection of the World Cultural and Natural Heritage and the

Convention on the Conservation of Migratory Species of Wild Animals. Each of these treaties is important in their own right, and collectively they represent an increasing global effort in wildlife management (Lyster, 1985). In effect, they represent the adoption of a global principle of conservation that parallels the public trust doctrine. Instead of a single state having a duty to protect wildlife for its own citizens, each nation has a similar duty for the benefit of every person.

Conclusion

We have tried to provide an understanding of the legal history supporting state and federal regulations. There are four important points in this chapter. First, animals are, and always have been, recognized as personal property capable of being owned by one or more people. Second, the free take doctrine led to the establishment of a market in wild game meat. Unfortunately, wildlife populations could not sustain the needs of a commercial market, and it became imperative to restrict the taking of wild game. Third, recognizing that the state owned the wildlife for the citizens created an obligation on the government to manage and conserve populations. And, fourth, as our scientific knowledge about wildlife populations has expanded and evolved, the need for international regulations, such as cohesive management plans for migratory birds, has arisen to ensure the continued success of wildlife conservation.

Cases Cited

Arnold v. Mundy [1821] 6 NJL 1.
Geer v. Connecticut [1896] 161 U.S. 519.
Ghen v. Rich [1881] 8 F. 159.
Hughes v. Oklahoma [1979] 441 U.S. 322.
Missouri v. Holland [1920] 252 U.S. 416.
Pierson v. Post [1805] 3 Cai. R. 175.
Takahashi v. Fish and Game Commissioner [1948] 334 U.S. 410.

References

Archer, J.H. *et al.* (1994) *The Public Trust Doctrine and the Management of America's Coasts*. Amherst, MA: University of Massachusetts Press.

Barta, P. (1999) Fear of sprawl prompts some cities to tighten up development rules. *The Wall Street Journal*, 3 February, T1.

Blackstone, W. (1979) *Commentaries on the Laws of England: A Facsimile of the First Edition of 1765–1796*, Vol. 2. Chicago: University of Chicago Press.

Blumm, M.C. and Lucus, R. (2005) Symposium article: the pioneer spirit and the public trust: the American rule of capture and state ownership of wildlife. *Lewis & Clark Law School Environmental Law*, **35**(Fall), 673–720.

Bravin, J. (2008) High Court further limits scope of patents. *The Wall Street Journal*, 10 June, A4.

Brinkley, D. (2009) *The Wilderness Warrior: Theodore Roosevelt and the Crusade for America*. New York: HarperCollins Publishers.

DeWitt, S.L. (1996) Note: the indigent criminal defendant, DNA evidence and the right to an expert witness: a comparison of the requirements of due process in State v. Dubose and Harris v. State. *The Boston University Public Interest Law Journal*, **6**(Fall), 267–291.

Environmental Law Institute (1977) *The Evolution of the National Wildlife Law*. Washington DC: author.

Freyfogle, E.T. and Goble, D.D. (2002) *Wildlife Law: Cases and Materials*. New York: Foundation Press.

Green, J.A. (1997) *The Aristocracy of Norman England*. Cambridge: Cambridge University Press.

Hemingway, E. (1952) *The Old Man and the Sea*. New York: Charles Scribner's Sons.

Kaile, D.K. (1993) Evolution of wildlife legislation in the United States: an analysis of the legal efforts to protect endangered species and the prospects for the future. *Georgetown International Environmental Law Review*, **55**, 441–478.

Lyster, S. (1985) *International Wildlife Law*. Cambridge: Grotius Publications.

Melville, H. (1949) *Moby Dick or the White Whale*, ed. by W. Maugham. Philadelphia, PA: The John C. Winston Company.

Panjwani, R. (2008) *Wildlife Law: A Global Perspective*. Chicago: ABA Publishing.

Rothman, H.K. (2000) *Saving the Planet: The American Response to the Environment in the Twentieth Century*. Chicago: Ivan R. Dee Publishers.

Thomas, H.M. (2008) *The Norman Conquest: England after William the Conqueror*. New York: Rowman & Littlefield Publishers, Inc.

Ward, K. (2006) *History in the Making: An Absorbing Look at How American History Has Changed in the Telling Over the Last 200 Years*. New York: The New Press.

Wilcove, D.S. (2008) *No Way Home: The Decline of the World's Great Animal Migrations*. Washington, DC: Island Press.

Wise, S.M. (1996) The legal thinghood of nonhuman animals. *Boston College Environmental Affairs Law Review*, **23**(Spring), 471–546.

Wood, M.C. (2000) The tribal property right to wildlife capital (Part I): applying principles of sovereignty to protect wildlife populations. *Idaho Law Review*, **37**, 1–102.

2

Society for Wildlife Forensic Science

DeeDee Hawk

Figure 2.1 The logo of the SWFS.

Introduction

We have come a long way in Wildlife Forensic Science since Dr. C. Robin and Dr. A. Salmon in 1887 determined that the red-colored stain on the smock of murder suspect was not duck blood as purported by the suspect. Now Wildlife Forensic laboratories have all the same state-of-the-art equipment one would expect to see in a human crime laboratory; and in some instances, much more sophisticated equipment. And the scientists, in almost all instances, are dedicated

Wildlife Forensics: Methods and Applications, First Edition. Edited by Jane E. Huffman and John R. Wallace.

not only to solving the crime involving the animal in question but also to the preservation of the resource.

Animal smuggling and poaching have grown to an estimated annual US$12 billion criminal industry (Interpol estimate but this does not include the illegal timber trade), and are exceeded only by the drugs and arms trades (Eccleston, 2007). This industry's illicit profits are a major source of funding for terrorist and militia groups, including Al-Qaida, and the snaring and slaughtering of animals are driving dozens of species to the brink of extinction. Many criminal gangs have links to warlords and militias, and an increasing body of evidence suggests animal smuggling is being used to bankroll civil wars. In 2008, the trades in bushmeat and ivory were found to be directly supporting rogue military gangs, and providing economic support for several persistent pockets of rebel activity (Fison, 2011). "Estimates are that more than a million tons of bushmeat are harvested from Central Africa each year, an amount equivalent of almost four million head of cattle" (*Mongabay Environmental News*, 2008) and that the bushmeat trade "is the most significant threat to Africa's wildlife" (Hance, 2008).

While non-human/wildlife forensics is not a totally new field, it is relatively novel compared to human forensics. The US Fish and Wildlife National Forensics Laboratory opened its doors for business in the summer of 1989 as the first crime laboratory dedicated strictly to law enforcement for thousands of animal species in the world. They were charged with the enforcement of the Endangered Species Act and the Convention on International Trade in Endangered Species of Wild Fauna and Flora (CITES) Treaty. One hundred and seventy five nations have now signed the CITES Treaty (It should be noted that the number of Parties that have signed the CITES agreement may fluctuate due to geopolitical situations in participating nations) (CITES, 2011). The number of countries and states involved in the illegal trade of animals and poaching increases every year and crimes involving non-human evidence encompass every corner of the world and the entire biodiversity of the planet. This, along with the increase in the number of states who now have felony and high level misdemeanor poaching violations in their state regulations; and the rise in fines assessed for poaching violations at the state and federal level, has increased awareness of this scientific field. These factors, as well as several others have made the demand for wildlife forensic services more of an issue and priority. Fines in excess of US$100,000 are no longer uncommon in the illegal trade and traffic of wildlife (Oswell, 2007; U.S. Department of Justice, 2009, 2011a, 2011b); and the harvesting and poaching of trophy animals can easily result in fines of over US$10,000 to US$30,000 as well as a jail sentence.

There are over one hundred laboratories world-wide now in operation that work with wildlife law enforcement officers to fight crimes against wildlife. However, the number of officers and Law Enforcement officials that utilize this relatively small number of laboratories highlights the fact that the request for wildlife forensic analysis is becoming more prevalent. A short list of the stakeholder groups utilizing this unique discipline include: Natural Resource Officers, such as Wildlife Officers or the USFWS (200 Special Agent Officers),

State wildlife agencies (thousands of officers); Marine Officers; Environmental Officers, including the EPA; Forestry Officers; US Customs; the over 150 foreign countries who have signed the UN's CITES Treaty; non-governmental organizations (NGOs), such as the Rocky Mountain Elk Federation, the Mule Deer Foundation, the National Turkey Foundation, and the Wild Sheep Foundation; those who enforce animal cruelty laws; criminal investigations officers (federal, state, local); and USFWS Conservation Genetics Community of Practice.

Wildlife forensics or non-human forensics (these two terms will be used interchangeably throughout this chapter) is a unique science with nothing else closely comparing to the depth, breadth, and variety of species and analyses types. In what other discipline can you be doing law enforcement (LE) on Black Coral in one laboratory, bighorn sheep in another and Asian catfish in a third? While there are numerous differences between human forensics and wildlife forensics, the major difference is, in most instances, when a wildlife forensic laboratory is involved, the animal is the victim of the crime and the goal is to link the crime scene to the suspect poacher or animal trafficker. In a human crime lab, the human is the victim as well as the perpetrator of the crime.

Another major difference from our counterparts in the human arena is that while a human crime laboratory is working with only one species, which allows for standardization of techniques, non-human/wildlife forensic personnel are often required to develop new procedures and protocols to determine the differences between very closely related species. This may be critical to making the case as some closely related species are protected while others are not. Rarely is the whole carcass of the animal in question presented to the forensic laboratory. Usually only smaller parts are confiscated and these parts often do not contain the defining characteristics of the species.

In short, many wildlife laboratories spend their days determining if the wildlife trade and harvest of thousands of different species comply with all the federal, state, and CITES requirements. While human forensics deal with only a single species (*Homo sapiens*), wildlife forensic scientists must be prepared to identify, genotype and determine statistical probabilities from evidence from any species in the world that is illegally killed, smuggled, poached or sold on an illicit market. Food safety and the proper labelling of seafood is large component of marine wildlife forensic work. This is also critical to protecting the livelihood of commercial fishermen. For example, consumer fraud is present when international catfish is sold in the USA as grouper which can also depress the market value of grouper, making it difficult for the legitimate fisherman to make a living.

There is no end to the list of evidentiary items that might be submitted to a non-human forensic laboratory or the type of answer the law enforcement officer is looking for to make his/her case. The law enforcement (LE) officer may need the laboratory to determine if different evidentiary items came from the same animal; or the laboratory may be asked to determine if items such as shark fins, coral or whale teeth originate from an animal/organism that is protected by state, Federal or International laws. LE officers may also need to know how many animals are represented by the packaged meat in the suspect's freezers. Common evidentiary items that have been involved in wildlife cases include caviar; fresh, frozen, cooked or smoked meats; loose hair and fur; clothing of every shape and variety; camping items (tents, sleeping bags, etc.); fur coats; reptile leather products, such as purses, belts, and shoes; loose feathers and down; carved ivory objects; sea turtle oil (suntan lotion); shell jewelry; powdered rhinoceros horn; bear gall bladders; trophy antlers and horns; gut piles and legs; shark fins; coral; or stomach contents.

While these types of cases make up the majority of the cases submitted to wildlife/non-human forensic laboratories, there are other non-human forensic laboratories who also work with an animal victim or an animal perpetrator as well as a more traditional victim, a human. These laboratories often work with domestic animals on cases of animal cruelty or theft, as well as instances where the animal was involved in an attack on another animal or a person. In some criminal cases of robbery, burglary and homicide, there is a need for non-human forensic science to solve the case. In these instances, the alleged assailant can be identified using their pet or the pet of their victim. The animal's DNA can be transferred from the victim's pet to the suspect or the crime scene, or from the suspect's animal to the victim. Numerous people have been convicted of various crimes, including murder, with the help of non-human forensic scientists. There are also laboratories that work with human victims who have been attacked by bears, mountain lions and other predatory animals. In these instances, it is very important to make sure the offending animal has been removed from population to insure the safety of the public. A genetic match from biological material retrieved from the crime scene or the victim to the suspect animal is critical to the public's and wildlife officer's peace of mind. Also, the public does not want indiscriminate killing of animals not involved in the attacks so it is important to identify the correct animal as quickly as possible.

Numerous DNA techniques are available in forensic laboratories but DNA is just the part of the work performed by non-human forensic experts. Phylogeny, chemistry, anthropology, entomology, morphology, serology and toxicology are also performed in different wildlife/non-human laboratories around the country. Wildlife laboratories can also be involved in the more "traditional forensic sciences," such as criminalistics, ballistics, fingerprint analysis, and digital/computer forensics. Pathologists in wildlife, like their human counterparts, examine carcasses and wounds for cause of death, in order to determine if a crime has been committed. Morphologists can often identify a species of animal based on characteristics and observations of the feathers, tusks or skeletal structure. Chemists in wildlife will do traditional testing to identify poisons and pesticides but they also use very high tech instruments to determine species identification; whether it is an evidentiary piece of suspect ivory or some internationally protected Black Coral. Whereas human forensic laboratories primarily use DNA to make comparisons between individuals and to match evidence from the crime scene to the suspect, forensic analysis of wildlife uses DNA in more varied ways: DNA sequencing is utilized to identify species – is this item from an elk, or mule deer or a protected/endangered species or its non-protected, closely related cousin?; population assignment – where did this animal originate from in Africa?; paternity – is this harvested mountain lion the mother of the orphaned cub?; and genotyping – do the samples from this gut pile originate from the trophy elk hanging on the wall?.

While there are many different wildlife/non-human forensic laboratories in the world, it is also true that no two laboratories do work on exactly the same species or have the same types of analyses available. These very large differences within the discipline as well as the difference between wildlife and traditional human forensic have fueled the need for some venue that would allow for increased communication between scientists. Thus the formation of a Society for Wildlife Forensic Science; which gives scientists in this field that are scattered across the world a common forum for discussion of the discipline and issues; was born. And with ever-increasing federal mandates in the United States, the Society will be a much needed resource to assist with unforeseen issues that are sure to arise in the future.

Formation of the Society

The Society for Wildlife Forensic Science (SWFS) (Figure 2.1) was officially formed in September 2009 with the mission to develop wildlife forensic science into a comprehensive, integrated and mature discipline. However, it is thriving because of a deep devotion to this science and the resource it protects. The Society's inception came about because of a need to bring some great minds together to collectively work on the issues, challenges and ideas that are unique to our discipline. While the Society was the brainchild of a few individuals, it took a great effort and hundreds of hours on the part of the new board and officers to get the concept of a Society off the ground and into a workable team. We knew if we could succeed in improving communication and techniques between scientists in different corners of the world, we could improve the science, thus accomplishing a greater good for the resource. It was understood from the beginning that an international group was needed to accomplish our mission. Only an international team could comprehend and address all the challenges that faced the assembly of committed scientists in the Society. For that reason, membership is open to all those who will impact the non-human/wildlife forensic community worldwide.

The vision of SWFS is as follows: (1) to become the pre-eminent professional organization in the world representing wildlife forensic scientists; (2) to promote the exchange of scientific and technical information; (3) to encourage research in wildlife forensics; and (4) to promote professional competence, uniform qualification, certification and ethical behavior among non-human/wildlife forensic scientists. The Society, still in its formative years at the printing of this book, plans on having a certification scheme as well as guidelines and protocols that will be the gold standard for all the laboratories having an affiliation with the Society. These programs will be set up within the Scientific Working Group for Wildlife Forensics (SWGWILD) and forwarded to SWFS as a recommendation to be adopted by the officers and directors after a consensus process has been put into place. There will also be a Wildlife Forensic journal which will be available in an electronic format within the next couple of years.

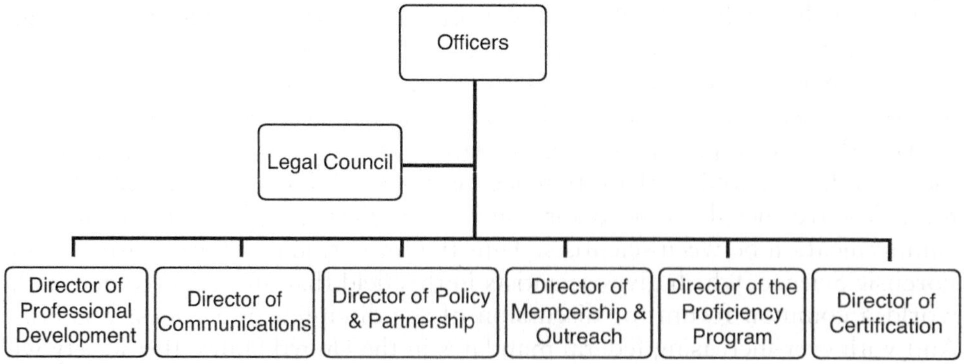

Figure 2.2 The structure of the SWFS.

The structure of SWFS was set up in such a manner that the directors and officers, while answering to the membership, generally determine the direction and goals of the Society. The structure of the Society is as shown in Figure 2.2.

Every director and officer has a responsibility to the Society and its membership which is well defined in the by-laws. The responsibilities of the board are as follows:

- *Director of Professional Development:* The Professional Development Director oversees all matters regarding the professional development of the members, including training, education, career development, case management, statistics and professional ethics. This will include the development of a "Guidelines" document which will be developed under the auspices of the SWGWILD group and forwarded to the Society in the form of a recommendation.
- *Director of Communications:* The Communications Director creates communication strategies to present a consistent message and professional depiction of the Society, and is responsible for the Society's bi-annual communication with the membership. The Communications Director is also responsible for the creation and maintenance of the Society web page as well as the abstract booklet and setting up presentations at all triennial meetings.
- *Director of Membership and Outreach:* The Outreach Director develops participant retention and recruitment strategies, sustains contact with and service to the current participants, and coordinates outreach campaigns and surveys of the membership and related communities, with the goal of generating greater interest in the Society's activities. This position is also responsible for obtaining endorsement from institutions, e.g. National Fish and Wildlife Forensic Laboratory, and attracting corporate membership and underwriting, e.g. Instrument vendors.
- *Director of Policy and Partnership:* The Policy and Partnership Director represents the perspective of the wildlife forensic science community in policy

matters under consideration by professional organizations and government agencies. Additionally, the Policy Director is the liaison with the membership, with the goal of attracting support and involvement in the Society and its activities as well as other forensic communities. The Policy Director interacts with and secures support from sponsors, develops initiatives beneficial to the Society and its members, and plans and coordinates the triennial conference of the Society, with the help of the sponsoring laboratory/organization. This position was also responsible for the creation of the Code of Ethics; signing of the said document is a requirement of membership. The Code of Ethics is given in Box 2.1.

- *Director of the Proficiency Program:* The Proficiency Program Director oversees the Wildlife Proficiency Testing program. The work of the Proficiency Program Director will be guided by the Wildlife Proficiency Testing Program Charter. The Proficiency Program is discussed below.
- *Director of Certification:* The Certification Director will oversee the implementation of a certification scheme which will be developed by the SWGWILD team and presented to the SWFS Board of Directors and Officers as a recommendation for implementation.
- *The President:* The President will supervise, direct, and control the affairs of the Society. The President also performs all duties commonly associated with the office of president and other duties prescribed by the board of directors.
- *The Vice President:* The Vice President will perform the duties of the president if the president is incapacitated. The Vice President also will perform all duties commonly associated with the office of Vice President and other duties prescribed by the board of directors or an authorized officer. The Vice President will be responsible for strategic planning of the Society and will automatically become the president at the subsequent tri-annual meeting.
- *The Treasurer:* The Treasurer will have general charge of and be responsible for all funds and securities of the Society; receive and give receipts for monies due and payable to the Society from any source and deposit the monies in the name of the Society in banks, trust companies, or other depositories selected by the board of directors; prepare an annual budget; prepare a report of the Society's finances for each triennial meeting and special meeting; make available all books, records, and accounts of the Society for inspection by the Society's directors, officers, and the members during normal business hours; and perform all duties commonly incident associated with the office of treasurer and other duties prescribed by the board of directors or an authorized officer.
- *The Secretary:* The Secretary will oversee the Society's awards program; prepare minutes of the directors' meetings and authenticate records of the Society; ensure that all notices by the Society, the Articles of Incorporation or these Bylaws are given; keep and maintain the records of the Society; and perform all duties commonly associated with the office of Secretary and other duties prescribed by the board of directors or an authorized officer.

The Code of Ethics

The Code of Ethics must be signed by potential members prior to them being admitted as a member of the Society. It was determined by the board and the officers to be a very important document which exemplified the core values that every forensic scientist should strive to attain. It was determined that those not willing to sign the document, would not be admitted to the Society. These ideals and values are critical for credibility issues as well as court testimony. The Code of Ethics is set out as shown in Box 2.1.

Box 2.1: The Code of Ethics

To promote the highest standards of professional and personal conduct among its members and affiliates, the following Code of Ethics and Conduct is endorsed by all members and affiliates of the Society for Wildlife Forensic Science:

Professionalism

Ethical and professionally responsible wildlife forensic scientists:

1. Are independent, impartial, and objective, approaching all examinations with due diligence and an open mind.
2. Conduct complete and unbiased examinations. Conclusions are based on the evidence and reference material relevant to the evidence, not extraneous information, political pressure, or other outside influences.
3. Render conclusions only within their area of expertise, and about matters which they have given formal consideration.
4. Honestly communicate with all parties (the investigator, prosecutor, defense, and other expert witnesses) about all information relating to their analysis, when communications are permitted by law and agency practice.
5. Report to the appropriate legal or administrative authorities any unethical, illegal, or scientifically questionable conduct of other forensic scientists or laboratory employees.
6. Report conflicts between their ethical/professional responsibilities and applicable agency policy, law, regulation, or other legal authority, and attempt to resolve them.
7. Do not accept or participate in any case on a contingency fee basis or in which they have any other personal or financial conflict of interest or an appearance of such a conflict.

Competency and proficiency

Ethical and professionally responsible wildlife forensic scientists:

1. Base their opinions and conclusions on scientifically validated and generally accepted methods and tests.
2. Are committed to career-long learning in their forensic disciplines and stay abreast of new equipment and techniques while guarding against the misuse of methods that have not been validated.
3. Are properly trained and competent through testing prior to undertaking the examination of evidence.
4. If applicable, complete regularly scheduled:
   (a) proficiency tests within their forensic discipline(s);
   (b) comprehensive technical reviews of fellow examiners' work;
   (c) verifications of conclusions.
5. Give utmost care to the treatment of all samples or items of potential evidentiary value to avoid tampering, adulteration, loss or unnecessary consumption.
6. Use appropriate controls and standards when conducting examinations and analyses. The Society for Wildlife Forensic Science will develop and maintain a list of best practices in the various disciplines of wildlife forensic science on the Society website (http://www.wildlifeforensicscience.org). The best practices document will be reviewed and, if necessary, updated prior to each tri-annual meeting of the Society.

Clear communications

Ethical and professionally responsible wildlife forensic scientists:

1. Accurately represent their education, training, experience and area of expertise.
2. Present accurate data in reports, testimony, publications and oral presentations.
3. Make and retain full, contemporaneous, clear and accurate records of all examinations and tests conducted, and conclusions drawn, in sufficient detail to allow meaningful review and assessment of the conclusions by an independent person competent in the field.
4. Do not alter reports or other records, or withhold information from a report for strategic or tactical litigation advantage.
5. Support sound scientific techniques and practices, and never pressure another examiner or technician to arrive at conclusions or results that are not supported by data.

6. Accept their moral obligation to assure that the court understands the evidence as it exists, and to present that evidence in an impartial manner.
7. Provide complete and informative testimony, for example, by qualifying their responses if needed when counsel attempts to elicit a simple yes or no answer.

Obligations of members to the Society for Wildlife Forensic Science

1. Every member and associate of the Society shall refrain from exercising professional conduct adverse to the best interests and objectives of the Society.
2. No member or associate of the Society shall materially misrepresent his or her education, training, experience, area of expertise, or membership status within the Society.
3. No member or affiliate of the Society shall issue public statements that appear to represent the position of the Society without specific authority first obtained from the Board of Directors.

Provisions for disciplinary action

Any member of the Society who has violated any of the above provisions of the Code of Ethics and Conduct may be subject to disciplinary measures by action of the Board of Directors. Such disciplinary action may include censure, suspension or expulsion from the Society, as detailed in the Policy Manual of the Society for Wildlife Forensic Science (http://www.wildlifeforensicscience.org/).

By accepting membership in the Society for Wildlife Forensic Science, I pledge to abide by the Society's Code of Ethics and Conduct.

Signed: ______________________________ Date: ______________________

Membership of the Society

The Society has different levels of participation so that anybody involved with wildlife forensics can find a niche. The voting members of SWFS, however, must be directly involved in the science. A person can join the Society through sponsorship by a voting member and upon approval of the Board of Directors. Other methods of joining the Society are located on the web page. The different levels of membership are as follows:

- *Voting member:* The Society may admit voting members who must be individuals actively or formerly employed in non-human/wildlife law enforcement in an analytical, intelligence or investigative capacity related to wildlife forensic science.

- *Regular member:* These individuals will be those who are not eligible to be a voting member but who are qualified by other professional attainments related to forensic analysis or in the government, academic or private sector in instruction, education, research or advocacy for study and/or protection of wildlife and who demonstrate support for wildlife forensic science.
- *Special Participant:* SWFS also has Special Participants under the following classifications: (a) Honorary Participants must be individuals who have an outstanding record of public or private service in the field of forensic wildlife science analysis (the board of directors will review Honorary Participants for their continued participation in the Society every two years); (b) Student Participant: Student Participants must be individuals who are enrolled as full-time students at an accredited college or university, as defined by such college or university.
- *Organization Participant:* The Society also has a membership class for Organization Participants under the following classifications: (a) Corporate Participant: Corporate Participants must be corporations or other business entities which demonstrate and continue to demonstrate support of the Society's purpose and functions; (b) Supporting Agency Participant: Supporting Agency Participants must be government agencies or entities which have demonstrated and continue to demonstrate support of the Society's purpose and functions; and (c) Academic Institution Participant: Academic Institution Participants must be accredited (or will hold an equivalent status if located outside the United States), academic institutions with a scientific analytical curricula that supports the Corporation's purpose and functions, as well as, wildlife forensic science.

Member Labs

There has been a large international response to the formation and development of SWFS. At the time of this publication, over 52 laboratories have members involved in the Society; this includes 11 countries (Australia, Brazil, Canada, Hong Kong, India, New Zealand, the United Kingdom, South Africa, Sweden, Norway, and Thailand) and 20 states in the United States of America (California, Colorado, Idaho, Illinois, Massachusetts, Maine, Mississippi, Montana, North Carolina, New York, Oklahoma, Oregon, Pennsylvania, South Carolina, South Dakota, Tennessee, Texas, Virginia, Washington and Wyoming). Table 2.1 lists the 59 laboratories that are part of the Society as of the Summer of 2011.

Proficiency Program

The current Proficiency Program, which has been in place since 2004 (and was administrated by the US Fish and Wildlife National Forensic Laboratory),

Table 2.1 Member laboratories in the Society for Wildlife Forensic Science.

1. Wildlife Genetics Laboratory, Murdoch University, School of Biological Sciences & Biotechnology, Perth, Australia
2. University of Queensland, School of Biological Science, Queensland, Australia
3. Australian Museum, DNA Laboratory, Sydney, Australia
4. Laboratorio de Biologia Evolutiva e Conservação de Vertebrados SOS Fauna Cidade Universitaria, Butanta, São Paulo, Brazil
5. Alberta Fish and Wildlife Forensic Unit, Edmonton, AB, Canada
6. Lethbridge Community College, Lethbridge Alberta, Alberta, Canada
7. Environment Canada, Pacific & Yukon Laboratory for Environmental Testing, North Vancouver, BC, Canada
8. Pacific Biological Station, Dept. of Fisheries and Oceans, Canada, Nanaimo, BC, Canada
9. Simon Fraser University, Burnaby, BC, Canada
10. Research and Productivity Council (RPC), Fredericton, NB, Canada
11. Trent University Wildlife Forensic DNA Laboratory, Peterborough, ON, Canada
12. Environment Canada, Wildlife Enforcement Directorate, Gatineau, Quebec, Canada
13. Cowan Vertebrate Museum, The Beaty Biodiversity Museum, University of British Columbia, Vancouver, BC, Canada
14. WWF Canada, Vancouver, BC, Canada
15. Hong Kong CITES Office, Agriculture, Fisheries and Conservation Department, Kowloon, Hong Kong Special Administrative Region, Hong Kong, China
16. St. Xavier's College, Mumbai, India
17. EcoGene Lancare Research, Auckland, New Zealand
18. TRACE Wildlife Forensics Network, c/o The Royal Zoological Society of Scotland, South Queensferry, Midlothian, Scotland, United Kingdom
19. University of Pretoria, Equine Research Center, Veterinary Genetics Laboratory, Pretoria, South Africa
20. National Veterinary Institute, Uppsala, Sweden
21. CITES Enforcement Task Force, Geneva, Switzerland
22. Forest Genetics and Biotechnology Group, Forest and Plant Conservation Research Office Dept of National Parks, Wildlife and Plant Conservation, Bangkok, Thailand
23. Fish and Wildlife Service, Conservation Genetics Laboratory, Anchorage, AK, USA
24. California Department of Fish and Game Forensics Laboratory, Rancho Cordova, CA, USA
25. California State University, Fresno, Clovis, CA, USA
26. Canorus Ltd., San Jose, CA, USA
27. Center for Accelerator Mass Spectrometry (CAMS), LLNL, Livermore, CA, USA
28. University of California, Berkley, Napa, CA, USA
29. Veterinary Genetics Forensic Laboratory, University of California, Davis, Davis, CA, USA
30. University of Colorado, Boulder, CO, USA

Table 2.1 (*Continued*)

31. Idaho Fish and Game, Wildlife Forensics Program, Caldwell, ID, USA
32. Microtrace, LLC, Elgin, IL, USA
33. University of Maine, Molecular Forensic Laboratory, Orono, ME, USA
34. NOAA National Seafood Inspection Laboratory, Pascagoula, MS, USA
35. US Department of Justice, Environmental Crimes Section – ENRD, Missoula, MT, USA
36. USDA Forest Service Rocky Mtn, Missoula, MT, USA
37. DNA Solutions, Inc. Analytical Research Laboratory, Oklahoma, OK, USA
38. University of Central Oklahoma, Edmond, OK, USA
39. Fish and Wildlife Service, National Forensic Lab, Ashland, OR, USA
40. Southern Oregon University, Ashland, OR, USA
41. East Stroudsburg University, Northeast Wildlife DNA Laboratory, East Stroudsburg, PA, USA
42. NOAA, Marine Forensic Laboratory, Charleston, SC, USA
43. Black Hills State University, CCBR/West Core, Spearfish, SD, USA
44. Tennessee Wildlife Resource Agency, Big Sandy, TN, USA
45. Texas Parks and Wildlife A.E. Wood Fish Hatchery, San Marcos, TX, USA
46. Smithsonian Institution, Feather Identification Lab, Fairfax, VA, USA
47. Stoney Forensic, Inc., Chantilly, VA, USA
48. NOAA/NMFS/NWFSC, Seattle, WA, USA
49. University of Washington, Biology, Seattle, WA, USA
50. University of Washington, Department of Biostatistics, Seattle, WA, USA
51. Washington State Department Fish and Game, Olympia, WA, USA
52. Wyoming Game and Fish Wildlife Forensic Laboratory, Laramie, WY, USA
53. University of Montana, Division of Biological Services, Missoula, MT, USA
54. NCSU-CVM Clinical Pathology Lab, Raleigh, NC, USA
55. New York State Department of Environmental Conservation, Wildlife Pathology Unit, Delmar, NY, USA
56. University of Central Lancashire, School of Forensic Investigative Sciences, England, UK
57. School of Biological Sciences, Flinders University, Adelaide, South Australia
58. Anglia Ruskin University, Department of Forensic Science, Cambridge England, UK
59. Wildlife DNA Forensics, Diagnostic and Molecular Biology Section, Science and Advice for Scottish Agriculture, Edinburgh, UK

was moved under the auspices of the Society for Wildlife Forensic Science in February of 2010. It is open to all non-human/wildlife forensic analysts who offer analytical services to law enforcement agencies and agree to the terms of the program. The participating analyst has to be a member of the Society to participate in the program. Currently the program offers a mammal's genetics test whereby participants analyze samples to identify species, gender, and individual identification; prepared from four different taxa, including North American black bear, North American elk, white-tailed deer and mule deer. As is found in the human crime labs, three proficiency samples are submitted to participating analysts and after a pre-determined amount of time, the results are returned to the Duty laboratory.

The Duty Laboratory then send out an anomalous consensus report to all the participating laboratories. The Consensus Report is a summary report for test subscribers and contain the compiled results reported from all participants; a description of the test design, test objective, and details of the origin of the test samples, results of pre-distribution testing or a statement that the results of pre-distribution testing confirmed the expected results; and a brief summary and/or analysis of all results plus any additional comments by subscribers. As is the standard with other American Society of Crime Lab Directors (ASCLD) laboratories, the proficiency is administrated to the participating laboratories once a year in the early Spring.

The Proficiency Test Program is under the direction of the Wildlife Forensic Proficiency Board. Analysts who miss a completion deadline will not be given an extension and the Consensus Report will indicate "Not Completed" for that analyst in that testing cycle. Analysts who miss two consecutive deadlines are excluded from further participation until they take corrective actions. Also, if an analyst fails consensus on any particular sample, as per the Proficiency Charter, they must write a letter to the board informing them of the cause of the error and the steps they will take to prevent the error in the future.

All corrective actions are reviewed and approved by the Board by simple majority before the analyst can be reinstated as a Member in the Proficiency Program. Labs or analysts that fail to respond to the Board within the 30-day period will be excluded from further participation until they take corrective actions or follow the dispute resolution process. The supervisor is notified that the analyst has been excluded from further participation. Corrective actions are reviewed and approved by the Board by simple majority before the analyst can be reinstated as a Member in the Proficiency Program.

The mission statement of the Proficiency Program is "to provide a reliable method by which participating Wildlife Forensic Laboratories can verify their technical procedures are valid and the quality of their examiners' work is being maintained." For these reasons, the Proficiency Program is invaluable to the members who use the service. The ability to articulate the fact that they participate in a Proficiency Program has bolstered analysts' credibility and had a very positive outcome in the judicial system. The American Society of Crime Lab Directors/ Laboratory Accreditation Board recognizes the Proficiency Program as a source for wildlife testing materials for laboratories accredited under ASCLD/LAB. As of this publication, the proficiency board is seeking formal recognition by the ASCLD/LAB as an approved provider for wildlife proficiency tests. Being an ASCLD approved proficiency provider would further increase the creditability of the program.

As mentioned earlier, currently the Proficiency Program has a mammal's genetic component that is utilized by SWFS members, but is working to add a fish component in the coming year. Morphological tests are also planned and may include both a bird and herpetology test. A survey is being developed to solicit information from SWFS members to determine the type of testing that would best suit their needs. These additional programs will also be a consensus-based test.

Scientific Working Group for Wildlife Forensic Sciences (SWGWILD)

The National Academy of Sciences (NAS) recently published a report critiquing forensic science entitled *Strengthening Forensic Science in the United States: A Path Forward* (Committee on Identifying the Needs of the Forensic Science Community, 2009). The NAS press release in February of 2009 was entitled: "Badly fragmented forensic science system needs overhaul: Evidence to support reliability of many techniques is lacking". The report says:

> A congressionally mandated report from the National Research Council (NRC) finds serious deficiencies in the nation's forensic science system and calls for major reforms and new research. Rigorous and mandatory certification programs for forensic scientists are currently lacking, as are strong standards and protocols for analyzing and reporting on evidence. And there is a dearth of peer-reviewed, published studies establishing the scientific bases and reliability of many forensic methods. Moreover, many forensic science labs are underfunded, understaffed, and have no effective oversight.
>
> (Frueh, 2009)

The report continues:

> But with the exception of nuclear DNA analysis, no forensic method has been rigorously shown able to consistently, and with a high degree of certainty, demonstrate a connection between evidence and a specific individual or source. Non-DNA forensic disciplines have important roles, but many need substantial research to validate basic premises and techniques, assess limitations, and discern the sources and magnitude of error.Even methods that are too imprecise to identify a specific individual can provide valuable information and help narrow the range of possible suspects or sources. In terms of a scientific basis, the disciplines based on biological or chemical analysis, such as toxicology and fiber analysis, generally hold an edge over fields based on subjective interpretation by experts, such as fingerprint and toolmark analysis. Nuclear DNA analysis enjoys a pre-eminent position not only because the chances of a false positive are minuscule, but also because the likelihood of such errors is quantifiable.

The report notes:

> Studies have been conducted on the amount of genetic variation among individuals, so an examiner can state in numerical terms the chances that a declared match is wrong. In contrast, for many other forensic disciplines – such as fingerprint and toolmark analysis – no studies have been conducted of large populations to determine how many sources might share the same or similar features. For every forensic science method, results should indicate the level of uncertainty in the measurements made, and studies should be conducted that enable these values to be estimated... What's more: there has been little rigorous research to investigate how accurately and reliably many forensic science disciplines can do what they purport to be able to do.
> (Committee on Identifying the Needs of the Forensic Science Community, 2009)

"Strong leadership is needed to adopt and promote an aggressive, long-term agenda to strengthen forensic science," the report says. To achieve this end, the report

> strongly urges Congress to establish a new, independent National Institute of Forensic Science to lead research efforts, establish and enforce standards for forensic science professionals and laboratories, and oversee education standards. Much research is needed not only to evaluate the reliability and accuracy of current forensic methods but also to innovate and develop them further.

As committee's co-chair Constantine Gatsonis, Professor of Biostatistics and Director of the Center for Statistical Sciences at Brown University said: "An organized and well-supported research enterprise is a key requirement for carrying this out" (Frueh, 2009).

This report was the impetus behind the formation of the Scientific Working Group for Wildlife Forensics (SWGWILD) in December, 2010. While much of the concern with forensic methods centered on human forensic laboratories, the non-human laboratories will be included in the sweeping legislative changes that are sure to occur in the next decade. The reform movement started in 2011 with the introduction of Senate Bill 132, the Criminal Justice and Forensic Science Reform Act of 2011, sponsored by Senator Patrick Leahy (D-VT). The bill, which aims to ensure consistency and scientific validity in forensic testing, would require the nation's forensic scientists and labs – whether they work with human or animal evidence – to be certified in their disciplines and conduct their work in accredited laboratories. While SWGWILD is very young, other various scientific and technical working groups (SWGs and TWGs) consisting of representatives from the fields of forensic, industrial, commercial, academic, and in some cases international communities, have been in practice for more than

20 years. These groups, like SWGWILD, were put together to support the efforts in the advancement of forensic standards, techniques, guidelines and to generally improve communications throughout their respective disciplines. In several instances, the FBI Laboratory and several other federal agencies provide financial and logistical support of these efforts. SWGWILD will produce a White Paper and attempt to receive the same type of funding for SWGWILD for members to travel to meetings and the costs associated with the pending Certification Program.

The NAS report and the Leahy Bill have two common themes that the SWGWILD group is addressing with two separate subcommittees: (1) a certification scheme committee; and (2) Standards and Guidelines Committee. An additional requirement that will come from the report will be accreditation of all forensic laboratories that receive any type of Federal funding. The need for standardization will be addressed through a "Guidelines" document that presents different levels of recommendations; "Standards" and "Guidelines". Standards are mandatory minimum practice necessary to ensure that accurate, precise, and unbiased finds are obtained and conveyed. Guidelines are (non-mandatory) best-case scenario suggestions that optimize the science and are practices that all non-human forensic laboratories and analysts should strive to achieve. At present, there are only three accredited non-human/wildlife labs in the country and there is not a program for certification in non-human/wildlife forensics. A future goal of the SWFS Board of Directors and Officers is to work with one or several accrediting bodies to ascertain standards that will be applicable to non-human forensics applications. The report also indicates that forensic laboratories need additional resources in regard to training, education, benchmarking and sustainable funding sources at all levels. At some point down the road, the SWGWILD committee and SWFS will begin to work on additional training and education opportunities other than just the triennial meeting.

Another area that warrants attention in the future is research. The NAS report indicates that lack of research is a major problem in forensics. There are certainly many areas in wildlife forensic that could be strengthened with additional research. At some time in the future, after a dedicated source of funding is achieved, SWFS will determine research priorities and put into place a research program to further the science.

While the NAS report presents the opportunity to evaluate and determine the status of forensic laboratories worldwide, it is critical that non-human laboratories have a say in the process that will be forthcoming. As was mentioned earlier, the differences between the two laboratory types are such that blanket legislation will be extremely difficult for smaller wildlife laboratories to achieve and will effectively close the doors of many laboratories. Awareness of the differences in issues between non-human and human forensic laboratories at the federal level is one of the main missions of the SWGWILD group, in addition to writing Guidelines and producing a Certification scheme. The invitation of a representative from SWGWILD to participate in a meeting of all SWG chairs is indicative that the SWGWILD group has started to make some inroads in the recognition of "Non-human/Wildlife Forensics" as a separate entity. Also, there has been communication between personnel at the National Institute of Justice and the National Institute of Standards and Technology with SWGWILD personnel. One of the most exciting opportunities proposed to the group came from an ISO accreditation organization. They have asked the SWGWILD membership to assist with setting up "wildlife field specific" ISO accreditation requirements. This is a very positive step for wildlife forensics and will greatly increase the likelihood that wildlife forensic laboratories will be able to be accredited.

Certification and accreditation will be necessary in the future, whether or not the currently proposed legislation passes. The SWGWILD group will produce documents that set up standards and certification, which will bolster the quality and credibility of scientific evidence that analysts associated with the Society for Wildlife Forensic Science present in criminal and civil trials.

Conclusion

The logo has special meaning for the Society and all aspects of the logo were adopted with the mission and the membership in mind. The double helix design was carefully chosen to show the advanced technological abilities of non-human wildlife forensic practitioners; the scale is a universal symbol of truth and fairness that dates back to ancient Egypt, the scale also reminds us of the quintessential moral and ethical obligations that we operate under as forensic scientists; and the Ovis species was chosen as wild sheep are among the most successful and universally recognized mammals on the planet, with a wide geographical distribution which extends from Europe to Siberia and Alaska to South America. This animal symbolizes the International nature of the Society for Wildlife Forensic Science. A wildlife forensic scientists, who understands all these concepts, was the designer of the logo and he captured the essence of the Society exceptionally well with his design.

Before the Society of Wildlife Forensic Science was formed, non-human forensic practitioners had few venues to exchange information and ideas. SWFS makes it possible for this small but motived international group of scientists to meet more often and learn and grow from one another. And with all the unprecedented challenges in forensics at this time, there has never been a better time to be an organized force to advance the discipline of non-human forensics. Membership is open to all who have an interest and/or impact on the field. As a group, we have more leverage and impact than we do as individual scientists.

To join the Society of Wildlife Forensic Science, go to the web site (www.wildlifeforensicscience.org) and click on the "Membership" tab. If an interested applicant is acquainted with a Voting member, the voting member can sponsor the new applicant; the applicant can also be sponsored by the head (director or manager) of a forensic laboratory or a professor from an accredited post-secondary institution. The membership fee can be paid at the triennial meeting or to the treasurer directly. This fee is set by the SWFS board and will be determined based on the needs of the Society.

Wildlife forensics personnel use modern highly technological procedures and protocols to assist law enforcement with the fight against those who would damage the wildlife resource through illegal trade, poaching, and the importation/exportation of thousands of different species of animals to other countries other than their native homelands. Wildlife forensic scientists are an important tool for law enforcement agencies who are struggling with this ever increasing drain on our natural resources. And the Society for Wildlife Forensic Science is there to support the scientists who do this critical work. "Individual commitment to a group effort – that is what makes a team work, a company work, a society work, a civilization work" (Vince Lombardi, football coach).

The goal of protecting and conserving wildlife is shared by all in the Society and it is an extraordinarily worthwhile pursuit! Come join our team!

References

Committee on Identifying the Needs of the Forensic Science Community (2009) *Strengthening Forensic Science in the United States: A Path Forward.* Washington, DC: National Academy Press.

Eccleston, P. (2007) Gangs moving into environmental crime. *The Telegraph.* Available at: http://www.telegraph.co.uk/earth/earthnews/3296580/Gangs-moving-into-environmental-crime.html (accessed 17 March 2011).

Fison, M. (2011) The £6bn trade in animal smuggling: it funds terrorists and civil wars, and brings more species closer to extinction. WildSingapore. Available at: http://wildsingaporenews.blogspot.com/2011/03/6bn-trade-in-animal-smuggling.html (accessed 12 January 2011).

Frueh, S. (2009) "Badly fragmented" forensic science system needs overhaul; evidence to support reliability of many techniques is lacking. Office of News and Public Information, National Academy of Science. Available at: http://www8.nationalacademise.org/onpinenews/newsitem.aspx?RecordID=12589 (accessed 10 January 2011).

Hance, J. (2008) Bushmeat trade "most significant" threat to Africa's wildlife says Richard Leakey. *Mongabay Environmental News.* Available at: http://news.mongabay.com/2008/0925-hance_bushmeat.html (accessed 8 March 2011).

Member Countries Available at: http://www.CITES.org/ (accessed 25 August 2011).

Mongabay Environmental News (2008) Commercial bushmeat trade is devastating wildlife. Available at: http://news.mongabay.com/2008/0915-bushmeat.html (accessed 7 February 2011).

Oswell, M. (2007) Seafood importer and associated corporations receive imprisonment and fines. NOAA News Releases 2007. Available at: http://www.publicaffairs.noaa.gov/releases2007/jan07/noaa07-r101.html (accessed 8 March 2011).

U.S. Department of Justice (2009) News Release. President of company that illegally imported catfish sentenced to more than five years in federal prison. Available at: http://justice.gov/opa/pr/2009/May/09-enrd-409.html (accessed 8 March 2011).

U.S. Department of Justice (2011a) Southern District of Florida News Release. Coral Gables seafood firm sentenced for illegal importation of Chilean sea bass. Available at: http://justice.gov/usao/fls/PressRelease/110203-01.html (accessed 8 March 2011).

U.S. Department of Justice (2011b) News Release. Seafood wholesaler owners plead guilty to selling falsely labeled fish, smuggling, and misbranding of seafood products. Available at: http://justice.gov/opa/pr/2011/January/11-ag-101.html (accessed 8 March 2011).

3

The Application of Forensic Science to Wildlife Evidence

John R. Wallace and Jill C. Ross

Introduction

Wildlife forensics can be broadly defined as the application of several integrated aspects of natural and cultural sciences, e.g. biology, chemistry, and anthropology in the court of law focused on the regulation of wildlife protection and conservation laws and statutes established in regional, national and international legislation. By definition, crime against wildlife (i.e., wild or undomesticated animals and plants) and their derivatives involves four major categories: (1) the illegal taking or poaching; (2) possessing; (3) trading, shipping or moving; and (4) inflicting cruelty to or persecution of wildlife in breach of these laws (Cooper and Cooper 2007; Cooper *et al.*, 2009; Lawton and Cooper, 2009). McDowell (1997) has categorized wildlife crime offenders into three groups: (1) minor offenders – those who violate permits and are more opportunistic, typically tracked through inadequate record keeping; (2) organized illegal trading – involves a more sinister contingent that delves into clandestine poaching for financial gain and generating and maintaining such markets with these activities; and (3) serious major criminal activity – differing from organized illegal traders in that it involves major professional criminal groups, is financially supported and deals with specific markets (e.g., bear gall bladders) (Wilson-Wilde, 2010). Unfortunately, committing such crimes can result in large financial gains for those involved, which explains the continued occurrence of these activities. Some reports suggest that the illegal side of wildlife trade is worth upwards of US$15–50 billion annually (Neme, 2009). Because of this aspect, U.S. Fish & Wildlife Service investigators have seen a 150% increase in wildlife cases over the past decade (Figure 3.1).

Wildlife Forensics: Methods and Applications, First Edition. Edited by Jane E. Huffman and John R. Wallace.

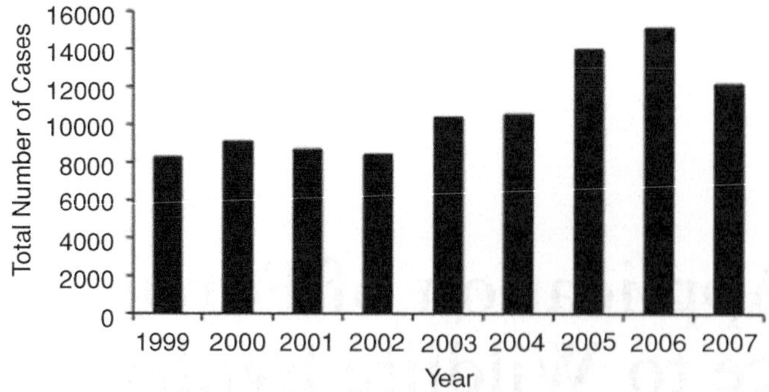

Figure 3.1 Total number of cases conducted from 1999–2007 by the U.S. Fish & Wildlife Services Wildlife Forensics Laboratory. USF&S: www.lab.fws.gov/publications.php.

The connections between forensic investigations involving humans as victims and wildlife (both animals and plants) as victims are vast and in fact, most methods and protocols involving all areas of science were initially developed, tested and validated for crimes against humans and were later adapted for crimes against wildlife. The drivers of this new discipline in forensic science typically have their underpinnings in conservation biology and illegal harvest (such as poaching) for personal or financial gain worldwide and are reflected in their prevalence in court. Over the past three decades, an important empirical development has been the introduction and application of various methodologies and technologies involving criminal investigations focused on humans to wildlife and plant evidence. The expansion of such methodological advancements among several disciplines within forensic science e.g., serology, anthropology, odontology, entomology, and trace evidence analysis have allowed conceptual queries commonly addressed involving crimes with human victims to be asked and tested for crimes involving wildlife and plant evidence (Table 3.1). A follow-up query for many of the questions presented in Table 3.1 might be "How might the outcome influence conviction/exoneration rates in the court of law?"

The specific aim of this chapter is to elucidate to the reader how forensic science principles and protocols can and have been applied to wildlife evidence in the court of law. An understanding of the evolution of wildlife protection legislation is essential in this process. This historical aspect sets the stage as to how human forensic methodologies and protocols have been adapted to wildlife crime investigations from both a conceptual and empirical perspective. This chapter will introduce the major laboratories in North America involved in providing assistance with federal and international cases as well as state or regional violations. The analytical assistance provided by these laboratories has been established with several areas of focus such as genetic, morphologic and pathological analyses, analytical chemistry, and criminalistics; these foci and others have been utilized in protocol and methodological development in human investigations and are applied in wildlife criminal investigations. These areas launch the premise of this text and will be discussed in depth in subsequent chapters.

Table 3.1 Examples of empirical and conceptual roles of forensic science in wildlife forensics.

1. Questions involving the species identification and suspects
   Examples:
   - Do genetic databases exist for species of wildlife?
   - Can wildlife DNA be distinguished at the species level using similar methodologies as those used for humans?
   - Besides molecular approaches, what other aspects of wildlife species morphology can be used in the identification of wildlife?
   - How does specimen degradation influence success rate in accurate identification?
   - Does sample condition, e.g., intact v. butchered, influence identification?
2. Questions evaluating wildlife crime scenes
   Example:
   - Are crime scene processing techniques standardized for terrestrial and aquatic crime scenes (e.g., coral reef pilfering)?
3. Questions evaluating and interpreting wildlife crime evidence
   Examples:
   - Does evidence analysis meet with the *Daubert* standard?
   - Is there reproducibility of research results in academic research to document the precision and accuracy of the evidence being interpreted?
   - Should laboratories assessing this evidence require certification?
   - How can this evidence be used to determine a minimum postmortem interval (mPMI)?
   - Can the geographic origin of an animal or plant be determined?
4. Questions involving acceptance in court and the Trier of fact
   Examples:
   - What are the qualifications of expert witnesses for this type of evidence?
   - How do international laws affect the laws in the country of trial?

Overview of Forensic Science

Forensic science in the broadest sense applies the knowledge and technology of science in the court of law. With specific relevance to this chapter, it involves the active debate of the application of natural and physical sciences as it pertains to wildlife evidentiary interpretation in the court of law in order to uphold and enforce both national and international laws. To understand the origins of wildlife forensics, it is important to trace how the field of forensic science in general developed that would in turn form the foundation of scientific protocols that are applied to wildlife crime.

Without any formal classification system, the origins of forensic science date back to the eighth century in China when fingerprints were used to establish identity and three centuries later, Quintilian, a Roman attorney, modified this approach that included using bloody palm prints to convict a blind man of his mother's murder (Inman and Rudin, 2001). In thirteenth-century China, the application of medical, as well as entomological, knowledge was used to solve several crimes (Mcknight, 1981). Through the 1800s, several areas of forensic

Table 3.2 Eleven sections within the American Academy of Forensic Sciences professional society.

Criminalistics*	Digital & Multimedia Sciences*
Engineering Sciences	General
Jurisprudence*	Odontology*
Pathology/Biology*	Psychiatry & Behavioral Sciences
Physical Anthropology*	Questioned Documents*
Toxicology (includes Analytical Chemistry)*	

Note: *Sections that have wildlife forensic relevance.

science began to develop such as the use of serology, latent print identification, hair fiber analysis, anthropometry, questioned documents and ballistic analysis (Inman and Rudin, 2001).

By the early to mid-twentieth century, forensic scientists were not only advancing the knowledge base in many areas within disciplines such as fingerprint, hair fiber analyses, serological techniques, comparative ballistics with improved microscopy methodologies, and trace chemical identification, but also creating forensic crime labs in Los Angeles, Chicago, and New York in the United States, and the first lab established by Rudolph Reiss at the University of Lausanne, Switzerland, as well as forming the American Academy of Forensic Science in North America and the European Network of Forensic Science Institutes (ENFSI) and Australian and New Zealand Forensic Science Society (ANZFSS) later in the twentieth century. The American Academy of Forensic Sciences, founded in 1950, consists of 11 areas or disciplines that represent a wide range of forensic specialties, many of which have direct application to wildlife forensics (Table 3.2).

During this time frame, the validity of scientific evidence was tested in the court of law with *Frye v. United States* with the end result prohibiting polygraph testing because it did not meet the criteria of general acceptance, and was ruled admissible from thenceforth (Inman and Rudin, 2001). This ruling introduced the concept of general acceptance criteria of scientific methods and protocols.

During the latter half of the twentieth century, analytical chemistry techniques, such as the use of gas chromatograph mass spectroscopy and thin layer chromatography, were developed. A forensic anthropological research facility was founded at the University of Tennessee for the purpose of conducting anthropological research on human remains. But, perhaps the single most important contribution to forensic science was the development of the first DNA profiling test in 1984 by Sir Alec Jeffreys and the actual application in 1986 by Jeffreys in a murder investigation in England that not only identified the murder suspect but also coincidentally was used to exonerate an innocent suspect in the same case (ibid.). DNA profiling was first used in the United States in 1987 but it was the later advent in the 1990s of polymerase chain reaction (PCR) techniques that would facilitate the use of DNA profiling in criminal and civil courts. Within the last 20 years, computer technological advances have accelerated the

Table 3.3 Checklist of questions regarding the *Daubert* factors used in Rule 702 by courts to decide the admissibility of scientific evidence.

1. Have either the scientific theory or method/protocol been tested?
2. Have the theory or methodologies in question been questioned by peer-review evaluation in the publication process?
3. Are there known or potential error rates to the theory or methods when applied in testing?
4. Are there standard operating procedures, quality controls and are they applied?
5. Has the relevant scientific community generally accepted the theory or methodology?

Source: Modified from Herrero (2005).

development of automated DNA (CODIS) fingerprint (AFIS) and ballistics (IBIS) imaging systems that facilitate the rapid identification of individuals and firearms associated with a human and wildlife crime. However, since the *Frey v. United States* decision, scientific advancements have necessitated similar jurisprudence advancements with respect to their acceptance in the court of law. Thus, in 1993, the U.S. federal court in *Daubert et al. v. Merrell Dow* modified the *Frey* standard for the admission of scientific evidence and established a checklist for trial experts to utilize in the assessment of the reliability of scientific expert testimony regarding these analyses (Table 3.3) (Herrero, 2005). These criteria or *Daubert* factors would later drive the moral imperative for the foundation of the United States Fish & Wildlife Forensic Crime lab in Ashland, Oregon. This forensic science timeline provides a basis to understand how the most recent advancements in molecular and morphological biology, analytical chemistry, crime scene investigation, anthropology, and criminalistics have provided the underpinning for the advent of the emerging new field of wildlife forensics.

History of Wildlife Forensics

In an attempt to streamline national and international laws and regulations concerning the protection and conservation of wildlife (animals and plants) as well as domesticated animals, those involved with wildlife forensics have been attempting to establish and test scientific procedures to identify and compare animal or plant evidence and their derivatives from crime scenes, ports of entry, clandestine markets or personal possession, but to link this physical evidence with a suspect and wildlife victim(s) (USF&WS: www.lab.fws.gov/publications.php). Compared to the forensic sciences, the historical chronology of events related to wildlife forensics is in its infancy when one examines the impetus that launched this field approximately 110 years ago, i.e., overexploitation of wildlife for commerce. It is no surprise that national and international laws designed to combat international wildlife trafficking (animals for personal or commercial keeping), poaching, e.g., elephants and rhinos for their ivory and horns, "legal" and illegal harvesting of native species, e.g., tigers in India for bounties assigned by British colonizers because they were viewed as pests, and millions of birds for their feathers around the world (Neme, 2009), as well as habitat destruction, were established at the beginning of the twentieth century.

Some early international attempts were made by colonial powers to provide protection for big game species under the mask of several treaties: (1) the 1900 London Convention Designed to Ensure the Conservation of Various Species of Wild Animals In Africa Which Are Useful to Man or Inoffensive; and (2) the 1933 London Convention to the Preservation of Fauna and Flora in Their Natural State. These, however, failed due to the lack of signatories (the former) and administrative and logistical problems within the institutions charged to carry out such regulation in addition to the imminent uncertainties soon to be created by decolonization (the latter) (ibid.). However, this international concern for the overexploitation of wildlife in Europe and Africa was also mirrored in the United States and spawned a suite of national and international legislative milestones over the next century. From the turn of the twentieth century, the number of legislative acts/treaties increased exponentially over the decades illustrating a growing interest to protect and conserve wildlife with legislation that would levy significant punishments if prosecuted (Figure 3.2). The end result of the enforcement of these laws was an increase in the numbers of cases prosecuted and corresponding fines and prison sentences. An abbreviated list of some of the most significant examples and their purpose in wildlife protection/conservation is provided in Table 3.4.

In terms of impact on wildlife forensic cases worldwide, probably the most significant regulations, laws and treaties in the United States today, have been the Lacey Act, the Migratory Bird Treaty Act (MBTA), the Endangered Species Act, the Convention on International Trade in Endangered Species (CITES) and the Marine Mammal Protection Act.

Considered to be the first wildlife protection law, the Lacey Act was passed and took effect in 1900 and prohibited interstate shipment or trafficking of illegally

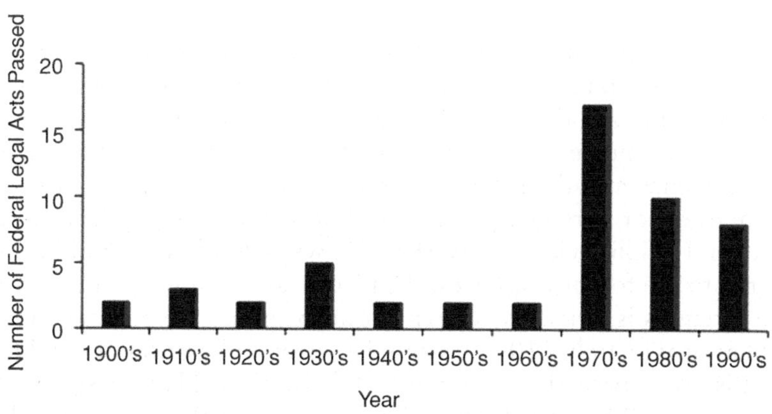

Figure 3.2 Number of legislative acts or treaties passed or signed over the decades from 1900–1990s. USFWS: www.lab.fws.gov/publications.php.

Table 3.4 Abbreviated list of key events in wildlife protection and conservation 1900–2009.

Date	Act/Treaty	Aim
1900	Lacey Act*	
1913	Federal Migratory Bird Law	Hunting regulations on migratory birds
1916	Migratory Bird Treaty	Signed with Great Britain and recognized migratory birds as international resource
1918	Migratory Bird Treaty Act*	
1926	The Black Bass Act	Prohibited interstate transport in commerce black bass taken, purchased, or sold in violation of state law
1930	The Tariff Act	Required a certificate of legal acquisition for imports of birds and mammals and their parts
1934	Division of Game Management	Created within Dept. of Agriculture, responsible for wildlife law enforcement
1935	Lacey Act (expanded)	Prohibited foreign commerce in illegally taken wildlife
1940	Bald Eagle Protection Act	Prohibited numerous activities involving Bald Eagles
1960	Migratory Bird Act	Amended to include waterfowl protection
1962	Bald Eagle Protection Act	Amended to include protection for Golden Eagles
1969	Endangered Species Act*	
1971	Airborne Hunting Act	Prohibited use of aircraft to hunt/harass wildlife
1972	Marine Mammal Protection Act	Moratorium on taking/importing marine mammals
1972	Bald/Golden Eagle Protection Act	Amended to increase penalties (both fines/ imprisonment)
1975	CITES Treaty*	
1976	TRAFFIC Network	The wildlife trade monitoring network works to ensure that trade in wild plants and animals is not a threat to the conservation of nature
1978	Antarctica Conservation Act	Established to protect plants/animals on the continent
1982	Endangered Species Act	Amended to include unlawful taking of plants on federal lands
1983	LEMIS Operational	USFWS Law Enforcement Management Information Service (LEMIS) activated
1988	African Elephant Conservation Act	Provided additional protection for African elephants
1988	FWFL founded	The National Fish and Wildlife Forensics Laboratory was dedicated in Ashland, Oregon
1990	10th Port of Entry	Portland, Oregon, became tenth port of entry for importation and exportation of wildlife

(*Continued*)

Table 3.4 (*Continued*)

Date	Act/Treaty	Aim
1992	11th Port of Entry	Baltimore, Maryland, became eleventh port of entry
1992	Wild Bird Conservation Act	Includes provisions to limit or prohibit US imports of exotic bird species and also set standards for qualifying bird breeding facilities and establishes the Exotic Bird Conservation Fund
1994	12th Port of Entry	Boston, Massachusetts, became twelfth port of entry
1994	Rhinoceros/Tiger Conservation Act	Prohibited unlawful taking of rhinoceros and tigers
1996	13th Port of Entry	Atlanta, Georgia, becomes thirteenth port of entry
1998	Rhinoceros/Tiger Conservation Act	Prohibited various activities associated with any reforms on substances derived from rhinoceros and tigers
2005	ESU Wildlife Forensics Lab	Founded with assistance from NSF funding as a private lab
2008	International Veterinary Forensic Science Association	Founded to promote the health, welfare and safety of animals
2009	Society of Wildlife Forensic Science	Formed to develop wildlife forensic science into an integrated comprehensive, and mature discipline

Sources: USFWS: www.lab.fws.gov/publications.php; Neme (2009).
Note: *Acts discussed in depth in text.

taken wildlife and also included the importation of injurious species (USFWS: www.lab.fws.gov/wildlife_laws.php). This Act included under its umbrella not just whole animals (including fish) or plants, but also live or dead specimens, their parts or products made from their bodies, possessed, transported, falsely recorded or labeled or sold in violation of a wildlife-related state, federal, foreign or tribal law or regulation (USFWS: www.lab.fws.gov/wildlife_laws.php). The Lacey Act was expanded in 1935 to prohibit foreign commerce in illegally obtained wildlife. Misdemeanor and felony penalties that require forfeiture of both wildlife involved as well as any vehicle used to assist in the commission of such crimes are provided by this Act. Later, the Act was amended in 1981 to include protection of migratory birds and to target commercial violators with higher fines and prison sentences, and again in 1988 to include felony provisions for commercial guiding violations (USFWS: www.lab.fws.gov/wildlife_laws.php).

By 1918, the United States and Great Britain signed the Migratory Bird Treaty Act into law, recognizing that migratory birds were an international resource, after having been signed by Great Britain two years earlier, but not by Mexico until 1936 and Japan in 1972. In 1918, the treaty offered protection for most migratory birds, making it illegal to pursue or hunt, take, capture, possess, sell, trade, buy, ship/export, or import any migratory bird, any part, nest, eggs or product from any of its derivatives (USFWS: www.lab.fws.gov/wildlife_laws.php). However, as of 1935, only half of the states had laws protecting hawks and none protected all hawk species, especially Accipters, such as falcons and Red-tailed hawks. Some states had bounties on hawks, encouraging shooting, such as the Pennsylvania Goshawk bounty (Goodrich, personal communication). Federal protection for all birds of prey occurred in 1972 when the treaty was amended to protect them and additional species.

The Endangered Species Act (ESA), initially proposed as the Endangered Species Conservation Act of 1969, prohibited the importation of those species "threatened with extinction worldwide" into the United States except for those permitted for zoological or scientific purposes as well as propagation in captivity (USFWS: www.lab.fws.gov/wildlife_laws.php). This Act amended several other important wildlife conservation legislatures, e.g., the Black Bass Act, in an attempt to regulate interstate and foreign commerce of fish illegally taken according to foreign law, and the Lacey Act in an effort to prohibit similar commerce both nationally and internationally of reptiles, mollusks, amphibians and crustaceans, with the primary goal of protecting North American alligators (USFWS: www.lab.fws.gov/wildlife_laws.php). Arguably the best-known wildlife protection law in America, the ESA became law in 1973 and unless permitted by regulation, it expanded the scope to prohibit the exportation along with importation (previously included in the Act), taking, possessing, selling, buying or receiving endangered or threatened animal species across interstate or foreign boundaries. The Act was amended in 1982 to include a prohibition of taking plants on federal lands. In addition, the Act also implements the CITES Treaty that is designed to regulate international commerce of those species at risk of extinction due to such activities.

Neme (2009) referred to the Convention on International Trade in Endangered Species (CITES) as the "Magna Carta for wildlife" as this international treaty regulates currently the transnational commerce of approximately 5000 species of endangered and threatened animals and 28,000 species of plants. Some of these taxa have explicit bans on their harvest. To date there are approximately 170 signatory nations of CITES, making it one of the most powerful and successful international agreements ever. The rigor in the enforcement of CITES is dependent on a mutual agreement between supplying nations with export restrictions and buying nations with import restrictions – an approach that can enforce controls at both country of origin (exit points of wildlife trade) and final destinations (ibid.). The magnitude of the movement of wildlife commerce internationally is three- to six-fold greater among designated ports of entry in the United States compared to undesignated or even unstaffed ports (Figure 3.3). Because shipments are being made through non-designated ports as well as unstaffed ports, strict regulations such as CITES are needed to reduce negative effects on wildlife populations in their country of origin.

The last of the major legislative coups to protect wildlife targeted those species in marine environments. The Marine Mammal Protection Act of 1972 became

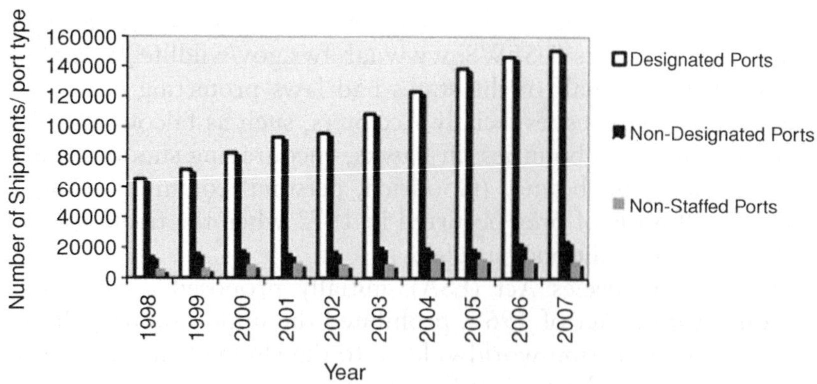

Figure 3.3 The number of shipments per port type to designated, non-designated and non-"staffed" ports of entry to monitor wildlife trade into the United States. Data from USFWS Annual Reports, 1999–2007. USF&WS: www.lab.fws.gov/publications.php.

law and provided protection for all large truly aquatic marine mammals such as whales, dolphins, porpoises, manatees, and dugongs as well as those that utilize both marine and terrestrial habitats e.g. polar bears, walruses, seals, sea lions and sea otters. The Act stated that it was unlawful to take, import, transport, buy, or sell any marine mammal or its derivatives unless the species was exempt from such regulation (USFWS: www.lab.fws.gov/wildlife_laws.php).

Enforcement of Wildlife Protection Policy

The enforcement of the many national and international legislative acts generally falls under the auspices of the National Fish & Wildlife Service (USF&WS) in the United States. However, many countries have established governmental agencies to protect wildlife and enforce international regulations. In the United Kingdom, any investigation into illegal action against wildlife is coordinated by the Department of Environment, Food and Rural Affairs (DEFRA) and assisted by the Partnership for Action Against Wildlife Crime (PAW), a multi-agency body comprised of the police, the UK Border Agency, and other representative government departments, in addition to voluntary organizations involved in wildlife law enforcement in the UK. In Australia, the Department of the Environment, Water, Heritage and the Arts (DEWHA) works with State and Territory wildlife personnel, the Customs Service, the Federal Police as well as other signatories of the CITES treaty, Interpol, and some non-government organizations (NGOs) such as the wildlife trade monitoring network (TRAFFIC) to coordinate intelligence resources in Australia and abroad in an effort to regulate international movement of wildlife and wildlife products for all species, except cetaceans under Part 13A of the Environment Protection and Biodiversity Conservation Act 1999 (EPBC Act) (Australian Government Department of Sustainability, Environment, Water, Population and Communities: see www.environment.gov.au/index.htm).

In 2005, several Asian nations formed the Association of South-East Asian Nations Wildlife Enforcement Network, including Brunei, Cambodia, Indonesia, Laos, Malaysia, Myanmar, the Philippines, Singapore, Vietnam, and Thailand. This is the largest intergovernmental wildlife law enforcement network involving police, customs, and environmental agencies in the world, charged with coordinating the regional response to illegal trade in protected species, which threatens biodiversity, endangers public health, and undermines economic well-being (ASEAN Wildlife Enforcement Network: see www.asean-wen.org/). In the Philippines, the Protected Areas and Wildlife Bureau regulates wildlife farming and permit services for importing and exporting wildlife (Protected Areas and Wildlife Bureau, Republic of the Philippines, Department of Environment and Natural Resources: see www.pawb.gov.ph/). The Wildlife Crime Control Bureau in New Delhi, India, was founded in 2007 as the nation's primary enforcer of the Wildlife Protection Act (1972) established to protect the wildlife of that country (The Wildlife Crime Control Bureau, India: see http://www.wccb.gov.in/).

Development of Wildlife Forensic Laboratories

As wildlife protection legislation has evolved, there has been a subsequent increase in cases appearing in court. The prosecution of individuals for alleged violations required that needed guilt be established beyond a reasonable doubt, a requirement of our criminal system. Some of the basic tenets in forensic investigations involving human suspects and victims include: (1) processing and investigating crime scenes; (2) determining cause and manner of death, and if a crime has occurred; (3) identifying and comparing physical evidence in order to either link or exonerate a suspect and/or victim to a crime scene; and (4) testifying as an expert in the field in question. The hurdles in dealing with wildlife evidence in the court of law were twofold: (1) prior to 1989, it was extremely difficult for federal and state law enforcement to identify individuals who could or would identify the evidence; most were university scientists who either lacked adequate security and analytical procedures or oftentimes refused to present and defend their findings in court; and (2) regular crime labs for human crimes could not justify working on animal cases above those involving humans. This distinct disadvantage when enforcing the law on violators could only be remedied through the establishment of a wildlife crime laboratory. In 1989, federal funds were allocated to construct a National Fish and Wildlife Forensics (NF&WS) Laboratory in Ashland, Oregon, designed to provide services (analytical techniques and expert witness testimony) so that serious wildlife violators, both nationally and internationally, could be successfully prosecuted.

The NF&WS forensic lab processes approximately 700–800 cases annually and utilizes the assembly of six team sections: criminalistics, pathology, morphology, genetics (molecular biology), analytical chemistry, and digital analysis. Agents on these teams evaluate wildlife evidence with the central purpose of: (1) identifying the species or animal or plant from the evidence collected whether is the entire organism, parts or pieces or even products such as clothing, jewelry, or processed meats; and (2) determining the cause-of-death (COD) of the organism in question.

However, prior to any evidentiary analysis, proper evidentiary collection and crime scene management are critical to the success of any investigation and NF&WS forensic lab agents are well skilled in both. In addition, trace evidence analysis and interpretation are essential to any forensic investigation, and the charge of the Criminalistics Unit is to evaluate the physical evidence collected from crime scenes such as ballistic evidence, tool marks, soils, entomological/anthropological (often charged to board-certified experts in each field to evaluate and interpret), questioned documents (such as falsified permits, licenses and other documents), and animal/human prints. Sometimes, both the Biology and Chemistry Units are integrated into trace evidence assessments.

The Pathology Unit functions much like the medical examiner's office that deals with human cases, in that the primary objective for this section is to conduct necropsies (animal autopsies) to determine the COD, mechanism of death (due to injury or disease) as well as the manner of death (i.e. circumstances initiating the COD). While the Pathology Unit generally works on intact carcasses, the Morphology Unit typically uses zoological and botanical form and structure from items such as fur/fibers, feathers, teeth/bones, claws, seeds, flowers, etc. to ascertain the species in question. This work is often facilitated with optical and scanning electron microscopy of this and other evidentiary items. Many times, intact carcasses, identifying morphological characters (such as feathers or fur) are not available or collected as evidence, therefore, it is the lab's Genetic (Molecular Biology) section that utilizes serological proteins and DNA analytical methods, mitochondrial and nuclear DNA for animal and plant species identification, for the individualization of taxa, using kinship analyses as well as geographic origin to establish genetic variation across the geographical range for a given taxon.

When questions such as the cause of death or species identification cannot be determined using biological analytical approaches, the Chemistry Unit of the NF&WS forensic lab can levy an opinion on these questions by using blood or tissue evidence, or any derivative product to examine the chemical and molecular structures for species identification and COD. In addition, this section can provide toxicological methodologies to identify toxins or poisons useful in determining the manner of death or geographic location where death may have occurred.

Evidence interpretation and, more importantly, the communication of this interpretation is paramount to successful convictions of violators of suspected wildlife crimes, therefore the NF&WS forensic lab employs a Digital Analysis Unit that not only utilizes state-of-the-art computer technology, but also audio and visual evidence collected to facilitate jury comprehension of the interpretations presented in court. The lab also has developed a user-friendly computer program for field use to assist agents with the determination of the time-of-death (TOD) civil and criminal wildlife cases.

There has been considerable pressure to augment DNA profiling in wildlife cases worldwide considering the increasing annual case-load of the NF&WS forensics lab. To address these needs, several labs have dovetailed wildlife forensics with natural resource management, conservation, and research. The Wildlife Forensic DNA laboratory within the Natural Resources DNA Profiling and Forensic Centre (NRDPFC) has partnered with Trent University in Ontario, Canada, and the Ontario Ministry of Natural Resources in Ontario, Canada, to assist conservation officers and law enforcement. At Murdoch University in Perth, Australia, Australian Wildlife Forensic Services is a non-profit laboratory aimed at reducing illegal wildlife trade across the country by offering DNA technology to screen a number of wildlife evidentiary substrates e.g., ivory, bones, eggs, traditional Asian medicines, and feathers (Australian Wildlife Forensic Services: see www.wildlifeforensics.com.au/). Most recently, TRACE Wildlife Forensics Network, an NGO based in the UK, is spearheading a project (partnered with TRAFFIC Southeast Asia) designed to train laboratory scientists in DNA techniques as well as enforcement officers in evidence collection and storage, to address wildlife crime in South-East Asian nations. This effort is part of a new initiative within the Association of South-East Asian Nations Wildlife Enforcement Network (ASEAN-WEN) (ASEAN Wildlife Enforcement Network: see www.asean-wen.org/).

Current Perceptions

Wildlife forensics is a nascent field within forensic science, however, it has not been immune to the CSI effect, as observed among a variety of other areas of forensic science, e.g., even in this age of social networking, even wildlife forensics has not been ignored by the Facebook society (Wildlife Forensic Facebook page: www.facebook.com/pages/WILDLIFE-FORENSICS/124098030967924). This increase in public interest most likely is a function of the expanding literature base and professional interest (Figure 3.4). Supplementing this growing list of literature are two textbooks that have been written on the subject, Linacre (2009) and Neme (2009). The former is probably the first book that focused on wildlife forensic molecular and microscopic techniques and targeted those people with a particular interest in wildlife forensics but who were not necessarily active in the field. The latter text is a popular reading account of a very thorough treatise of the evolution of the National Fish & Wildlife Service Forensics Laboratory and the case studies that made it possible. In contrast, our textbook is aimed at practitioners of forensic science, wildlife forensic investigations, students and the public in general.

The NGO, TRACE (Tools and Resources for Applied Conservation and Enforcement) was established in 2006 and has been one of the flagship organizations dedicated to the application of forensic science in wildlife conservation and law enforcement and has served as a template for similar organizations (TRACE – The Wildlife Forensic Network: www.tracenetwork.org/). As with emerging

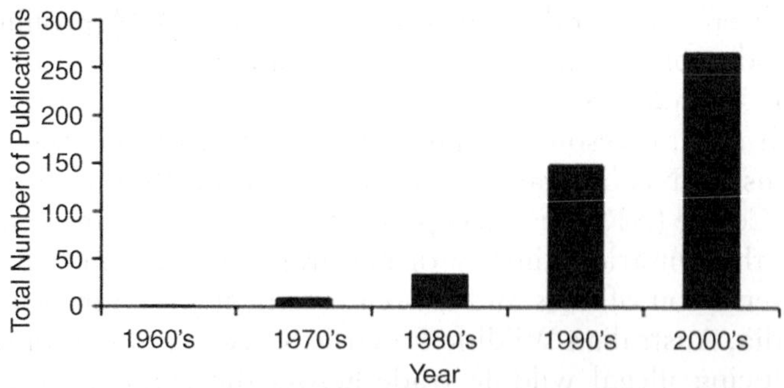

Figure 3.4 Approximate total of publications dealing with wildlife forensics including protocol/methods advancements and case studies found in Biological Abstracts, Greenfile, and JSTOR by searching wildlife forensics and listed according to the decade in print.

areas of forensic science, e.g., forensic entomology – which has close ties to wildlife forensics and its own professional society (North American Forensic Entomology Association: www.nafea.net/NAFEA/Home.html), wildlife forensic science has recently spawned the Society for Wildlife Forensic Science (Society of Wildlife Forensic Science: www.wildlifeforensicscience.org/ and Chapter 2 in this volume) to develop the field as a comprehensive, integrated science including annual professional international conferences as well as a peer-reviewed process to validate new techniques and methodologies.

Conclusion

Illegal poaching and trafficking of wildlife (both animals and plants) are not only one of the most lucrative criminal trades but also have strong ties to organized crime (Neme, 2009). Some reports indicate that less than 10% of all illegal wildlife smuggling is intercepted, and this figure may even be less than 1% (see: www.laurelneme.com/). Sadly, actual numbers of animals and plants trafficked annually are unknown, the diversity of illegal wildlife products is huge and while profits continue to soar due to this illegal business, so do prosecutions of violators of wildlife crime, both on the small and large scale. Wildlife conservation officers, investigators and jurisprudence personnel rely on the advancement of evidence analysis and interpretation to protect wild and domestic animals as well as the conservation of endangered and threatened wildlife and plants. The methods and protocols used by a variety of forensic scientists and the validation of these protocols in a peer-reviewed process have proven effective in this quest of reducing wildlife crime.

The exciting evolution of wildlife forensics in the field of forensic science can be attributed to the following sequence of activities: (1) the development of the NF&WS forensics lab and others around the world; (2) the constant amending of wildlife conservation legislation that ensures increased protection and punishment for violators; (3) the creative application of already established forensic methodologies to the evaluation of wildlife evidence; (4) the establishment of international NGO watchdogs that assist national governments with monitoring illegal wildlife trade and trafficking; and (5) the increase in professional and scientific involvement reflected in the creation of new professional societies, conferences, and publications. The practitioner's understanding of the application of current and new forensic methods and protocols can influence the direction of wildlife investigations but also public comprehension of how this evidence is interpreted may direct the overall outcome of civil and criminal trials.

Acknowledgements

We would like to acknowledge Dr. Martin Hall (Natural History Museum of London) for providing valuable details for the chapter.

References

ASEAN Wildlife Enforcement Network. Available at: www.asean-wen.org/.

Australian Government Department of Sustainability, Environment, Water, Population and Communities. Available at: www.environment.gov.au/index.htm.

Australian Wildlife Forensic Services Available at: www.wildlifeforensics.com.au/.

Avise, J.C. (1996) Introduction: the scope of conservation genetics. In J.C. Avise and J.I. Hamrick (eds) *Conservation Genetics: Case Histories from Nature*. New York: Chapman and Hall, pp. 1–9.

Cooper, J.E. and Cooper, M.E. (2007) *Introduction to Veterinary and Comparative Forensic Medicine*. Oxford: Blackwell Publishers.

Cooper, J.E., Cooper, M.E. and Budgen, P. (2009) Wildlife crime scene investigation: techniques: tools and technology. *Endangered Species Research*, **9**, 229–238.

Herrero, S. (2005) Legal issues in forensic DNA. In S.H. James and J.J. Nordby (eds) *Forensic Science: An Introduction to Scientific and Investigative Techniques*. Boca Raton, FL: CRC Press.

Inman, K. and Rudin, N. (2001) *Principles and Practices of Criminalistics: The Profession of Forensic Science*. Boca Raton, FL: CRC Press.

Laurel Neme: www.laurelneme.com.

Lawton, M.P.C. and Cooper, J.E. (2009) Wildlife crime scene visits. *Applied Herpetology*, **6**, 29–45.

Linacre, A. (2009) *Forensic Science in Wildlife Investigations*. Boca Raton, FL: CRC Press.

McDowell, D. (1997) *Wildlife Crime: Policy and the Law*. Canberra: Australian Government Publishing Service.

Mcknight, B.E. (1981) The washing away of wrongs: forensic medicine in the thirteenth century China by Sung T'zu. In S.H. James and J.J. Nordby (eds.) *Forensic Science: An Introduction to Scientific and Investigative Techniques*. Boca Raton, FL: CRC Press, pp. 136–137.

Merck, M.D. (2007) *Veterinary Forensics: Animal Cruelty Investigations*. Oxford: Blackwell Publishing.

Neme, L.A. (2009) *Animal Investigators*. New York: Scribner Publishers.

North American Forensic Entomology Association. Available at: www.nafea.net/NAFEA/Home.html.

Protected Areas and Wildlife Bureau, Republic of the Philippines, Department of Environment and Natural Resources. Available at: www.pawb.gov.ph/.

Sinclair, L., Merck, M. and Lockwood, R. (2006) *Forensic Investigation of Animal Cruelty: A Guide for Veterinary and Law Enforcement Professionals*. New York: Humane Society Press.

Society of Wildlife Forensic Science. Available at: www.wildlifeforensicscience.org/.

TRACE, The Wildlife Forensics Network. Available at: www.tracenetwork.org/.

United States Fish & Wildlife Service. Available at: www.lab.fws.gov/publications.php.

Wildlife Crime Control Bureau, India. Available at: http://www.wccb.gov.in/.

Wildlife Forensics Facebook Page. Available at: www.facebook.com/pages/WILDLIFE-FORENSICS/124098030967924.

Wilson-Wilde, L. (2010) Combating wildlife crime. *Forensic Science Medical Pathology*. DOI 10.1007/s12024-010-9179-4.

4

Defining a Crime Scene and Physical Evidence Collection

Jason H. Byrd and Lerah K. Sutton

Introduction

Science stands as a witness to almost every crime. It is the duty and task of law enforcement and forensic investigators to analyze and interpret physical evidence, applying relevant and reliable testing to speak for the evidence in a court of law. The task at hand is daunting. An investigator must be able recognize, document, collect, and preserve nearly any item he or she may encounter. This must be done properly, without error, at every crime scene if the evidence is to stand in a court of law. The quote "Science does not start at the laboratory door" holds true for all aspects of forensic science (Shaler and Pizzola, 2004). Scientific and legal principles for evidence must be met without fail from an objective, thorough, and thoughtful approach. Although each crime scene is unique, there are fundamental standards and principles which should be factored into how each crime scene is processed. The investigation techniques for wildlife-related crimes are similar to procedures recommended for any crime scene investigator (Adrian, 1996). This chapter will address the basic scientific and legal principles for physical evidence, with a focus on crime scenes which contain animals as evidence.

Definition of a Crime Scene

Strictly defined, a crime scene is the location where an illegal act has occurred in which physical evidence of the action can be recovered (Horswell, 2004). It is the "tip of the spear" upon which all subsequent methodologies in the forensic sciences will be applied. The objective of a crime scene investigation is to locate,

Wildlife Forensics: Methods and Applications, First Edition. Edited by Jane E. Huffman and John R. Wallace.

document, preserve, and collect physical evidence that can lead to the identity of the offender(s). Any mistake (errors of commission or omission) made at the scene may be impossible to rectify, and the errors could be magnified at each step of the analytical process, up to and including trial. The wildlife crime scene, as with all crimes scenes, is an environment of continual change. Nothing can be done to halt the inevitable change that will happen. The mere act of entering a scene changes it, and these changes can be insignificant or disastrous, depending on your actions and knowledge of crime scene processing and the forensic sciences.

Questions to Be Asked

For each crime scene, the investigator must consider what they wish to accomplish by processing the scene. As a general rule, the scientific method is applied to each and every scene as a guide to assist in the proper collection of physical evidence. It is the job of the crime scene investigator, conservation officer, or law enforcement officer to translate legal questions into scientific questions that can be reliably and repeatedly tested. Therefore, the law enforcement official seeks information that will help answer certain questions commonly encountered at a scene. Common questions for all legal investigations include the following: What happened? Who was involved? When did the event happen? Where did the event happen? How did it happen? For wildlife crime, the investigator must often seek to answer additional questions specific to wildlife or animal investigations. What species was involved? Is the specimen or sample from a male or female? What is the age of the animal?

Physical evidence is collected in an effort to provide answers to these questions as a result of scientific analysis and interpretation. If the collected evidence is found to have probative value, then it may be introduced into court as forensic evidence.

Scene Priority

At all crime scenes, the first priority is to check for survivors, which could include victims, witnesses, the perpetrator, and animals in need of immediate veterinary care. Many conservation officers will arrive at a crime scene and find the perpetrator in the act of committing the offense, or still in the immediate area. Therefore, wildlife officers must constantly be aware of the possibility and dangers associated with human activity at the wildlife crime scene. With all crime scenes, priority is given to any medical care or life-saving efforts that are medically necessary to people and animals even if physical evidence must be sacrificed in the process. Due to the high incidence of weapons and drug trafficking associated with wildlife crime scenes, the discovery of individuals in need of medical attention is commonplace. Weapons should be immediately rendered safe, but no attempt should be made to "clean up" any drugs or other illegal paraphernalia before scene processing begins. Any statements or comments made by individuals already present on scene to the first responding officer or medical personnel should be documented and held as part of the crime scene record. Identifying information for the responding medical and veterinary personnel should also be documented.

First Responding Officer

The most important aspect of crime scene investigation is to preserve the scene with minimal disturbance and change to any of the physical evidence. Often, this duty falls to the first responding officer who is first person to encounter and interact with the physical evidence of potential forensic science value. They will be the initial response effort for an agency and in receipt of all initial information. As a general practice, the first officer on scene should make notation of date, time, location, type of call, and individuals involved. Immediately upon arrival, the officer should ensure the safety and well-being of other response personnel, victims (human and animal), and witnesses by identifying and controlling any dangerous situations. This may be indicated by the activity of individuals, sounds, smells, or sights that may indicate dangers present. All situations should be approached so that human and animal safety is paramount. Once any dangerous situation has been mitigated and officer safety assured, emergency care should be provided to injured individuals. Animals needing immediate veterinary care should be treated at this time. Once on scene, the first officer should guide responding medical and veterinary personnel in a manner that will minimize alteration of the crime scene and contamination of physical evidence. Additionally, the first officer should insure that medical staff preserves all personal effects, and veterinary staff preserves all items in association with the animal (collars, leashes, identification tags, and microchips). Transportation information should be recorded for all medical transports away from the scene. A thorough documentation of all personal property items recovered at the scene should be conducted. This is particularly important with wildlife crimes due to the many seizure laws that apply to wildlife crime.

Securing the Scene

Once any needed medical or veterinary attention has been provided, the first responding officer must then secure the scene to preserve physical evidence. This includes identifying individuals and vehicles at the scene and limiting their movement, as well as separating suspects and witnesses. All individuals present at the scene should be identified and a determination should be made as to what aspects of the crime they may have witnessed. Initial documentation of the number and type of animals present should be conducted at this time.

Securing the scene also includes defining the physical space of the crime scene and demarcating this area with some type of physical barrier. This physical barrier can be established using nearly anything that can create a barrier, including crime scene tape, vehicles, and people. The requirement is that a physical boundary is created and can be monitored for access. Boundaries can be established by starting at the center of the crime scene in the area possessing the most physical evidence and radiating outward to include any and all potential points of ingress and egress of the suspect and/or victims, and all items determined to be physical evidence. This act limits the number of people entering the crime scene and protects the evidence it contains from further deterioration and possible compromise until the scene can be thoroughly documented and processed by the appropriate individuals. Written notations should be made of any individuals or vehicles exiting the crime scene as well as any individuals and vehicles in the immediate vicinity. For all instances the location should be treated as a crime scene until further assessment may prove otherwise.

Once physical barriers have been established, the entry and exit of all individuals should be documented in a crime scene log (Figure 4.1). Only personnel having an immediate need to document and collect physical evidence should be allowed into the crime scene. Within a crime scene, it is important to establish a path for authorized crime scene personnel to use that is the least likely path of the perpetrator. This reduces the likelihood of contamination or destruction of physical evidence potentially left by the perpetrator during his or her travel through the scene. Priority should be given to physical evidence such as shoe and tire impressions that can easily be degraded by environmental factors (e.g., rain and wind). At this time, 4th Amendment Search and Seizure issues should be considered to determine the need for search warrants or consent prior to the collection of physical evidence.

CRIME SCENE SECURITY LOG

Agency Number: Case Number:
Location of Scene, City, State. Case Type:
Securing Officer: Badge Number:
Securing Date: Access Point:
Beginning Time: Ending Time:

Name	Agency	Title	Reason for Entry	Time In	Time Out

Figure 4.1 Standard Crime Scene Log for documentation of personnel activities.

EVIDENCE CHAIN OF CUSTODY RECEIPT

Agency Name: Case Number:

Item #	Description

I hereby acknowledge receipt to the listed evidence items which were taken into my custody on the listed date and received from the listed individual.

From	Name/Signature		Date		Time	
To	Name/Signature		Date		Time	

Figure 4.2 Standard chain of custody log sheet for the transfer of evidence.

Chain of Custody

In order to meet one of the legal standards for evidence, each physical item collected from the crime scene must have the "chain of custody" or "chain of evidence" maintained. This can be defined as a documentation of the location and handling of the item of evidence from the time of collection, and maintained throughout the testing phase until the eventual presentation in court and subsequent disposition or destruction. The minimum amount of information required to establish the chain of custody is item number, date and time of collection, name of collector, and written description of the item. In order to assist in creating a chain of custody, an example log sheet can be found in Figure 4.2. Any break in this "chain" irreparably weakens the association to the scene and leaves open the possibility of undocumented alteration of the evidence.

Processing the Scene

It is important to note that all observations and actions at the scene be documented as soon as possible to preserve the maximum amount of information possible. Never rely on memory. This "contemporaneous" documentation will be maintained as a permanent record. This record should be started by the first responding officer and include such observations as the location and appearance of objects and individuals within the crime scene. No attempt should be made to reposition items that have been moved, and no new items, including scene processing equipment, should be brought into the crime scene until the initial scene documentation is completed. Situational evidence should also be documented at this time (lights on/off, thermostat setting, position of doors and windows, smells, ambient temperature).

Scene assessment

Eventually, control of the scene will shift from the first responding officer to a lead investigator. The investigator will be tasked with determining the type and intensity of investigation to be conducted and will assign specific investigation responsibilities to responding personnel. The first officer should ensure that all notes, observations, and activities are reported to the investigator in charge. The investigator should then re-assess the scene boundaries, resolve search and seizure issues, and establish a pathway for scene ingress and egress. Also, at this time a secure area for equipment, responding personnel, witnesses, and temporary evidence storage should be established. Separate areas should be established for media and the public to gather at a safe distance away from the crime scene.

When processing a scene, there are a number of main functions of a crime scene analyst. Successfully identifying, locating, collecting, and preserving physical evidence as well as documenting the crime scene and submitting the evidence to a laboratory for analysis all aid in achieving the overall goals of a death scene. In order to fulfill these goals of identifying the victim, determining time of death, and cause and manner of death, it is important to select your team members appropriately. The team leader (crime scene analyst) should ideally be the member of the team with the most experience, as he or she is responsible for the overall coordination of the forensic aspects of the case. Other roles include photographer, sketcher/note taker, excavator, soil sifter, and evidence custodian. Since the number of individuals present at each scene may differ, it may occasionally be necessary for some members of the team to be assigned multiple duties.

Depending on the nature of the scene at hand, the lead investigator may decide it is necessary to call in additional specialized personnel to assist with scene processing. These specialists may include a forensic anthropologist, forensic odontologist, forensic entomologist, forensic botanist, medical examiner, search dogs and handlers, wildlife biologist, or a surveyor to assist in mapping the scene. It is the job of the lead investigator to coordinate the efforts of additional personnel as well as to arrange for any public works type equipment that may be necessary such as aerial photography, water for wet screening, or heavy equipment.

Initial Documentation

In order to create a plan for processing the crime scene, an initial "walk-through" should be conducted by the lead investigator and crime scene personnel. This will allow everyone involved to develop a concise and logical approach to processing the crime scene and ensure that all relevant evidence will be collected. The walk-through helps prevent the primary error often made at crime scenes of not collecting vital evidence. The walk-through will provide an overview of the entire scene and identify the order in which physical evidence will be processed. Generally speaking, the most relevant evidence will be processed first. However, consideration must also be given to any items of evidence that are easily degraded or damaged and may require special precautions to protect from change until they can be fully documented. Every procedure at the crime scene should have the basic objective of preserving the integrity of the evidence, limiting degradation, preventing contamination, and providing the maximum information about their relationships to each other.

Before evidence can be collected, it must first be "recognized." Since forensic evidence can be defined as "physical evidence of probative value," the crime scene analyst must have in mind a preliminary hypothesis as well as a few plausible alternatives. Any item of physical evidence that could support any of the hypotheses should be collected. Therefore, a crime scene search is not a blind search for "anything," it is a directed search designed to minimize the inherent oversights by an attempt to search with mindless purpose.

Based on the nature of the crime scene in terms of size and environment, different types of searches may be conducted, with the most common types being grid, strip/line, and zone searches (Figure 4.3). Generally speaking, most searches are a modification of a grid search but a strip/line search is most often used in outdoor scenes. A line search is conducted by aligning personnel along the outer perimeter of the scene, standing fingertip to fingertip. The line then moves forward as a whole unit and stops when a piece of potential evidence is recognized. Once the piece of evidence has been flagged, the line continues to move forward. Once the line has reached the opposite end of the scene, it should then walk through the scene in the other direction so that it is searched once from north to south and again from east to west. This allows the entire area to be searched twice by two different individuals which decreases the chances of overlooking items of physical evidence. Keep in mind that there are several unsuitable conditions for searching and processing outdoor scenes including

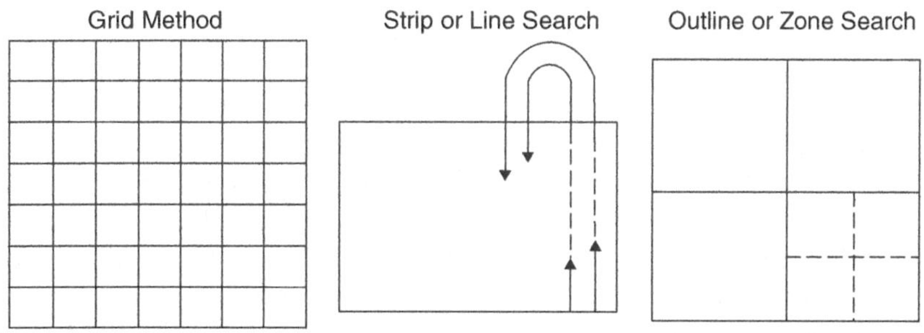

Figure 4.3 Typical search patterns that can be employed to locate physical evidence.

darkness, rain, severe weather, or other unsafe conditions. Establish safe and appropriate conditions first, then begin the search.

When flagging evidence located during the walk-through search, it may be helpful to use different colored flags to indicate specific types of evidence. Consider flagging biological evidence (e.g., tissue, bone, hair, teeth, nails, etc.) with one color and other physical evidence with another.

It is vital to know what you are searching for as the type of scene may alter the search techniques employed. Consider whether it is the primary crime scene or a dump site, a surface scene or a burial. Surface scenes may have skeletonized, decomposed, concealed, or scattered remains while burial scenes may have an extended time interval, making detection more difficult, or it may be recent. If the case is recent, it may be useful to look for the body itself, hair, blood, rope, tape, or other artifacts such as clothing and personal effects. It may also be useful to look for differences in the natural environment to indicate potential human influence. If a large amount of foliage is present, depressed areas of foliage or broken branches may be indicators of a path to a grave or dump site. Scattering by scavengers may also be an issue with surface scenes as scattered remains may be difficult to distinguish from the surrounding environment and vegetation. Despite scattering, it is important to determine a "core area," the location of the body when decomposition began. This is usually the area with the highest concentration of skeletal material, in particular vertebrae and ribs.

To assist in the search, a basic written and photographic record of the scene should be made at this time to provide a permanent record of the initial scene before intentional or inadvertent change may occur. This initial scene assessment will determine the nature and extent of the scene documentation that will be required. The walk-through will also allow for the opportunity to assess the need for additional personnel, forensic specialists, and equipment. This phase of the investigation will determine the number and type of personnel needed and their duty assignments.

Scene Documentation

Once the walk-through is complete, it will be apparent to the forensic investigator what type and level of documentation will be necessary. For most any scene, combinations of documenting techniques are utilized. The most widely utilized type of scene documentation is photography. Supplemental videography is utilized, as are sketches, measurements, and written notations.

Once photography is complete, preliminary sketches should be completed to show the relative location of items of evidence. These sketches are not required to be "to scale" provided a footnote is indicated on the sketch with the disclaimer "not to scale." However, each sketch should include a "North" marker and a unique identifier label for each item of evidence. Distance to reference points (i.e., datum, subdatum, corner of room, adjacent buildings, and other landmarks) should also be included. They should also include the title of the scene portrayed, location, case number, date, and name of person preparing the sketch. Only essential items of evidence should be contained within a sketch; it is not necessary to include every item found on scene. If symbols are used to represent specific items within the sketch, a legend should also be included to explain these symbols. It may also be necessary to draw more than one sketch to fully document the scene (e.g., position of physical evidence, bones within a grave, physical evidence within a grave, etc.).

Photography

All scenes should be documented utilizing overall, mid-range, and macro (close-up) photographs. Overall shots of the entire scene show the relationships of all items of evidence within the scene to the surrounding area. These photographs should be the first ones taken upon arrival and should show the scene "as is" without photo scales, evidence markers, personnel, or other equipment in the photograph. Should you feel it necessary to take additional overall shots once evidence has been marked, this can be done once mid-range and macro photographs have been completed. Moving from general to more specific, mid-range photographs should show relationships of items of evidence within the scene. Macro photography should show detail of individual items of evidence and can be used for comparison purposes (e.g., fingerprints, fabric marks, shoe or tire impressions, injuries, wounds, bite marks, etc.). For these photographs, each item of evidence should ideally fill the entire field of view of the camera lens. All evidence to be collected should be documented photographically without size scales and evidence labels, and then photographed again with specific identifying labels and scales. If possible, photographs should be taken at a 90° angle to the item of evidence. Using a photographic scale such as those from the American Board of Forensic Odontology may be helpful as the coloration of these scales is 18% gray, which allows for correction for color distortion using photo editing software. These scales also contain circles which help to correct any angle distortion in the photograph, indicated by the circles appearing as ellipses in the photographs. As a matter of routine, photographs should be made of all victims, suspects, witnesses, onlookers, and vehicles and each photograph taken should be recorded in a photo log (Figure 4.4). Even if duplicates or mistake photographs are taken, none should be deleted or altered in any way. As a general rule, you can never take too many photographs; a seemingly insignificant item may turn out to be of great importance. Video can be taken to supplement photography, but it should never be utilized to replace or substitute still photos.

At all crime scenes, with wildlife crime being no exception, properly executed documentation and processing of evidence are essential to presentation in court and successful persecution. Therefore, it is necessary to ensure that all aspects of the scene are fully and appropriately documented. While small errors in documentation, collection, or preservation at the crime scene may appear insignificant at the time, they can prove to be detrimental to the outcome of a case.

DIGITAL PHOTOGRAPH LOG

Agency Name: Case Number:

Scene Location:
City, State:

Photo	Digital File Number	Description

Use additional forms as necessary to document each photograph taken on the scene.

Figure 4.4 Standard photographic log sheet for documentation of photographs.

Note taking

Taking notes at a crime scene is very useful because it forces crime scene personnel to commit their observations to writing and to keep a record detailing actions pertaining to the crime scene. Note taking should begin the moment personnel arrives on scene and should continue in chronological order throughout the duration of the investigation. When arriving on scene, initial notes should contain a brief narrative description of the scene as well as time of call out, time of arrival, names of all individuals present, and a description of the geographical and physical location of the scene and the surrounding area. Other situational evidence such as temperature, sounds, smells, lighting, and pertinent weather conditions should also be included in the written notes. All notes should be neat and thorough as sloppy or incomplete notes can be misinterpreted at a later date.

During scene processing, note taking continues to play an important role. Written notes should contain a description of any evidence collected and the location in which it was found. If a body is present, detailed notes should be made as to location and position of the body. This description should include as much information as possible such as gender, hair color, positioning, measurements, wounds (if present), and any other additional items present on or around the body. Any specific evidence marking system being used should be indicated in written notes to further aid in photographic interpretation. Techniques for processing burial scenes or dump sites for animals are presented in Chapter 5 in this volume.

Remains in an Aquatic Environment

Regardless of the type of scene an investigator may encounter, each scene should be processed utilizing the same basic techniques and principles. Unique scenes such as aquatic environments are no exception to this rule. If remains are located on a seabed, photographs should still be taken, a grid should still be created, and all evidence should be documented and processed exactly as it would be in a surface scene. However, some specialized equipment (e.g., underwater camera, waterproof paper, underwater pens, scuba equipment, etc.) is required. To properly process an underwater scene, the assistance of individuals possessing both crime scene specialties and scuba certification is an absolute necessity. Before processing the scene, the investigator should consider the type of aquatic environment (i.e. open water, swift water, etc.).

The underwater crime scene poses a myriad of dangers for the investigator. However, the biggest danger of recovering remains and processing evidence in an aquatic environment is the possible presence of seemingly innocuous silt. Some forms of silt such as sand are harmless as it is heavy and settles quickly when disturbed. Mud and red clay pose greater threats in underwater scenes as they can cause a "silt-out condition" with a cloud-like effect causing zero visibility when disturbed. This condition could take several days to clear (Eliopulos, 1993), and this would make processing the scene extremely difficult and dangerous, if not impossible. Only fully certified and experienced scuba divers should attempt to recover remains from an aquatic environment.

Collection of Evidence

During the walk-through, the sequence of evidence collection should have been prioritized with consideration for the durability of the evidence (most easily degraded or changed should be collected first), and to conserve movements of the crime scene personnel at the scene (evidence located close to points of access should be collected prior to evidence in out-of-the-way areas). Also, evidence located between points of access and the body, if present, should be collected first so forensic investigators can gain access to the animal remains for documentation and processing. Finally, the entire scene should be processed in a manner such that initial collection procedures will not jeopardize any subsequent collections that may be required. This prioritization is a complex process, and requires an awareness of all methods to document, collect, and preserve physical evidence to ensure the entire scene is processed without compromising any evidence.

In order to ensure the integrity of physical evidence, scene security must be maintained until all processing is complete and the scene is released. For each item of evidence collected, its unique identifier label should be recorded, as well as its location at the scene, date and time of collection, and the name of the collector. This is the minimum information required to establish the "chain of custody." Standard samples (reference samples) should also be collected. If necessary, elimination samples should be obtained while the scene is still secure. It is important to always consider digital evidence. This includes computers, hard drives, and portable/external memory, as well as video tapes, cell phones, and cameras.

At the time of collection, the physical evidence is often changed, and preservation to prevent further change becomes the main objective. The first rule of

EVIDENCE LOG

Agency Name: Case Number:

Scene Location:
City, State:

Item #	Description	Location	Disposition

Figure 4.5 Standard evidence log sheet for the documentation of physical evidence.

evidence is to minimize change while doing no harm. All collected evidence should be packaged to avoid contamination and damage and recorded in an evidence log (Figure 4.5). Proper evidence containers should be utilized for differing types of evidence, and each container should be uniquely labeled with an identifier, name of collector, date and time of collection, and location. All evidence should be handled minimally, and maintained in a manner to minimize change, degradation, or loss.

Review of Scene Processing

Everyone involved in the collection of evidence from the crime scene should meet to review the scene processing that occurred prior to releasing the scene. During this meeting, the collected evidence should be reviewed; any preliminary findings and potential forensic testing should be discussed. This meeting also provides the opportunity for personnel to suggest collection of additional evidence, consider any special requests, and establish various responsibilities for having evidence analyzed post-scene.

Final Inspection

The investigator in charge should conduct a final walk-through to ensure each area of the crime scene has been processed, all collected evidence is accounted for, and all equipment and materials from the investigation are removed from the scene. After the final inspection is complete, and after consultation with all investigative personnel involved, the crime scene can be released from law enforcement control. Any subsequent physical evidence discovered and recovered from the scene may lack the legal protections necessary to be presented as courtroom evidence in any future legal proceedings.

Each crime scene is unique, and the specific requirement to properly collect and preserve the multitude of physical evidence items is beyond the scope of this chapter. However, certain basic legal and scientific requirements must be met for all types of physical evidence at all scenes. Unfortunately, these basic requirements are often not met and as a result a large amount of physical evidence with probative value is kept from being presented in the courtroom. Therefore, it is critical that all investigative personnel are well versed in the minimum scientific and legal standards for evidence.

References

Adrian, W.J. (ed.) (1996) *Wildlife Forensic Field Manual*. Colorado: Association of Midwest Fish and Game Law Enforcement Officers.

Eliopulos, L.N. (1993) *Death Investigator's Handbook: A Field Guide to Crime Scene Processing, Forensic Evaluations, and Investigative Techniques*. Boulder, CO: Paladin.

Horswell, J. (2004) The practice of crime scene investigation. In J. Horswell (ed.) *International Forensic Science and Investigation Service*. Boca Raton, FL: CRC Press.

Shaler, R.C. and Pizzola, P.A. (2004) Forensic scientists at the crime scene: lab directors' perspective. In *Proceedings of the American Academy of Forensic Sciences*, Vol. 10.

5

Forensic Evidence Collection and Cultural Motives for Animal Harvesting

Michelle D. Hamilton and Elizabeth M. Erhart

Introduction

Use of wild animals by humans has a long history, with evidence of consumption dating back over 2 million years (Asfaw *et al.*, 1999), documented use as trade goods dating to 6,000 years ago (Maisels, 1993), and use as medicines documented for millennia (Lev, 2003). These and other cultural practices continue today (Davies, 2005). Further, as the ecological and spatial overlap of humans and animals has intensified in recent times due to human population expansion that covers much of the earth's surface, so too have the use and trade of wildlife intensified (TRAFFIC, 2008). Use and trade may be local, such as hunting for meat for direct consumption, or take place many thousands of miles away, as products passing through a complex sequence of individuals from harvester to end consumer.

Today, wild animals continue to be a critically important resource, meeting the food requirements of human communities in many areas of the world. In at least 62 countries wildlife constitute at least 20% of the animal protein consumed and is often the only form of protein (Prescott-Allen and Prescott-Allen, 1982; Robinson and Redford, 1991; Townsend, 2000). Whereas most hunted wildlife is consumed locally, there has been a distinct upsurge in the amount that now goes into regional and international trade networks (Bennett and Robinson, 2000).

There is also great economic value attached to the subsistence use of, and the commercial trade in, wild meat, making it an important source of livelihood for

Wildlife Forensics: Methods and Applications, First Edition. Edited by Jane E. Huffman and John R. Wallace.

both rural and urban communities. There is no clear break between subsistence and market hunting in terms of technologies or prey, but market hunting is obviously motivated by commercial considerations (Rabinowitz, 1998). The increased use of guns has also made it easier to kill large, wary, and/or arboreal prey (Kramer, 2001). Although the major portion of meat harvested by forest hunters are large animals, particularly the larger ungulates and primates, a huge range of other species contributes to the numbers (Redford and Robinson, 1987; Bennett and Robinson, 2000; Nooren and Claridge, 2001; Rao *et al.*, 2005). As the impetus for hunting, urban wealth is increasingly replacing rural poverty (Robinson and Bennett, 2002; Polet and Ling, 2004), and the preferred prey of hunters are more often trade species such as elephants, tigers, and bears rather than food species such as deer, pigs, primates (Rao *et al.*, 2005; Williamson, 2002). The use of wildlife in medicines has increased, particularly in Asia (Nooren and Claridge, 2001; Wilkie and Lee, 2004). The value of wild meat harvested in the Amazon Basin exceeds \$175 million per year, in Côte d'Ivoire, the value of meat eaten each year is estimated to be \$200 million (Lamarque, 1995; Tratado de Cooperación Amazonica, 1995), and the total estimated value of the wild meat sold in Sarawak is about \$83 million per year (Wildlife Conservation Society and Sarawak Forest Department, 1996). Illegal resource use can provide alternative livelihood strategies to marginalized people and substantial profits to poachers of prized species (Rao and McGowan, 2002; Pratt *et al.*, 2004), but legitimate resource users can suffer significant revenue losses as a result of illegal use of resources, and biological impacts range from declines in genetic diversity and species richness to changes in community composition and ecosystems (Gigliotti and Taylor, 1990; Pauly *et al.*, 2002; Edirisinghe, 2003; Brashares *et al.*, 2004; Okello *et al.*, 2008).

Wild Animals as Pharmacopeias

Animals and products derived from their various organs have been used as medicinal substances for at least 4,000 years since the ancient Assyrian, Chinese, and Egyptian civilizations (Adeola, 1992; Anageletti *et al.*, 1992; Veith, 2002; Lev 2003). Currently, the World Health Organization estimates that 80% of the world's developing countries rely on animal and plant-based medicines because they are often the only accessible and affordable treatment available, and that traditional medicines are quickly gaining in popularity in developed countries where Western medicines are readily available (WHO, 1999). Although traditional human populations have a large pharmacopoeia consisting of wild plant and animal species, these ingredients are also increasingly valued as raw materials in the preparation of modern medicines and herbal preparations (Kang and Phipps, 2003).

The extensive practice of traditional medicine in developing countries, and the rapidly growing acceptance of alternative therapies in developed countries, have resulted in the field of zootherapy, which is the use of medicines obtained from animals or ultimately derived from them (Labadie, 1986; Puri, 2000). Wild and domestic animals and their organs and by-products (e.g., gallbladders, hooves, paws, skins, bones, feathers, horns, tusks) form important ingredients in the preparation of curative, protective and preventive medicine (Adeola, 1992; Anageletti *et al.*, 1992; Shephard *et al.*, 2004). For example, in traditional Chinese medicine, which dates back at least 3,000 years, more than 1,500 animal species have been recorded to be of some medicinal use (China National Corporation of Traditional and Herbal Medicine, 1995). In India nearly 20% of the Ayurvedic medicine is based on animal-derived substances (Unnikrishnan, 1998). In Bahia State, in the north-east of Brazil, over 180 medicinal animals have been recorded (Costa-Neto, 2004).

Zootherapeutical products are used to treat a wide variety of human health problems that vary from the promotion of good health, to the treatment of specific illness and disease, to use as aphrodisiacs. The most frequently used animal taxa in medicines and for magical or religious purposes are primates with at least 101 species from 38 genera and 10 families affected. The greatest concentration of primate use (over 46%) is in Asia (Alves *et al.*, 2010), which reflects the overall increase in zootherapy in this area of the world (Nooren and Claridge, 2001; Wilkie and Lee, 2004). China and its surrounding regions are particularly dangerous for primates where their use as zootherapeutics is growing to the point that it is unsustainable (Corlett, 2007; Nijman and Shepherd, 2007) and the primary threat to their conservation (Mittermeier *et al.*, 2007).

Throughout history, primates have produced a range of different and sometimes conflicting views among people, leading to veneration and denigration. Various folktales represent primates as human ancestors, with some seen as capable of warding off the evil eye or spirits (Nekaris *et al.*, 2010). Although cultural rules often forbid the harming or killing of these species, it is not the case that they are never used in medicines or for magical or religious purposes.

Trade in Wild Animals

Utilitarian and non-utilitarian trade in wild animals was first documented with the beginnings of the urban, literate societies about 6,000 years ago (Maisels, 1993). Aspects of urbanization included increasingly large human populations, social stratification, civil administration, common defense, cooperative and specialized labor, and foreign trade to obtain materials not available locally. Although most of the urban population had little leisure time or money, wealthy individuals, who included royalty, government officials, priests, merchants, and landowners, were able to indulge in animal collecting (Hawkes, 1973; Hughes, 1975; Menzies, 1994). Trade in animals expanded to urban centers across the Old World with the advent of the Silk Routes (collectively known as the "Silk Road"), named from the lucrative Chinese silk trade that began during the Han Dynasty (206 BC–220 AD) (Elisseeff, 2000). Beginning in the fifteenth century, trade in animals intensified as Europeans explored, mapped and colonized much of the planet, making direct contact with cultures in Africa, the Americas, Asia and Oceania (Mancall, 1999). Thus, records of animal trade and collections began with the ancient civilizations of Mesopotamia, Egypt, China, India, the central Andes, and Mesoamerica, and expanded to urban centers around the world and through time. Trade in wild animals has continued to be a major source of foreign exchange in the twentieth century (Martin and Phipps, 1996).

Recovering Evidence at Poaching Scenes

Worldwide, the illegal procurement and harvesting of endangered or out-of-season animal species are tied to subsistence-based hunting practices, traditional medicinal therapies, culturally patterned sport activities, or black market trade use. As a result, the quality and quantity of evidence left behind at a poaching scene will vary depending on the animal species harvested, the specific organ or body parts targeted, the cuts of meat preferred, and the weapon or hunting technique employed. For example, in the United States, poaching involves species such as deer (*Odocoileus virginianus*) for meat resources, the gallbladders of black bears (*Ursus americanus*) for exported medicinal use, and the feathers of bald eagles (*Haliaeetus leucocephalus*) for sale or trade on the black market. The proper documentation, collection, and preservation of evidence from scenes where suspected illegal poaching activities have occurred are crucial for the purposes of prosecution of individuals involved with these practices. In this section, a general methodology for locating, identifying, and preserving evidence found at suspected animal harvesting scenes is presented. These procedures are adapted from methods and techniques used in forensic anthropological casework (see France *et al.*, 1997; Galloway *et al.*, 2001), and they are intended to serve as a baseline for the wildlife investigator who has access to minimal resources or equipment.

As noted, the collection of information is invariably accompanied by the loss of information (Skinner and Lazenby, 1983), and the act of investigating the crime destroys the integrity of the scene in ways that make future reconstruction difficult, if not impossible. Documentation is therefore crucial to maintaining the integrity of the investigation and building a case for court and prosecutorial purposes. Documentation has been addressed in Chapter 4 in this volume.

Proper reference documents (written notes, photographs, sketch maps, etc.) are essential to insure a permanent record of the scene exists and to note the procedures used to collect evidence. Photographs should be taken with the goal of preserving the scene and documenting the recovery process, since the very act of processing and collection of evidence destroys the scene. Photography at crime scenes is addressed in Chapter 4 in this volume.

Evidence collection proceeds using established investigative and crime scene protocols (e.g., Fox and Cunningham, 1973), with the goal of ensuring full recovery of items of evidentiary value and to minimize contamination and/or modification of evidence. Establish security and chain of custody protocols beginning from the initiation of collection at the scene. In addition to collecting known or suspected evidentiary items, also collect reference/control samples for comparative items such as soil, water, botanical remains, and insect specimens present at the scene. Begin collection starting with the most fragile or ephemeral items first. Physical evidence at poaching scenes may include items related to animal procurement, preparation, disposal, and transportation. Items to be aware of include ballistic/projectile material, trapping equipment, footprints, tire marks, shovel and other tool marks, and items such as cigarettes, drink containers, and other personal items which may retain DNA or latent fingerprint evidence. Biological evidence at poaching sites may include animal remains (including skeletal elements, decomposing tissues, feathers, skin, blood, fur, offal, and discarded paws), entomological evidence (i.e., fly larvae indicative of time since death), or botanical evidence (such as roots, pollen, and leaves which may indicate location or time since death).

Prior to collecting and transporting the evidence, record the location of each item using notes, photographs, and sketch maps. Label each evidence container and identify who collected the evidence, the date and time of collection, the location where the evidence was recovered from, and the nature of the evidence. Insure that the evidence collection containers (paper or plastic bags, paper or plastic envelopes, vials, jars, boxes, etc.) are appropriate for each item and will not result in damage to the specimen. For example, bones should always be collected in paper versus plastic bags to inhibit mold growth and potential damage from moisture, fleshed remains should be placed in plastic or rubber containers to avoid leakage and contamination, and insect evidence should be preserved according to established entomological collection protocols (see Tomberlin and Sandford, Chapter 6 in this volume).

Initial overview of scene: establishing site boundaries

Access to crime scene areas where illegal poaching activities have occurred should be limited to those investigators directly tasked with processing the scene and collecting evidence, in order to maintain evidentiary integrity and site security (Bureau of Alcohol, Tobacco and Firearms, 1999; U.S. Department of Justice, National Institute of Justice, 2004). Prior to processing the scene, the wildlife investigator should conduct an initial scene walk-through (Table 5.1).

Locating the evidence: line and spiral searches

Depending on the nature of the outdoor crime scene, evidence may be left on the surface (and further scattered by additional animal or environmental agents), or it may be buried in clandestine graves in an effort to prevent discovery. These scenarios represent two possible disposal methods, and the investigator can take advantage of various search strategies and techniques for locating both types of scenes.

Table 5.1 List of tasks the wildlife investigator should consider when evaluating a wildlife crime scene for zooanthropological evidence.

1. Set up established entry and exit points in order to minimize damage and limit contamination of the scene
2. Outline areas of interest (for example, areas of ground disturbance, burn pits, campsites, butchering spots, or trapping areas)
3. Identify and protect physical evidence (such as soft tissue or skeletal remains, field dressing byproducts, ballistic evidence, or items that might retain perpetrator DNA)
4. Determine if a larger search strategy is necessary to recover more items of evidentiary value

Established search and recovery protocols should be utilized in order to identify areas or items of interest (Fox and Cunningham, 1973; Bureau of Alcohol, Tobacco and Firearms, 1999; U.S. Department of Justice, National Institute of Justice, 2004). If there are multiple personnel available, a line search should be initiated with participants standing at arm's length apart, with the entire line proceeding first in a parallel and then in a perpendicular plane, so that the site is eventually covered in a grid pattern (Figure 5.1) (Morse *et al.*, 1983; Killam, 1990; Connor, 2007). For smaller evidentiary items, or in cases where the vegetation makes visibility difficult, participants can stand shoulder to shoulder with 20–30% of the searcher's visual field overlapping (Dirkmaat and Adovasio, 1997). To ensure a complete recovery, searchers can even proceed on hands and knees to perform fingertip searches. If the investigator is alone while conducting a search over a wide area, a more effective strategy would be in a spiral pattern, starting in the center of the search area (i.e., where evidence has initially been spotted), scanning left and right, and slowing spiraling outwards (Figure 5.1) (Morse *et al.*, 1983; Killam, 1990; Connor, 2007).

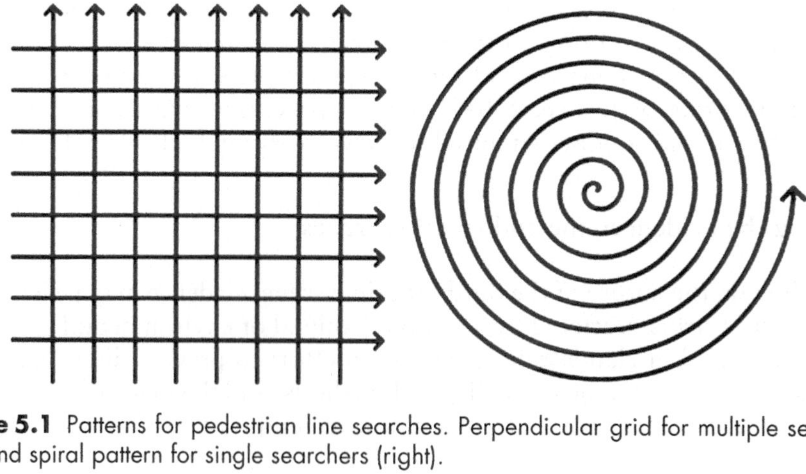

Figure 5.1 Patterns for pedestrian line searches. Perpendicular grid for multiple searchers (left) and spiral pattern for single searchers (right).

All items of potential evidence found during these searches must be flagged, photographed with a scale, and documented prior to disturbing or removing them from their initial discovery location. If the evidence is confined to the surface, thorough and repeated line searches will ensure maximum recovery of all available elements. However, if the remains are suspected to have been buried, additional approaches may be necessary to identify the location of the grave if it is not immediately identifiable.

Locating the Burial: Anomalies on the Surface

When remains have been clandestinely buried in an effort to hide evidence of illegal poaching, there are a series of techniques the investigator can use in order to identify the location of the burial, excavate the grave, and retrieve items of associated evidentiary value. While these protocols have been developed for the discovery and recovery of human remains in forensic anthropological contexts, these techniques also have application to situations where animal remains are suspected to have been buried. Locating clandestine graves is best accomplished by observing anomalies in vegetation, topography, and environment (Hochrein, 2002). Essentially, the observer is looking for markers of surface disturbance, including:

- *Anomalous ground features:* The action of digging a grave into previously undisturbed soil alters site topography in ways that can very clearly differentiate it as a potential burial site. The presence of disturbed soil such as dirt piles and subsurface soils on the surface (i.e., layers such as clays normally found below other soil types), as well as depressions or mounded areas, unusually compact or loose soils, bald spots, and/or cracks in the soil are all potentially indicative of disturbance. The investigator must determine if these are natural (i.e., old tree falls can leave mounded dirt piles as a result of the root ball breaking the surface), or unnatural (i.e., as a result of perpetrator actions). Utilizing a probe in a suspect area and in a nearby control area for comparison will help ascertain whether the soil is compacted (undisturbed) or loose (possibly disturbed) (Morse *et al.*, 1983; Owsley, 1995; Connor, 2007). Loose areas should be flagged in an effort to outline the grave boundary based on the border between disturbed and undisturbed probe tests.
- *Anomalous vegetation:* Plants react to soil disturbance in a variety of ways that may signify the presence of a burial. The act of digging a pit will kill the vegetation located on the surface, and backfill dirt from the grave may be thrown on surrounding vegetation, also causing it to die. Different plant species from those normally found in the area may be attracted to freshly disturbed/aerated soils (such as dandelions), so the investigator should be alert for anomalous plant growth (Figure 5.2). Additionally, the presence of decomposing tissue in a burial may affect plant growth on the surface in one

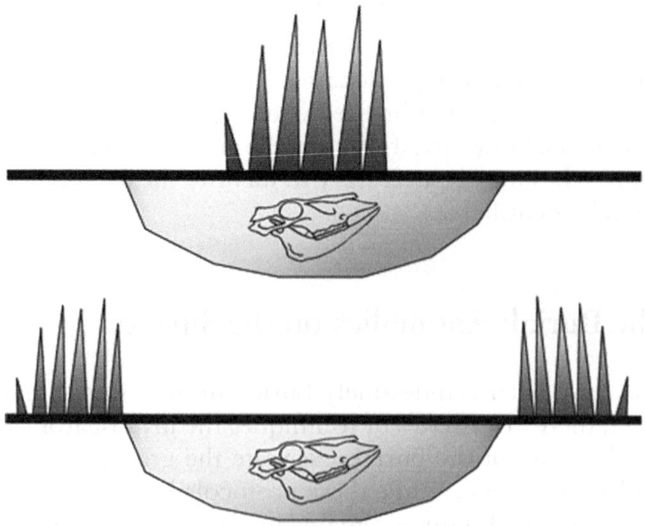

Figure 5.2 Anomalous vegetation over gravesites showing unusual plant growth patterns as a result of remains buried below the surface releasing additional nutrients into the soil (top), and vegetation that has died over a grave site due to soil disturbance and the release of acidic decompositional by-products (bottom).

of two ways; volatile body acids can leach into the soil and kill the plants via the root systems, or the plants may respond favorably to the presence of decomposing material and experience a growth as a result of increased nutritive chemicals in the soil (Figure 5.2). All of these indicators, ranging from unexpected plant types, to patches of ground with no plants on them or areas where plants are flourishing in comparison to the surrounding environment should be flagged and investigated as possible burial locations.

- *Human artifacts:* The human byproducts of digging a grave include tamped-down grass and other vegetation, dirt left on the surface, shoe prints in the soil, as well as shovel or other tool marks in the grave walls (Hochrein, 2002; Hunter and Cox, 2005). Additionally, there may be obvious attempts to hide the grave by deliberately placing rocks, branches, or trash on top of the burial.

Burial mapping and excavation strategies

Once the grave has been located, for proper documentation and recovery purposes it must be excavated and mapped using protocols adapted from archaeological practice (Roskams, 2001) in order to preserve evidence location and context within the burial (Figure 5.3).

The simplest way to map a burial is to superimpose a grid over it. Begin by establishing a datum point of known coordinates from which everything will be measured and which will be the reference point for the map. The datum

Figure 5.3 Series showing the excavation of buried juvenile pig remains. Image a: Using probes for assessment of soil pressure changes in the ground indicative of disturbed earth. Image b: After identifying a likely burial location based on probing, laying out a 1 meter by 1 meter square using measuring tapes to triangulate right angles. Image c: The grave outline becomes visible as the difference between the compaction of disturbed and undisturbed soil is revealed while using trowels to gently scrape the surface of the earth. Image d: Screening the excavated soil for biological or material evidence. Image e: Pig bones revealed at base of shallow burial. Image f: After photographic and written documentation is complete, the bones are removed from the grave and placed in paper evidence bags for transportation to the laboratory.

should be a permanent feature such as a geological survey marker or the corner of a permanent structure, but often when dealing with outdoor crime scenes a permanent datum is not available. In this case, driving a metal rebar or a large nail into the ground and then mapping in its coordinates can establish a site datum. Once the recovery of evidence is complete, the datum can be driven below the level of the ground (to avoid injuries by people or animals tripping over it) so that investigators can return and find the scene at a later time using metal detectors.

The datum traditionally is placed in the southwest corner of the area to be excavated, and from the corner of the datum, squared grids are imposed over the burial area. The grids are assigned individual numbers/letters, and measurement readings of items recovered from within the grave can be taken using the datum as a fixed reference point (Figure 5.4).

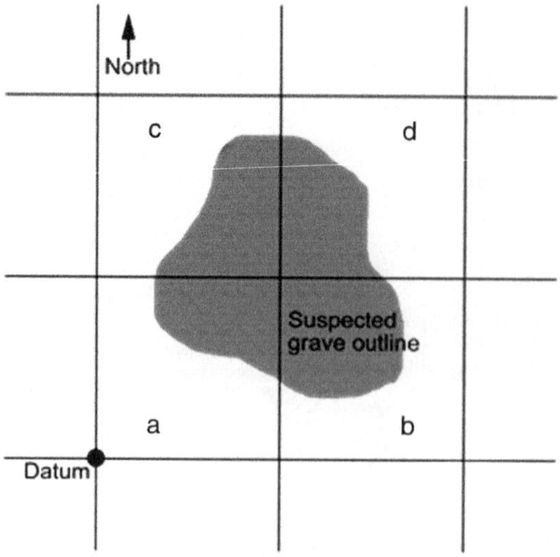

Figure 5.4 Depiction of an imposed 1x1 meter grid system over a suspected grave site showing a datum located in the southwest corner.

Burial excavation must proceed in a controlled and standardized manner (Schultz *et al.*, 2006). It is important to remember that evidence may be located throughout the grave, and not just at the level of the remains. For this reason, it is advisable to excavate graves using a standard level approach; that is, to determine an arbitrary depth that each level will consist of (i.e., 5 or 10 centimeters), and to excavate each grid to that level before moving on the next level. The soil from each grid and each level within the grid is then screened separately in order to preserve contextual information. This approach can be useful in determining associations of items to the crime scene; for example, a bullet found in Grid B, Level 1 (0–10 centimeters depth) may represent an unassociated bullet found near surface depth, while a bullet found deeper in Grid C, Level 9 (81–90 centimeters depth) may be of evidentiary value.

Excavation of the levels should be undertaken using pointed trowels, which allows for finer control and better recovery of items *in situ*. Flat shovels can be used to skim the surface, and pointed shovels can be used to dislodge large rocks or to sever roots, but they should never be used to excavate graves due to their potential to inflict massive damage in the hands of careless or over-enthusiastic excavators.

When evidentiary or skeletal items are located within the grave feature isolated from the main component, it is important to photograph, measure, and map in place using the established datum and grid coordinate system. After the item has been documented, it can then be removed and placed into an evidence container marked with the appropriate identifying information. Excavation can continue from this point.

Once body parts or bones are discovered, the excavators need to proceed cautiously. The correct technique is to "pedestal" the remains. This means that the entire set of remains (for example, a partial deer skeleton) should be excavated at an equal level, leaving the entire body "pedestalled" on a base of soil, instead of excavating around each bone and pulling each element out as it is uncovered. This technique allows for assessment of body positioning and distribution, which would be lost utilizing a more haphazard method. Once the remains have been "pedestalled," mapped, and photographed, they can then be removed for transport and analysis. The dirt just below where the remains were found should also be screened until sterile soil is reached. This is done in case evidence such as bullets are present.

Once all mapping and photography documentation are complete, removal of the remains can occur. If possible, elements should be grouped and identified in the field and then placed in marked evidence bags (e.g., left front leg, right hind leg, cervical vertebrae), since it can be very difficult once back at the laboratory to identify bones once they have been mixed and commingled.

Crime scene equipment checklist

This list is not intended to be comprehensive; in fact, it represents the minimum equipment necessary to process a small-scale scene. Many of these items are available via archaeology and forestry supply websites, and through select hardware outlets (Table 5.2).

Table 5.2 List of equipment a wildlife officer may require to collect zooanthropological evidence.

1. Personal Protective Equipment (including latex gloves, eye protection)
2. Note paper, graph paper, pencils, pens, indelible permanent markers
3. Camera (35 mm or digital with good macroscopic capabilities)
4. Measurement scale/ruler
5. Evidence containers (multi-size paper bags, Ziploc bags, plastic containers, etc.)
6. Evidence flags/markers
7. Compass
8. Tape measures
9. String
10. Large metal nails/wooden stakes
11. Probe
12. Shovels (flat and pointed)
13. Trowels (pointed)
14. Toothbrushes, paintbrushes, and wooden picks for delicate excavations
15. Gardening gloves (for sifting)
16. Buckets
17. Heavy-duty dustpan and hand broom
18. Sifting screen

Acknowledgements

The authors would like to acknowledge Elizabeth Richards and Kelly Sauerwein for assistance with the excavation of the pig remains.

References

Adeola, M.O. (1992) Importance of wild animals and their parts in the culture, religious festivals, and traditional medicine, of Nigeria. *Environmental Conservation*, **19**, 125–134.

Alves, R.R.N. and Alves, H.N. (2001) The faunal drugstore: animal-based remedies used in traditional medicines in Latin America. *Journal of Ethnobiology and Ethnomedicine*, **7**, 1–43.

Alves, R.N.N., Souto, W.M.S. and Barboza, R.R.D. (2010) Primates in traditional folk medicine: a world overview. *Mammal Rev*, **40**, 155–180.

Anageletti, L.R., Agrimi, U., Curia C. *et al.* (1992) Healing rituals and sacred serpents. *Lancet*, **340**, 223–225.

Asfaw, B., White, T.D., Lovejoy, O., *et al.* (1999) *Australopithecus garhi:* a new species of early hominid from Ethiopia. *Science*, **284**, 629–635.

Bennett, E.L. and Robinson, J.G. (2000) Hunting for sustainability: the start of a synthesis. In J.G. Robinson and E.L. Bennett (eds.) *Hunting for Sustainability in Tropical Forests*. New York: Columbia University Press, pp. 499–519.

Brashares, J.S., Arcese, P., Sam, M.K., *et al.* (2004) Bushmeat hunting, wildlife declines, and fish supply in West Africa. *Science*, **306**, 1180–1183.

Bureau of Alcohol, Tobacco and Firearms (1999) *Crime Scene and Evidence Collection Handbook*. Washington, DC: Author.

China National Corporation of Traditional and Herbal Medicine (1995) *Materia Medica Commonly Used in China*. Beijing: Science Press.

Connor, M. (2007) *Forensic Methods: Excavation for the Archaeologist and Investigator*. New York: AltaMira Press.

Corlett, R.T. (2007) The impact of hunting on the mammalian fauna of tropical Asian forests. *Biotropica*, **39**, 292–303.

Costa-Neto, E.M. (2004) Implications and applications of folk zootherapy in the state of Bahia, Northeastern Brazil. *Sustainable Development*, **12**, 161–174.

Davies, B. (2005) *Black Market: Inside the Endangered Species Trade in Asia*. Berkeley, CA: Ten Speed Press.

Dirkmaat, D.C. and Adovasio, J.M. (1997) The role of archaeology in the recovery and interpretation of human remains from an outdoor forensic setting. In W.D. Haglund and M.H. Sorg (eds.) *Forensic Taphonomy: The Postmortem Fate of Human Remains*. Boca Raton, FL: CRC Press, pp. 39–64.

Edirisinghe, U. (2003) Sustainable aquatic resources management in the 21st century: some important issues. *Tropical Agriculture Research and Extension*, **6**, 122–127.

Elisseeff, V. (2000) *The Silk Roads: Highways of Culture and Commerce*. New York: UNESCO Publishing/Berghahn Books.

Fox, R.H. and Cunningham, C.L. (1973) *Crime Scene Search and Physical Evidence Handbook*. Washington, DC: U.S. Department of Justice, National Institute of Justice.

France, D.L., Griffin, T.J., Swanburg, J.G., *et al.* (1997) NecroSearch revisited: further multidisciplinary approaches to the detection of clandestine graves. In W.D. Haglund and M.H. Sorg (eds.) *Forensic Taphonomy: The Postmortem Fate of Human Remains*. Boca Raton, FL: CRC Press, pp. 497–510.

Galloway, A., Walsh-Haney, H. and Byrd, J.H. (2001) Recovering buried bodies and surface scatter: the associated anthropological, botanical, and entomological evidence, in J.H. Byrd and J.L. Castner (eds.) *Forensic Entomology: The Utility of Arthropods in Legal Investigations*. Boca Raton, FL: CRC Press, pp. 223–262.

Gigliotti, L.M. and Taylor, W.W. (1990) The effect of illegal harvest on recreational fisheries. *North American Journal of Fisheries Management*, **10**, 106–110.

Hawkes, J. (1973) *The First Great Civilizations: Life in Mesopotamia, the Indus Valley, and Egypt*. New York: Knopf.

Hochrein, M.J. (2002) An autopsy of the grave: recognizing, collecting, and processing forensic geotaphonomic evidence. In W.D. Haglund and M.S. Sorg (eds.) *Advances in Forensic Taphonomy: Method, Theory, and Anthropological Perspectives*. Boca Raton, FL: CRC Press, pp. 45–70.

Hughes, J.D. (1975) *Ecology in Ancient Civilizations*. Albuquerque, NM: University of New Mexico Press.

Hunter, J. and Cox, M. (2005) *Forensic Archaeology: Advances in Theory and Practice*. New York: Routledge.

Kang, S. and Phipps, M. (2003) *A Question of Attitude: South Korea's Traditional Medicine Practitioners and Wildlife Conservation*. Hong Kong: TRAFFIC East Asia.

Killam, E.W. (1990) *The Detection of Human Remains*. Springfield, IL: C. C. Thomas Press.

Kramer, K. (2001) *Legal Controls on Small Arms and Light Weapons in Southeast Asia*. Geneva: Small Arms Survey.

Labadie, R.P. (1986) Problems and possibilities in the use of traditional drugs. *Journal of Ethnopharmacology*, **15**, 221–230.

Lamarque, F.A. (1995) The French cooperation's strategy in the field of African wildlife. In J. A. Bissonette and P.R. Krausman (eds.) *Integrating People and Wildlife for a Sustainable Future*. Bethesda: Wildlife Society, pp. 267–270.

Lev, E. (2003) Traditional healing with animals (zootherapy): medieval to present-day Levantine practice. *Journal of Ethnopharmacology*, **86**, 107–118.

Maisels, C.K. (1993) *The Near East: Archaeology in the Cradle of Civilization*. New York: Routledge.

Mancall, P.C. (1999) The age of discovery. In L. Masur (ed.) *The Challenge of American History*. Baltimore, MD: Johns Hopkins University Press, pp. 26–53.

Martin, E.B. and Phipps, M. (1996) A review of the wild animal trade in Cambodia, *TRAFFIC Bulletin*, **16**, 45–60.

Menzies, N.K. (1994) *Forest and Land Management in Imperial China*. New York: St. Martin's Press.

Mittermeier, R.A., Ratsimbazafy, J., Rylands, A.B., *et al.* (2007) Primates in peril: the world's 25 most endangered primates, 2006–2008. *Primate Conservation*, **22**, 1–40.

Morse, D., Duncan, J. and Stoutamire, J. (1983) *Handbook of Forensic Archaeology and Anthropology*. Tallahassee, FL: Rose Printing Co.

Nekaris, K.A.I., Shepherd, C.R., Starr, C.R., *et al.* (2010) Exploring cultural drivers for wildlife trade via an ethnoprimatological approach: a case study of slender and slow lorises (Loris and Nycticebus) in South and Southeast Asia. *American Journal of Primatology*, **72**, 877–886.

Nijman, V. and Shepherd, C.R. (2007) Trade in non-native, CITES-listed, wildlife in Asia, as exemplified by the trade in freshwater turtles and tortoises (Chelonidae) in Thailand. *Contribution to Zoology*, **76**, 207–212.

Nooren, H. and Claridge, G. (2001) *Wildlife Trade in Laos: The End of the Game*. Amsterdam: Netherlands Committee for IUCN.

Okello, J.B.A., Wittemyer, G., Rasmussen, H.B., *et al.* (2008) Effective population size dynamics reveal impacts of historic climatic events and recent anthropogenic pressure in African elephants. *Molecular Ecology*, **17**, 3788–3799.

Owsley, D.W. (1995) Techniques for locating burials, with emphasis on the probe. *Journal of Forensic Sciences*, **40**, 735–740.

Pauly, D., Christensen, V., Guenette, S., *et al.* (2002) Towards sustainability in world fisheries. *Nature*, **418**, 689–695.

Polet, G. and Ling, S. (2004) Protecting mammal diversity: opportunities and constraints for pragmatic conservation management in Cat Tien National Park, Vietnam. *Oryx*, 38, 186–196.

Pratt, D.G., Macmillan, D.C. and Gordon, I.J. (2004) Local community attitudes to wildlife utilisation in the changing economic and social context of Mongolia. *Biodiversity and Conservation*, **13**, 591–613.

Prescott-Allen, R. and Prescott-Allen, C. (1982) *What's Wildlife Worth? Economic Contribution of Wild Plants and Animals to Developing Countries*. London: IIED-Earthscan.

Puri, K. (2000) Is traditional or cultural knowledge a form of intellectual property? *Oxford Electronic Journal of Intellectual Property Rights*. Available at: http://www.oiprc.ox.ac.uk/EJWP0100.pdf.

Rabinowitz, A. (1998) Findings: killed for a cure. *Natural History*, **107**, 22–24.

Rao, M.H. and McGowan, P.J. (2002) Wild-meat use, food security, livelihoods, and conservation. *Conservation Biology*, **16**, 580–583.

Rao, M.H., Myint, T., Zaw, T. and Htun, S. (2005) Hunting patterns in tropical forests adjoining the Hkakaborazi National Park, north Myanmar. *Oryx*, **39**, 292–300.

Redford, K.H. and Robinson, J.G. (1987) The game of choice: patterns of Indian and colonist hunting in the Neotropics. *American Anthropologist*, **89**, 650–667.

Robinson, J.G. and Bennett E.L. (2002) Will alleviating poverty solve the bushmeat crisis? *Oryx*, **36**, 332.

Robinson, J.G. and Redford, K.H. (1991) *Neotropical Wildlife Use and Conservation*. Chicago: University of Chicago Press.

Roskams, S. (2001) *Excavation, Cambridge Manuals in Archaeology*. Cambridge: Cambridge University Press.

Schultz, J.J., Williams, L.J., Wheeler, S.M. and Dupras, T.L. (2006) *Forensic Recovery of Human Remains: Archaeological Approaches*. Boca Raton, FL: CRC Press.

Shepherd, C.R., Sukumaran, J., and Wich, S.A. (2004) *Open Season: An Analysis of the Pet Trade in Medan, Sumatra, 1997–2001*. Petaling Jaya, Malaysia: TRAFFIC Southeast Asia.

Skinner, M. and Lazenby, R.A. (1983) *Found! Human Remains: A Field Manual for the Recovery of the Recent Human Skeleton*. British Columbia, Canada: Archaeology Press Burnaby, Simon Fraser University.

Townsend, W.R. (2000) The sustainability of substance hunting by the Sirionó Indians of Bolivia. In J.G. Robinson and E.L. Bennett (eds.) *Hunting for Sustainability in Tropical Forests*. New York: Columbia University Press, pp. 267–281.

TRAFFIC (2008) Wildlife trade monitoring network. Available at: www.traffic.org.

Tratado de Cooperación Amazonica (1995) *Uso y conservación de la fauna silvestre en la Amazonia*. Lima, Peru: Tratado de Cooperación Amazonica.

Unnikrishnan, P.M. (1998) Animals in Ayurveda. *Amruth*, **1**, 1–15.

U.S. Department of Justice, National Institute of Justice (2004) *Crime Scene Investigation: A Reference for Law Enforcement Training*. Washington, DC: U.S. Government Printing Office.

Veith, I. (2002) *Huang ti nei ching su wen: The Yellow Emperor's Classic Internal Medicine*. Berkeley, CA: University of California Press.

Wildlife Conservation Society and Sarawak Forest Department (1996) *A Master Plan for Wildlife in Sarawak*. Kuching, Sarawak: Wildlife Conservation Society and Sarawak Forest Department.

Wilkie, D.S. and Lee, R.J. (2004) Hunting in agroforestry systems and landscapes: conservation implications in West-Central Africa and Southeast Asia. In G. Schroth, G.A.B. da Fonseca, C.A. Harvey, C. Gascon, H.L. Vasconcelos and A.M.N. Izac (eds.) *Agroforestry and Biodiversity Conservation in Tropical Landscapes*. Washington, DC: Island Press, pp. 346–370.

Williamson, D.F. (2002) *In the Black: Status, Management, and Trade of the American Black Bear (Ursus Americanus) in North America*. Washington, DC: World Wildlife Fund.

World Health Organization (1999) *Traditional, Complementary and Alternative Medicines and Therapies*. Washington, DC: WHO Regional Office for the Americas/Pan American Health Organization.

6

Forensic Entomology and Wildlife

Jeffery K. Tomberlin and Michelle R. Sanford

Introduction

A seasoned forensic investigator will often recognize the presence of entomological evidence in animal abuse or wildlife death investigations long before actually seeing any specimens. This ability is due to the investigator recognizing the association between the smell of decay and decomposition with arthropod activity. The aim of this chapter is to provide a cursory review of entomology and the use of insects as evidence in forensic investigations as they pertain to wildlife crimes. Those seeking greater depth should consult their regional forensic entomologist for guidance. These individuals can be located through the American Board of Forensic Entomology that is the certifying body for this discipline.

Animals in the Phylum Arthropoda are invertebrates and these organisms share several unifying characteristics, including an external skeleton or exoskeleton, an open circulatory system that bathes the organs and an independent respiratory system decoupled from the circulatory system, among many other characters. Entomology is the study of insects and their relatives, such as spiders, ticks and mites. Insects have six legs, a tripartite body plan consisting of a head, thorax and abdomen and are the only arthropods capable of flight. Some of the more commonly encountered insects are flies, beetles, dragonflies, honeybees, and butterflies. While these examples represent the various forms of insects encountered either crawling across a sidewalk or buzzing around a person's head, the diversity of insects and their relatives is truly impressive. The current estimate of known arthropods exceeds one million species. However, some experts speculate there could be as many as 30 million species waiting for identification

---

Wildlife Forensics: Methods and Applications, First Edition. Edited by Jane E. Huffman and John R. Wallace.

(Tomberlin, 2008; Byrd and Castner, 2010). This diversity is due to their remarkable adaptability and their ability to live in most habitats including those considered extreme, such as tar pits, hot springs, the Arctic, and decomposing human or animal remains (Tomberlin, 2008; Byrd and Castner, 2010).

Forensic entomology involves the use of insects and their relatives collected from living or dead humans and animals as forensic evidence. Specimens collected represent a unique form of evidence well accepted in legal proceedings on a global scale. Litigation involving insect evidence can take the form of criminal cases related to homicide or neglect and civil cases such as the infestation of food or malpractice for neglect (Tomberlin, personal communication) (Byrd and Castner, 2010). This acceptance in the courtroom is predominantly due to the long history of using entomological material collected from a victim or scene as evidence. Initial cases date back to thirteenth-century China (Byrd and Castner, 2010) and extend into the twenty-first century in North America (Tomberlin *et al.*, 2005; Schoenly *et al.*, 2007) and South America (Battan Horenstein *et al.*, 2007; Gomes *et al.*, 2009), Europe (Grassberger and Frank, 2004), Australia (Archer, 2004; George *et al.*, 2009), and other regions of Asia (Singh and Bharti, 2008; Pritam and Jayaprakash, 2009). Death investigations that use arthropod evidence are more commonly associated with people than animals; however, information gleaned from these investigations, and the resulting research conducted are applicable in wildlife investigations (Anderson, 1999). We hope to demonstrate this point throughout this chapter.

There are many potential uses for arthropod or insect-based evidence and perhaps the most well known is the development of an estimate of time of colonization which specifically refers to the estimated amount of time that the insects or other arthropods have been associated with the human or animal tissue (Tomberlin *et al.*, 2011). Under certain circumstances it may directly correlate with the initiation of an infected wound or with the minimum postmortem interval but this is not always the case. As we will discuss, the life history of the arthropods associated with decay and decomposition is exceedingly diverse and intricately associated with the environment which infuses it with a certain level of variability inherent to any living system. Yet arthropod-based evidence can provide the best estimate of these time intervals that incorporates the history of the animal from which they were collected and the history of the environment from which they came.

Application of Forensic Entomology to Wildlife Crimes

The analysis of entomological evidence in criminal and civil investigations is not new to the forensic sciences. Its application in wildlife forensics has been limited but appears to be gaining momentum (Stroud, 1998). The forensic entomology applications discussed below will be presented as they relate to information currently available in the literature. We will attempt to bridge information from human death or abuse investigations, and demonstrate that such information is applicable to the wildlife arena.

How long have the arthropods been on the body and what does it mean?

The presence of arthropods on animal remains can be used to infer much information. The presence of arthropods on living individuals can be used to infer abuse or neglect. Proper hygiene and periodic baths reduce the accumulation of filth, such as fecal material in the hair of the animal and thus reduce the attraction of many of the flies that would typically colonize this material. In most cases, once colonization has occurred, larvae would feed on the fecal material and could eventually begin feeding on the animal itself (myiasis). However, caution should be observed when drawing conclusions of neglect in some cases. Myiasis can occur within a relatively short period of time and may be due to the basic nature of the arthropods involved rather than negligence on the part of the caregiver (i.e., bot flies). Myiasis has been documented for a number of animals and is a major economic concern in some livestock and wildlife industries.

In addition to the use of the insects to determine if neglect has occurred, they can also be used to estimate the time of the colonization event or period of insect activity (Tomberlin *et al.*, 2011). Two methods are primarily used to estimate the period of insect activity. Arthropods are poikilothermic and as such development of the arthropod is based on a rate of growth as it relates to temperature. As temperatures increase, development time decreases and vice versa. However, upper and lower developmental thresholds exist. When temperatures get too high or low, development can be suppressed and the arthropods can potentially die. This method is a common method used for estimating the age of what is presumed to be the oldest immature arthropod collected from the remains. Time of colonization estimates for arthropods collected from deceased wildlife can be used to determine a minimum postmortem interval (Anderson, 1999). We would like to emphasize that these estimates rely on proper identification of the immature arthropod collected from the remains as development rates vary among species. Furthermore, we caution the application of a data set for one species with another species even though they may be closely related. Such uses open the door for error in the conclusions being drawn and are likely to be challenged in court. Also, it should be noted that the forensic entomologist is assuming that the specimen being analyzed represents the oldest on the remains. Consequently, proper collection and curation are essential.

The second method of determining period of insect activity is the use of arthropod succession patterns. Arthropods progress through a natural succession pattern on animal remains. Over time, the remains are utilized by different arthropods and the species composition will shift with the decomposition of the remains. Samples of the arthropod community from remains could provide estimates of where the remains are in the succession process and thus represent a minimum postmortem interval. This ecological process has been well documented for decomposing animal remains.

Toxicology

Arthropods can also be useful in determining the presence of foreign substances in the remains which can be essential for an investigation. Entomotoxicology is the analysis of arthropods sampled from decomposing remains in the absence of soft tissues or fluids for toxins (Goff and Lord, 1994; Gagliano-Candela and Aventaggiato, 2001; Introna *et al.*, 2001). A variety of substances have been detected in arthropods collected from decomposing remains including but not limited to morphine (Bourel *et al.*, 2001; Gunn *et al.*, 2006), amitriptyline, temazepam, trazodon, (Sadler *et al.*, 1995), and 3,4-methylenedioxyamphetamine (Sadler *et al.*, 1997). Detection of these substances could prove crucial for determining accidental or intentional poisoning or overdose. This information is also important for refining estimates of the period of insect activity as many of these substances can accelerate or suppress arthropod development. Substances such as amitriptyline (Goff *et al.*, 1993), hydrocortisone, sodium methohexital (Musvasva *et al.*, 2001), and codeine (Kharbouche *et al.*, 2008), can accelerate arthropod development. In contrast, drugs such as amitriptyline (Goff *et al.*, 1993) can suppress arthropod development. It should be noted that these compounds have been tested on a limited number of species and caution should be used when comparing their effects across species.

The leap from entomotoxicology in humans to animal application is not that great as many model systems used in entomotoxicology studies are non-human. Swine carcasses are the most common model for human decomposition and thus have been used in a number of forensic entomology studies. However, the same cannot be said for entomotoxicology studies (Shahid *et al.*, 2003; Schoenly *et al.*, 2005; Tabor *et al.*, 2005; Zurawski *et al.*, 2009) as other animal models, such as rabbits (Bourel *et al.*, 1999), pet mince (i.e., mixture of kangaroo and lamb) (George *et al.*, 2009), raccoons (Joy *et al.*, 2002), and dogs (Reed, 1958) are used. Data gathered from these studies most likely could be used to extrapolate information from wildlife cases suspected to involve poisoning. However, caution should be used when analyzing entomological evidence for foreign substances. While these compounds can be detected, it is not possible at this time to estimate the level of ingestion or exposure (Tracqui *et al.*, 2004).

Movement of remains between locations

Arthropod distribution in a given locality can be used to aid investigators in determining if animal remains have been moved from one location to another. This determination hinges on the species in question and the geographic scale being investigated. Some arthropods, such as blow flies, have broad distribution reaching a global scale. However, if correctly analyzed, their distribution within a given area can lead to critical information regarding the movement of remains.

For example, certain species are more apt to colonize remains in sunlit versus shaded areas. *Phormia regina* and *Lucilia* spp. larvae were collected from carrion in the sun and shade; however, *Sarcophaga* sp. was only collected from carrion in the sun (Joy *et al.*, 2002). Other species are more likely to colonize remains located in urban than in rural regions (Sukontason *et al.*, 2007).

Arthropod infestations and transmission of pathogens

Many arthropods are known to transmit pathogens to wildlife. We suggest readers refer to *Medical and Veterinary Entomology* (Mullen and Durden, 2009) for a detailed description of these pathogens and their associated vectors. In addition, an excellent review of potential threats of introduction of foreign pathogens to the United States is available in the literature (Bram *et al.*, 2002).

Patterns of colonization by arthropods are well documented

Arthropod colonization of animals before or after death is well documented. The location site of colonization on an animal prior to death may be associated with a specific wound or decay location. After death, colonization also occurs at predictable sites. These sites include the natural orifices of the body, such as the eyes, mouth, nose and ears. Other sites, such as the urogenital region, will be colonized within a similar time frame as those on the head. However, wounds inflicted to the body of the animal produce alternate sites for colonization. These sites could be the result of abuse, gunshot wounds, stabbing wounds, or any other mechanical method of producing such injuries. When dealing with decomposing animal remains, it is vital that the sites of colonization be recorded as such information may lead to the conclusion of injury prior to death. Furthermore, if these sites are colonized long before the animal dies, the arthropods collected from these sites would be more indicative of when the wound was inflicted and not when the animal died.

DNA can be isolated from arthropods collected from a scene

DNA collected at a suspected crime scene, or from associated remains, represents a tremendous amount of pertinent information. In most cases, DNA is recognized for its use in identifying or eliminating individuals as suspects (Saks and Koehler, 2005), however, in the case of forensic entomology, DNA can yield additional important information. Insects and other arthropods that are obligate blood-feeders can often be collected from the body. Examples of these arthropods include lice (Phthiraptera: Pediculidae) (Replogle *et al.*, 1994), bed bugs (Hemiptera: Cimicidae) (Szalanski *et al.*, 2006), ticks (Pichon *et al.*, 2009), and mosquitoes (Diptera: Culicidae) (Oshaghi *et al.*, 2006). DNA isolated from arthropods collected from decomposing remains can be used to identify the animal species on which the arthropods were feeding (Lord *et al.*, 1998; Wells and

Stevens, 2008). Ross *et al.* (2009) determined that DNA isolated from blow fly larvae feeding on deer and other wild game tissue could be identified. They also found that wild game DNA could be isolated and identified from multiple stages of fly larval development as well as multiple species. These findings provide encouraging preliminary results to elaborate the interpretation of entomological evidence from wildlife crime scenes.

In cases where the arthropods cannot be morphologically identified, analysis of DNA isolated from the arthropod can be used for identification (Amendt *et al.*, 2004; Wells and Stevens; 2008). As previously mentioned, estimates of the age of arthropods collected from remains are primarily based on past development studies (Byrd and Butler, 1996; Grassberger and Frank, 2003). Development of these arthropods, even within species, can vary geographically (Tarone and Foran, 2006; Gallagher *et al.*, 2010). Some suggest these differences in development can be due to variation in methods used (Tarone and Foran, 2006; Byrd and Castner, 2010), time scale (i.e., every 12 hr versus 24 hr observations) measured (Kamal, 1958; Anderson, 2000), and food moisture and sampling techniques employed (Tarone and Foran, 2006). Thus, accurate identification to the species and even population can be accomplished with DNA analyses.

Arthropods Commonly Encountered

In terrestrial systems (i.e., on land, hanging, or buried) two major insect Orders are typically implicated with respect to colonization of animal tissues in life or death: Diptera, the true flies, and Coleoptera, the beetles. Both flies and beetles are characterized by holometabolous development in which they progress from an egg stage to three progressively growing larval stages or instars that are mediated by ambient temperature. For the groups of flies discussed here, the instar of the larva can be determined by observing the number of spiracular slits (the larva breathes from these slits located at the posterior end, that can be kept out of liquefied food; one slit that is extremely difficult to see and a lack of an anterior spiracle = first instar, two slits = second instar, three slits = third instar). The last larval stage is then followed by a transitional pupal stage where the insect body changes form drastically until the adult stage is formed (Figure 6.1). The adult stage in insects is the only stage to possess wings.

In aquatic systems, the arthropod community is quite different. There are few aquatic arthropods that specialize on carrion decomposition as compared to those found in terrestrial habitats, such that many aquatic species use the animal remains more as a substrate on which to live or locate food rather than for food itself (Keiper and Casamatta, 2001). The same principles apply to aquatic systems in terms of temperature-dependent growth and development, however, the organized successional sequence often encountered in terrestrial decomposition is usually less clear due to the lack of decomposition specialists (ibid.). In most instances, aquatic arthropods and associated microbial growth can be used to estimate the postmortem submergence interval (Wallace *et al.*, 2008; Merritt and Wallace, 2010). There is often also the potential interaction

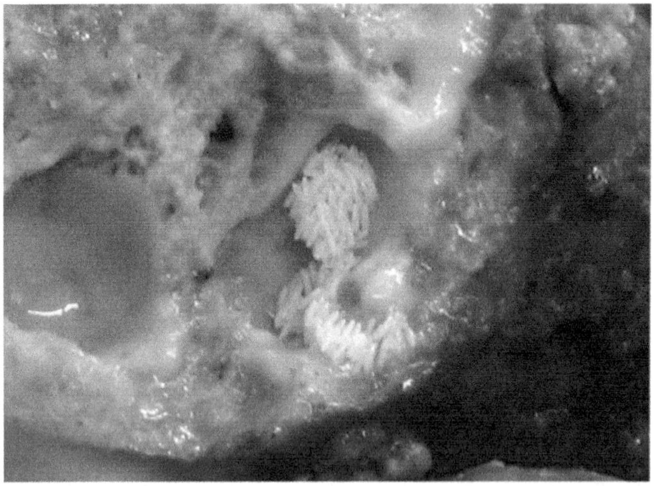

Figure 6.1 Blow fly (Diptera: Calliphoridae) eggs (Photo credit: Michelle R. Sanford).

between the aquatic and terrestrial insect communities because carcasses will often bloat due to microbial generation of gases and float to the surface of a body of water and allow for colonization by terrestrial insects (Keiper and Casamatta, 2001; Merritt and Wallace, 2010). Most of the current knowledge with respect to aquatic arthropod decomposition is from freshwater systems where insects represent the most numerous arthropod group, however, this is not the case for marine systems. In marine systems, crustaceans and other invertebrates dominate and different factors must be taken into account for colonization of decomposing remains in a saltwater environment (Anderson, 2010). The application of aquatic arthropod ecology to forensic investigations is a relatively new area and thorough reviews on methodology and principles can be found for both freshwater habitats (Keiper and Casamatta, 2001; Merritt and Wallace, 2010) and marine habitats (Anderson, 2010).

Parasitic interactions with wildlife can be characterized as either obligatory, meaning the insect requires a living host to complete development, or facultative, meaning the insect will take advantage of an opportunity to infest a living host but it is not a requirement for the completion of development. In Diptera, the infestation of living tissues by the larval stages of flies is known as myiasis and is often initiated by an adult female fly laying eggs (Figure 6.1) directly on the host. In Coleoptera, infestation of living tissues by the immature stages is termed canthariasis, while infestation by adults is referred to as scarabaeisis, however, it is much rarer than in Diptera.

Diptera

Flies (Diptera), or true flies, are defined by the possession of only one pair of wings. The flies typically associated with myiasis and colonization of remains are in the Suborder Cyclorrapha which is characterized by flies with a compact

Figure 6.2 Examples of blow fly (Diptera: Calliphoridae) larvae and pupae (Photo credit: Michelle R. Sanford).

streamlined appearance, a three-segmented antenna with an arista (a thick hair-like projection from the third antennal segment), and a pupal case (Figure 6.2) that the adult fly exits via a circular hole.

Obligatory myiasis flies

There are several fly families that exhibit obligatory myiasis which require living hosts to complete development. More thorough discussions of these parasites can be found in texts on veterinary entomology as they are often parasites of domestic animals (Mullen and Durden, 2009) as well as texts on parasitic diseases of wildlife (Samuel *et al.*, 2001). Here, we will briefly discuss those obligate parasitic flies that are most commonly encountered in wildlife, as they may also be encountered in decomposing remains. Comparatively less is known about how obligate parasites can be used to determine time of colonization of decomposing remains.

Oestridae

This Family of flies is also known as the bot flies and warble flies. Many groups of wild and domestic animals are infested by flies in the Oestridae including deer, rabbits, squirrels, horses, cattle, elephants and others (Pape, 2001). Oestridae either infest the nasal cavities and sinuses, the gastrointestinal system or under the skin. As adults, these flies are stout-bodied, typically hairy and may have reduced mouthparts. The larvae are also stout and often described as being grub-like in appearance. They can be quite large with lengths up to 23 mm as observed in the final instar of the sheep nasal bot fly, *Oestris ovis* (Diptera: Oestridae) (Colwell *et al.*, 2006). Oestridae are not generally known to cause significant mortality under normal circumstances but may be observed in wild

Figure 6.3 Blow fly (Diptera: Calliphoridae) larval mass (Photo credit: Michelle R. Sanford).

animals and are, under most circumstances, not indicative of maltreatment or neglect of an animal in and of themselves.

Calliphoridae (obligate parasites)

The name of this Family, *Calliphoridae* (Obligate Parasites), refers to the fact that these flies are typically very shiny with various shades of metallic blues and greens as adults (Calliphoridae = jewel-bearing). The identification of adult Calliphoridae in North America was recently updated by Whitworth (Whitworth, 2006). The larvae of the flies (Figure 6.3) in this family are commonly referred to as maggots and are generally creamy white in color with a tapered cylindrical appearance. The tapered end of the maggot is the feeding end and contains the mouth-hooks used to feed, whereas the enlarged end of the maggot contains the spiracular plate which is the main respiratory opening for the larva (there is also a small anterior spiracle that looks like a tiny appendage near the tapered/head end of large/late instar larvae). Most larvae in this group are smooth but some may be covered in tubercles (spiny projections) that are very useful for identification. Many of the calliphorids are not considered obligate parasites but for those groups that are, they are more likely to be encountered in wildlife than in domestic animals or humans.

The primary or new world screwworm fly, *Cochliomyia hominovorax* is an obligate parasite of mammals, including wild and domestic animals and humans. It has been successfully eradicated from the United States, Mexico, Belize, Guatemala, El Salvador, Honduras, Nicaragua, and Costa Rica with current efforts in Panama and into South America (USDA, 2001). The screwworm eradication program is perhaps the best example of the successful use of the sterile insect technique to eradicate a pest in entomological history. The primary screwworm does not create wounds by itself but lays its eggs in existing wounds, that need not be infected, and feeds on living tissues (Norris, 1965). *Chrysomya bezziana*, the old world screwworm fly is also an obligate parasite of mammals that lays its eggs in open wounds. Its known distribution currently includes the Old World (Europe, Africa, and Asia) and has the potential to spread into Australia (OIE, 2008).

Larvae of Calliphorid genus, *Protocalliphora* spp. feed on the blood of a wide variety of nestling birds (Bennett and Whitworth, 1991). They are restricted in larval life to bird nests. These flies are somewhat unusual among the blow flies as they feed on blood flowing from wounds. Bennett and Whitworth (1991) observed larvae using their mouthparts to create a wound in the skin of the nestling bird. The wound was maintained for approximately one hour by mechanically sustaining the blood flow. This fly genus is not well known and is not generally considered a major source of mortality for birds. It may, however, cause significant problems in nestling birds that are compromised by other factors (Baumgartner, 1988).

A group of obligate parasitic blow flies belonging to the genus, *Bufolucilia* spp. is associated, as the name suggests, with amphibians. *Bufolucilia silvarum* lays its eggs on the exterior of the host, and newly hatched larvae migrate under the skin during development. Completion of development by *B. silvarum* has been known to result in the death of Eastern American toads (Bolek and Coggins, 2002). Infestation by *B. bufonivora*, a European species is almost always fatal to the amphibian (Baumgartner, 1988).

Sarcophagidae (obligate parasites)

Sarcophagidae (Figure 6.4) are commonly known as the flesh flies and tend to be larger than blow flies (Calliphoridae) with a duller appearance that can include tessellation (a black and white checkerboard appearance) and black and white stripes. The striking life history difference between the flesh flies and the other flies associated with myiasis and decomposition is that a sarcophagid female retains eggs in her body, allowing them to develop into the first instar before depositing them in a wound or on decomposing flesh. Sarcophagids are very difficult to identify based on basic morphological features as adults and accurate identification often requires specialized training. These insects are morphologically inseparable as larvae, so if species identification is required, a portion of the collected larvae must be reared to the adult stage.

There are several members of the Sarcophagid genus *Wohlfahrtia* spp. that are aggressive myiasis-causing flies that can lead to death of the infested animal (Baumgartner, 1988). The most commonly encountered members of this genus are parasites of small mammals (e.g., fox, squirrel, minks, etc.). The larvae of this genus tend to infest animal nests and have been found to be commonly associated with the anus, ears and the umbilical scar of newborn animals. The larvae create a wound to gain access to the animal (Craine and Boonstra, 1986). Domestic animals can also host these flies, which can result in economic losses (Baumgartner, 1988).

Figure 6.4 Adult flesh fly (Diptera: Sarcophagidae) (Photo credit: Michelle R. Sanford).

Facultative myaisis flies and those associated with decomposition

Diptera in this group are those typically associated with the decomposition of filth and carrion. They can opportunistically infest infected wounds and dying tissues. In some species, the larvae continue to feed beyond the decay into living tissue. This is the primary distinction between flies associated solely with decomposition and those that may cause myiasis. In the case of flies that do not feed on living tissue, some species have been evaluated for their use in wound debridement or "maggot therapy" as an alternative to surgical removal of decaying tissue (for a detailed review, see Sherman *et al.*, 2000, and for a review with respect specifically to veterinary practice, see Jones and Wall, 2008). However, under certain circumstances, almost any fly species associated with decomposition can be considered as a potential facultative myiasis-causing species, thus, the differentiation is often difficult to make. For the purposes of this discussion, we lump together the flies that are not considered obligate parasites and point out the different species that are commonly associated with facultative myiasis.

Calliphoridae

For the remainder of those fly species belonging to the family Calliphoridae, there are no physical characteristics that separate the obligate from facultative parasites in this family, thus both the adults and larvae have similar appearances as those described for the obligate myiasis-causing blow flies. A few exemplary species are described here to demonstrate the breadth of life history and environmental conditions that can be found within the Family Calliphoridae.

The Australian sheep blow fly or bronze bottle fly, *Lucilia cuprina*, is a significant pest in the sheep industries of Australia where it causes flystrike. This condition is a common name given to myiasis of sheep or other animals that starts out as infestation associated with a wound or soiled fur or wool and continues into the flesh of the animal. *Lucilia cuprina* has a very wide distribution in the temperate areas of the world and has been introduced to New Zealand where it is responsible for approximately 50% of the flystrike incidences caused by *Lucilia* spp. among sheep herds with the other 50% attributed to *L. sericata* (Heath and Bishop, 2006). Adults of this species are often a coppery bronze and metallic green color particularly on the thorax but variation exists in coloration. The larvae of this species are not particularly morphologically distinct and share many of the same characters as other members of the Calliphoridae. This species is a potential myiasis-causing fly species and is also important to estimating time of colonization.

The other common *Lucilia* species, *Lucilia sericata*, is often referred to as the sheep blow fly because it is a significant flystrike-causing species in New Zealand and Europe. Interestingly, *L. sericata* is among the most widely utilized maggots for debridement therapy. It has been shown that the secretions of the larvae have significant antibacterial properties (Kerridge *et al.*, 2005). Thus, depending on the circumstances, it appears that this fly can be implicated in myiasis that is invasive while in other instances it may be more an artifact of an infected wound. As an adult, this fly is metallic green and can have similar coloration to *L. cuprina* and other *Lucilia* spp. The larval stages are not morphologically distinct and typify the calliphorid larval morphology with a creamy white color, tapered body and smooth appearance. *Lucilia sericata* is a potential myiasis-inducing species and is important to estimates of time of colonization on decomposing remains.

Members of the genus *Calliphora* spp. are connected by the common life history trait of being associated with cooler temperatures and temperate latitudes. In the seasonal succession of fly species that occurs in the transition from winter to spring in temperate areas, this species is among the first to become active. Members of this genus have been found to be significant contributors to the movement of nutrients from decaying salmon carcasses back into the environment in rivers of British Columbia (Hocking and Reimchen, 2006). *Calliphora* spp. are not generally considered significant producers of myiasis but have been associated with incidents of wound myiasis (e.g. Knotek *et al.*, 2005). Adult *Calliphora* spp. are typically large and hairy in appearance with a dusty blue coloration. The larvae of this genus are also generally large but not otherwise morphologically distinct. Species level identification of larvae often requires dissection and observation of the internal mouthpart structures. Members of this genus are important for determination of time of colonization estimates.

The secondary screwworm fly, *Cochliomyia macellaria*, is generally restricted to the warmer latitudes of the Nearctic and is widely distributed in the neo-tropics. This species is one of the most commonly encountered fly species on decomposing carrion and is distributed from the southeastern US (Byrd and Butler, 1996), southward into Peru (Baumgartner and Greenberg, 1985), and Argentina (Mariluis and Mulieri, 2003). *Cochliomyia macellaria* can be associated with wound myiasis, but is not generally considered a significant pest in that regard. The adults are metallic blue-green with a characteristic three stripe pattern on the thorax which is similar to the pattern observed in *C. hominivorax*. In live specimens, late stage larvae can often be distinguished from other species by the darkened color of the tracheal trunks that extend internally from the terminal spiracular slits into the body of the larva like two stripes on the dorsal surface of the larva. The tracheal trunk coloration is often difficult to observe in preserved specimens. This species is an important indicator species for determination of time of colonization estimates.

An introduced species in North and South America from the Oriental faunal region, *Chrysomya rufifacies* is important as a facultative predator of other larval flies. It was predicted that the introduction of this fly would have significant implications for native fly species (Baumgartner, 1993) and ongoing research is investigating the interactions it has with native blow fly species. *Chrysomya rufifacies* has been implicated in cases of wound myiasis but is not considered a significant myiasis-causing fly species in its introduced range (Baumgartner, 1993). The adults of this species are metallic blue-green and do not have any striping on the body. The larvae are morphologically distinct and are covered in pointed tubercles that run in lines parallel to the long axis of the larval body. The ease of larval identification coupled with the available development data (Byrd and Butler, 1997) and its common presence during the hottest times of the year in the US, have made it an important species for determination of time of colonization estimates.

Sarcophagidae

For the remainder of those fly species belonging to the family Sarcophagidae and similar to the blow flies, there are no morphological differences between obligate and facultative parasitic flesh flies. In fact, most sarcophagids are so difficult to identify they are not taken to taxonomic resolution beyond the family level. Most species-level identifications are made based on dissected male genitalia, and larval identifications require rearing of the specimens to adults. Nevertheless flesh flies are a component of the entomological fauna associated with both myiasis and decomposing remains and literature is available on larval development if accurate identification can be reliably accomplished (Villet *et al.*, 2006).

Most of the members of the genus *Sarcophaga* spp. are considered incidental wound myiasis flies and this is perhaps due to the difficulty inherent to identification rather than a true lack of this life history trait. Females have the potential to spread their offspring among multiple habitats much more easily than calliphorid females who lay all of their eggs in a single large mass. Thus flesh flies may have the opportunity to occupy small wounds and because they are already prepared to feed when they arrive at a wound site or carrion (females deposit larvae rather than eggs) (Tomberlin, 2008), these maggots penetrate the tissues faster and may, in turn, complete development faster than their presumed competition, the blow flies. Literature examples of *Sarcophaga* spp. infesting wildlife are rare and this is also likely due to the difficulty in identification. Members of this genus are potentially useful in determining a time of colonization estimate and a portion of the larvae should be reared to the adult stage if definitive identification will be required (Tomberlin, 2008; Byrd and Castner, 2010).

Muscidae

The muscid family includes many of the most common pest flies, including the house fly, *Musca domestica*, horn fly, *Haematobia irritans*, stable fly, *Stomoxys calcitrans*, face fly, *Musca autumnalis*, and many others. These flies are typically known for their association with filth and the breakdown of feces. Both the horn fly and stable fly complete their larval development in manure or other moist high organic materials. Myiasis caused by these flies is not common and is often associated with infected wounds or attributed to accidental introduction. When compared to the Calliphoridae and Sarcophagidae, which are considered early colonizers of decomposing remains, the Muscidae are usually considered late stage decomposition colonizers and tend to be present at the very moist advanced decay stages (Tomberlin, 2008; Byrd and Castner, 2010). Adult Muscidae have a typical house fly appearance with a black head and thorax and a brown abdomen which may have light patches on the sides. Muscid fly larvae tend to be more slender than calliphorid larvae and have an even stronger taper to the body with a more rounded posterior end.

This genus, *Musca* spp. contains the most common muscid known, *M. domestica* which is considered a synanthropic fly, meaning that it lives among humans. Myiasis caused by *Musca* spp. appears to be mostly accidental introduction and is less common than in the blow flies or flesh flies. The members of this genus are not usually associated with the early stages of decomposition unless feces or gut contents are exposed. Otherwise, they are have been described as being among the later succession of insects associated with advanced decay. *Musca* spp. are typically brown to black flies that are slightly smaller, on average, than the Calliphoridae. The larvae are typically very light in color being almost translucent white in some cases and they are also, on average, smaller and more slender than blow fly larvae. The spiracular plate is much smaller and darker than in the Calliphoridae and on close inspection the slits are sinuous rather than straight as in the blow flies and flesh flies (Tomberlin, 2008; Byrd and Castner, 2010).

Flies belonging to the genus, *Fannia* spp. are also known as lesser house flies. As in the *Musca* spp., *Fannia* flies are not generally associated with early decomposition but can colonize during advanced decomposition stages and are most commonly associated with filth and feces. *Fannia* flies are not considered significant myiasis-causing flies and, where documented, it has been suspected that infestation is accidental (Tomberlin, 2008; Byrd and Castner, 2010). Adults closely resemble house flies but are smaller in appearance. *Fannia* larvae are morphologically distinct in that they are dorso-ventrally flattened and have lateral projections or tubercles running in a single line along both sides of the larva.

Coleoptera

The beetles are the largest and most diverse group of insects on the planet. Thus, it is not surprising to find them to be one of the two most important groups associated with decomposition. However, the utility of beetles in determining time of colonization is limited because beetles have less clear patterns of colonization and their association with the stages of decomposition is less well defined. Nevertheless, beetles play an important ecological role and are often among the last insects remaining at carrion well into the late stages of decomposition.

Adult beetles are characterized by the presence of a pair of hardened or leathery protective wing covers known as elytra. The elytra protect the membranous wings that are typically folded underneath the elytra when the beetle is not in flight. Coleoptera are also holometabolous insects and go through multiple larval instars followed by a pupal stage. However, the number of instars in the life cycle of a beetle can be more variable than in the flies as well as the fact that pupal beetles are not encountered as often as in the flies. One unifying trait that helps to organize the beetles associated with decomposing tissues is that their morphology is closely tied to their life history. For example, those beetles that are predatory, as larvae or as adults, will have mouthparts that are large, sickle-shaped and well adapted for capturing prey. There are two major life history divisions among beetles associated with decomposition: predation and scavenging. The infestation of living tissues with beetle adults (scarabaeisis) or larvae (canthariasis) is relatively rare compared to myiasis, and is often accidental and results from the ingestion of the insects. However, there are instances where arthropod activity does not result in the typical smell of rotting flesh, such as associating pathogen infections with their arthropod vector or gastrointestinal infestation by arthropods.

Predators

Beetles can be predatory as either larvae, adults or during both life stages. Those associated with decomposition feed upon the large numbers of larvae associated with a maggot mass (Figure 6.3). The impact these beetles have on the population dynamics of dipteran larvae, if any, is largely unknown, however, they can often be observed feeding at the periphery of a maggot mass. The lack of a tight correlation between beetle development and the stages of decomposition limits their usefulness in the determination of a time of colonization, but they can aid in other ways. For example, if predatory beetles and or beetle larvae are observed in the area it may provide an indication that a carcass is nearby or was recently present in the area. In the following sections, we describe two predatory beetle families that vary drastically in their morphology but have a similar life history and ecological role at decomposing remains.

Histeridae

Hister beetles (Family: Histeridae) are commonly known as clown or hister beetles and are characterized by a rounded appearance with shortened elytra. Adults are small, shiny-black beetles that are very fast moving and are often found either at the edge of a maggot mass or just underneath the decomposing remains (Tomberlin, 2008; Byrd and Castner, 2010). Larval histerids are rarely observed at decomposing remains but may be concealed in the soil. Both larvae and adults are predatory, and thus are typically present during the active stages of decay when there are large aggregates of Diptera larvae present (Tomberlin, 2008; Byrd and Castner, 2010).

Staphylinidae

The Staphylinidae family includes a wide variety of generalist predators known as rove beetles. These beetles tend to be long and slender with large mandibles adapted for capturing prey. As in the histerids, they also have truncated elytra, leaving some of the abdominal segments are visible. Staphylinid larvae have prominent mandibulate mouthparts that are highly mobile. They are aggressive predators (Tomberlin, 2008; Byrd and Castner, 2010). One of the more common species of staphylinds, *Creophilus maxillosus*, has the common name of "hairy rove beetle" due to its hairy appearance. It can be observed rapidly running in and out of the maggot mass while hunting and consuming Diptera larvae (Tomberlin, 2008; Byrd and Castner, 2010). The available information on the development of Staphylinidae beetles is not well established, and thus these predators are not usually used to determine of a time of colonization estimate.

Scavengers

Most beetles associated with decomposing remains can be classified as scavengers on this type of food resource. Scavenging beetles can feed directly on the tissues or on the fluids associated with decomposition. There are a number of families that can arrive at or near a carcass as generalist scavengers without any established direct link to the decomposition process. Some of these families are associated with stored products (Cleridae, Ptinidae, and Nitidulidae), while others are broadly associated with decaying organic matter (Scarabaeidae, including the dung beetles).

Dermestidae

A scavenger beetle family, Dermestidae, commonly known as dermestid beetles or carpet beetles (Figure 6.5) are perhaps the best-known beetles of forensic importance associated with decomposition (Kulshrestha and Satpathy, 2001).

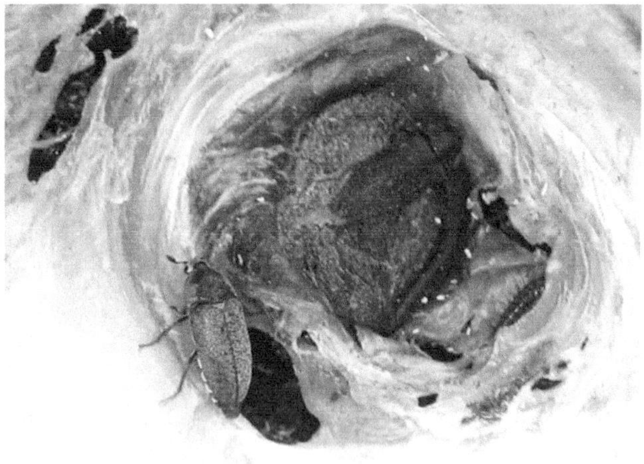

Figure 6.5 Adult dermestid beetle (Coleoptera: Dermestidae) (Photo credit: Michelle R. Sanford).

Larval development rates have been estimated and can be used to estimate time of colonization. However, the range offered by the use of dermestids is much wider than what can be obtained from Diptera larvae and less accurate. Dermestids are also known for their ability to invade seemingly tightly sealed containers where they consume natural fibers, taxidermy specimens, insect specimens, and a wide variety of museum specimens that contain any natural component. Therefore, for those wildlife cases where specimens are being smuggled into another country, dermestid beetles may provide some valuable information in wildlife investigations. Damage caused by Dermestidae is often in the form of small round holes (Byrd and Castner, 2010) and a small pile of dust-like debris. Dermestids are often used to clean skeletons for museum or taxidermy display because they are very skilled at reaching every bit of tissue remaining on a skeleton. Adult dermestids are dark to light brown or tan and can vary in size from 2–12 millimeters in length and have a hairy or scaly appearance that varies among species (ibid.). The larvae (Figure 6.6) have a generally hairy appearance and are highly mobile generalist scavengers as well. The appearance of dermestids in insect succession on a carcass appears to be highly variable.

The burying beetles, Silphidae, are perhaps one of the best-known beetles associated with decomposing remains. They are usually 1.5–2.5 cm long with clubbed antennae, five segmented tarsi and shortened elytra (Haskell and Williams, 2008). Though it is generally thought that silphid larvae are sequestered in a provisioned den, the larvae can be observed at carrion and are typically brown to black. They look very similar to a pill bug or isopod (Figure 6.6). Adult silphids may arrive at carrion throughout the decay process and some debate exists as to whether they are feeding exclusively on the carrion or are also predatory on the maggots as well. The larvae of those silphids observed at carrion are generally considered predaceous, but they have also been observed feeding on the carrion itself (Figure 6.7).

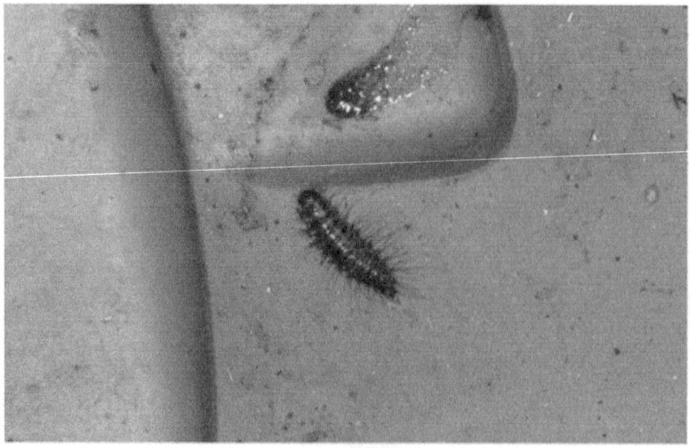

Figure 6.6 Larval dermestid beetle (Coleoptera: Dermestidae) (Photo credit: Michelle R. Sanford).

Sampling

Collection

An entomology sampling checklist is provided as Figure 6.8 in the Appendix. The collection of entomological evidence typically occurs at either the location where the carcass was discovered or during necropsy (Stroud, 1998). The most informative specimens in either instances of myiasis or in developing an estimate of time of colonization are typically immature stages of flies or beetles as they are dependent on the body of the victim for food.

A DVD entitled, *Forensic Entomology* demonstrates the identification, collection, and preservation of entomological evidence has been developed by Mer-

Figure 6.7 Larval silphid beetle (Coleoptera: Silphidae) (Photo credit: Michelle R. Sanford).

ritt and colleagues at Michigan State University and can be purchased online at http://www.filmbaby.com/films/3475. Fly larvae are easily collected with a gloved hand. There are various entomological supplies such as forceps and scoops that also accomplish this function but are not required for effective collection. Once collected, larvae can be fixed and preserved in a solution (discussed in the next section) to increase their usefulness in subsequent analyses, and another portion of which can be kept alive to confirm identification by rearing them to the adult stage at a known temperature. When collecting larvae, representative specimens of all stages and sizes present should be sampled. Multiple larvae should be collected from the wound or carcass as this can aid in identification and specimens can be taken from separate areas if there appear to be differences (specimens from different body locations should be kept separate). Essential information required upon collection include the date, time, and location where the specimens were collected, should be recorded to aid in the development of a time of colonization estimate. Additional data that are potentially useful are details related to weather (e.g., rain or extreme wind), the location of the carcass with respect to whether there was full sun or shade, or whether an attempt was made to conceal the carcass. All of these factors have the potential to affect insect colonization and development (Byrd and Castner, 2010).

In addition to larvae, adult flies can be collected with either an insect-collecting, sweep net or a sticky board trap (similar to those used to catch mice) folded into a tent which will catch the flies as they perch on the trap. Adult flies can help to confirm identification of any larvae collected at the site. Flies collected with the use of a net can be either frozen in the net or killed in a jar with a sponge soaked in ethyl acetate (nail polish remover) and later moved to a box or jar of preservative solution. Adults are more difficult than larvae to maintain after collection due to their fragile nature. Once dry, insects may break if not properly curated (this involves mounting each specimen on an entomological pin), or there may be deterioration of coloration with placement in preservative. There may be some benefit to using a sticky board trap to collect adult flies as this technique facilitates the killing of the insects in a standard freezer and if required they can be stored until they can be shipped to a forensic entomologist. Beetle larvae and adults are most easily collected by hand and can be placed directly into a preservative.

Preservation

Preservation of larval specimens is critical for the determination of a time of colonization estimate. The preservation method used to maintain specimens can have important implications for the properties of the larval tissues that in turn have the potential to change the physical properties of the specimen. The two most important pieces of information that can be obtained from preserved larval Diptera are identification of the species and the length of the specimen. Proper preservation provides for flexible specimens and minimizes alterations in larval length. This facilitates identification and provides for accurate measurements of the larval length. Larval length is used to estimate the age of the larva and can be affected by preservation technique (Adams and Hall, 2003).

The recommended procedure for preserving immature insects is fixation and then placement into a preservative solution of 80% ethanol (Amendt *et al.*, 2007). Fixation of the tissues can be accomplished by placing the larvae into near boiling hot water (hot water killing: HWK) for a few seconds (< 30 seconds). However, this technique is only necessary when dealing with immature flies as beetles are more sclerotized (hardened exterior) and can be placed directly into liquid-proof containers filled with 80% ethanol. Fixed immature flies should be placed in similar containers with ethanol. The use of solutions like formalin renders the specimens very stiff, damages the larval cuticle (Huber, 1998), degrades extractable DNA from the specimens (Dillon *et al.*, 1996) and should, therefore, be avoided if at all possible. The only risk to the specimens at this point is the loss of the preservative by evaporation or leakage of the container. This can be avoided by using standard liquid specimen containers for biological samples or obtaining entomological vials with polyethylene cone caps to prevent evaporation during storage and shipment.

Shipping

Shipment of specimens to a forensic entomologist for identification and generation of a time of colonization estimate should be accomplished in a manner that prevents damage to the specimens and follows chain of custody. Adult insect specimens become fragile after they dry and can easily break in transit. They should be packed to minimize crushing and shifting. If specimens are to be shipped in preservative, there are restrictions and regulations with respect to the amounts and concentrations of flammable liquids that can be shipped through the US Postal Service (USPS, 2010). If the specimens will need to be maintained with chain of custody requirements, a shipment method should be selected that allows for documentation and tracking.

Conclusion

Forensic entomology is well established in criminal and civil litigation involving people, however, information from research and case studies that has accumulated over time can easily bridge with wildlife investigations. As pointed out, most decomposition research has been conducted using swine as the model and recent efforts have branched out to examine insect succession (Anderson, 1999; Watson and Carlton, 2003, 2005; Nelder *et al.*, 2009) and development (Kaneshrajah and Turner, 2004; Boatright and Tomberlin, 2010) using other animal models. With that in mind, entomology can be a valuable tool in forensic wildlife investigations and should be evaluated when such evidence is present in a case.

Appendix

Date:______________________________	Collector:______________________________
Case Number:_____________________	Agency:________________________________
Location (GPS coordinates, nearest city, state, country):	
Animal's country of origin if non-native:	
Animal species/common name:	
Sex of the animal: ☐ male ☐ female ☐ undetermined	Is the animal: ☐ juvenile ☐ adult ☐ undetermined
Date and time reported:	Date and time collected:
Condition of the carcass: ☐ whole ☐ partial	If partial, what part ofthe carcass is present:
Presence of wounds: ☐ yes ☐ no ☐ unknown	Evidence of scavenging: ☐ yes ☐ no ☐ unknown
Type of carcass concealment, if any: ☐ none ☐ plastic bag ☐ burial, depth:_______________	☐ container, type: ☐ other:
Location(s) of insect activity: ☐ head including: ☐ mouth ☐ eyes ☐ chest ☐ completely encompassing carcass	(check all that apply) ☐ anus ☐ genitals ☐ abdomen ☐ wound(s), location(s):
Where on the body were insect specimens collected?: ☐ head including: ☐ mouth ☐ eyes ☐ chest ☐ other:	(check all that apply) ☐ anus ☐ genitals ☐ abdomen ☐ wound(s), location(s):
Approximate stage of decomposition: ☐ fresh ☐ bloated ☐ active decay ☐ saponification	(can check more than one) ☐ advanced decay ☐ skeletonized ☐ mummification
Collection Site: ☐ indoor ☐ outdoor ☐ aquatic	
Indoor: Type of structure: ☐ house ☐ shed or outbuilding ☐ other:	Outdoor: Type of predominant vegetation: ☐ grass ☐ trees/forest ☐ brush ☐ other:

Figure 6.8 Forensic entomology data collection form for wildlife. Byrd and Castner (2010).

Was the structure closed to outside access by insects?: ☐ yes ☐ no ☐ unknown Was the structure temperature controlled?: ☐ yes, temperature:_____F_____C ☐ no ☐ unknown	Carcass sun exposure: ☐ full sun ☐ partial shade all day ☐ full shade ☐ partial shade/sun depending on time of day
Aquatic: Type of water body: ☐ freshwater ☐ marine ☐ running water ☐ standing water ☐ other: Water temperature: :_____F_____C Was the carcass floating on the surface: ☐ yes ☐ no ☐ unknown	Notes on the collection site/carcass condition:
Current air temperature:	
Temperature of the maggot mass if available:	
Method of insect preservation for soft-bodied specimens: ☐ hot water kill and 80% ethanol ☐ 80% ethanol ☐ isopropyl alcohol (rubbing alcohol) ☐ other:	How many specimen containers were prepared with specimens: ☐ preserved: ☐ alive:
Were specimens kept alive: ☐ yes ☐ no	How are they being maintained: ☐ room temperature at: _________ ☐ other:
Where were the specimens sent:	

Figure 6.8 *(Continued)*

Acknowledgements

The authors would like to thank F. Baxendale for comments on an earlier draft of this chapter. The Department of Entomology and Agrilife Research at Texas A&M University provided financial support for J. Tomberlin and M. Sanford.

References

Adams, Z.J.O. and Hall, M.J.R. (2003) Methods used for killing and preservation of blowfly larvae, and their effect on post-mortem larval length. *Forensic Science International*, **138**, 50–61.

Amendt, J., Campbasso, C.P., Gaudry, E., *et al.* (2007) Best practice in forensic entomology – standards and guidelines. *International Journal of Legal Medicine*, **121**, 90–104.

Amendt, J., Krettek, R. and Zehner, R. (2004) Forensic entomology. *Naturwissenschaften*, **91**, 51–65.

Anderson, G.S. (1999) Wildlife forensic entomology: determining time of death in two illegally killed black bear cubs. *Journal of Forensic Science*, **44**, 856–859.

Anderson, G.S. (2000) Minimum and maximum development rates of some forensically important Calliphoridae (Diptera). *Journal of Forensic Science*, **45**, 824–832.

Anderson, G.S. (2010) Decomposition and invertebrate colonization of cadavers in coastal marine environments. In J. Amendt, M.L. Goff, C.P. Campbasso and M. Grassberger (eds) *Current Concepts in Forensic Entomology*. New York: Springer Science+Business Media, B. V., pp. 223–272.

Archer, M.S. (2004) The effect of time after body discovery on the accuracy of retrospective weather station ambient temperature corrections in forensic entomology. *Journal of Forensic Science*, **49**, 553–559.

Battan Horenstein, M., Linhares, A.X., Rosso, B., *et al.* (2007) Species composition and seasonal succession of saprophagous calliphorids in a rural area of Cordoba: Argentina. *Biological Research*, **40**, 163–171.

Baumgartner, D.L. (1988) Review of myiasis (Insecta: Diptera: Calliphoridae, Sarcophagidae) of Nearctic wildlife. *Wildlife Rehabilitation*, **7**, 3–46.

Baumgartner, D.L. (1993) Review of *Chrysomya rufifacies* (Diptera: Calliphoridae). *Journal of Medical Entomology*, **30**, 338–352.

Baumgartner, D.L. and Greenberg, B. (1985) Distribution and medical ecology of the blow flies (Diptera: Calliphoridae) of Peru. *Annals of the Entomological Society of America*, **78**, 565–587.

Bennett, G.F. and Whitworth, T.L. (1991) Studies on life history of some species of *Protocalliphora* (Diptera: Calliphoridae). *Canadian Journal of Zoology*, **69**, 2048–2058.

Boatright, S.A. and Tomberlin, J.K. (2010) Effects of temperature and tissue type on the development of *Cochliomyia macellaria* (Diptera: Calliphoridae). *Journal of Medical Entomology*, **47**, 917–923.

Bolek, M.G. and Coggins, J.R. (2002) Observations on myiasis by the Calliphorid, *Bufolucilia silvarum*, in the Eastern American Toad (*Bufo americanus americanus*) from southeastern Wisconsin. *Journal of Wildlife Diseases*, **38**, 598–603.

Bourel, B., Fleurisse, L., Hedouin, V. *et al.* (2001) Immunohistochemical contribution to the study of morphine metabolism in Calliphoridae larvae and implications in forensic entomotoxicology. *Journal of Forensic Science*, **46**, 596–599.

Bourel, B., Hedouin, V., Martin-Bouyer, L. *et al.* (1999) Effects of morphine in decomposing bodies on the development of *Lucilia sericata* (Diptera: Calliphoridae). *Journal of Forensic Science*, **44**, 354–358.

Bram, R.A., George, J.E., Reichard, R.E. and Tabachnick, W.J. (2002) Threat of foreign arthropod-borne pathogens to livestock in the United States. *Journal of Medical Entomology*, **39**, 405–416.

Byrd, J.H., and Butler, J.F. (1996) Effects of temperature on *Cochliomyia macellaria* (Diptera: Calliphoridae) development. *Journal of Medical Entomology*, **33**, 901–905.

Byrd, J.H. and Butler, J.F. (1997) Effects of temperature on *Chrysomya rufifacies* (Diptera: Calliphoridae) development. *Journal of Medical Entomology*, **34**, 353–358.

Byrd, J.H. and Castner, J.L. (2010) *Forensic Entomology: The Utility of Arthropods in Legal Investigations*. Boca Raton, FL: CRC Press.

Colwell, D.D., Hall, M.J.R. and Scholl, P.J. (eds.) (2006) *The Oestrid Flies: Biology, Host-Parasite Relationships, Impact and Management*. Cambridge, MA: CABI Publishing.

Craine, I.T.M. and Boonstra, R. (1986) Myiasis of *Wohlfahrtia vigil* in nestling *Microtus pennsylvanicus*. *Journal of Wildlife Diseases*, **22**, 587–589.

Dillon, N., Austin, A.D. and Bartowsky, E. (1996) Comparison of preservation techniques for DNA extraction from hymenopterous insects. *Insect Molecular Biology*, **5**, 21–24.

Gagliano-Candela, R. and Aventaggiato, L. (2001) The detection of toxic substances in entomological specimens. *International Journal of Legal Medicine*, **114**, 197–203.

Gallagher, M.B., Sandhu, S. and Kimsey, R. (2010) Variation in development time for geographically distinct populations of the common green bottle fly, *Lucilia sericata* (Meigen). *Journal of Forensic Science*, **55**, 438–442.

George, K.A., Archer, M.S., Green, L.M. *et al.* (2009) Effect of morphine on the growth rate of *Calliphora stygia* (Fabricius) (Diptera: Calliphoridae) and possible implications for forensic entomology. *Forensic Science International*, **193**, 21–25.

Goff, M.L., Brown, W.A., Omori, A.I. and LaPointe, D.A. (1993) Preliminary observations of the effects of amitriptyline in decomposing tissues on the development of *Parasarcophaga ruficornis* (Diptera: Sarcophagidae) and implications of this effect to estimation of postmortem interval. *Journal of Forensic Science*, **38**, 316–322.

Goff, M.L. and Lord, W.D. (1994) Entomotoxicology: a new area for forensic investigation. *American Journal of Forensic Medical Pathology*, **15**, 51–57.

Gomes, L., Gomes, G. and Desuo, I.C. (2009) A preliminary study of insect fauna on pig carcasses located in sugarcane in winter in southeastern Brazil. *Medical and Veterinary Entomology*, **23**, 155–159.

Grassberger, M. and Frank, C. (2003) Temperature-related development of the parasitoid wasp *Nasonia vitripennis* as forensic indicator. *Medical and Veterinary Entomology*, **17**, 257–262.

Grassberger, M. and Frank, C. (2004) Initial study of arthropod succession on pig carrion in a central European urban habitat. *Journal of Medical Entomology*, **41**, 511–523.

Gunn, J.A., Shelley, C. and Lewis, S.W. (2006) The determination of morphine in the larvae of Calliphora stygia using flow injection analysis and HPLC with chemiluminescence detection. *Journal of Analytical Toxicology*, **30**, 519–523.

Haskell, N.H. and Williams, R.E. (2008) *Entomology and Death: A Procedural Guide*. Clemson, SC: East Park Printing.

Heath, A.C.G. and Bishop, D.M. (2006) Flystrike in New Zealand: an overview based on a 16-year study, following the introduction and dispersal of the Australian sheep blowfly, *Lucilia cuprina* Wiedemann (Diptera: Calliphoridae). *Veterinary Parasitology*, **137**, 333–344.

Hocking, M.D. and Reimchen, T.E. (2006) Consumption and distribution of salmon (*Oncorhynchus* spp.) nutrients and energy by terrestrial flies. *Canadian Journal of Fisheries and Aquatic Science*, **63**, 2076–2086.

Huber, J.T. (1998) The importance of voucher specimens, with practical guidelines for preserving specimens of the major invertebrate phyla for identification. *Journal of Natural History*, **32**, 367–385.

Introna, F., Campobasso, C.P. and Goff, M.L. (2001) Entomotoxicology. *Forensic Science International*, **120**, 42–47.

Jones, G. and Wall, R. (2008) Maggot-therapy in veterinary medicine. *Research in Veterinary Science*, **85**, 394–398.

Joy, J.E., Herrell, M.L. and Rogers, P.C. (2002) Larval fly activity on sunlit versus shaded raccoon carrion in southwestern West Virginia with special reference to the black blowfly (Diptera: Calliphoridae). *Journal of Medical Entomology*, **39**, 392–397.

Kamal, A.S. (1958) Comparative study of thirteen species of sarcosaprophagous Calliphoridae and Sarcophagidae (Diptera) I. Bionomics. *Annals of the Entomological Society of America*, **51**, 261–271.

Kaneshrajah, G. and Turner, B. (2004) *Calliphora vicina* larvae grow at different rates on different body tissues. *International Journal of Legal Medicine*, **118**, 242–244.

Keiper, J.B., and Casamatta, D.A. (2001) Benthic organisms as forensic indicators. *Journal of the North American Benthological Society*, **20**, 311–324.

Kerridge, A., Lappin-Scott, H. and Stevens, J.R. (2005) Antibacterial properties of larval secretions of the blowfly, *Lucilia sericata. Medical and Veterinary Entomology*, **19**, 333–337.

Kharbouche, H., Augsburger, M., Cherix, D. *et al.* (2008) Codeine accumulation and elimination in larvae, pupae, and imago of the blowfly *Lucilia sericata* and effects on its development. *International Journal of Legal Medicine*, **122**, 205–211.

Knotek, Z., Fischer, O.A., Jekl, V. and Knotkova, Z. (2005) Fatal myiasis caused by Calliphora vicina in Hermann's tortoise (*Testudo hermanni*). *Acta Veterinaria Brunensis*, **74**, 123–128.

Kulshrestha, P. and Satpathy, D.K. (2001) Use of beetles in forensic entomology. *Forensic Science International*, **120**, 15–17.

Lord, W.D., DiZinno, J.A., Wilson, M.R. *et al.* (1998) Isolation, amplification, and sequencing of human mitochondrial DNA obtained from human crab louse, *Pthirus pubis* (L.), blood meals. *Journal of Forensic Science*, **43**, 1097–1100.

Mariluis, J.C. and Mulieri, P.R. (2003) The distribution of the Calliphoridae in Argentina (Diptera). *Revista de la Sociedad Entomologica Argentina*, **62**, 85–97.

Merritt, R.W. and Wallace, J.R. (2010) The role of aquatic insects in forensic investigations. In J.H. Byrd and J.L. Castner (eds.) *Forensic Entomology: The Utility of Arthropods in Legal Investigations*. Boca Raton, FL: CRC Press, pp. 271–320.

Mullen, G. and Durden, L. (eds.) (2009) *Medical and Veterinary Entomology*. San Diego, CA: Academic Press.

Musvasva, E., Williams, K.A., Muller, W.J. and Villet, M.H. (2001) Preliminary observations on the effects of hydrocortisone and sodium methohexital on development of *Sarcophaga* (Curranea) *tibialis* Macquart (Diptera: Sarcophagidae), and implications for estimating post mortem interval. *Forensic Science International*, **120**, 37–41.

Nelder, M.P., McCreadie, J.W. and Major, C.S. (2009) Blow flies visiting decaying alligators: is succession synchronous or asynchronous? *Psyche*, **2009**, 1–7.

Norris, K.R. (1965) The bionomics of blow flies. *Annual Review of Entomology*, **10**, 47–68.

OIE (2008) OIE Terrestrial Manual, in *T. W. O. f. A. H. (OIE)*, Chapter 2.1.10. New World screwworm (*Cochliomyia hominivorax*) and Old World screwworm (*Chrysomya bezziana*). OIE. Online.

Oshaghi, M.A., Chavshin, A.R., Vatandoost, H. *et al.* (2006) Effects of post-ingestion and physical conditions on PCR amplification of host blood meal DNA in mosquitoes. *Experimental Parasitology*, **112**, 232–236.

Pape, T. (2001) Phylogeny of oestridae (Insecta: Diptera). *Systematic Entomology*, **26**, 133–171.

Pichon, B., Egan, D., Rogers, M. and Gray, J. (2009) Detection and identification of pathogens and host DNA in unfed host-seeking *Ixodes ricinus* L. (Acari: Ixodidae). *Journal of Medical Entomology*, **40**, 723–731.

Pritam, H.M.H. and Jayaprakash, P.T. (2009) Nocturnal ovivposition behavior of necrophagous dipterans in Kelantan, Malaysia. *Journal of Forensic Science*, **54**, 1135–1140.

Reed, J.H.B. (1958) A study of dog carcass communities in Tennessee, with special reference to the insects. *The American Midland Natural Journal*, **59**, 213–245.

Replogle, J., Lord, W.D., Budowle, B. *et al.* (1994) Identification of host DNA by amplified fragment length polymorphism analysis: preliminary analysis of human crab louse (Anoplura: Pediculidae) excreta. *Journal of Medical Entomology*, **31**, 686–690.

Ross, J.C., Wallace, J.R. and Huffman, J.E. (2009) Detection of game DNA in maggot tissue. In *American Academy of Forensic Sciences*. Denver, CO: Publication Printers, Corp.

Sadler, D.W., Fuke, C., Court, F. and Pounder, D.J. (1995) Drug accumulation and elimination in *Calliphora vicina* larvae. *Forensic Science International*, **71**, 191–197.

Sadler, D.W., Seneviratne, C. and Pounder, D.J. (1997) Effects of 3,4-methelenedioxymethamphetamine in decomposing tissues on the development of *Parasarcophaga ruficornis* (Diptera: Sarcophagidae) and detection of the drug in postmortem blood, liver tissue, larvae and pupae. *Journal of Forensic Science*, **42**, 1212–1213.

Saks, M.J. and Koehler, J.J. (2005) The coming paradigm shift in forensic identification science. *Science*, **309**, 892–895.

Samuel, W.M., Pybus, M.J. and Kocan, A.A. (eds.) (2001) *Parasitic Diseases of Wild Mammals*. Ames, IA: Iowa State University Press.

Schoenly, K.G., Haskell, N.H., Hall, R.D. and Gbur, J.R. (2007) Comparative performance and complementarity of four sampling methods and arthropod preference tests from human and porcine remains at the Forensic Anthropology Center in Knoxville, Tennessee. *Journal of Medical Entomology*, **44**, 881–894.

Schoenly, K.G., Shahid, S.A., Haskell, N.H. and Hall, R.D. (2005) Does carcass enrichment alter community structure of predaceous and parasitic arthropods? A second test of the arthropod saturation hypothesis at the Anthropology Research Facility in Knoxville, Tennessee. *Journal of Forensic Science*, **50**, 134–142.

Shahid, S.A., Schoenly, K. and Haskell, N. H. (2003) Carcass enrichment does not alter decay rates or arthropod community structure: a test of the arthropod saturation hypothesis at the Anthropology Research Facility in Knoxville, Tennessee. *Journal of Medical Entomology*, **40**, 559–569.

Sherman, R.A., Hall, M.J.R. and Thomas, S. (2000) Medicinal maggots: an ancient remedy for some contemporary afflictions. *Annual Review of Entomology*, **45**, 55–81.

Singh, D. and Bharti, M. (2008) Some notes on the nocturnal larviposition by two species of Sarcophaga (Diptera: Sarcophagidae). *Forensic Science International*, **177**, e19–20.

Stroud, R.K. (1998) Wildlife forensics and the veterinary practicioner. *Seminars in Avian and Exotic Pet Medicine*, **7**, 182–192.

Sukontason, K., Narongchai, P., and Kanchai, C. (2007) Forensic entomology cases in Thailand: a review of cases from 2000 to 2006. *Parasitology Research*, **101**, 1417–1423.

Szalanski, A.L., Austin, J.W., McKern, J.A. *et al.* (2006) Time course analysis of bed bug, Cimex lectularius L., (Hemiptera: Cimicidae) blood meals with the use of polymerase chain reaction. *J. Agric. Urban Entomology*, **23**, 237–241.

Tabor, K.L., Fell, R.D., Brewster, C.C. *et al.* (2005) Effects of antemorteum ingestion of ethanol on insect successional patterns and development of *Phormia regina* (Diptera: Calliphoridae). *Journal of Medical Entomology*, **42**, 481–489.

Tarone, A.M. and Foran, D.R. (2006) Components of developmental plasticity in a Michigan population of *Lucilia sericata* (Diptera: Calliphoridae). *Journal of Medical Entomology*, **43**, 1023–1033.

Tomberlin, J.K. (2008) Arthropods Associated with Decomposing Human Remains. In Entomology & Death: A Procedural Guide. N.H. Haskell and R.E. Williams, eds. East Park Printing, Clemson, SC.

Tomberlin, J.K., Benbow, M.E., Tarone, A. and Mohr, R. Invited paper (2011) Evolutionary ecology approaches in decomposition research enhances forensics: entomology as a case example. *Trends in Ecology & Evolution*, **26**, 53–55.

Tomberlin, J.K., Sheppard, D.C. and Joyce, J.A. (2005) Black soldier fly (Diptera: Stratiomyidae) colonization of pig carrion in South Georgia. *Journal of Forensic Science*, **50**, 152–153.

Tracqui, A., Keyser-Tracqui, C., Kintz, P. and Ludes, B. (2004) Entomotoxicology for the forensic toxicologist: much ado about nothing? *International Journal of Legal Medicine*, **118**, 194–196.

USDA, APHIS (2001) Screwworm. In USDA, APHIS (ed) *Veterinary Services*. North Carolina.

USPS (2010) 601 Mailability: 10.0 Hazardous Materials. In U. S. P. Service (ed.) Mailing Standards of the United States Postal Service Domestic Mail Manual. Washington, DC: U.S. Government Printer.

Villet, M.H., MacKenzie, B., and Muller, W.J. (2006) Larval development of the carrion-breeding flesh fly, *Sarcophaga* (*Liosarcophaga*) *tibialis* Macquart (Diptera: Sarcophagidae), at constant temperatures. *African Entomology*, **14**, 357–366.

Wallace, J.R., Merritt, R.W., Kimbirauskas, R. *et al.* (2008) Caddisflies assist with homicide case: determining a postmortem submersion interval using aquatic insects. *Journal of Forensic Science*, **53**, 219–221.

Watson, E.J. and Carlton, C.E. (2003) Spring succession of necrophilous insects on wildlife carcasses in Louisiana. *Journal of Medical Entomology*, **40**, 338–347.

Watson, E. J. and Carlton, C. E. (2005) Insect succession and decomposition of wildlife carcasses during fall and winter in Louisiana. *Journal of Medical Entomology*, **42**, 193–203.

Wells, J.D. and Stevens, J.R. (2008) Application of DNA-based methods in forensic entomology. *Annual Review of Entomology*, **53**, 103–120.

Whitworth, T. (2006) Keys to the genera and species of blow flies (Diptera: Calliphoridae) of America north of Mexico. *Proceedings of the Entomological Society of Washington*, **108**, 689–725.

Zurawski, K.N., Benbow, M.E., Miller, J.R. and Merritt, R.W. (2009) Examination of nocturnal blow fly (Diptera: Calliphoridae) oviposition on pig carcasses in mid-Michigan. *Journal of Medical Entomology*, **46**, 671–679.

7

Wildlife Forensic Pathology and Toxicology in Wound Analysis and Pesticide Poisoning

Douglas E. Roscoe and William Stansley

Introduction

Fish and wildlife agencies seldom have crime scene investigative units. The conservation officer must provide the observations, field measurements, collection, preservation and laboratory submission of samples with appropriate continuity of evidence forms. The officer, knowledgeable in the potential forensic tests which could be employed, can formulate questions and determine how and what samples to be collected or actually perform the tests at the scene. More often than not, it is the field observations of the investigator, or those gleaned from interviews with witnesses that provide the critical information needed to solve the case. These observations will also determine what sampling and testing should be conducted. The key is to know which observations to make and which questions to ask. This chapter will describe methods for investigations of wounds and poisonings, which, in the experience of the authors, have been commonly employed by New Jersey Conservation Officers.

Wound Analysis

Entrance vs. exit wounds

Wounds of animals characterized by circumscribing abrasions of the skin (Figure 7.1) are typical of entrance wounds of projectiles from firearms. Cut

Wildlife Forensics: Methods and Applications, First Edition. Edited by Jane E. Huffman and John R. Wallace.

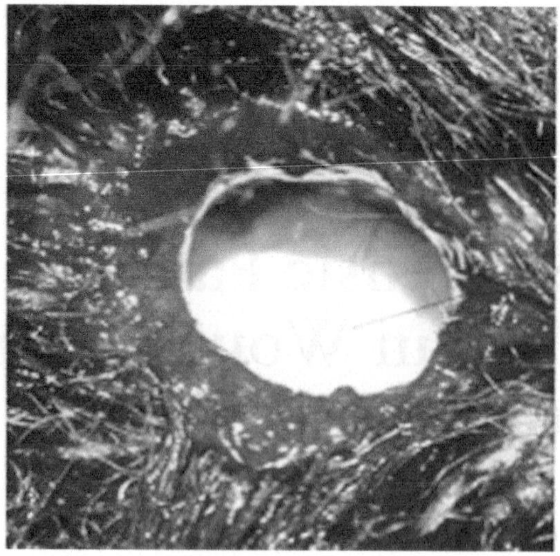

Figure 7.1 A bullet entrance wound characterized by circumscribing abrasion and hemorrhage. (*See plate insert for color representation of this figure.*)

hair (Figure 7.2) or feathers surrounding a puncture or incised wound of the skin or with hairs or feathers drawn into the wound also suggest an entrance wound. Entrance wounds are the most useful to examine.

Exit wounds lack circumscribing abrasion of the skin. An exception to this, described in humans, is a shored exit wound when skin is supported by a firm surface where the bullet exits (Denton *et al.*, 2006). If there is an exit

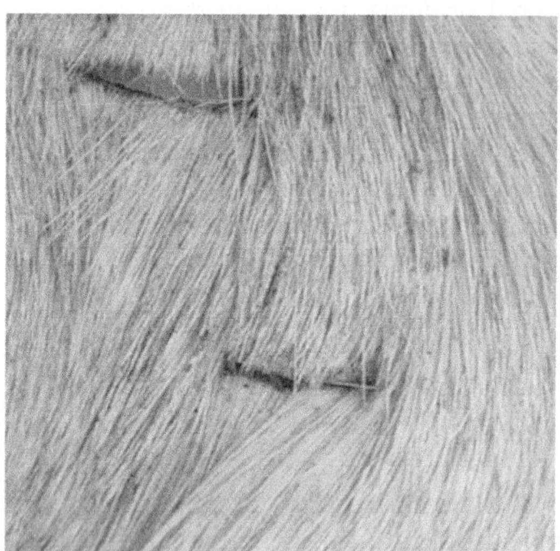

Figure 7.2 Cut hair typifies incised entrance wounds. (*See plate insert for color representation of this figure.*)

wound, deformation or fragmentation of a projectile as it passes through bone and soft tissue diminishes the value of the wound shape and size in identifying the projectile.

Wounds in live animals vs. wounds in dead animals

The best way to examine an entrance wound to see if it was inflicted in a live animal is to remove the skin surrounding and including the wound and look at the subcutaneous side (Figure 7.3). With a sharp knife or scalpel, the pooled blood and the subcutaneous muscle layer may be cut away to reveal the white connective tissue underside of the skin. Skin is elastic. In the case of an entrance wound, a projectile passes through the skin drawing it into the wound channel. The projectile compresses the margins of the wound in the skin against the tissues of the wound channel. In a live animal the traumatized blood vessels and capillaries in the skin release blood, which is propelled under pressure from the pumping heart into the surrounding tissues at the margins of the wound (Figure 7.4). This circumscribing hemorrhage defines a wound inflicted in a live animal. If there is no circumscribing hemorrhage, the wound was inflicted in a dead animal (Spraker and Davies, 1994).

Attempts to disguise the true cause of death may involve inflicting wounds in dead animals. A bullet, shot or arrow wound inflicted in the live animal may be altered to resemble another projectile (i.e. four-bladed vs. three-bladed broadhead, bullet vs. broadhead) after the animal has died. In such circumstances the margin of hemorrhage will not follow the margin of the altering post-mortem wound (Figure 7.5).

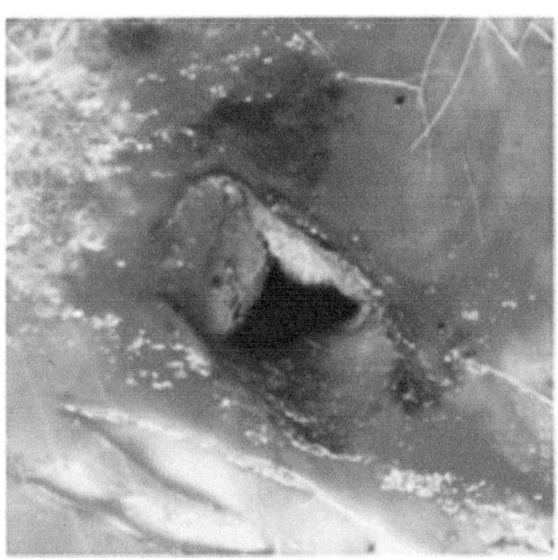

Figure 7.3 Subcutaneous view of an entrance wound in the hide of a deer from a three-bladed broadhead. (*See plate insert for color representation of this figure.*)

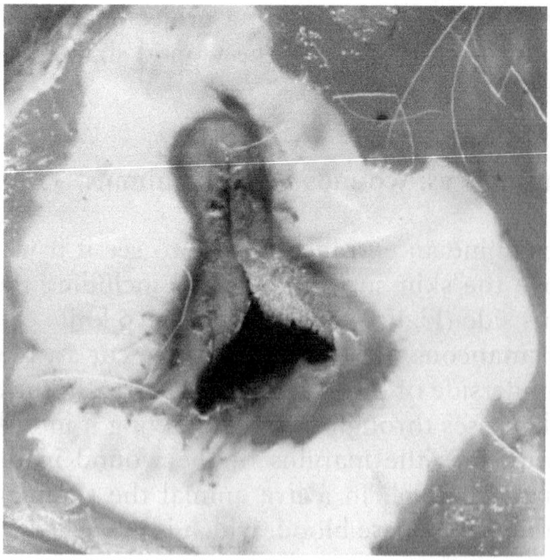

Figure 7.4 Subcutaneous muscle scraped away from the hide in Figure 7.3 revealing hemorrhage circumscribing the wound. (*See plate insert for color representation of this figure.*)

Wound shape and size

The size and shape of a wound are useful in identifying the inflicting implement or projectile. Some investigators find it useful to have a collection of bullets, slugs, broadheads and shot for comparison to wounds (Figure 7.6). Wound shape and size can be distorted in the skin. The wounds in the thoracic area of the deer

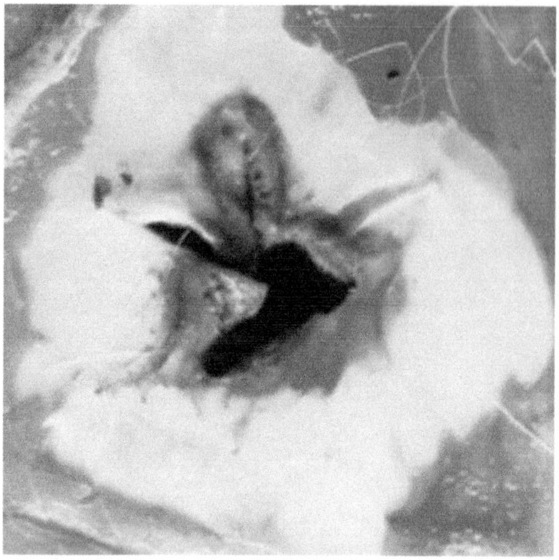

Figure 7.5 The three-bladed broadhead wound in Figure 7.4 altered by a knife cut to the left margin of the wound post-mortem. (*See plate insert for color representation of this figure.*)

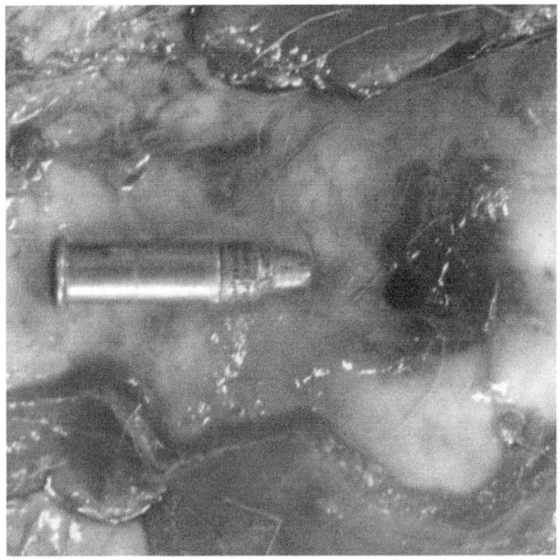

Figure 7.6 The bullet in the cartridge approximates the diameter of the wound in the hide. (*See plate insert for color representation of this figure.*)

hide in Figure 7.7 appear oval or circular. Examination of the wound channels in the underlying thorax showed less circular distortion and more slit-like wounds. By pulling the hide to align the edges of the wounds, they become straight slit-like incisions (Figure 7.8). Examination of the hair side of the hide reveals a straight line cut of the hairs overlying the slits (Figure 7.2). Both ends of the slits terminate in an acute angle suggestive of an object with two opposing cutting edges. A two-bladed broadhead or a dagger blade might inflict such wounds.

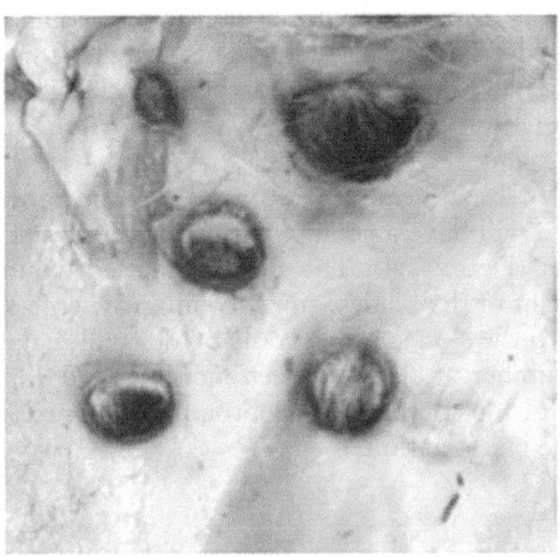

Figure 7.7 Wounds in the hide pulled in one direction appear circular. (*See plate insert for color representation of this figure.*)

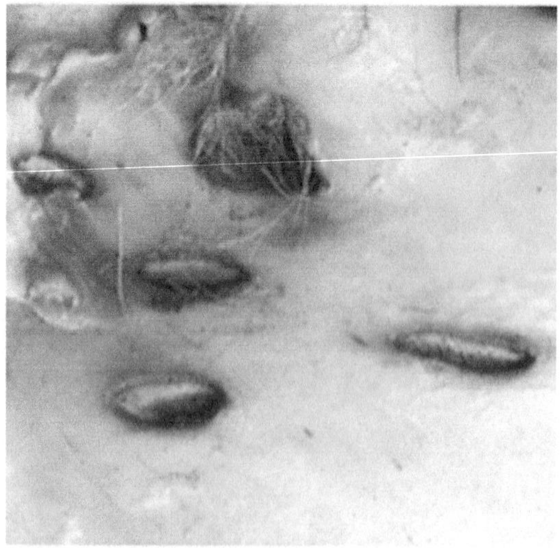

Figure 7.8 Pulling the hide in Figure 7.7 in another direction aligns the margins into slits. (*See plate insert for color representation of this figure.*)

Three observations argue against an arrow tipped with a broadhead: (1) there are five wounds inflicted in the hide of a live (circumscribing hemorrhage) deer illustrated in Figures 7.7 and 7.8. This would require unrealistic, rapid, accurate shooting of arrows; (2) the wound slits are not all the same length; and (3) there were no exit wounds in the carcass. However, there were three small lacerations evident on the inside wall of the thorax 7 inches from the entrance wounds on the opposite thoracic wall.

The explanation provided by the suspect to the investigating officer that the deer, near death, was dispatched with a dagger possessing a 7-inch blade was supported by the analysis of the wounds. The varying lengths of the slits were the result of a tapered dagger penetrating to varying depths. The longest slit wounds in the thoracic hide conformed to the widest portion of the dagger blade examined.

With multi-bladed broadheads the entrance wound, after alignment of the margins in the skin, will have a stellate pattern with incised wounds projecting out from the center (Figure 7.4). The shortest incised wound most closely approximates the height of the blades, since if the arrow enters at any angle other than a right angle to the skin surface, some blades will make longer lacerations than others. The number of blade-induced incisions and approximate length of the shortest is useful for comparison to broadhead tipped arrows collected or observed during the investigation.

Shot wound patterns

Shotgun shot wound patterns in animal skin may indicate the distance from the animal to the shooter. Multiple shot wound patterns in the skin combined with the anatomical locations may further indicate the sequence of the shots.

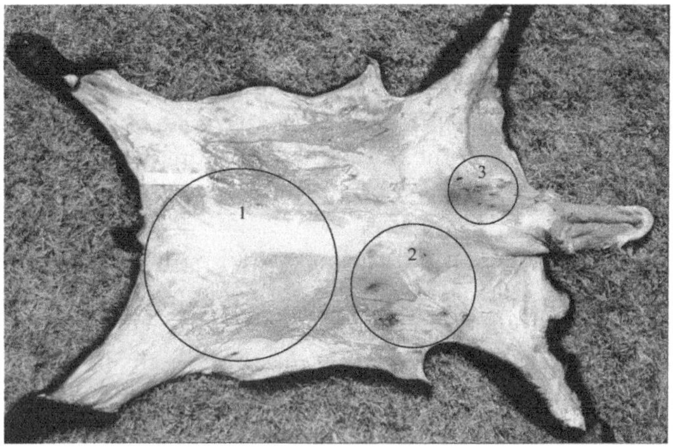

Figure 7.9 The three buckshot wound patterns in the hide become more lethal in anatomical location and decrease in diameter as the shooter gets closer to the bear. (*See plate insert for color representation of this figure.*)

The bear hide in Figure 7.9 has three discernible patterns of buckshot pellet holes. Investigation revealed a single shooter was using a shotgun with the same buckshot load for each shot. As the distance from a target increases, the diameter of a shot pattern increases. The first shot wounds at the longest distance are within the largest circle containing the fewest pellets on the hindquarters of the bear and were not immediately lethal. The second shot wounds at a closer distance are within the mid-size circle on the left thorax of the bear and would be quickly disabling and lethal. The final shot wounds at the closest distance are within the smallest circle on the right neck of the bear and would be immediately lethal.

To develop an approximation of the distances for each of the shots illustrated, the investigator must shoot the shotgun in question with a specific choke or a similar one at varying distances from a target using the same buckshot loads used by the suspect. The diameter of the circle enclosing the outer pellet holes in the target is related to the distance from the target. The diameter of the circle in the target most closely corresponding to that of the shot wound pattern is then correlated to the approximate distance between the animal and the shooter.

Wound paths

The path that a projectile follows through the body of an animal may be used to determine the orientation of the animal relative to the shooter. Sometimes this is done to locate the position of a shooter at the scene or support/refute a claim of self-defense.

Wound paths, which pass through soft tissue, are preferred but not essential for analysis. Projectiles, which pass through bone close to the entrance wound, may have been deflected. If the bone strike is well into the body, the wound path prior to the bone strike may be long enough for analysis.

Wound paths that lead to a bone strike may provide evidence of the direction of the projectile and therefore the location of the entrance wound. The fragments of lead or bone sheared off in the bone strike will be present along the wound channel as the projectile continues its path after the strike. In the case of flat bones in the skull or ribs, a conical defect in the bone occurs as the bullet exits. The narrow tip of the conical defect points in the direction of the entrance wound (Denton *et al.*, 2006).

A probe or rod inserted gently into the wound path so as not to create a new channel provides a guide to visualize the path (Figure 7.10). An animal, which has an exit wound without evidence of projectile deformation, may be suitable for probe insertion even after intervening internal organs have been removed. If

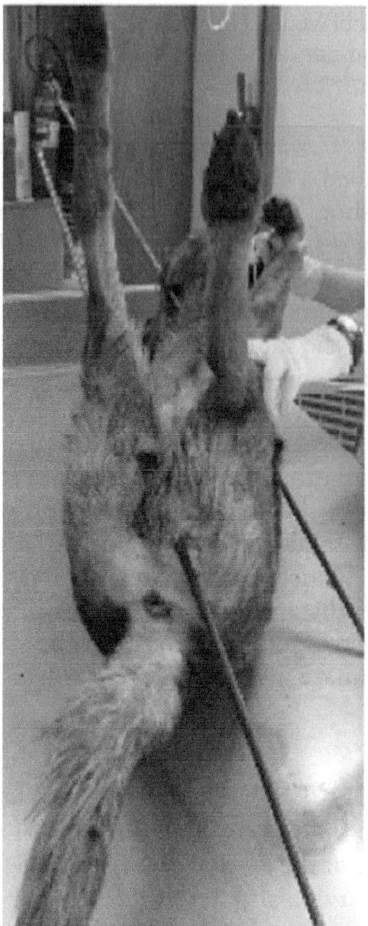

Figure 7.10 Rods mark two wound channels through the animal. (*See plate insert for color representation of this figure.*)

the investigator removes the organs, confirmation of the straight-line passage of the projectile through those organs should be determined during dissection.

A wound path, which has an entrance wound dorsal (higher on the back) to the exit wound or terminus within the body, suggests the shooter is above the standing animal (i.e. uphill, tree stand) or behind the back of one lying down. The reverse of the wound locations would place the shooter below the standing animal (i.e. downhill, shooter lying down) or in front of the ventral surface of one lying down.

A wound path, which has an entrance wound anterior (head end) to an exit wound or terminus within the body, suggests the shooter is in front of the animal. The reverse of wound locations would put the shooter behind the animal.

A wound path, which has an entrance wound in one side of the animal places the shooter on that side.

A combination of measurements at the scene and examination of wound paths may provide quantitative evidence of the location of the shooter relative to the animal. If it is assumed a suspect shot an animal standing at a nearby bait pile from a tree stand, the following measurements could be useful. The height of the stand from the base of the tree and from the base of the tree to the suspected animal location (blood and/or bait pile) will provide two sides of a right triangle, assuming the ground is level from the tree to the suspected animal location. By drawing these two measurements to scale one can draw the projectile path (hypotenuse) by connecting the ends of each line (Figure 7.11). A protractor may be used to measure the angle of the projectile path relative to the horizontal ground line. This angle can be compared to the angle of the wound path in the animal carcass, which is determined in a similar manner using a probe in the wound channel. Marking the probe at the entrance wound and exit wounds provides the length of the hypotenuse. A carpenter's square can be used to help measure the other two legs of the right triangle. Then if the angle of the wound path approximates the angle of the projectile path, the assumptions developed at the scene are supported.

Projectile residues and recovery

The presence of lead residues in wound channels can help differentiate gunshot wounds from other types of wounds. Residues can be determined in a manner similar to that used for gunshot residues on hands (Newton, 1981). The wound channel is swabbed with a plastic cotton-tipped swab moistened with 5% ultrapure nitric acid. Preferred sites for swabbing are places where the projectile has penetrated bone or hide because these tend to abrade the projectile more than muscle tissue. Control swabs should also be collected. Depending on the kind of wound swabs collected, these can be swabs of incisions made in an intact portion of hide or muscle or swabs of undamaged bone. The heads of the control and wound swabs are clipped off and leached overnight in acid-washed 2 mL microcentrifuge tubes containing 1 mL of 5% nitric acid. The tubes are then

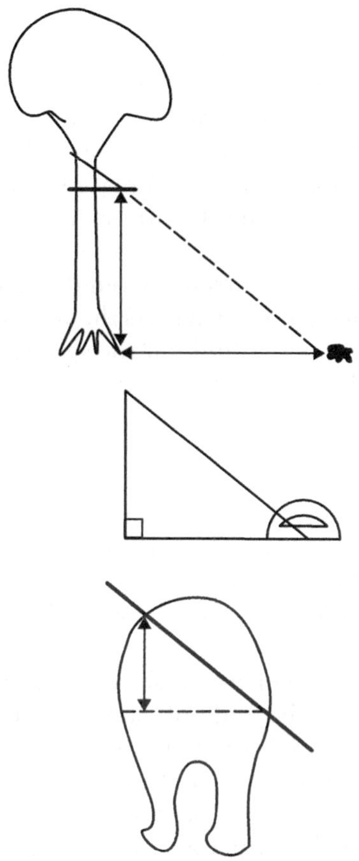

Figure 7.11 The angle of a projectile path from a tree stand to a bait pile where the animal was shot is measured on a scaled drawing of the right triangle using a protractor and then compared to the angle of a wound channel through the animal.

vortex-mixed for 30 seconds and centrifuged. The supernatant is analyzed for lead by graphite furnace atomic absorption spectrophotometry. Residues from a bullet or shot are usually many hundredfold the residues in control samples.

Colorimetric, rhodizonic acid-based test kits to detect lead are easy to use in the field and can be prepared by the investigator (Stone *et al.*, 1978) or purchased at hardware stores where they are sold to test for lead-based paint. The area of suspect lead residue is swabbed and the red color produced on the swab is indicative of lead. The drawback is that a high frequency of false negative results has been observed with some colorimetric tests (Spraker and Davies, 1994). The negative results are more likely when very small traces of lead are present and may be minimized by selection of a sample site where the bullet or shot passes through bone, leaving a visible gray residue (Figure 7.12). Wound locations should also be blotted of excess blood, which masks the red color change on the swab. These colorimetric tests when combined with a magnet are useful in distinguishing steel and lead shot, recovered from a carcass.

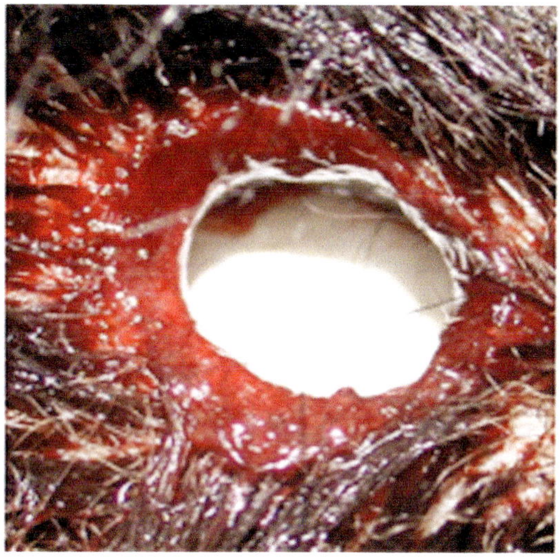

Plate 7.1 A bullet entrance wound characterized by circumscribing abrasion and hemorrhage.

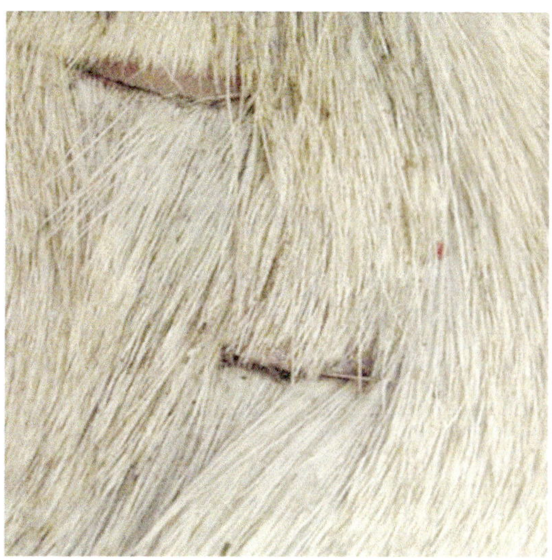

Plate 7.2 Cut hair typifies incised entrance wounds.

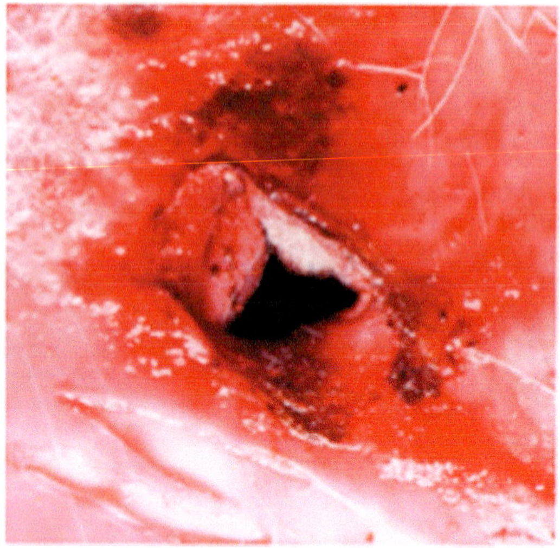

Plate 7.3 Subcutaneous view of an entrance wound in the hide of a deer from a three-bladed broadhead.

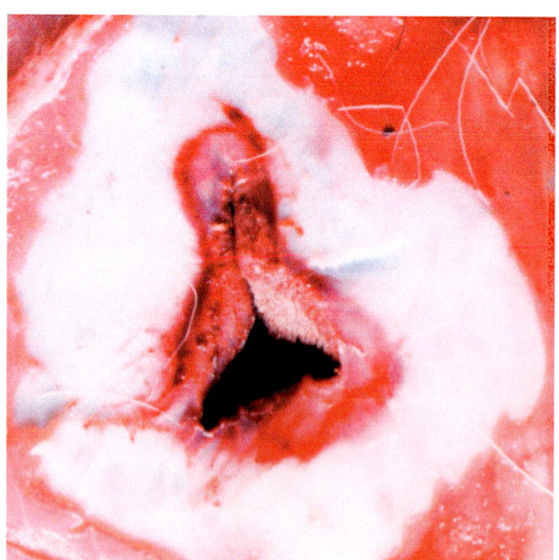

Plate 7.4 Subcutaneous muscle scraped away from the hide in Figure 7.3 revealing hemorrhage circumscribing the wound.

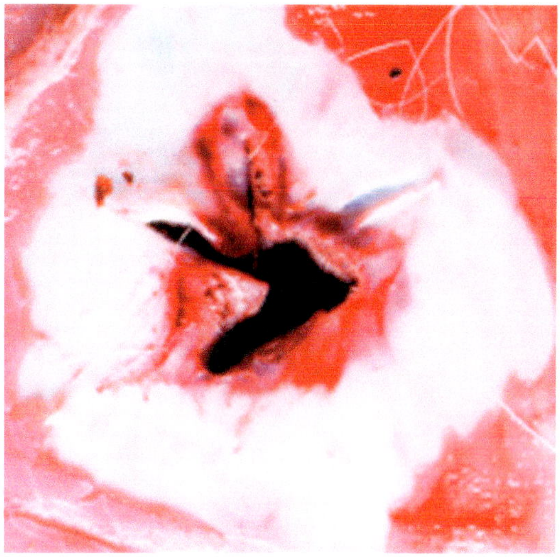

Plate 7.5 The three-bladed broadhead wound in Figure 7.4 altered by a knife cut to the left margin of the wound post-mortem.

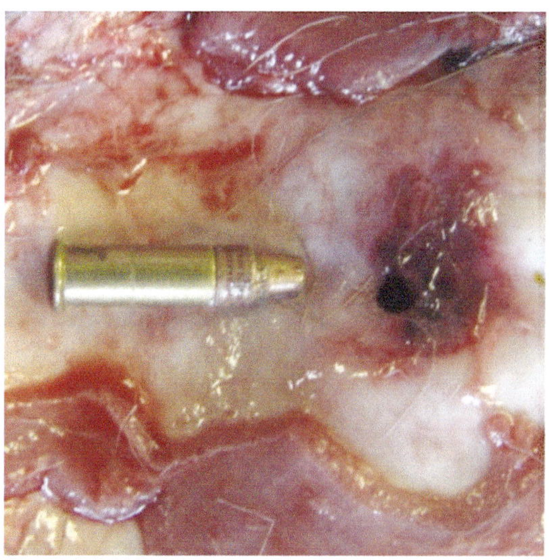

Plate 7.6 The bullet in the cartridge approximates the diameter of the wound in the hide.

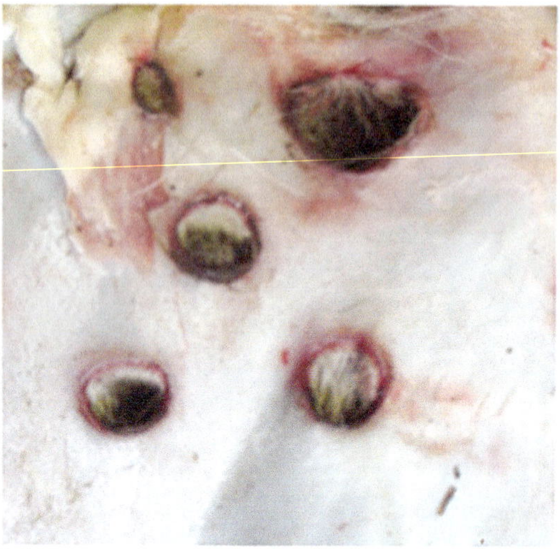

Plate 7.7 Wounds in the hide pulled in one direction appear circular.

Plate 7.8 Pulling the hide in Figure 7.7 in another direction aligns the margins into slits.

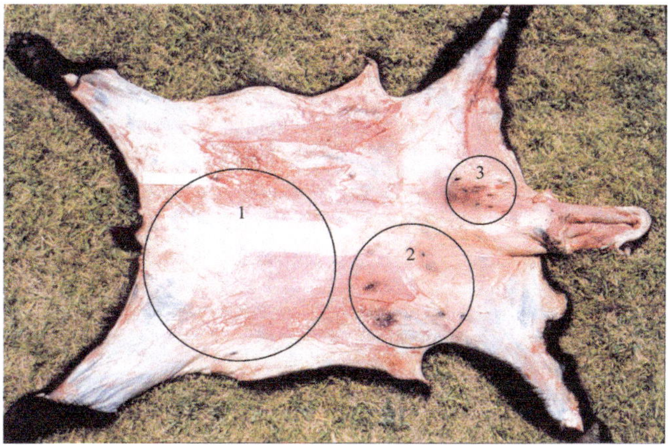

Plate 7.9 The three buckshot wound patterns in the hide become more lethal in anatomical location and decrease in diameter as the shooter gets closer to the bear.

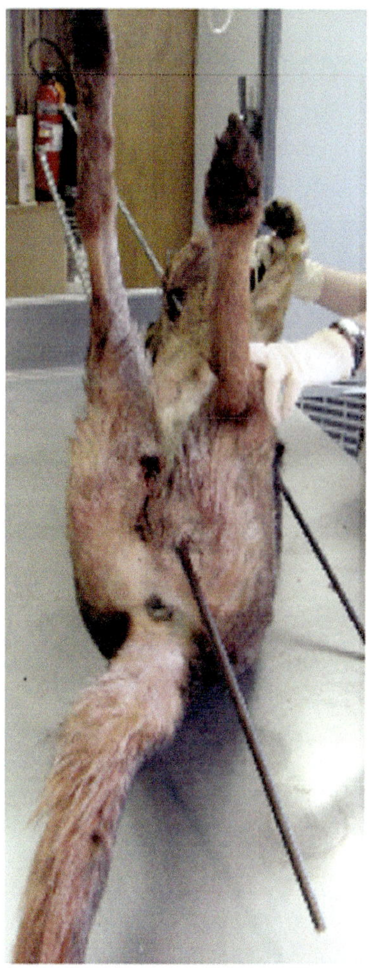

Plate 7.10 Rods mark two wound channels through the animal.

Plate 7.12 Wounds through bone are best for lead residue sampling.

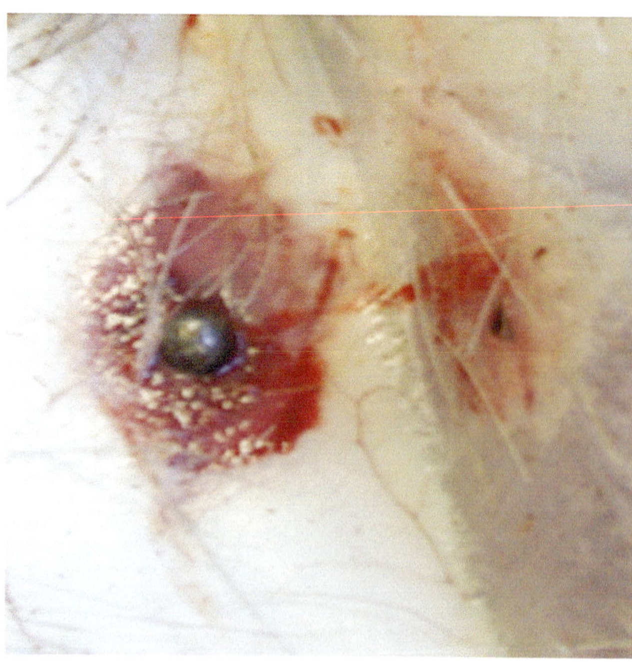

Plate 7.13 Buckshot pellets and other projectiles are often captured just under the tough hide on the side of the animal opposite the entrance wound.

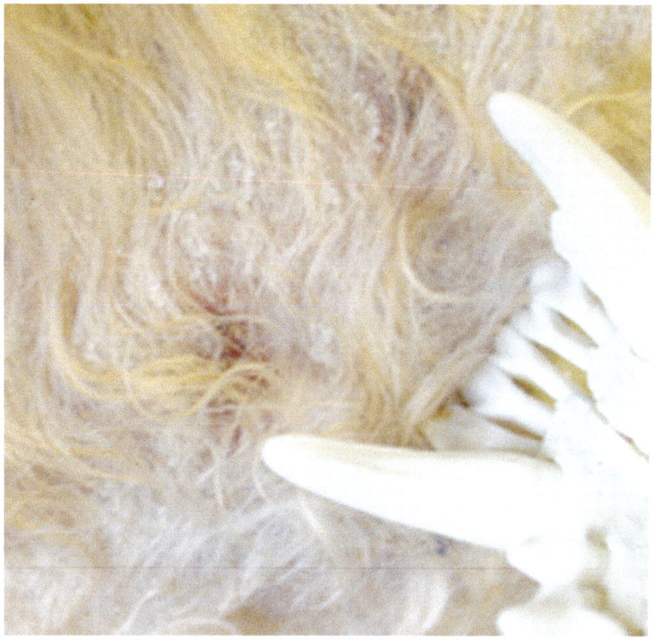

Plate 7.14 Coyote upper canine teeth compared to shallow puncture wounds in a suspect prey animal.

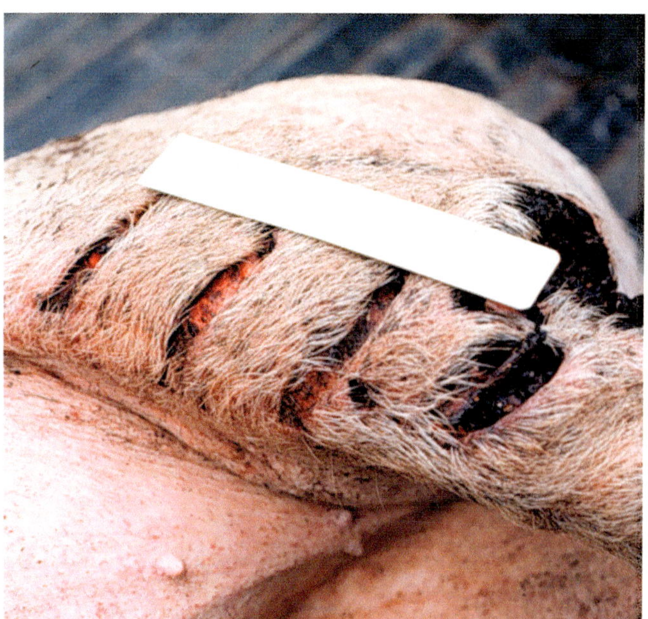

Plate 7.15 Parallel, shallow, linear lacerations with spacing consistent with that of bear claws.

Figure 7.12 Wounds through bone are best for lead residue sampling. (*See plate insert for color representation of this figure.*)

Projectiles are often trapped just beneath the tough elastic hide (Figure 7.13) or against flat bones like the scapula (shoulder blade) opposite the entrance wounds. Bullets, slugs and shot can sometimes be detected by carefully running the hands over the hide. Metal detectors (Stockdale, 1994) for field application and radiographs (X-rays) in laboratory settings simplify the search.

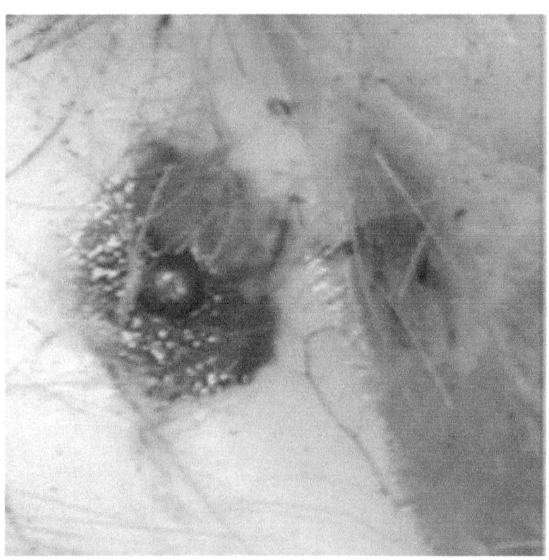

Figure 7.13 Buckshot pellets and other projectiles are often captured just under the tough hide on the side of the animal opposite the entrance wound. (*See plate insert for color representation of this figure.*)

Figure 7.14 Coyote upper canine teeth compared to shallow puncture wounds in a suspect prey animal. (*See plate insert for color representation of this figure.*)

Non-projectile-induced wounds

Wounds, superficially resembling bullet or knife wounds, occasionally are puncture wounds from teeth (Figure 7.14), talons or deer antlers. Parallel lacerations characterize wounds from claws (Figure 7.15). Blunt trauma from an automobile strike to a protuberance of the hip or head of a bone may crush the overlying skin causing the bone to break through, which superficially may appear to be

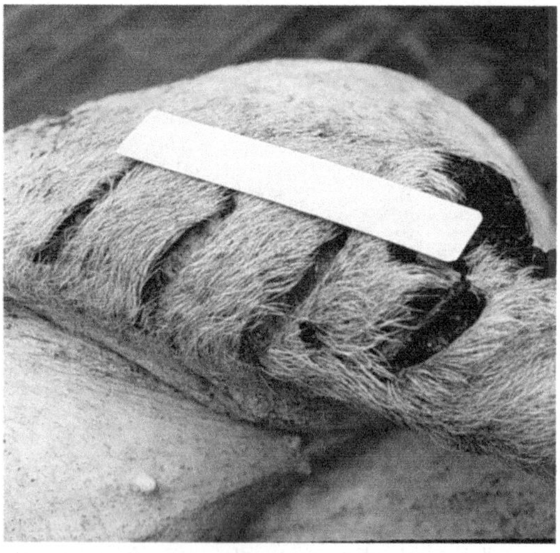

Figure 7.15 Parallel, shallow, linear lacerations with spacing consistent with that of bear claws. (*See plate insert for color representation of this figure.*)

a circular wound typical of a slug. The most obvious distinction of these non-projectile wounds is the short depth of the wound channels. Collections of skulls, jaws, claws and talons can be useful references when hypothesizing the origins of animal-inflicted wounds.

Wildlife Poisoning by Insecticides

Organophosphate and carbamate insecticides, collectively referred to as anti-cholinesterase compounds, came into widespread use as replacements for banned chlorinated pesticides. They are neurotoxins that disrupt the transmission of nerve impulses by inhibiting the action of the enzyme acetylcholinesterase at nerve synapses (Grue *et al.*, 1991). Although these newer compounds are not environmentally persistent as were chlorinated pesticides such as DDT, they are acutely toxic to fish and wildlife. Granular formulations are especially problematic because the granules can be mistaken for food or grit by foraging birds (Best and Fisher, 1992). In addition to causing inadvertent poisonings, these compounds have also been used to deliberately poison nuisance birds and mammals (Flickenger *et al.*, 1986; Wobeser *et al.*, 2004). In 2010, there were 32 organophosphate (OP) and 9 carbamate (CB) pesticides registered for use in the United States (U.S. Environmental Protection Agency, 2010). However, two compounds that were responsible for numerous bird poisonings have been totally or partially banned. In 1988, the U.S. EPA banned the use of the OP pesticide diazinon on golf courses and sod farms because of large bird kills associated with these uses. All outdoor residential uses of diazinon were cancelled on December 31, 1994, although product purchased before that date can still be legally used. As a result of the ban, we have not documented a case of diazinon poisoning in New Jersey since 2004. Carbofuran is a CB pesticide that has caused numerous bird poisonings (Fleischli *et al.*, 2004). Most uses of carbofuran were cancelled in 2009, and the U.S. EPA has proposed a total ban for all uses. Carbofuran poisonings continue to occur in New Jersey, and it has become the most commonly used compound in cases of deliberate poisoning.

Field observations and sample collection

Organophosphates and carbamates are acutely toxic to birds and cause death very quickly. Therefore, the presence in the same area of a large number of birds that appeared to have died around the same time may be a sign of OP or CB poisoning. These poisons act on the nervous system, affecting control of the muscles. If dying birds are observed at the scene, they may show a lack of coordination, inability to walk or fly, excessive salivation, spasms or convulsions, and arching of the head over the back (Grue *et al.*, 1991).

The presence of bait piles in the vicinity of large numbers of dead birds is characteristic of deliberate poisonings. The poison-treated bait may be the same as the planted grain, to disguise the presence of obvious piles. Samples of any suspect bait should be collected for pesticide residue analysis in anticipation of comparison to the crop and stomach contents of dead birds. Species of birds (e.g. hawks, turkeys), not intended to be targets of intentional poisonings, may also be found at the scene. Hawks that feed on poisoned birds may be poisoned by the pesticide-treated grain in the crops of their prey.

Accidental poisonings tend to occur during the growing season when the pesticides are being applied to control insect pests. However, while deliberate poisonings may occur at any time, those intended to control nuisance birds (Canada geese, blackbirds) in agricultural settings often occur during planting of cover crops in the fall and early winter, when large numbers of migrating birds may feed on the newly planted seeds or seedlings. Chlordane poisonings of roosting blackbirds, starlings and grackles may be confused with OP or CB poisoning, because of the involvement of large numbers of birds in a relatively small area and time interval. Chlordane poisonings occur most frequently in older suburbs peaking in July in the mid-Atlantic area (Okoniewski and Novesky, 1993; Stansley *et al.*, 2001). These mortalities are the result of the birds feeding on emerging Japanese beetles, which are resistant to and enhance the toxicity of the chlordane residues concentrated from the contaminated soils. Poisonings can also occur in the spring when beetle larvae are available to birds. Chlordane kills much more slowly than OP or CB pesticides. After feeding, birds are able to return to the roost, where they become too sick to leave and eventually die. Large numbers of birds are often reported dead or convulsing on the ground. At one such roost in New Jersey, 425 dead birds were recovered over a three-week period (Stansley and Roscoe, 1999).

Necropsy findings and sample collection

The presence of granules and/or freshly ingested food in the upper gastrointestinal tract may be an indication of anticholinesterase pesticide poisoning, especially when the same material is found in multiple animals from the same location. Feathers or fur in the upper gastrointestinal tract of raptors are often seen in cases of secondary poisoning by anticholinesterase pesticides (U.S. Geological Survey, 1999). Lesions are non-specific and may be absent. Lung congestion due to respiratory failure and reddening or hemorrhage of the intestinal wall may be observed (ibid.).

Crop and stomach contents should be collected for pesticide residue analysis. Whole or medially bisected brain should be collected for cholinesterase determination.

Diagnosis

The diagnosis of anticholinesterase pesticide poisoning in birds typically involves the demonstration of depressed brain cholinesterase activity and the presence of pesticide residue in the ingesta (Hill and Fleming, 1982). Brain cholinesterase inhibition of 50% or more is generally considered diagnostic of lethal poisoning (Ludke *et al.*, 1975). Brain cholinesterase inhibition in suspect animals can be determined relative to normal activity in control specimens or to in-vitro reactivated samples from the suspect animal (Martin *et al.*, 1981; Hill and Fleming, 1982; Stansley, 1993; Smith *et al.*, 1995). Carbamate-inhibited brain cholinesterase can undergo spontaneous postmortem reactivation. Therefore, brain cholinesterase activity may be inhibited less than 50% in CB-poisoned birds collected under varying field conditions. In such cases, the use of cholinesterase reactivation techniques is particularly useful for demonstrating carbamate exposure (Hill, 1989).

The presence of the same pesticide in both the ingesta of dead birds and the suspect bait is evidence that the pesticide was used in an illegal, extra-label manner to treat bait for the purpose of poisoning birds. Linking the poison to the suspect is difficult, requiring witnesses to the bait distribution or evidence linking the suspect to the purchase or possession of the pesticide or pesticide-treated bait that was used to poison the birds.

Wildlife Poisoning by Rodenticides

Pesticides used for rodent control include first generation anticoagulants such as warfarin and chlorophacinone, second generation anticoagulants such as brodifacoum and bromadiolone, and non-anticoagulant compounds such as zinc phosphide. Anticoagulants interfere with the formation of blood clotting factors through the inhibition of the enzyme vitamin K epoxide reductase. The resulting production of non-functional clotting factors predisposes the affected animals to lethal hemorrhaging from minor trauma, exertion, or other factors (Stone *et al.*, 2003; Valchev *et al.*, 2008). Wildlife may be poisoned by direct ingestion of rodenticide baits or by secondary poisoning after consuming poisoned rodents. Second generation anticoagulants, particularly brodifacoum, have a greater potential for secondary poisoning because they are both highly toxic and physiologically persistent in animal tissues (Albert *et al.*, 2010). Zinc phosphide liberates toxic phosphine gas in the acidic environment of the stomach. The risk of secondary poisoning is low and most cases result from the direct ingestion of zinc phosphide baits (Poppenga *et al.*, 2005). While some instances of intentional poisoning of game species (i.e. squirrels) occur, most are inadvertent through improper, extra-label, application of the rodenticide. Rodenticide use should include monitoring and rapid clean-up of poisoned rodents and/or covering the poisoned bait in bait stations or with shingles to limit access by non-target species.

Field observations and sample collection

Clinical signs of anticoagulant rodenticide poisoning are non-specific and may include drowsiness, weakness, anorexia, increased thirst, rapid and easy exhaustion, and decreased locomotion and perception (Valchev *et al.*, 2008). Effects on perception and locomotion may pre-dispose sublethally-poisoned animals to death by predation, accidental trauma or other causes (Stone *et al.*, 2003).

Clinical signs of zinc phosphide poisoning are also non-specific and may include listlessness, anorexia diarrhea, stiffness and muscle spasms (Poppenga *et al.*, 2005).

Numerous poisonings have been reported near orchards or nurseries where anticoagulants or zinc phosphide were applied for rodent control. When the granular bait is broadcast without bait station or shingle covers, birds are at risk and wild turkey poisonings have been documented in New Jersey. Any suspected rodenticide-containing bait should be collected for residue analysis.

Necropsy findings and sample collection

Internal hemorrhage in the absence of traumatic injury is a characteristic sign of anticoagulant poisoning (Stone *et al.*, 1999). Lesions caused by zinc phosphide are non-specific and include organ congestion and pericardial, pleural and peritoneal effusions. When zinc phosphide has been ingested, gastrointestinal contents may have the odor of acetylene or rotten fish (Poppenga *et al.*, 2005). Gastrointestinal contents and liver should be collected for residue analysis when rodenticide poisoning is suspected.

Diagnosis

Diagnosis of acute anticoagulant poisoning is based on the finding of internal hemorrhage typified by watery unclotted blood without traumatic injury in combination with pesticide residues in the liver or ingesta. Diagnosis of zinc phosphide poisoning is based on the finding of zinc phosphide or phosphine gas in the ingesta.

A spot test for the presence of zinc phosphide in gastrointestinal contents can be performed using a Dräger-Tube™ to detect the phosphine gas liberated when zinc phosphide reacts with acid. Attach a 2.5 cm length of clear PVC tubing (4.8 mm I.D. x 1.6 mm wall thickness) to a plastic female Luer-Lok™ x 4.8 mm hose barb fitting and secure the fitting to a 30 cc plastic syringe barrel. Snap off both ends of a phosphine gas Dräger Tube™ (0.01–1 ppm) and set the tube aside. Holding the syringe horizontally, remove the plunger from the syringe barrel and place 1–2 grams of sample inside the barrel. Replace the plunger, hold the syringe vertically, and tap the barrel to shake the sample to the bottom (in contact with the plunger). Introduce 5 mL of 1N HCl into the syringe barrel with a Pasteur pipette and quickly fit one end of the Dräger-Tube™ snugly into the end of the clear PVC tubing, being careful to hold the syringe in a vertical position throughout the procedure. The flow direction arrow on the

Dräger-Tube™ should point away from the syringe. After 30–60 seconds, slowly advance the plunger to expel any evolved gas through the Dräger-Tube™, being careful not to expel any liquid. If zinc phosphide is present, phosphine gas will cause a purple color reaction in the Dräger-Tube™.

Sampling and analytical considerations in pesticide poisoning investigations

To prevent contamination with other organic compounds, field-collected samples of suspected pesticide-containing bait should either be wrapped in aluminum foil or placed in jars that have been specially pre-cleaned for pesticides. Pre-cleaned sample jars can be obtained from many scientific supply companies. As a general rule, gastrointestinal contents, liver and brain should be collected during necropsy whenever pesticide poisoning is suspected. These samples should also be wrapped in aluminum foil or placed in pre-cleaned jars. If zinc phosphide poisoning is suspected, the gastrointestinal contents should be stored in an airtight container. All samples for pesticide residue analysis or brain cholinesterase assays should be frozen as soon as possible and kept frozen until analyzed. It is also important to maintain chain-of-custody records for all samples that may potentially be used in a legal case.

A detailed discussion of analytical procedures for pesticide residues is beyond the scope of this chapter. A number of veterinary schools throughout the country have toxicology laboratories that are capable of analyzing tissues and gastrointestinal contents for pesticides and other toxins. It is important to consult with the laboratory in advance to discuss their sample submission policies and requirements. For example, some veterinary toxicology laboratories require that a veterinarian be involved in sample submissions, and many laboratories charge extra fees for out-of-state submissions.

References

Albert, C.A., Wilson, L.K., Mineau, P., Trudeau, S. and Elliott, J.E. (2010) Anticoagulant rodenticides in three owl species from western Canada, 1988–2003. *Archives of Environmental Contamination and Toxicology*, **58**, 451–459.

Best, L.B. and Fisher, D.L. (1992) Granular insecticides and birds: factors to be considered in understanding exposure and reducing risk. *Environmental Toxicology and Chemistry*, **11**, 1495–1508.

Denton, J.S., Segovia, A. and Filkins, J.A. (2006) Practical pathology of gunshot wounds. *Archives of Pathology & Laboratory Medicine*, **130**, 1283–1289.

Fleischli, M.A., Franson, J.C., Thomas, N.J., Finley, D.L. and Riley, W. Jr. (2004) Avian mortality events in the United States caused by anticholinesterase pesticides: a retrospective summary of National Wildlife Health Center records from 1980 to 2000. *Archives of Environmental Contamination and Toxicology*, **46**, 542–550.

Flickinger, E.L., Mitchell, C.A., White, D.H. and Kolbe, E.J. (1986) Bird poisoning from misuse of the carbamate furadan in a Texas rice field. *Wildlife Society Bulletin*, **14**, 59–62.

Grue, C.E., Hart, A.D.M. and Mineau, P. (1991) Biological consequences of depressed brain cholinesterase activity in wildlife. In P. Mineau (ed.), *Cholinesterase-Inhibiting Insecticides: Their Impact on Wildlife and the Environment*. New York: Elsevier.

Hill, E.F. (1989) Divergent effects of postmortem ambient temperature on organophosphorus- and carbamate-inhibited brain cholinesterase activity in birds. *Pesticide Biochemistry and Physiolology*, **33**, 264–275.

Hill, E.F. and Fleming, W.J. (1982) Anticholinesterase poisoning of birds: field monitoring and diagnosis of acute poisoning. *Environmental Toxicology and Chemistry*, **1**, 27–38.

Ludke, J.L, Hill, E.W. and Dieter, M.P. (1975) Cholinesterase (ChE) response and related mortality among birds fed cholinesterase inhibitors. *Archives of Environmental Contamination and Toxicology*, **1**, 1–21.

Martin, A.D., Norman, G., Stanley, P.I. and Westlake, G.E. (1981) Use of reactivation techniques for the differential diagnosis of organophosphorus and carbamate pesticide poisoning in birds. *Bulletin of Environmental Contamination and Toxicology*, **26**, 775–780.

Newton, J.T. (1981) Rapid determination of antimony, barium, and lead in gunshot residue via automated atomic absorption spectrophotometry. *Journal of Forensic Science*, **26**, 302–312.

Okoniewski, J.C. and Novesky, E. (1993) Bird poisonings with cyclodienes in suburbia: links to historic use on turf. *Journal of Wildlife Management*, **57**, 630–639.

Poppenga, R.H., Ziegler, A.F., Habecker, P.L., Singletary, D.L., Walter, M.K. and Miller, P.G. (2005) Zinc phosphide intoxication of wild turkeys (*Meleagris gallopavo*). *Journal of Wildlife Diseases*, **41**, 218–223.

Smith, M.R., Thomas, N.J. and Hulse, C. (1995) Application of brain cholinesterase reactivation to differentiate between organophosphorus and carbamate pesticide poisoning in wild birds. *Journal of Wildlife Diseases*, **31**, 263–267.

Spraker, T.R., and Davies, R.B. (1994) Differentiation of wounds in carcasses. In W. Adrian (ed.) *Wildlife Forensic Field Manual*. Ft. Collins, CO: Association of Midwest Fish and Game Law Enforcement Officers, Colorado Division of Wildlife, pp. 131–138.

Stansley, W. (1993) Field results using cholinesterase reactivation techniques to diagnose acute anticholinesterase poisoning in birds and fish. *Archives of Environmental Contamination and Toxicology*, **25**, 315–321.

Stansley, W. and Roscoe, D.E. (1999) Chlordane poisoning of birds in New Jersey. *Environmental Toxicology and Chemistry*, **18**, 2095–2099.

Stansley, W., Roscoe, D.E., Hawthorne, E. and Meyer, R. (2001) Food chain aspects of chlordane poisoning in birds and bats. *Archives of Environmental Contamination and Toxicology*, **40**, 285–291.

Stockdale, M. (1994) Metal detectors for wildlife forensics. In W. Adrian (ed.) *Wildlife Forensic Field Manual*. Ft. Collins, CO: Association of Midwest Fish and Game Law Enforcement Officers, Colorado Division of Wildlife, pp. 139–141.

Stone, W.B., Butkas, S.A., Kellogg, C.F. and Kebabjian, D.E. (1978) A lead detection kit for determining bullet wounds. *NY Fish and Game Journal*, **25**, 165–168.

Stone, W.B., Okoniewski, J.C. and Stedelin, J.R. (1999) Poisoning of wildlife with anticoagulant rodenticides in New York. *Journal of Wildlife Diseases*, **35**, 187–193.

Stone, W.B., Okoniewski, J.C. and Stedelin, J.R. (2003) Anticoagulant rodenticides and raptors: recent findings from New York, 1998–2001. *Bulletin of Environmental Contamination and Toxicology*, **70**, 34–40.

U.S. Environmental Protection Agency (2010) Pesticide reregistration status. Available at: http://www.epa.gov/oppsrrd1/reregistration/status.htm (accessed October 2010).

U.S. Geological Survey (1999) Section 7: chemical toxins. In M. Friend and J.C. Franson (eds.) *Field Manual of Wildlife Diseases: General Field Procedures and Diseases of Birds*. Washington, DC: U.S. Geological Survey, Biological Resources Division, Information and Technology Report 1999–001.

Valchev, I., Binev, R., Yordanova, V. and Yordan, N. (2008) Anticoagulant rodenticide intoxication in animals – a review. *Turkish Journal of Veterinary Animal Science*, **32**, 237–243.

Wobeser, G., Bollinger, T., Leighton, F.A., Blakley, B. and Mineau, P. (2004) Secondary poisoning of eagles following intentional poisoning of coyotes with anticholinesterase pesticides in western Canada. *Journal of Wildlife Diseases*, **40**, 163–172.

8
The Use of Hair Morphology in the Identification of Mammals

Lisa Knecht

Introduction

The scientific study of hair is called trichology and this field dates to the mid-1800s. Hair is not easily destroyed, even with exposure to moisture and decomposition of accompanying tissue and can be important physical evidence at a crime scene. Hair examination compares a variety of factors, including color, coarseness, granule distribution, hair diameter, scales and the presence or absence of a medulla. This chapter will address a number of different characteristics of hairs in order to determine whether they have a common source.

Hausman (1920, 1924, 1930, 1944) was a pioneer in characterizing mammal hairs and wrote several early papers on the microscopy and structural characteristics of hair. Amman, Owen and Bradley (2002) proved the utility of hair structure for taxonomic discrimination in bats, showing that if a variety of characters are used, identification to species is possible. Numerous keys for the identification of hairs have been written for mammals, which are based solely upon hair characteristics (Mathiak, 1938; Mayer, 1952; Moore *et al.*, 1974). Such keys have been used in regional surveys and investigations of food habits (Williams, 1938; Stains, 1958; Day, 1966, 1968), forensic medicine (Stoves, 1942; Hausman, 1944), and archaeology (Brown, 1942; Douglas, 1965; Appleyard and Wildman, 1969).

In 1977, Hicks authored an introductory manual for the microscopic examination and identification of human and animal hairs for investigation and prosecution of crimes. Deedrick and Koch (2004a, 2004b) developed a manual for identification of human and animal hair from crime scenes, and Tridico

Wildlife Forensics: Methods and Applications, First Edition. Edited by Jane E. Huffman and John R. Wallace.

(2005) reported on the examination and analysis of hair and its application in forensics.

Scanning electron microscopy (SEM) has enhanced our understanding of hair morphology. Homan and Genowyas (1978) analyzed hair structure and its phylogenetic implications in heteromyid rodents using light microscopy and SEM. Their findings supported earlier works that species can be characterized and distinguished through hair structure. Moore and Braun (1983) developed a key to the hairs of the families Soricidae, Vespertilionidae, and Muridae in Tennessee using light microscopy and SEM. Most species could be separated with at least a 95% chance of making the correct identification.

The Ohio Bureau of Criminal Identification and Investigation has provided a web page (www.iamaweb.com) with light and SEM animal hair images. Gonzalez and Miller (2010) have developed HAIRbase^{TM}, (http://web.me.com/kwpmiller/HAIRbase/Welcome.html), which is intended to show variability and subtleties of animal hair structure and function. In the microscopic comparison of hairs, it is important to always use a comparative standard to (hair from an identified source) compare like to like.

Types of Hair

There are four types of mammal hair: vibrissae, overhairs, guard hairs, and underfur (Mathiak, 1938; Tridico, 2005). Vibrissae (singular: vibrissa), or whiskers, are specialized hairs usually employed for tactile sensation. Vibrissae hairs commonly grow around the nostrils, above the lips, and on other parts of the face of most mammals, as well as on the forelegs and feet of some animals. Vibrissae are usually thicker and stiffer than other types of hair.

Overhairs are the longest hairs of a mammal's coat and sparsely distributed. Close examination of animal pelts will reveal that some sparsely distributed hairs are distinctly longer than the remainder of the hairs. These hairs are not particularly useful as many of the characteristics necessary to determine species may not be present or not visible if the hairs are heavily pigmented (Tridico, 2005).

Guard hairs are long and the coarsest hairs in a mammal's coat, forming the top coat (or outer coat). They taper to a point and protect the underfur from the elements. They are often water-repellent and stick out above the rest of the coat. Guard hairs add the sheen to the coat of an animal. All hairs that are described in this chapter are dorsal guard hairs and were sampled from the back/shoulder region of the mammal. Guard hair can differ in morphology from one region of the body to another on most mammals. Guard hair can also differ in morphology from an immature to mature mammal (Stains, 1958).

Underfur, also called the undercoat, is the very fine, fluffy hairs closest to the skin on some mammals. The hairs are short and often crimped, which makes them highly efficient for trapping air and insulating the animal.

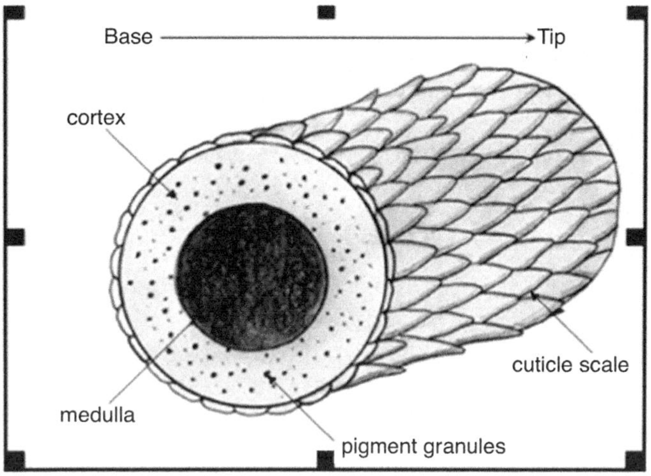

Figure 8.1 Cross-section of hairshaft. *Source:* http://www.ecobyte.com.au/using_.html.

Hair Structure

A strand of hair consists of three parts: the cuticle (the outer most layer), the cortex (the middle layer) and the medulla (the inner layer) (Mathiak, 1938). Hair is made up of cornified dead cells and consists of keratin (a protein). Melanin (a pigment) is found in the cortex. Figure 8.1 shows a cross-section of a hair shaft.

Regions of the hair

A hair shaft is divided into three regions. The proximal region near the root, the medial region in the middle and the distal region near the tip of the hair. The regions of the hair shaft are important when examining the scales and medullas of mammal hairs as they can change significantly from region to region of the hair shaft (Figure 8.2) (Adorjan and Kolenosky, 1969). The regions are also important when identifying the location of hair bands, which may appear in any of the three regions of the hair.

Cuticle structure

The cuticle is the translucent outer layer of the hair shaft consisting of scales that cover the shaft. Cuticular scales always point from the proximal or root end of the hair shaft to the distal or tip end of the hair shaft (Moore *et al.*, 1974; Hicks, 1977). An example of cuticular scales can be seen in Figure 8.3. Further details and examples of types of cuticular scales are described below in Classification of cuticle.

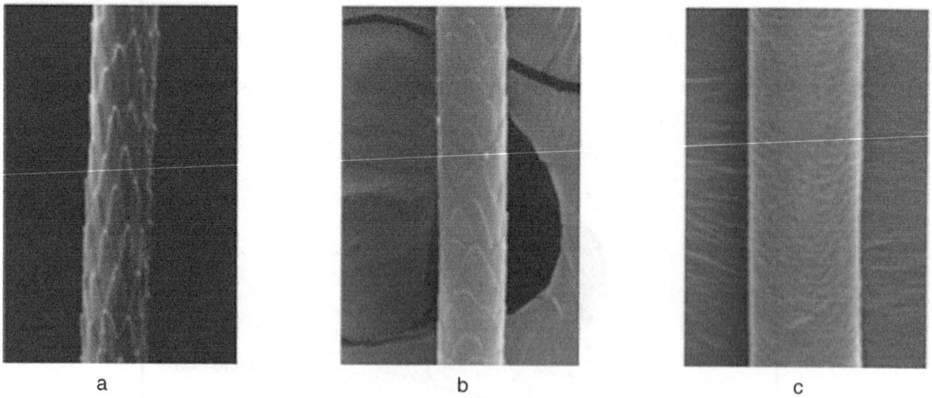

Figure 8.2 SEM microphotographs of a dorsal guard hair from an American Marten (*Martes americana*) – a. Proximal, 590X b. Medial, 585X c. Distal, 585X, illustrating the change in scale patterns between the three regions of the hair shaft.

Classification of cuticle

Cuticular scales are the surface pattern of the hair, which appear as regular or irregular, shingle-like, sometimes overlapping, clear cells of various configurations (Moore *et al.*, 1974). Only scale patterns will be described in this section. Scale margin crest, distance, and overlapping will not be described herein;

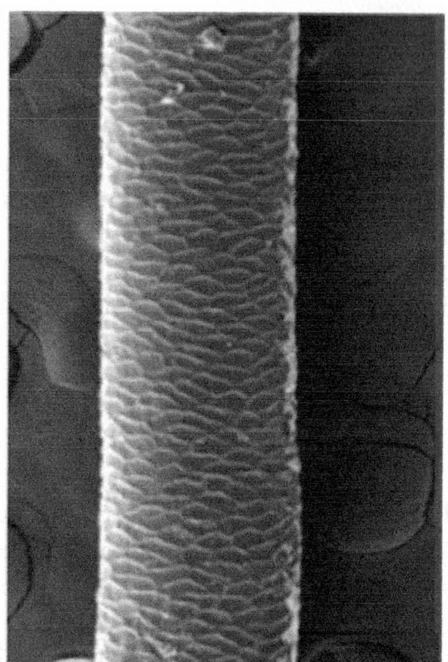

Figure 8.3 SEM of Caribou (*Ranger tarandus*) proximal cuticular scales, 134X.

however, the details of these characteristics for a limited number of mammals are described in Moore, Spence and Dugnolle (1974).

Scales appear in definite patterns. Some scale patterns are intermediate between two or more types. These are referred to by combining names of the basic patterns (i.e. diamond petal). The scale pattern may change along the length of the hair shaft from the proximal to the distal end, and there may be points or regions where one type of scale pattern changes into another type. Even hairs from different regions of the same mammal may vary greatly. Because of the variability of the scale patterns, the dominant scale pattern in the proximal region of the guard hair was selected for imaging purposes. The descriptions of scale patterns generally follow that of Moore, Spence and Dugnolle (1974).

Coronal scales are shaped like a crown, each scale completely encircling the hair shaft (Figure 8.4a). The upper rim is frequently oblique to the hair axis (i.e. Eastern pipistrelle (*Perimyotis subflavus*) proximal region). Figure 8.4b illustrates diamond petal overlapping scales giving the appearance of a diamond pattern, with the long axis oriented in a base-to-tip direction. Usually the tip of one scale touches or nearly contacts the trough of the scale above it (i.e. Red Squirrel (*Tamiasciurus hudsonicus*) proximal region). Non-overlapping scales appearing as waves with both crests and bottoms of troughs narrow and V-shaped are classified as a double chevron pattern (Figure 8.4c) (i.e. Appalachian Cottontail (*Sylvilagus oscurus*) proximal region). Non-overlapping scales that are non-uniform in size and shape represent an irregular mosaic (Figure 8.4d) (i.e. domestic Cat (*Felis catus*) proximal region). Irregular petal overlapping scales are similar to flower petals that are not uniform in size and shape (Figure 8.5a) (i.e. Gray Fox (*Urocyon cinereoargenteus*) proximal region). Irregular wave non-overlapping scales are wavy in appearance and usually continuous, but with the length of the waves on the same and different scales unequal,

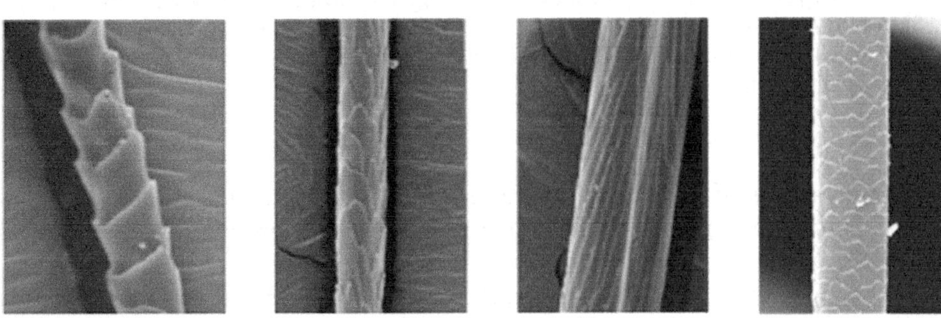

a b c d

Figure 8.4 a. SEM of an Eastern pipistrelle (*Perimyotis subflavus*) proximal scale showing a coronal scale pattern, 2040X, b. SEM of a Red Squirrel (*Tamiasciurus hudsonicus*) proximal scale showing a diamond petal scale pattern, 895X, c. SEM of an Appalachian Cottontail (*Sylvilagus oscurus*) proximal scale showing a double chevron scale pattern, 1,160X, d. SEM of a domestic obscurus Cat (*Felis catus*) proximal scale showing an irregular mosaic scale pattern, 384X.

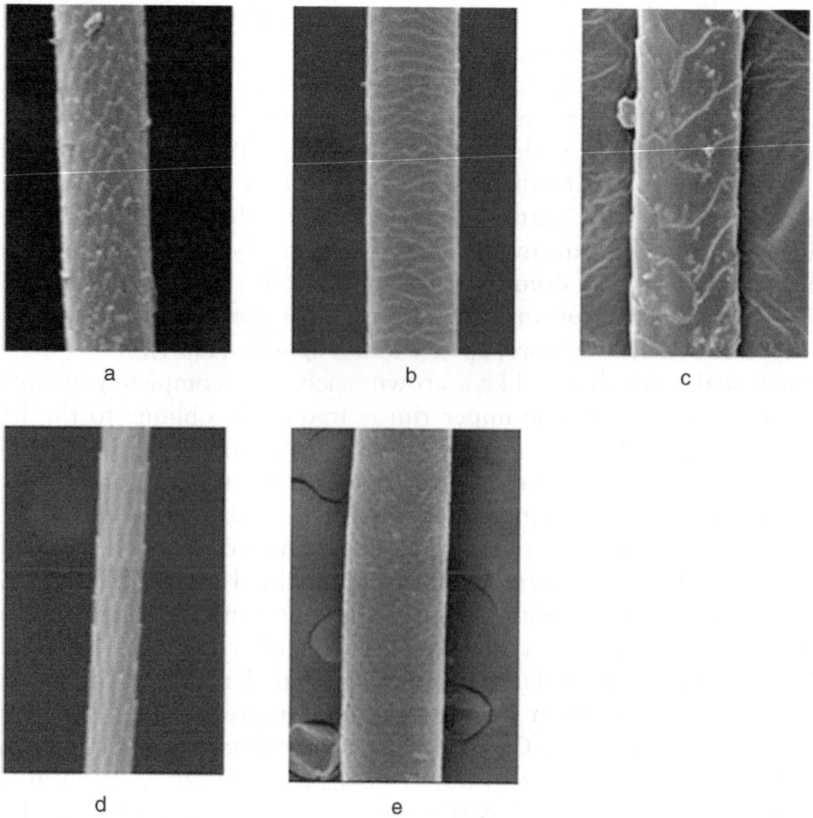

Figure 8.5 a. SEM of a Gray Fox (*Urocyon cinereoargenteus*) proximal scale showing an irregular petal scale pattern, 294X, b. SEM of a domestic Dog (*Canis lupus familiaris*) proximal scale showing an irregular wave scale pattern, 342X, c. SEM of an Allegheny Woodrat (*Neotoma magister*) proximal scale showing an irregular-waved mosaic scale pattern, 920X, d. SEM of a Mink (*Mustela vison*) proximal scale showing a pectinate scale pattern, 416X, e. SEM of a White-tailed Deer (*Odocoileus virginianus*) proximal scale showing a regular mosaic scale pattern, 115X.

as are the heights of the crests (Figure 8.5b) (i.e. domestic Dog (*Canis lupus familiaris*) proximal region). Irregular-waved mosaic is a combination of the waves and mosaic patterns, where the waves formed by the margins are not continuous, but divided by the scale edges, and each scale is non-uniform in size and shape (Figure 8.5c) (i.e. Allegheny Woodrat (*Neotoma magister*) proximal region). Pectinate elongated overlapping scales resemble a comb, forming a series of regular waves which often run obliquely to the long axis of the hair shaft (Figure 8.5d) (i.e. Mink (*Mustela vison*) proximal region). Crests of the waves in one row alternate with the troughs of the row above it. There is rarely overlapping of the trough so common in diamond petal. Regular mosaic non-overlapping scales that are quite uniform in size and shape as are seen in the proximal region of White-tailed Deer (*Odocoileus virginianus*) hair (Figure 8.5e). Regular petal

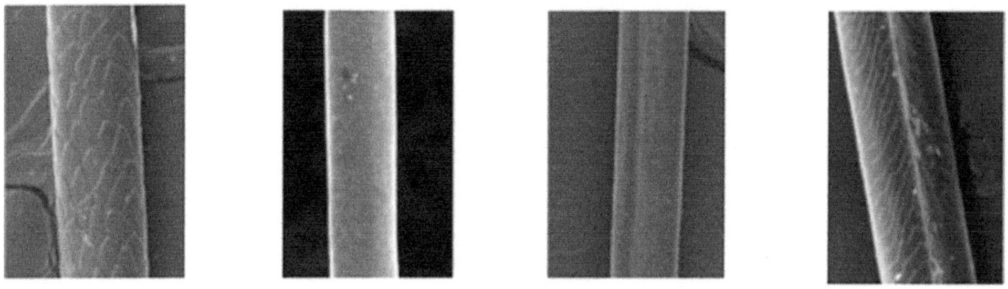

Figure 8.6 a. SEM of a Fisher (*Martes pennanti*) proximal scale showing a regular petal scale pattern, 545X, b. SEM of a Beaver (*Castor canadensis*) proximal scale showing a regular wave scale pattern, 240X, c. SEM of a Snowshoe Hare (*Lepus americanus*) proximal scale showing a single chevron scale pattern, 496X, d. SEM of an Appalachian Cottontail (*Sylvilagus oscurus*) proximal scale showing a streaked wave scale pattern, 1,160X.

overlapping scales similar to flower petals that are uniform in size and shape are seen in the proximal region of Fishers (*Martes pennanti*) (Figure 8.6a). Regular wave non-overlapping, wavy appearing scales, usually continuous, with the length of the waves on the same and different scales equal, as are the heights of the crests (i.e. Beaver (*Castor canadenis*) proximal region) (Figure 8.6b). Single chevron non-overlapping scales appearing as high waves with either crests or bottoms of troughs, but not both, narrow and V-shaped are found in the proximal region of Snowshoe Hares (*Lepus americanus*) hair (Figure 8.6c). Streaked wave non-overlapping wavy scales similar to irregular wave, but the waves are interrupted at regular intervals by longitudinally-running columns of scales having steeply inclined margins (i.e. Eastern Cottontail (*Sylvilagus oscurus*) proximal region) (Figure 8.6d).

Cortex

The cortex is the main body of the hair and is composed of elongated and fusiform (spindle-shaped) cells. The cortex may contain cortical fusi, pigment granules, and/or large oval-to-round-shaped structures called ovoid bodies (Hicks, 1977). An example of an ovoid body can be seen in Figure 8.10c on p. 139. Details and examples of cortical fusi, pigment granules, and ovoid bodies observed in the cortex are described in further detail in the section on distinguishing characteristics of the cortex on p. 139.

Medulla

The medulla is a central core of cells that may be present in the hair. If it is filled with air, it appears as a black or opaque structure (see Figures 8.8b–8.8j on p. 137) (Hicks, 1977). If it is filled with mounting medium or some other

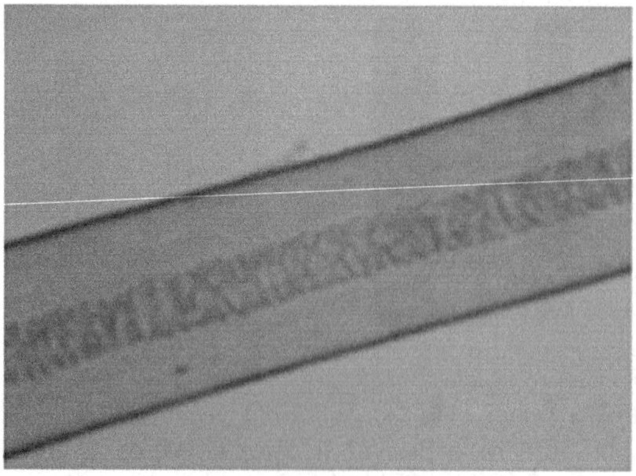

Figure 8.7 Medulla in Nutria (*Myocaster coypus*) hair 40X.

clear substance, the structure appears clear or translucent (Figure 8.7) (Moore *et al.*, 1974; Hicks, 1977). In human hairs, the medulla is generally amorphous in appearance (see Figure 8.8a on p. 137), whereas in animal hairs, its appearance is frequently very regular and well defined (Deedrick and Koch, 2004a, 2004b; Hicks, 1977).

Classification of medullae

The medulla is the innermost layer of the hair shaft and is a valuable aid to identification (Tumlison, 1983). It is composed of a series of discrete cells or an amorphous spongy mass. The cell may be cornified and shrunken with intercellular spaces filled with air (as in unbroken with cortical intrusions). The medulla often does not extend the entire length of the hair and may be sporadically interrupted. It is absent in bat hair and some human head hair. The medulla in hairs of mammals is normally continuous and very regularly structured and generally occupies an area of greater than one-third the overall diameter of the hair shaft (Hicks, 1977).

The descriptions of medullae generally follow that of Moore, Spence and Dugnolle (1974). The medullar appearance classified as absent is where no medulla is visible, and the cortex is continuous throughout the hair as seen in some human hair and all bat hair (Figures 8.8a and 8.8b, respectively). A fragmented medulla is sporadically interrupted by cortical material as seen in human hair (Figure 8.8c). A uniserial ladder medulla is a continuous single column of discrete cells formed by transverse septa (Figure 8.8d). Multiserial ladder medulla is a continuous column of rectangular cells, found only in Leporid hairs (Figure 8.8e). A simple unbroken amorphous medulla is a continuous tube, garden hose-like, appearing darkened without structural detail in uninfiltrated hairs (Figure 8.8f) or spongy with no distinct cells in hairs (Figure 8.8g). An unbroken cellular medulla is a continuous tube with distinct irregular shaped

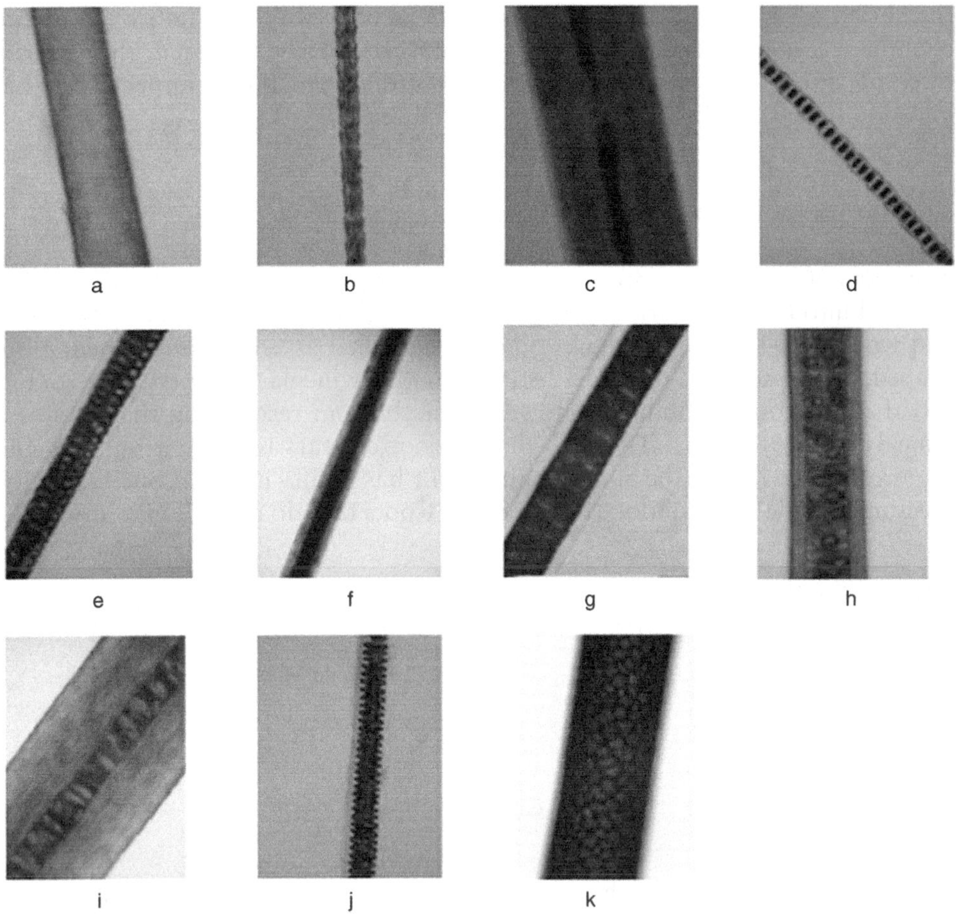

Figure 8.8 a. Human (*Homo sapiens*) hair with medulla absent, 400X, b. Eastern Pipistrelle (*Perimyotis subflavus*) with medulla absent, c. Mongoloid Human (*Homo sapiens*) hair with fragmented medulla, 400X, d. Deer Mouse (Prairie) (*Peromyscus maniculatus bairdii*) hair with uniserial ladder medulla, 400X, e. Appalachian Cottontail hair (*Sylvilagus oscurus*) with multiserial ladder medulla, 400X, f. American Bison (*Bison bison*) hair with simple unbroken amorphous medulla, 400X, g. Canadian Lynx (*Lynx canadensis*) hair with simple unbroken amorphous medulla, 400X, h. American marten (*Martes americana*) hair with unbroken cellular medulla, 400X, i. Black Bear (*Ursus americanus*) hair with unbroken vacuolated medulla, 400X, j. Least Shrew (*Cryptotis parva*) hair with unbroken with cortical intrusions medulla, 400X, k. Elk (*Cervus elaphus*) hair with unbroken lattice medulla, 400X.

cells. Infiltrating with mounting media by cutting or breaking the hair may be necessary to bring out this detail (Figure 8.8h). An unbroken vacuolated medulla is a continuous tube with distinct cells, some of which appear as large vacuoles extending entirely across a wide medulla (i.e. Black Bear hair (*Ursus americanus*)) (Figure 8.8i). The unbroken with cortical intrusions medulla is a continuous tube with cortical material appearing as projections and/or islands in the medulla (i.e. Least Shrew hair (*Cryptotis parva*)) (Figure 8.8j). An unbroken lattice medulla is a continuous tube of many small, irregularly arranged, thin-walled, often polygonal cells in hairs with a narrow cortex which may appear absent as in cervid hair (i.e. Elk (*Cervus elaphus*)) (Figure 8.8k).

Classification of roots

The roots of human hair are commonly club-shaped. The roots of animal hairs may fall into four categories and are highly variable between animals (Deedrick and Koch, 2004b). Animal hair roots are classified as wineglass-shaped, club-shaped, spade-shaped and not distinct. In the wineglass-shaped, the root is broad at the top, becoming narrower at the bottom resembling the stem of a wineglass (Figure 8.9a). The club-shaped root appears to have a bulbous end (Figure 8.9b) whereas the spade-shaped root has a curvature on one side only, creating a spade-shaped look (Figure 8.9c). Roots that do not fall into any of the

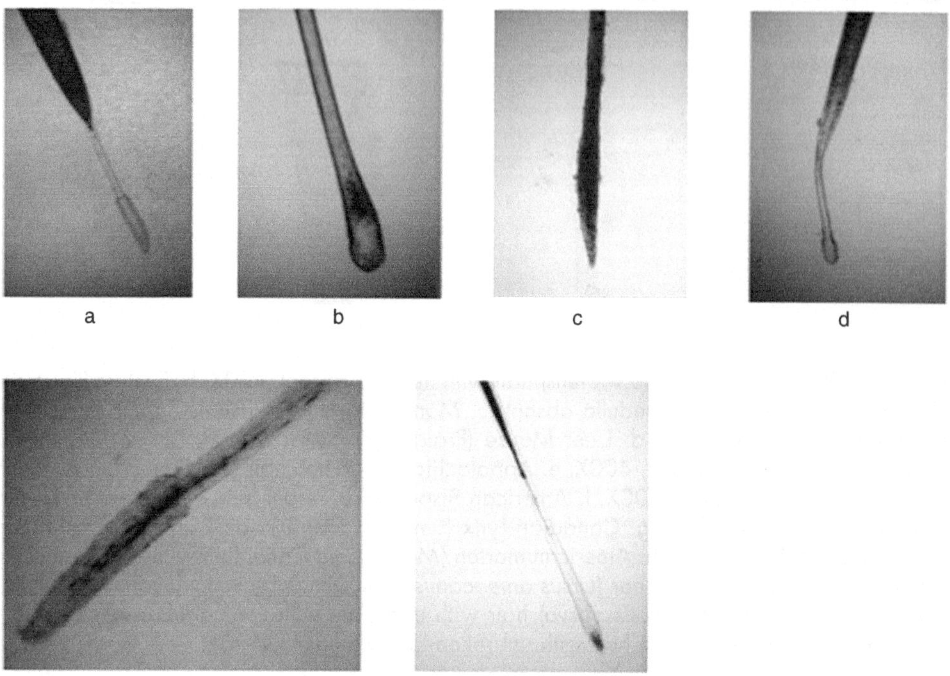

a b c d

e f

Figure 8.9 a. Wineglass-shaped root of the White-tailed Deer (*Odocoileus virginianus*), 400X, b. Club-shaped root from Human hair (*Homo sapiens*), 100X, c. Spade-shaped root from domestic Dog (*Canis lupus familiaris*) hair, 100X, d. No distinct shape to root from Meadow Jumping Mouse (*Zapus hudsonius*), 100X, e. Elongated with medulla continuing into root of Cattle hair, 100X, f. Fibrils frayed at base of root from the domestic cat (*Felis catus*), 400X.

categories listed above are designated not distinct (Figure 8.9d). Other morphological characteristics which may be observed in mammal roots are the medulla extending into the root area (Figure 8.9e) or frayed fibrils at the base of the root (Figure 8.9f).

Distinguishing characteristics of the cortex

Under microscopic examination, the cortex may contain pigment granules and/or large oval-to-round-shaped structures called ovoid bodies as seen in Figure 8.10c (Deedrick and Koch, 2004b). Ovoid bodies are much larger than pigment granules and are dark, solid structures that are spherical to oval in shape, with very regular margins, as seen in dog hair.

Pigment granules are small, dark, solid structures that are granular in appearance and considerably smaller than cortical fusi, which give the hair its unique color, as seen in beaver hair (Figure 8.10a). Pigment granules vary in color, size, and distribution in a single hair and among animal species. Cortical fusi are irregular-shaped airspaces of varying shapes and sizes, as seen in human hair (Figure 8.10b).

Hair pigmentation

Hair pigment may be studied on the basis of color, distribution, and type. Hair gets its color from a type of pigment called melanin. The color of hair depends upon the distribution, type and amount of melanin in the middle layer of the hair shaft or cortex. There are two types of pigments: dark (eumelanin – black to brown pigment) and light (phaeomelanin – yellow to red pigment). They blend together to make up the wide range of hair colors.

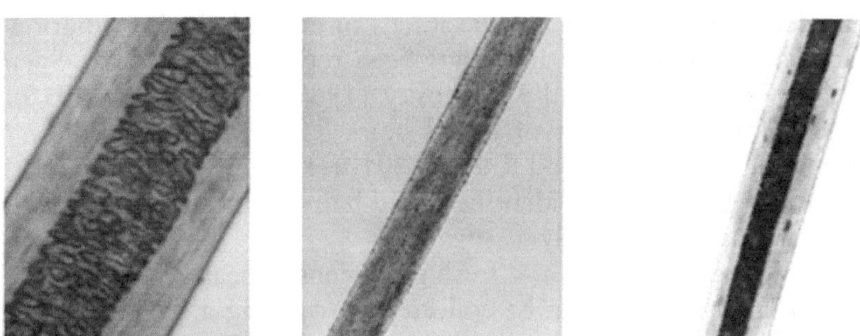

a b c

Figure 8.10 a. Pigment granules in Beaver (*Castor canadensis*) hair, 40X, b. Cortical fusi – human (*Homo sapien*) hair (Deedrick and Koch 2004a), c. Medulla and ovoid bodies in dog hair (Deedrick and Koch, 2004b).

Color varies greatly over different parts of the body, but also varies with the season, the stage of molt, wear, fading, and many other conditions; and therefore, great reliance on coloration should not be used for identification (Mayer, 1952).

Pigment granules are small, dark, and solid structures that are granular in appearance. Pigment granules or aggregate pigments may be arranged in well-defined areas or arranged in streaked patterns (Sahajpal and Goyal, 2009). They vary in color, size, and distribution in a single hair. In humans, pigment granules are commonly evenly distributed toward the cuticle, except in red-haired individuals. Animal hairs have the pigment granules commonly distributed toward the medulla (Deedrick and Koch, 2004a).

While pigment in the medulla, cortex, and cuticular scales is important, the way in which the pigment is distributed along the length of the shaft is equally important. Due to the presence of pigment in certain areas and its absence or reduction in another area, many mammalian hairs present a banded appearance. In most banded hair, the distal tip is dark, followed by a succession of light and dark bands in the medial and proximal area. In non-banded hair, the heaviest pigment concentration is in the distal area with the proximal areas almost always being lighter (Mayer, 1952). Additional information on banding can be found in Moore (1974).

Techniques for Studying Hair Structure

Sampling strategy and methods

Hair samples can be collected from live animals, vehicle strikes, skin mounts, study skins, and taxidermied mounts. Complete guard hairs with distal, medial and proximal regions intact should be selected for examination. The length and diameter measurements, scale patterns, medulla types, and pigment locations should be determined from intact specimens of guard hair. Information on the length and diameter of guard hairs has been reported by Moore, Spence and Dugnolle (1974), Adorjan and Konenosky (1969) and Knecht (2010). Color bands and color arrangement of guard hairs have been reported by Moore, Spence and Dugnolle (1974) and Knecht (2010). Hairs from sites other than the dorsal area may be less easily identified, and hairs from different regions of the same mammal may vary greatly.

Hair morphology of tanned and fresh specimens appears to be identical (Hess *et al.*, 1985). Hair samples can be collected by running a finger or hand down the shoulder/back region of the specimen and collecting the guard hairs that have been released naturally from the skin, and samples from tanned skins or taxidermied mounts may be obtained by pulling out the hairs. Frozen specimens should be allowed to thaw before sampling in order to avoid the breakage of roots from the hair shaft.

Hair storage and cleaning

To preserve hair specimens for future reference, a representative sample of the mammal hair can be stored in clear plastic bag with a Ziploc closure and labeled with common name and genus/species. If reference specimens are not stored in this manner, the hairs from some families such as Cervidae may dry out and become too brittle for future handling. A permanent mount on a glass slide can be prepared for each mammal and made part of a reference collection for future use. Hairs can be cleaned by immersing them in distilled water and then patting them dry with a paper towel to remove natural oils, or debris such as dirt prior to preparing the slides for scale casts or SEM.

Slide preparation and examination

Hair is best examined using a microscope at 200 to 800x. The use of oil immersion, 1000x, is not recommended because at higher magnifications, the depth of field of viewing is reduced. Wet mount slides are prepared using water as the mounting medium. A droplet of water is placed on a clean microscope slide. The sample hair is looped in a figure eight or cut to size, if necessary, and placed on the slide with the water droplet. A cover slip is then placed on top. The slide is immediately examined with a light microscope. Following the same technique as the wet mount slides, the permanent mount slides are prepared using Permount™ mounting medium. A drop of Permount™ is placed on a clean slide. The sample hair is looped in a figure eight or cut to size, if necessary, and placed on the slide with the Permount™. A cover slip is then placed on top. The slide is allowed to set overnight and is examined with a light microscope. These slides may be stored and used in the future as part of a reference collection. Under 100x, locate the hair for viewing. Once the hair is centered and focused, increase the magnification to 200x, 300x, 400x, or 800x. The cortex and medulla of the hair should be visible. If a hair has simply fallen out of a follicle, the root should be visible at one end and the hair may taper to almost a point at the other end. If the hair has been cut, then the end where it was cut will show a flat or blunt end. If the hair has been pulled out, then some of the follicle should be attached to the root.

Scale cast slides are prepared using a clean microscope slide and clear nail polish. A thin layer of nail polish is painted onto a clean microslide and then allowed to dry for approximately 20 seconds when the polish should become tacky. The sample hair is looped in a figure eight or cut to size, and placed on the tacky nail polish, leaving a small portion of the hair exposed at the edge for easy removal, and allowed to dry overnight. The hair should not sink into the nail polish. If it does, the polish is still too wet. Once dry, the hair is removed with tweezers leaving an impression of the hair in the polish. Adjust the microscope to 100x to locate the hair impression for viewing. Once the impression is centered and focused, increase the magnification to 300x or 400x. Gradually adjust the fine focus to view the impression of the cuticle surface of the hair. The impression is best viewed by reducing the illumination on the slide to produce a dark field creating shadows of the hair impression.

Scanning electron microscope

Using metal stubs covered with double-coated carbon tape, the sample hair should be cut to size, when necessary, and positioned with the tips towards the uncovered part of the stub. Two or three guard hairs usually can be mounted on the stub. The samples are gold coated with a DESK-1 Model Sputter Coater with Denton Vacuum for 60 seconds to ensure good resolution in the SEM. An Amray Model 1810 Diffusion Pumped SEM without an ion pump is used and images are recorded.

Conclusion

The features to be examined during hair analysis include length, shape, size, color, stiffness, curliness, pigmentation and the appearance of the medulla. It is important to always use a comparative standard (an actual hair from an identified source). Compare like to like.

References

Adorjan, A.S. and Kolenosky, G.B. (1969) A manual for the identification of hairs of selected Ontario mammals. *Ontario Department of Lands Forestry Research Report (Wildlife)*, No. 90. Ontario: Ontario Lands and Forests Department.

Amman, B.R., Owen, R.D. and Bradley, R.D. (2002) Utility of hair structure for taxonomic discrimination in bats, with an example from the bats of Colorado. *Occasional Papers, Museum of Texas Tech University*, No. 216, 1–15.

Appleyard, H.M. and Wildman, A.B. (1969) Fibers of archaeological interest: their examination and identification. In D. Brothwell and E. Higgs (eds.) *Science in Archaeology*. London: Thames and Hudson Ltd, pp. 624–633.

Brown, F.M. (1942) The microscopy of mammalian hair for anthropologists. *Proceedings of the American Philosophical Society*, **85**, 250–274.

Day, M.G. (1966) Identification of hair and feather remains in the gut and feces of stoats and weasels. *Journal of Zoology*, **148**, 201–217.

Day, M.G. (1968) Food habits of British stoats (*Mustela ermineas*) and weasels (*Mustela nivalis*). *Journal of Zoology*, **155**, 485–497.

Deedrick, D.W. and Koch, S.L. (2004a) Microscopy of hair Part I: a practical guide and manual for human hairs. *Forensic Science Communications*, **6**(1).

Deedrick, D.W and Koch, S.L. (2004b) Microscopy of hair Part II: a practical guide and manual for human hairs. *Forensic Science Communications*, **6**(3).

Douglas, C.L. (1965) Biological techniques in archaeology. *American Antiquity*, **312**, 193–201.

Gonzalez, M.V. and Miller, K.W.P. (2010) HAIRBase™. Available at: http://web.me.com/kwpmiller/HAIRbase/Welcome.html.

Hausman, L.A. (1920) Structural characteristics of the hair of mammals. *The American Naturalist*, 5, 496–523.

Hausman, L.A. (1924) Further studies of the relationships of the structural characters of mammalian hair. *The American Naturalist*, **58**, 544–557.

Hausman, L.A. (1930) Recent studies of hair structure relationships. *The Scientific Monthly*, **30**, 258–277.

Hausman, L.A. (1944) Applied microscopy of hair. *The Scientific Monthly*, **59**, 195–202.

Hess, W.M., Flinders, J.T., Pritchette, C.L. and Allen, J.V. (1985) Characterization of hair morphology in families Tayassuidae and Suidae with scanning electron microscopy. *Journal of Mammalogy*, **66**, 75–84.

Hicks, J.W. (1977) *Microscopy of Hairs: A Practical Guide and Manual*. Washington, DC: US Government Printing Office.

Homan, J.A. and Genoways, H.H. (1978) An analysis of hair structure and its phylogenetic implications among heteromyid rodents. *Journal of Mammalogy*, **59**, 740–760.

Knecht, LA. (2010) Hair atlas of mammals native to Pennsylvania. Master's thesis, East Stroudsburg University, PA.

Mathiak, H.A. (1938) A key to hairs of the mammals of southern Michigan. *The Journal of Wildlife Management*, **2**, 251–268.

Mayer, W.V. (1952) The hair of California mammals with keys to the dorsal guard hairs of California mammals. *American Midland Naturalist*, **48**, 480–512.

Moore, D.W., and Braun, J.K. (1983) Keys to the hairs of the families Soricidae, Vespertilionidae, and Muridae within Tennessee. *Journal of the Tennessee Academy of Science*, **58**, 40–43.

Moore, T.D., Spence, L.E. and Dugnolle, C.E. (1974) *Identification of the Dorsal Guard Hairs of Some Mammals of Wyoming*. Laramie, Wyoming: Wyoming Game and Fish Department.

Sahajpal, V. and Goyal, S.P. (2009) Microscopic examinations in wildlife investigations. In A. Linacre (ed.) *Forensic Science in Wildlife Investigations*. Boca Raton, FL: CRC Press, pp. 19–59.

Stains, H.J. (1958) Field key to guard hair of Middle Western furbearers. *The Journal of Wildlife Management*, **22**, 95–97.

Stoves, J.L. (1942) The history of mammal hair. *Analyst*, **67**, 385–387.

Tridico, S. (2005) Examination, analysis, and application of hair in forensic science – animal hair. *Forensic Science Review*, **17**, 18–28.

Tumlison, R. (1983) An annotated key to the dorsal guard hairs of Arkansas game mammals and furbearers. *The Southwestern Naturalist*, **28**, 315–323.

Williams, C.S. (1938) Aids to the identification of mole and shrew hairs with general comments on hair structure and hair determination. *Journal of Wildlife Management*, **2**, 239–250.

9

Plants and Wildlife Forensics

Christopher R. Hardy and David S. Martin

Introduction

Plants (including other photosynthetic organisms such as algae) may be involved in forensic investigations by wildlife authorities in a multitude of ways. As this book is concerned with the forensic investigation of animal wildlife crimes, this chapter will provide an overview of the more common ways in which plant evidence will figure in the investigation of animal theft, injury, or death. For information about wildlife crimes involving plants directly, such as the illegal farming of drug plants on park lands and wilderness areas, or the illegal trade in protected plant species, the reader is referred to other literature (e.g., Kessler, 2005; Lane *et al.*, 1990; Pittman, 2005; Anonymous, 2006). The use of anomalous vegetation as a guide to disturbed ground and the location of animal burial sites associated with the illegal harvest of animal parts is discussed in Chapter 5 of this volume.

Plants as Trace Evidence

There is increasing awareness that plant evidence can be a powerful supplement to traditional evidence, such as fingerprints and ballistics, in forensic investigations of crimes (Lane *et al.*, 1990; Coyle *et al.*, 2005; Hall and Byrd, forthcoming). Although the literature on forensic botany deals primarily with human, rather than wildlife crime, virtually all of the principles of forensic botany regarding human crime are equally applicable to wildlife crime, and so such literature is still of utility to the investigator of wildlife crime.

Whether the evidence is as large and readily visible as fruits and leaves, or as small as seeds or microscopic pollen, plants and their products make up the

Wildlife Forensics: Methods and Applications, First Edition. Edited by Jane E. Huffman and John R. Wallace.

majority of the biological matter in terrestrial and aquatic ecosystems (80% or more), and thereby are more likely than animal or fungal material to be accidentally carried away from a crime scene by criminals or physical evidence. Examples include small grass flowers, leaf fragments, fibers, fruits or seeds that are easily lodged in pants cuffs, shoe laces, or carried away with mud from the crime scene in the tread of car tires, or transferred from a perpetrator's shoes to the floor of his automobile (Figure 9.1). Indeed, some plant parts, such as seeds or fruits, are especially adapted to latch onto and be carried away by animals (e.g., perpetrators of wildlife crime, see Figure 9.1a, b). A match between the plant matter collected from the suspect animal or material possessions with that known to exist at the crime scene is compelling circumstantial evidence placing the said suspect at the scene of the crime. In natural aquatic systems, algae (and other aquatic plants) can provide evidence analogous to that of terrestrial plants. Hardy and Wallace (in press) provide an in depth consideration of many types of algae and how they can be used to investigate human crimes.

Microscopic plant evidence is ubiquitous and so even though it cannot be seen with the naked-eye, a capable forensic botanist would know when and where sampling for microscopic analysis would be useful. For example, a wildlife criminal that committed some part of the crime in a wildflower meadow will most certainly have pollen evidence preserved on his/her shoots and pants. Moreover, since the timing of flowering and other plant life-history events is restricted in a species-specific manner to certain seasons or months during the year, pollen evidence can help to place a suspect not only at a particular crime scene, but at a particular time of year (Bryant *et al.*, 1990). In fact all plants, whether or not they produce flowers, do produce microscopic pollen or spores that can be used as trace evidence in an analogous manner. In natural water bodies, unicellular algae known as "diatoms" are especially useful for forensic analysis because, like pollen and spores, they are particularly abundant, resistant to decay, and their species-specific diagnostic features are not lost or remain largely undistorted upon desiccation (Figure 9.2).

Plant DNA could also be used to identify plant evidence to species, and it is particularly useful in this regard when the plant fragments collected as evidence from a suspect or suspect's belongings are too small to make a confident, positive ID based on morphology alone. DNA barcodes are short segments of DNA that can be used to identify the correct species to which an unknown plant specimen belongs (Kress and Erickson 2008). Whereas barcoding scientists have identified one gene, *COI* (cytochrome oxidase I), that works well in animals, *COI* is not sufficiently variable in plants and so plant barcoding scientists have instead identified a combination of two genes, *matK* (pronounced matt-kay) and *rbcL* (pronounced ar-bee-cee-el), as the "barcode" for plants (Ferri *et al.*, 2009; CBOL Plant Working Group 2009). The application of DNA barcoding to wildlife forensics is currently limited by the fact that there are not yet comprehensive data bases of *matk* and *rbcL* sequences for many plant species. There are ongoing efforts by an international barcoding consortium to complete such databases, but the community is years away from such a goal.

Figure 9.1 Barbed fruits, flowers, and small or spiny seeds from a crime scene may be unknowingly carried away on the clothing of a wildlife criminal. All scale bars = 1 mm. a, b: Small fruits often have small hooks or barbs on them, allowing them to be easily picked up from a crime scene by unsuspecting passers-by: a fruit of the common daisy relative "beggar-ticks" (*Bidens frondosa*) is pictured here. c Small flowers or fruits, such as those from many grasses, easily break away from the stalk and are picked up among the laces of shoes and cuffs of pants legs: those of panic-grass (*Panicum depauperatum*) are pictured here. d Small seeds also may be picked up among shoe laces and cuffs of pants legs, may be found in tire treads, or they may indicate the components of a last "meal" when found in the stomach or stool of deceased accident or crime victims; here, the seed of the edible fox grape (*Vitis labrusca*, left) is pictured alongside the seeds of very similar, yet poisonous berries of Virginia creeper (*Parthenocissus quinquefolia*, middle) and moonseed (*Menispermum canadense*, right), all of which grow in the same habitat in eastern North America. Photo of fox grape seed courtesy of Daniel J. Yoder.

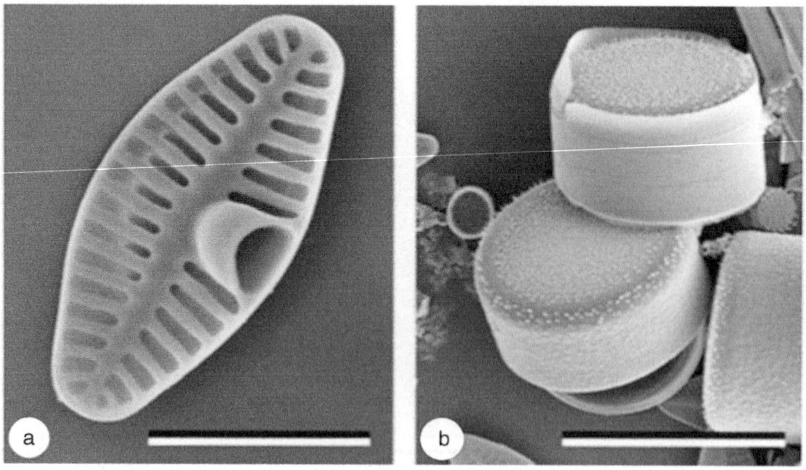

Figure 9.2 Diatoms are unicellular algae with ornate, yet tough cell walls called "frustules." a A single cell of *Planothidium lanceolatum*, a common freshwater, pennate diatom of south-eastern United States; scale bar = 4 μm. b Three cells of *Melosira varians*, a common freshwater, centric diatom of the south-eastern United States; scale bar = 20 μm. Scanning electron micrographs courtesy of Akshinthala K. S. K. Prasad, Department of Biological Science, Florida State University.

Even when morphology-based ID of the species is confident, however, DNA is a powerful tool that can be used to link a suspect, by way of plant material evidence on him, to a particular plant or population of plants at the crime scene. The level of precision necessary to match plant evidence with a single plant or population of plants from a crime scene, however, exceeds that typically possible with barcoding. Instead, hypervariable DNA markers such as AFLPs and microsatellites are the tools of choice for workers attempting this (e.g., Craft *et al.*, 2007). The limitations of this is that these techniques (generally called "DNA profiling" or "DNA typing") take much more time and money than DNA barcoding to develop, and may need to be developed on a case-by-case basis.

Plants as Trace Evidence Case Studies

Case study 1: plants in slain grizzly's gut contradict man's alibi for grizzly slaying

In the 1980's, a guide for horseback hunting expeditions in Wyoming, USA was caught having shot and killed a grizzly bear (*Ursus arctos* ssp. *horribilis*; Lane *et al.*, 1990). The grizzly is an endangered species and killing one is illegal except under extenuating circumstances. In his defense, the guide told Wyoming state game officials that he had shot it because the grizzly had been eating the alfalfa hay he had supplied for his horse stock. Analysis of the grizzly carcass's stomach contents by botanists at the Rocky Mountain Herbarium, University of Wyoming revealed wild grasses, sedges, and various wild forbs typical of streamside vegetation in Wyoming, but no alfalfa hay. At trial, the man's guide license was rescinded and he was fined and jailed on the basis of this and other evidence.

Case study 2: diatoms on teenagers' shoes link them to pond and brutal mugging

Although this case study does not involve a wildlife crime, it is chosen here to illustrate how aquatic plants (diatoms) and microscopy can be used to link suspects to crime scenes and victims. In 1992, three male teenagers were convicted of felonies for their involvement in the brutal mugging of two younger boys that were fishing at a rural Connecticut, USA pond (Siver *et al.*, 1994). In an attempt to steal the boys' bicycles, the teenagers bound the victims with tape, beat them with baseball bats, and left them in the pond to drown. The boys eventually managed to free themselves and rally area neighbors and police to find the perpetrators. A microscopic analysis of the mud on the perpetrators' shoes by limnologists at nearby Connecticut College found the same diatom species as on the victims' shoes and in the pond at the crime scene. The teenage suspects were convicted to a lengthy imprisonment based upon this and other evidence.

Case studies 3 & 4: plant DNA and the potential to match plant fragments on suspects to plants found at the crime scene

Although these case studies do not involve wildlife crimes, they are chosen here to illustrate how plant DNA can be used to identify a plant not only to species, but to a particular individual plant or population at a crime scene as well. Craft *et al.* (2007) presented DNA profiling data that exonerated a murder suspect in Florida, USA, data demonstrating that the fragments of oak leaves found in a murder suspect's car trunk did not come from any tree of the same species at the site where they victim's body had been dumped. In contrast, Yoon (1993) presented a case in which DNA was used to show that the fruits of a paloverde tree found in a murder suspect's pickup truck bed came from the same tree near to where the victim's body had been dumped in Arizona, USA, thereby implicating the suspect in the murder.

Poisonous Plants

Determining the cause of death of a protected animal is the important first step in determining whether or not a wildlife crime has been committed or, in the case of a death due to noncriminal factors, seeking to identify the causal environmental agent so that steps can be taken to prevent further deaths. The recovery in a conservation area of the carcass of a protected animal that had been mutilated by the removal of teeth, claws, or organs is an obvious sign of poaching for illegal sale of the removed items. In contrast, the carcass of an otherwise young and healthy animal with no apparent external injuries does not point to poaching, yet it is still something that should be investigated and understood in order to determine if there is a plausible threat to other animals.

Many plants produce toxins that may serve them as a deterrence of herbivory. Not surprisingly, some of these plants can occasionally cause illness and even death if consumed by wildlife. Mysterious deaths of young, otherwise healthy wildlife with no external signs of injury should alert wildlife investigators of the possibility that poisonous plants are the cause of death. Discovery of poisonous plants amongst the carcass's stomach contents is something that might lead to efforts by a park's authorities, for example, to locate and eradicate an infestation in the park of the responsible plants. In fact, many such plants are defined as Noxious Weeds by state or provincial laws and land owners may anyway be bound by law to take efforts to eradicate such plants. Much information about poisonous plants is available from large veterinary hospitals or state agricultural extension offices as they relate to illness and deaths in domestic animals. Not all plants toxic to one animal species are necessarily toxic to another, but such resources can be used as a guide for further investigation. Table 9.1 provides some useful Web resources on North American plants known to be toxic to animals.

In aquatic environments, algae are the dominant primary producers and, whereas most species are beneficial and nontoxic, some species are toxic and can cause illness or death in animals, including humans (Figure 9.3). The threat of such poisonings is typically only present during occasional and sporadic blooms (massive, temporary population growths) of toxic species. Illness or death may result from drinking from an affected water supply or, for deaths of animals that live and feed in the affected waters, simple exposure to toxins or consumption

Table 9.1 Some useful Web resources on North American plants known to be toxic to animals.

- Cornell University Department of Animal Science's *Plants Poisonous to Livestock and Other Animals* (http://www.ansci.cornell.edu/plants/)
- Canadian Biodiversity Information Facility's *Canadian Poisonous Plants Information System* (http://www.cbif.gc.ca/pls/pp/)
- University of Pennsylvania's *Poisonous Plants Home Page* (http://cal.vet.upenn.edu/projects/poison)
- Spokane County (Washington, USA) Noxious Weed Control Board's *A Guide to Plants that Are Poisonous to Horses and Livestock* (http://www.co.cowlitz.wa.us/noxiousweeds/download%20documents/Other%20sources/Guide%20to%20Plants%20Toxic%20to%20Horses%20and%20Livestock.pdf)

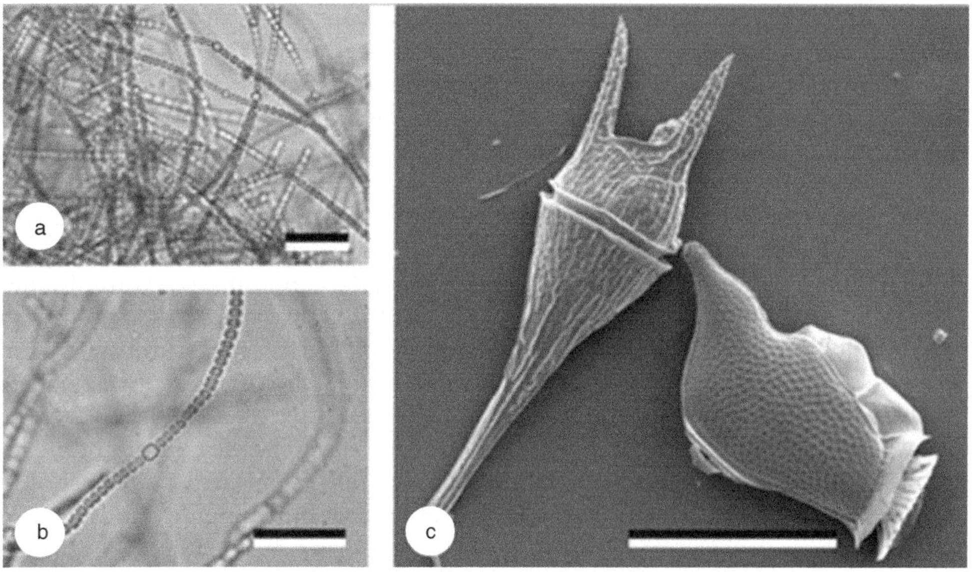

Figure 9.3 Some algae are toxic and can sicken or kill animals, including humans. a, b *Anabaena*, a filamentous, blue-green alga common in freshwater ponds and lakes. Photographs by Christopher R. Hardy. c *Ceratium hircus* (left) and *Dinophysis caudata* (right) are both components of marine phytoplankton. The latter is a red-tide species that is associated with massive fish kills in subtropical and tropical waters. Scale bar = 50 μm in all photographs. Scanning electron micrograph courtesy of Akshinthala K. S. K. Prasad, Department of Biological Science, Florida State University.

of filter-feeding shellfish that have accumulated the toxins. Such poisonings are not common and will not typically be criminal; however, investigators of mysterious wildlife deaths should be familiar with the circumstances under which poisonings are likely to occur.

The principal toxic algae of saltwaters are certain species of dinoflagellates (Figure 9.3c). Although most are harmless, the toxic species produce extremely potent neural toxins generally called "dinotoxins" (Hardy and Wallace, in press). It is during blooms in coastal waters (generally called "red tides" because of the color they may have) that sufficient amounts of dinotoxin can accumulate and lead to large fish die-offs, as well as accumulation in oysters, clams, mussels and other filter-feeding shellfish. During red tides, therefore, beaches may be closed to swimming and afflicted waters are closed to shellfishing since ingestion of dinotoxins can lead to paralytic shellfish poisoning (PSP). Though PSP has not much been studied in wild animals, symptoms in humans start with numbness around the mouth (if ingested orally) and limbs, vertigo, incoherent speech, general nerve dysfunction, nausea, vomiting, and may lead to respiratory paralysis and subsequent death within hours (Gessner *et al.*, 1997; CDC, 2011; Holstege, 2011).

The principal toxic algae of freshwaters are certain species of blue-green algae (Figure 9.3a, b; also known as cyanobacteria) that produce liver, neural, or skin toxins (generally called "cyanotoxins;" Graham *et al.*, 2010). These cyanotoxins may reach harmful concentrations during blooms. These blooms will be expansive masses of algae near the surface and their growth is fueled by the periodic convergence of sufficient nutrients (e.g., a recent rain and soil-erosion event), warm temperatures, and sunlight. Farmers and veterinarians are generally more familiar than most others with the danger posed by such blooms since domestic animal illness and deaths that arise from drinking the contaminated water bodies are common (Francis, 1878; Stewart *et al.*, 2006). Skin rashes associated with nerve or liver damage, and eyewitness accounts of "dirty" or "scummy" green, brown or blue-green masses in nearby water bodies should alert investigators to the possibility that blue-green algae are the causative agents. Because these toxic blooms also frequently produce malodorous but nontoxic compounds, eyewitness accounts of the water having distinctive musty or earthy odors should also alert investigators to the possible involvement of blue-green algae (Graham *et al.*, 2010).

Poisonous Plant Case Studies

Case study 1: blue-greens kill sea otters

In September 2010, the California Department of Fish & Game and the University of California, Santa Cruz, published their collaborative findings that the blue-green alga *Microcystis* and its potent liver toxin, microcystin, were responsible for the deaths of at least 21 southern sea otters (*Enhydra lutris* ssp. *nereis*) from Monterey Bay, California, USA (Gabel, 2010; Fimrite, 2010). The southern sea otter is listed by the United States as a federally endangered species. Although the algae were affecting the marine waters of Monterey Bay, scientists determined that the algae and their toxins had likely originated upstream in Pinto Lake, which drains into Corralitos Creek and then into the Pajaro River, one of three main rivers that feeds into Monterey Bay. It is at the mouth of the Pajaro where the toxins were subsequently picked up and accumulated by shellfish eaten by otters.

Case study 2: dinoflagellates kill coral

In 2010, scientists studying coral reefs in the Gulf of Oman concluded that blooms of the potentially toxic dinoflagellate *Cochlodinium polykrikoides* (assumed but not yet confirmed to be toxic) were likely responsible for the complete or near death of the coral as well as the reduction of fish in those waters by 70% (Davies, 2010), beneath the large blooms. One of these blooms measured over 500 km^2.

Case study 3: lichen kills elk

During February-April 2004, an estimated 400–500 free-ranging elk (*Cervus elaphus*) developed paresis, became recumbent, and died or were euthanized in the Red Rim Wildlife Habitat Management Area, Wyoming, USA. Diagnostic testing ruled out common infectious, inflammatory, toxic, and traumatic causes. Tumbleweed shield lichen, *Xanthoparmelia chlorochroa* (syn. *Parmelia chlorochroa*), is a common ground lichen in Wyoming and elsewhere in western North America. It was found in the area and in the rumen of several elk. The lichen produces usnic acid that may break down muscle tissue. The pathogenesis of the lichen in the elk remains unknown. That the usnic acid may play some role seems reasonable, but other contributing synergistic compounds in the lichen could not be ruled out (Cook *et al.*, 2007).

The Basics of Collecting and Preserving Botanical Evidence

Exploiting plants as evidence requires being aware of its probable existence, knowing how to collect and preserve it at a crime scene, and where and how to collect it from a suspect or physical evidence. Detailed protocols for the collection and preservation of plant evidence can be found in Hall and Byrd (forthcoming). Consideration of issues such as chain of custody and avoidance of contamination, discussed elsewhere in this volume, is paramount. Ideally, authorities involved in the initial stages of the investigation will have a forensic botanist present during evidence collection, since the botanist will best know precisely what to look for in terms of evidence. In summary, reference plant samples should be collected from a crime or accident scene for preservation and later comparison to trace plant evidence collected off a suspect's person, clothing, or vehicle. Upon collection, samples/evidence and its precise location should be photographed and notes taken and archived since location of evidence may prove vital to the case at a later time, and diagnostic attributes of the plants, such as color, can be preserved in photographs long after they have faded from the physical specimens taken. The following is but a brief overview of some of the procedures for collection of plant evidence. The reader is referred to Hall and Byrd (forthcoming) or Coyle (2005) for more detailed information.

DNA Evidence

Although all plant tissue has DNA in it, fresh leaves are the standard organ collected by professional botanists for DNA extraction and analysis. Rather than being collected into alcohol, as is often done with animal material, standard practice among botanists is to place the leaf material (one to four 1 × 1 cm squares cut from the leaf) into fine- or coarse-grained silica gel desiccant (Chase and Hillis, 1991). The silica gel quickly dries the tissue, preventing excessive degradation of the DNA. Short and long term storage of the tissue in the silica gel at room temperature is an acceptable practice, though many practitioners place the material in a $-80°$ Celsius for long-term storage on the order of months to years. Either way, it is important to voucher the plant from which DNA samples were taken by making a herbarium specimen (see below). This specimen can be kept in the investigator's possession or deposited in a herbarium where it will be archived with many other specimens – most of which were collected for various basic scientific, rather than forensic, investigations. If there is ever a question as to the identity of the species from which the DNA results came, the herbarium specimen represents a physical specimen that can be returned to for the purposes of confirming or refuting the original identification in question. Additionally, should the identity of the species from which the DNA came from ever be challenged, the specimen can be returned to for further extraction. Although not preserved in silica gel, DNA of sufficient quality may still be extracted from a dry herbarium specimen for years, depending in part on the storage conditions at the herbarium. The New York Botanical Garden curates a Website, *Index Herbariorum* (Thiers, continuously updated), that can be consulted to find the herbarium closest to an investigator for the deposition of a voucher specimen.

Organismal Evidence

Organismal evidence is defined here as plant matter for which species determination will be generally based on characteristics observable using the naked-eye or a microscope. This class of evidence, rather than DNA evidence, still represents the vast majority of evidence used in forensic botany because it is a time-tested, reliable, cost-effective means of determining the species-identity of the plant material in question. Whereas, the trace evidence from a suspect's person or belongings is expected to be fragmentary, thereby making the identification more difficult, the reference material purposely collected from the crime scene should be as complete as possible (with leaves, flowers, fruits) to ensure accurate and confident identification, and to facilitate comparison to the fragmentary trace evidence.

Large plant parts such as twigs, stem, and leaves should be pressed flat and held uniformly compressed until dry in order to prevent the shriveling that would otherwise occur during drying. This is best done with a plant press, which can be easily constructed or purchased from online herbarium or forestry supply companies. The procedure standard among professional botanists is to lay the plant material flat between two sheets or one folded sheet of newsprint (e.g., one leaf of a used newspaper). The plant itself is labeled using jeweler's tags or the newsprint is labeled with some collection number that links to a more complete description of the material in a notebook. Then, the newsprint with plant is sandwiched between two 12×18 inch rectangular pieces of corrugated cardboard and they are then sandwiched between two sturdy ca. $12\frac{1}{2} \times 19$ inch

Table 9.2 Some commonly used liquid preservatives for the preservation of botanical evidence.

FAA	*For land plants.* Preserves organ and cell morphology and structure, without drying. Natural coloration typically lost	Per 100 ml of sample, mix 10 ml formalin, 10 ml acetic acid, and 80 ml of 50% ethanol
Formaldehyde solution (Britton and Greeson, 1989)	*For algae.* Preserves color but may distort cell shape and cause loss of any flagella that are present	Per 100 ml of sample, add 3 ml of formalin, 0.5 ml of 20% detergent solution, and 0.1 ml cupric sulfate solution
Lugol's solution (Britton and Greeson, 1989)	*For algae.* Preserves cell morphology and flagella but stains cells brownish yellow	Per 100 ml of sample, add 1 ml of Lugol's solution containing 10% acetic acid.

pieces of wood (e.g., plywood) and bound firmly by two straps until dry. Moist climates may require that the press be placed in a plant dryer or over a safe, low heat source to prevent molding during the 1–3 day drying process. Once dry, the specimen can be stored flat and will be preserved indefinitely (e.g., centuries). Smaller presses that can fit into a backpack also can be made or purchased. Wildlife authorities should always have an empty plant press available in the trunk of their vehicle or in the office.

Smaller plant parts, such as seeds, flowers, or fragments, may be removed as trace evidence from a tire tread or pants cuff. In search of such evidence, the hand lens, or loupe, is a valuable, inexpensive, and highly portable tool offering anywhere from 10X to 20X magnification. Once found, such evidence should be removed with forceps and placed inside breathable, paper envelopes, labeled, and then placed into larger, standard evidence bags that are thoroughly labeled. Alternatively, plant material can be wet-preserved in glass jars using alcohol or a fixative solution based on formaldehyde (Table 9.2).

Pollen and spore sample collection is more complicated than for other plant parts, since they are microscopic and there is the opportunity for the collector to introduce contaminants that he/she cannot see and is unaware of their presence (Bryant *et al.*, 1990). A forensic botanist with expertise in pollen analysis will ensure that his collection vessels (typically plastic bags for pollen collection), solutions and vessels for subsequent processing are sterile and void of contaminant pollen or spores. That said, pollen will be found 1) in any soil or encrusted mud (a sample of 15–30 g of dirt is ideal), 2) trapped in woven materials such as clothing, bags, ropes or baskets, or 3) in packing materials for packages (e.g., those containing the illegally harvested animal parts) that were packed outdoors, exposed to the ambient pollen. The reader is referred to Bryant *et al.* (1990) or Hall and Byrd (forthcoming) for further details of pollen/spore collection and analysis.

Algae can be collected a variety of ways, depending on the size of the organism and the desire of the collector. Macroscopic algae (e.g., seaweeds) can be collected directly onto a water-color paper or standard herbarium paper by suspending the alga in water and then lifting the paper up and into it from beneath. As the paper with alga is lifted out of the water, the alga will stick to the paper in a semi-permanent manner due to glue like substances on the algal surface. Once dry, the algal body will be preserved flat and expanded as in life, rather than shriveled as would happen without affixing the alga to the paper. Filamentous or microscopic algae should be collected with the surrounding water into glass jars from and below the water surface. The microscopic algae in these samples will be various and the water samples may be examined microscopically for these various species as is or following preservation (Table 9.2). The exact procedure and volume needed in the collection of microscopic algae will vary with the type of algae and analysis to be done. See Hardy and Wallace (in press) for an overview of these methods.

Finding a Forensic Botanist

The majority of forensic botany applications require the accurate identification of plant material. Currently there is no national or international registry of forensic botanists in North America, for example, and relatively few members of the American Academy of Forensic Sciences (www.aafs.org) are listed in the membership directory explicitly as forensic botanists. Since there are relatively few botanists who explicitly specialize in forensic botany per se, botanists known as plant systematists or ecologists will generally have the identification skills and general knowledge of a regional flora sufficient to assist in an investigation. Since most plant systematists and ecologists specialize in the identification of terrestrial plants, however, the identification of aquatic plants such as algae may require botanists known as *algologists*, *phycologists* (phycology is the study of algae), *algal systematists*, *aquatic biologists*, or *freshwater* or *marine ecologists* may be needed. Such biologists are employed as educators/researchers at institutions such as universities or natural history museums. Since successful forensic investigations often rely on timeliness of evidence collection and processing, willing and capable forensic botanists should be identified by wildlife authorities ahead of time, *before* they are needed.

Conclusion

Botanical evidence is increasingly being used to supplement traditional evidence in forensic investigations. Two recent books on forensic botany, however, focus on its use regarding human crime (Coyle *et al.*, 2005; Hall and Byrd, forthcoming), and the only previous book dealing specifically with wildlife forensics (Linacre, 2009) lacks content regarding the application of forensic botany to wildlife crime. It is important to raise the awareness of the potential utility of plant evidence in wildlife forensics, since the mere fact of the ubiquity of plant matter in nature positions botany as potentially relevant in every wildlife forensic investigation imaginable.

Case studies of plants used as trace evidence to link suspects to crime scenes or physical evidence abound in the human criminal forensics literature. Fortunately, however, the principles and procedures revealed by such case studies are fully applicable to wildlife forensics, and it is only a matter of time before awareness will bring more case studies regarding wildlife crime to light. If wildlife authorities are not confident in their ability to collect and identify botanical evidence properly, then they should seek to ascertain the identity and availability of capable forensic botanists before they will be inevitably needed.

A more direct role of plant evidence in the outcome of a wildlife forensic investigation is when the plants themselves are the cause of death or injury to an animal. Poisonous plants and algae have been implicated in the deaths of several different rare or endangered species in North America. Although such incidents are not criminal, determining the cause of death of an animal is the important first step in ruling out criminal activity such that efforts can be focused on eradicating the toxic plants or otherwise managing the threat in order to prevent further deaths.

Many other applications of plant science are known in the human criminal forensics literature, such as the use of diatoms to confirm cases of human drowning, and the use of DNA profiling of drug plants and their products in the prosecution of drug traffickers. Such applications were purposely excluded from this chapter since they will not generally be relevant to wildlife forensics. For these, the reader is referred to more comprehensive works on forensic botany (e.g., Coyle, 2005; Hall and Byrd, forthcoming). Other direct roles of plants in wildlife crime, such as the illegal trade in protected plant species, are beyond the scope of this book and, therefore, also not included. For a discussion of these, the reader is referred to other literature (e.g., Kessler, 2005; Pittman, 2005; Anonymous, 2006).

Acknowledgements

We thank the editors and publishers of this book for their helpful review and critique of an earlier version of this manuscript. We also thank Akshinthala K. S. K. Prasad for his excellent scanning electron micrographs of diatoms and dinoflagellates.

References

Anonymous (2006) 'You can get off alcohol and drugs, but you never get off orchids. Never.' The Telegraph, 22 January 2006. http://www.telegraph.co.uk/news/uknews/1508457/You-can-get-off-alcohol-and-drugs-but-you-never-get-off-orchids.-Never.html.

Britton, L.J. and Greeson, P.E. (eds.) (1989) *Methods for Collection and Analysis of Aquatic Biological and Microbiological Samples.* U.S. Geological Survey Techniques of Water-Resources Investigations.

Bryant, V.M., Jones, J.G. and Mildenhall, D.C. (1990) Forensic palynology in the United States of America. Palynology, **14**, 193–208.

CBOL Plant Working Group (2009) A DNA barcode for land plants. *Proceedings of the National Academy of Sciences (USA)*, **106**, 12794–12797.

CDC (2011) Harmful algal blooms (HABs). Available at: http://www.cdc.gov/hab/cyanobacteria/default.htm.

Chase, M.W. and Hills, H.H. (1991) Silica gel: an ideal material for field preservation of leaf samples for DNA studies. *Taxon*, **40**, 215–220.

Cook, W.E., Raisbeck, M.F., Cornish, T.E. *et al.* (2007) Paresis and death in elk (*Cervus elaphus*) due to lichen intoxication in Wyoming. *Journal of Wildlife Diseases*, **43**, 498–503.

Coyle, H.M. (2005) *Forensic Botany: Principles and Applications to Criminal Casework.* CRC Press, Boca Raton, Florida, USA.

Craft, K.J., Owens, J.D. and Ashley, M.V. (2007) Application of plant DNA markers in forensic botany: genetic comparison of Quercus evidence leaves to crime scene trees using microsatellites. *Forensic Science International*, **165**, 64–70.

Davies, E. (2010) Toxic algae rapidly kills coral. *BBC News*, 8 October.

Ferri, G., Alú, M., Corradini, B. and Beduschi, G. (2009) Forensic botany: species identification of botanical trace evidence using a multigene barcoding approach. *International Journal of Legal Medicine*, **123**, 395–401.

Fimrite, P. (2010) Monterey sea otters killed by toxic algae. *SFGate.com*, 11 September.

Francis, G. (1878) Poisonous Australian lakes. *Nature*, **18**, 11–12.

Gabel, D.A. (2010) Toxic algae killing sea otters. ENN: Environmental News Network, 13 September. Available at: http://www.enn.com/wildlife/article/41767/.

Gessner, B.D., Bell, P., Doucette, G.J., *et al.* (1997) Hypertension and identification of toxin in human urine and serum following a cluster of mussel-associated paralytic shellfish poisoning outbreaks. *Toxicon*, **35**, 711–722.

Graham, J.L., Loftin, K.A., Meyer, M.T., *et al.* (2010) Cyanotoxin mixtures and taste-and-odor compounds in cyanobacterial blooms from the midwestern United States. *Environmental Science and Technology*, doi:10.1021/es1008938.

Hall, D. and Byrd, J. (forthcoming) *Forensic Botany: A Practical Guide.*

Hardy, C.R. and Wallace, J.W. (in press) Algae in forensic investigations. In D.A. Hall (ed.) *Forensic Botany*. Boca Raton, FL: CRC Press.

Holstege, C.P. (2011) Saxatoxin. In C.P. Holstege, T.M. Neer, G.B. Saathoff, R.B. Furbee. (eds.) *Criminal Poisoning: Clinical and Forensic Perspectives*. Sudbury, Massachusetts, USA: Jones and Bartlett Publishers, LLC., pp. 141–144.

Kessler, L. (2005) *The cult of the cycads*. The New York Times, 28 August.

Kress, W.J. and Erickson, D.L. (2008) DNA barcodes: genes, genomics, and bioinformatics. *Proceedings of the National Academy of Sciences (USA)*, **105**, 2761–2762.

Lane, M.A., Anderson, L.C. and Barkley, T.M. *et al.* (1990) Forensic botany: plants, perpetrators, pests, poisons, and pot. *BioScience*, **40**, 34–39.

Linacre, A. (2009) *Forensic Science in Wildlife Investigations*. CRC Press, Boca Raton, FL. 162 pp.

Siver, P.A., Lord, W.D. and McCarthy, D.J. (1994) Forensic limnology: the use of freshwater algal community ecology to link suspects to an aquatic crime scene in southern New England. *Journal of Forensic Science*, **39**, 847–853.

Stewart, I., Seawright, A.A., Schluter, P.J., *et al.* (2006) Primary irritant and delayed-contact hypersensitivity reactions to the freshwater cyanobacterium Cylindrospermopsis raciborskii and its associated toxin cylindrospermopsin. *Dermatology*, **6**, 1–12.

Thiers, B. (continuously updated) Index Herbariorum: a global directory of public herbaria and associated staff. New York Botanical Garden's Virtual Herbarium. http://sweetgum.nybg.org/ih/.

Yoon, C.K. (1993) Botanical witness for the prosecution. *Science*, **260**, 894–895.

10

Identification of Reptile Skin Products Using Scale Morphology

David L. Martin

Introduction

The international trade in wildlife and wildlife products is a multibillion dollar a year business. One of the larger consumer markets for international wildlife products is the United States of America. The trade in reptile skins and reptile skin products is a large component of the international wildlife commodities market, and the US is a major consumer for those products. The impact of this market on animal species, including reptiles, is considerable, with millions of reptiles being killed every year to support this trade despite international and national efforts to control the trade and the impact on wildlife and reptile species. One of the tools needed to combat the exploitation of reptile species is a reliable methodology by which to identify the reptile species entering the trade. Unfortunately, when reptiles are processed into tanned skins or leather and ultimately the products manufactured from those skins, many of the identifying morphological features traditionally used to identify a particular reptile to species are lost. In light of these difficulties, a study of the morphological features of reptile scales was initiated to determine if macro- and/or micro-morphological features of reptile scales can be used to identify reptile skin and skin products to species even in the absence of more traditional identifying features. The unique attribute of this study is that it utilizes preserved natural history specimens with known geographic and taxonomic data to document and confirm the suitability of the morphological features measured during this ongoing project.

Wildlife Forensics: Methods and Applications, First Edition. Edited by Jane E. Huffman and John R. Wallace.

International Trade in Reptile Skins

The value of the international trade in reptile skins and skin products

The legal international trade in wildlife and wildlife products had an estimated value of nearly US$332.5 billion in 2005 (Engler, 2008), which, when adjusted for inflation, represents an increase of about 70% over the US$158.9 billion estimated value of the wildlife trade in the early 1990s (Broad *et al.*, 2003; Engler, 2008). The largest component of the trade estimates above, 82% and 91% respectively, is represented by timber and fisheries, but the legal international trade in other wildlife and animal products was valued at nearly US$61 billion in 2005. This US$61 billion estimate includes the live reptile trade, valued at US$38 million (or ~0.5%), and trade in reptile skins and leather, valued at US$339 million (or ~5%) (Engler, 2008), which underscores the fact that the trade in live reptiles is dwarfed by the trade in reptile skins and skin products (Pernetta, 2009). Unfortunately, these trade values greatly under-estimate the true worth of the global trade in wildlife for a number of reasons. First, the estimates of wildlife trade values are based on the wholesale values rather than the considerably higher market values (Jenkins and Broad, 1994; Fernandez and Luxmoore, 1997; Engler, 2008). Second, these values are based largely on the trade reported by the countries or Parties to the 1973 Convention on International Trade in Endangered Species of Wild Fauna and Flora (CITES, enacted in 1975), which requires the Parties to report the quantity of wildlife that are listed in the Appendices of the Convention traded annually. Thus, the only portion of the wildlife trade reported to CITES is the legal international trade of CITES-listed species. This means neither the domestic wildlife trade, which can be considerable, especially in Asian countries, nor the trade in species not listed in the CITES Appendices are included in the estimates (see Groombridge and Luxmoore, 1991; Jenkins and Broad, 1994; Zhou and Jiang, 2004; Lin, 2005; Nijman, 2009; Auliya, 2010; USA and China 2010). Third, the trade between countries that are not Parties to the Convention is not reported and thus is not included in the estimates of the value of international trade in wildlife (Jenkins and Broad, 1994; Fernandez and Luxmoore, 1997; Zimmerman, 2003; Zhou and Jiang, 2004; Schlaepfer *et al.*, 2005; Engler, 2008; Auliya, 2010; USA and China 2010). Fourth, the quantification of trade in wildlife is not reported to CITES in a consistent manner by all the Parties. Some countries report trade in numbers of heads or skins, while others report trade by weight, and still others report trade in skin length or square area; and the trade in products manufactured from reptile skins is often reported as items even though a single item can be manufactured from many individual reptiles of different species (Jenkins and Broad, 1994; Fernandez and Luxmoore, 1997; Zhou and Jiang, 2004; Schlaepfer *et al.*, 2005; Arroyo-Quiroz *et al.*, 2006; Caldwell, 2007; Nijman, 2010; Rosen and Smith, 2010). Fifth, the illegal trade in wildlife is not included in these estimates as the very nature of the illegal trade makes it difficult to quantify this trade, but estimates of the illicit international wildlife trade range from at least

US$5 billion to over US$20 billion annually (UNEP, 1998; Roe *et al.*, 2002; Wyler and Sheikh, 2008; Rosen and Smith, 2010), which makes the illegal trade in wildlife among the most lucrative illicit economies in the world, behind illegal drugs and on par with human and arms trafficking. The size of this illicit trade attracts, and is bolstered by, organized criminal groups that use the high profits resulting from wildlife smuggling coupled with the low risk of incarceration and/or relatively small fines to supplement their income from trafficking in other illicit commodities (Jenkins and Broad, 1994; Ferrer, 1995; Roth and Merz, 1997; Cook *et al.*, 2002; Vince, 2002; Zimmerman, 2003; Shinawatra, 2004: Lin, 2005; Wyler and Sheikh, 2008; Barber-Meyer, 2010; Rosen and Smith, 2010; USA and China, 2010). The United States Fish and Wildlife Service (USF&WS), for example, seizes over US$10 million in illegal wildlife annually, and this likely represents only a small percentage of the illegal wildlife trade to the US alone (Perez, 2008). This illicit wildlife trade is driven by the demand for CITES-listed species that are otherwise banned from commercial trade and/or the demand for larger specimens or hides than can be legally produced in an economically feasible manner by the CITES approved farming or ranching operations (Jenkins and Broad, 1994; Rosen and Smith, 2010). For example, there were over 67,740 sea turtle products seized in 1994–2003 by the USF&WS despite sea turtle products, including eggs, meat, shell products and leather, being banned from trade for over 25 years (Rice and Moore, 2008), and in 2007 wildlife smugglers offered undercover USF&WS Special Agents over 4,000 sea turtle leather hides (Perez, 2008). Finally, the estimated value of the international wildlife trade does not consider the very real damage caused by this trade to species viability, ecosystems or the impact this trade can have on biodiversity (Hoover, 1998; Wilcove *et al.*, 1998; Gibbons *et al.*, 2000; Zhou and Jiang, 2004; Schlaepfer, *et al.*, 2005; Stuart *et al.*, 2006; Rosen and Smith, 2010; USA and China, 2010).

The volume of international trade in reptile skins and skin products

The vast majority of the reptiles entering the international trade in reptile skins and reptile skin products are collected from the wild with only a relatively few (~100,000 animals) farmed crocodilians being produced in captivity (Jenkins and Broad, 1994). There are several hundred snake farms in China alone that produce over 427,000 specimens, largely comprised of three species, but the majority of these facilities serve to raise wild-caught juvenile snakes to a marketable size in less than a year, so the animals still largely come from the wild even when reported as farmed (Pernetta, 2009; USA and China, 2010). Again, it is difficult to accurately estimate the number of individual animals represented in the international reptile skin trade for the same reasons as those listed above for the estimations of the value of the wildlife trade. There are, however, reports of reptile skin exports that suggest the commercial trade in reptile skins has a long history of heavy exploitation. As far back as 1926, there was a sizable trade in reptile skins for the production of luxury articles manufactured from reptile skins with 2 million reptile skins reportedly being exported from the Dutch East Indies (now Indonesia) in 1931 and 2 million reptile skins being exported from India in 1932 (Parker, 1933), which is comparable in volume to the roughly 6 million reptile skins exported annually in Asia today (Jenkins and Broad, 1994). The number of reptiles taken for the skin trade from the 1940s through the 1970s is not well quantified, but at least 10 million wild-collected reptiles were killed annually in the 1980s for the international skin trade, and the number of reptiles taken each year for the trade has generally continued to grow (Jenkins and Broad, 1994; Holden, 1998; Caldwell, 2007, 2010; Engler, 2008; Nijman, 2009). For example, an average of 2.2 million tegu lizards (*Tupinambs* sp.), 2.3 million monitor lizards (*Varanus* sp.), 39,000 boas (*Boa* sp.), 30,000 anacondas (*Eunectes* sp.), 764,000 pythons (*Python* sp.) and at least 4.3 million other snakes were taken from the wild annually in the 1980s for the international trade in skins and skin products, and these numbers do not include the number of individual reptiles taken that are not reported to the CITES database because the animals taken were used domestically or were from species not listed on the CITES Appendices or were traded illegally (Jenkins and Broad, 1994). More recent estimates of the number of individual reptiles taken from the wild for the skin trade are incomplete, but over 1 million water monitor lizards (*Varanus salvator*) are reportedly taken from the wild every year from Indonesia alone (Luxmoore and Groombridge, 1990; Shine *et al.*, 1998). Mexico reported the importation of nearly 9 million reptile skins in 1980–2001 with a nearly constant rise in the numbers of skins and species imported annually (Arroyo-Quiroz, *et al.*, 2006). China reported the importation of 8.5 million snake skins in 1991–2001, but these numbers do not reflect the number of snakes taken and used within China, nor does it include the number of snakes imported to China that are comprised of species not listed in the CITES Appendices due to China's policy of not reporting these numbers (Zhou and Jiang, 2004). The international trade in crocodile skins has gradually increased from 954,000 skins in 1996 (Caldwell, 2004) to over 1.3 million skins in 2005 (Caldwell, 2007), peaking at 1.8 million skins in 2006 but then decreasing to nearly 1.2 million by 2008 (Caldwell, 2010). Indonesia set the 2006 quota for the maximum number of individual Oriental rat snakes (*Ptyas mucosa*) that can be harvested annually at 100,000 after an export ban of this species in 1993–2005 failed to prevent the export of some 50,000–100,000 skins annually (Auliya, 2010). Despite the reported take of over 10 million reptiles annually for the skin trade, there is little to no knowledge regarding the ability of the reptile species included in the trade to tolerate the current levels of take (Luxmoore and Groombridge, 1990; Groombridge and Luxmoore, 1991; Wilcove *et al.*, 1998; Zhou and Jiang, 2004; Schlaepfer *et al.*, 2005; Roe, 2008; Nijman, 2009; USA and China, 2010; Auliya, 2010).

While the majority of the international trade in reptile skins is centered on Asia with a significant portion of the reptile skin trade in Asia going unreported (Zhou and Jiang, 2004; Lin, 2005; USA and China, 2010), at present, the US is considered the single largest consumer market for reptile skins and reptile skin products in the world. During the period between 1984 and 1990 the

US imported 2.5 million reptile skins and 27.3 million manufactured products containing reptile skins annually with an estimated value of US$49 million and US$257 million, respectively, or an estimated total value of US$306 million in reptile skin and reptile skin products imported to the US annually from 1984 to 1990. Over this same period the total value of the US trade in wildlife, excluding timber and fisheries, was estimated to be valued at over US$566 million (Jenkins and Broad, 1994; Arroyo-Quiroz *et al.*, 2006), which means reptile skins and reptile skin products account for approximately half of the value of wildlife reportedly imported to the US annually between 1984 and 1990. Overall, the US purchases approximately 20% of the legal international trade in wildlife and wildlife products (Wyler and Sheikh, 2008), which makes the US a major market for the international wildlife trade and for the international trade in reptile skins and reptile skin products.

Legal protection of species represented in the international reptile skin trade

At present, there are some 9,285 described reptile species (Uetz *et al.*, 2010), and of those, 594 reptile species, or approximately 6%, are listed as Critically Endangered, Endangered or Vulnerable on the 2010 International Union for the Conservation of Nature (IUCN) Red List (IUCN, 2010). CITES provides the chief form of protection from international commercial exploitation of 708 reptile species, including 78 reptile species listed as Appendix I or species threatened with extinction that are generally banned from commercial trade, 571 reptile species listed as Appendix II or species that are not necessarily now threatened with extinction but may become so unless trade is strictly regulated, and 59 reptile species listed as CITES Appendix III or species that one or more countries regulate to prevent exploitation (CITES, 2010). Additionally, there are 119 reptile species afforded protection from exploitation in the US by the Endangered Species Act of 1973 (16 U.S.C. §§1531–1544; P.L. 93-205, as amended; USF&WS, 2010), which also prohibits any person to engage in trade in any species contrary to the provisions of CITES. The US Lacey Act (16 U.S.C. §701; 31 Stat. 187, as amended) and its subsequent Amendments of 1981 (16 U.S.C. §§3371 *et seq.*; P.L. 97-79, as amended) further protect wildlife entering the US by making it unlawful to import, transport, sell or purchase any wildlife taken or sold in violation of any state, federal or foreign wildlife laws or regulations, including CITES, and require that all shipments of wildlife or wildlife products be accurately marked or labeled, thereby making it a violation to transport wildlife and wildlife products in falsely marked containers. Finally, the state of California, which is home to two of the largest ports of entry into the US for cargo originating in Asia, also helps reduce the exploitation of reptile species for the skin trade by prohibiting the importation of cobra, python and sea turtle parts or products including tanned skins into the state, and will prohibit the commercial importation of any crocodile or alligator parts or products as of January 1, 2015 (California Penal Code § 653o).

Given these laws, and in particular the Lacey Act, the legal shipment of wildlife and wildlife products into and within the US requires a declaration as to the animal species contained within the shipment and, in the case of CITES-listed species entering the US, a CITES Export Permit issued by the country of origin (CITES Appendix I listed species also require a CITES Import Permit) that also identifies the wildlife species contained within the shipment (Wyler and Sheikh, 2008). The species identification listed on these documents must be confirmed during import and/or export inspections to ensure that the shipment does not contain any wildlife or wildlife products manufactured from protected species and/or species not declared in the shipment. Thus, the inspection of shipments of wildlife and wildlife products requires some form of a forensic identification of the species contained within a given shipment to ensure the authenticity of the documents accompanying the shipment and that the shipment contains only those species listed on those documents. Further, criminal charges and legal proceedings resulting from falsely labeled wildlife shipments, smuggled wildlife and/or other enforcement issues will require the forensic identification of the species concerned that will withstand judicial scrutiny (Brazaitis, 1986b; Baker, 2006, 2008; Cooper, 2008).

Challenges to Species Identification of Reptile Skin Products

There are four key challenges faced by the forensic herpetologist when trying to identify a given reptile skin or skin product to species: (1) there is little to no, or worse misleading and often fraudulent, information included with the shipment documentation regarding the geographic origin of the evidence being examined; (2) the species identification provided with the shipment is often suspect and may have been provided with the intent to misdirect law enforcement personnel by identifying a closely related, but non-protected, species in an effort to obfuscate the species contained in the shipment; (3) the evidence usually only represents a portion of the original animal, such as a tanned skin or product manufactured from a portion of a tanned skin, such that many of the morphological features traditionally used to identify animal species are missing; and (4) the evidence being examined, and particularly in the case of commercially tanned leather products, is often unsuitable for genetic analysis due to degradation of the genetic material resulting from chemical processing during the manufacturing/tanning process or due to a lack of appropriate assays for novel species (King and Brazaitis, 1971; Brazaitis, 1984, 1986a, 1986b, 1987, 1989; Busack and Pandya, 2001; Baker, 2006, 2008; Baker *et al.*, under review).

The traditional methods used by herpetologists to identify reptile species include keys and species catalogs with a global (e.g. Ernst and Barbor, 1989), continental (e.g. Cogger, 1992), regional (e.g. Grismer, 2002) or taxonomic (Pianka *et al.*, 2004) focus as well as local field guides (e.g. Branch, 1998) and ultimately the original published species descriptions (e.g. Weijola and Sweet,

2010), but these tools often require some knowledge as to the geographic origin of the animal being identified in order to be effective. Further, these guides often use morphological features to identify specimens that may not be included with the evidence being analyzed. The identification or taxonomy of reptile species was historically based on morphometrics or the quantification of observable morphological attributes of whole zoological specimens. The attributes typically used to classify reptiles included standardized body measurements, standardized scale counts, skull morphology, dentition, hemipenal morphology, scale shape and scale ornamentation. Some of these characteristics are still useful in the identification of whole reptile skins or taxidermic mounts where much of the external structure of the animal can still be observed; but many of these characteristics are no longer present after an animal has been processed into a tanned skin or other product. Cogger (1992), for example, uses head scalation to differentiate between sea snake genera, but a tanned sea snake skin rarely has the head still attached even when it is a whole skin and the problem only gets worse once the skin has been made into a product such as a wallet. There are a few forensic identification guides for reptiles that are specifically designed to address the problem of the lack of reliable geographic data and focus on the morphological attributes of the animal (e.g. Charette, 1999; McCloud, 2008) particularly for crocodilians (Charette, 1995), and whole crocodilian skins (King and Brazaitis, 1971; Brazaitis, 1973, 1987, 1989; Busack and Pandya, 2001; Fuchs, 2006); but aids for the identification of turtle, snake and lizard skins are limited to the CITES *Identification Manual*, which includes only a few of the commercially exploited reptile species, and *The Reptile Skin* by Fuchs and Fuchs (2003), which provides information on the identification of 61 reptile species that are commonly exploited for the commercial leather industry. However, both of these guides use somewhat outdated taxonomy that is particularly troubling given that they provide descriptions of morphological characteristics of several CITES Appendix I listed species based on data gathered before those species were divided into two or more species, which calls into question the validity of the data they present (Martin, 2010; see also Thiele and Yeates, 2002; Mace, 2004). Further, both of these guides focus on the identification of whole reptile skins that are often traded commercially and not on the identification of reptile skin products that represent an even smaller sample of the original animal, and thus are more difficult to identify. Morphometric counts such as the number of belly scale rows or the number of mid-body scales often cannot be taken on manufactured products. Despite these serious limitations, these references provide some of the only available data on the morphological features of reptile skin that can be useful in the identification of reptile skin products.

This chapter pulls together data on reptile scale morphology from a number of published sources, first-hand evaluation of natural history museum specimens with known taxonomic identification and geographic origin data, attempts to correct the taxonomic nomenclature inconsistencies, and presents, wherever possible, the features and data that can best be used to identify reptile skin and skin products based on scale morphology.

Species and Products Represented in the Reptile Skin Trade

In total, there are something in excess of 101 reptile species reported in both the legal and illegal international reptile leather trade, but the majority of the commercial trade in reptile skin products is produced from 11 reptile species (Table 10.1) (Jenkins and Broad, 1994). "Native craft" products, on the other hand, are produced from whatever reptile species can be easily obtained in the local area where these cottage industries occur, so there are many more reptile species involved in this largely unregulated component of the reptile skin trade. For example, Kundu drums (Figure 10.1) are manufactured by the aboriginal inhabitants of Papua New Guinea and sold to tourists. There are no factories in the jungles where these instruments are manufactured and the crafts people use local materials including the skins of goanna or monitor lizards that are generally not otherwise seen in the trade (Anon, 1987).

The kinds of products manufactured from reptile scales or skins can be divided into five categories: (1) the keratinous scutes or scales of sea turtles, mostly hawksbill (*Eretmochelys imbricata*), known as "tortoise shell" or "Bekko" that are generally manufactured into art objects, jewelry and personal items resembling plastic; (2) whole reptile skins, which are usually tanned in commercial facilities and sold to product manufacturers in other countries; (3) commercially manufactured leather goods such as footwear, handbags, clothing and jewelry; (4) whole animal taxidermy mounts that are usually positioned in an unrealistic or comical manner and sold as curios; and (5) "native craft" or cottage industry products such as curios, musical instruments, wallets and purses, which are manufactured from raw or primitively tanned skins. Each of these categories presents different challenges for the identification of the species used to manufacture a given product. Tortoise shell is manufactured from individual scales, so all of the features used to identify the species are lost other than the scale itself, and

Table 10.1 Eleven reptile species that make up nearly 85% of the international reptile skin trade.

Species	Common name
Tupinambis rufescens	Red Tegu
Tupinambis teguixin (=nigropunctatus)	Golden Tegu
Varanus niloticus	Nile Monitor
Varanus salvator	Water Monitor
Acrochordus granulatus	Wart Snake
Acrochordus javanicus	File Snake or Karung
Broghammerus (=Python) reticulatus	Reticulated Python
Ptyas mucosus	Oriental Ratsnake
Cerberus rhynchops	Dog-faced water snake
Homalopsis buccata	Puff-faced water snake
Caiman crocodilus	Common caiman

Source: Jenkins and Broad (1994).

Figure 10.1 Kundu drum from Papua New Guinea with the skin of a mangrove monitor (*Varanus indicus)* used as a drum head.

even then the shape of the scale, and thus its morphology, are greatly altered. Fortunately, there are primarily only two species of sea turtle used to manufacture tortoise shell products. Commercially tanned reptile skins retain a good amount of morphological information that can be used to identify the species from which the tanned skin came if the natural coloration and surface structure of the skin are retained. Unfortunately, a large percentage of the skins tanned for the commercial reptile skin trade are bleached and dyed dark colors that obscure or obliterate the natural color pattern of the skin, thereby making it difficult to identify the species (pers. observation, though, see Baker *et al.*, under review). Further, commercial tanneries often alter the surface of the skin by sanding, scraping or flattening it, thereby altering the scale morphology making species identification difficult to impossible (pers. observation). Commercially produced reptile leather products have the added disadvantage of having the entire skin reduced to small pieces, thereby making scale counts and other commonly used morphometric characteristics functionally impossible to obtain (Brazaitis, 1984, 1987, 1989; Baker, 2008). The identification of whole animal taxidermic mounts is a relatively simple task when compared with the identification of incomplete reptile skins and products, but the quality of work performed on such curios is often suspect, with inferior tanning techniques and body part substitutions that can obscure morphological features needed for identification. The chief problem in identifying native craft items, aside from the principal difficulties of identifying products manufactured from portions of a skin rather than a whole animal, is that these items are often manufactured from unusual species that are not generally seen in the commercial skin trade (pers. observation), so the knowledge and experience gained from identifying thousands of reticulated python products are of little value when trying to identify a novel species that is often associated with native craft items. The morphological characteristics discussed in this chapter can be used to identify whole reptile skins that retain their original coloration and morphology and can certainly be used to identify whole taxidermic mounts, but the focus of this chapter will be the identification of reptile skins that are incomplete, due to having been used to manufacture products or reptile skins that have been dyed or otherwise altered, thereby obscuring characteristics typically used for species identification.

Reptile Scale Morphology Basics and Current Limitations

The general morphology of reptile scales can be sub-divided into five general categories: scale outline, scale size and shape uniformity, scale topography, scale micro structure and scale arrangement. These categories are treated as independent characters, as two species of snake can have keeled scales; but those same two species can have very different scale shapes, and thus, the identification of a particular species using these characteristics is based on the totality of the traits in parallel rather than as a stepwise function so often found in standard taxonomic keys. The reason for this approach is due to the fact that thus far only about 72 of the 101 species occurring in the reptile skin trade have been examined for these features, and while several hundred individuals of each of the more common species have been examined thus far, some of the species examined have only been represented by a few individuals and this sampling only examines a small number of the diversity that is likely to be found within 9,285 known species of reptile. This uneven and ongoing sampling effort dictates that a fair amount of caution be exercised when using the data provided in this chapter to identify reptile products to species, especially when being held up to the scrutiny of a court of law. The one firm conclusion the work has provided thus far is that there is a considerable amount of variability with respect to these traits within and between individuals of a given species. This variability may at some point in the future be explained by geographic variability, which is one of the reasons this research effort is focusing on the examination of natural history museum specimens with known geographic origins. The identification methodology presented herein is very much a work-in-progress (Martin, 2010); and while at some point in the future this technique will likely produce sound, reliable results, at present, this methodology should only be used as a guide to species identification, which should then be confirmed using more traditional methods whenever possible.

Figure 10.2 Tanned skin of an African rock python (*Python sebae*) with lanceolate-shaped scales.

Scale outline

The scale outlines used in this technique are based on geometric descriptors of the scale shapes observed. The most common scale type for snakes is lanceolate or shaped like the head of a lance with a rounded base tapering to a broad point with the widest part of the scale being in the middle as can be seen in the *Python* sp. (Figure 10.2). Guttiform is a closely related water drop scale shape that has a narrower point owing to the widest part being the base of the scale. A rhomboid is a more straight-sided member of this class of scale shape where the sides of the scale are parallel and bilaterally symmetrical but of unequal length such that an upside-down kite shape is produced. An elongated form of this straight-sided scale shape where the sides are of more equal lengths is a diamond, and a horizontally wider than long shape resembling a diamond on its side is a rhombus. A rather long and narrow form of scale can be referred to as elongated, and a squared diamond shape with equal sides and angles is a quadrangular-shaped scale as commonly occurs on *Xenopeltis unicolor* (Figure 10.3). Scales, particularly those on the ventral surface of lizards and crocodiles can be square or rectangular in shape, and the dorsal scales of some Elapid species, and *Lapemis hardwickii* in particular, can be hexagonal in shape (Figure 10.4).

Uniformity of scale size and shape

The uniformity of scales can be evaluated based on the size of the scales in a given area or region such as a scale row, or it can be evaluated based on the similarity of scale shapes within a given region, or both. The ventral scutes and body scales of a water snake, for example, are quite different from each

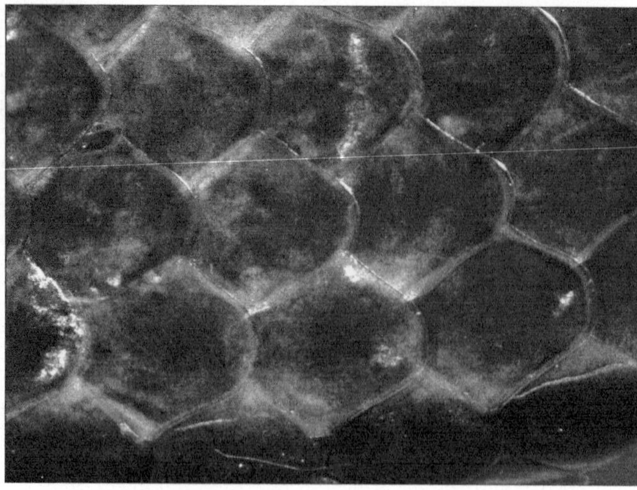

Figure 10.3 Flank scales of a preserved sunbeam snake (*Xenopeltis unicolor*, specimen No. CAS-241771) showing the transition from the ventral rhomboidal scales to the more quadrangular scales of the dorsum (see also Figure 10.18).

other, but regionally they are very uniform (Figure 10.5). The dorsal scales of a monitor lizard are comprised of relatively large shield scales that are surrounded with much smaller granular scales. The combination of large and very small scales may at first appear to be heterogeneous, but the underlying structure of relatively large shield scales with a consistent number of granula rows arranged

Figure 10.4 Hexagonal shaped scales of a Hardwicke's spine-bellied sea snake (*Lapemis hardwickii*, specimen No. CAS-23651). Note the central tubercle or spine on each scale that increases in size toward the ventral surface.

Figure 10.5 Transition between the enlarged belly scutes (bottom) and the keeled dorsal scales of a dog-faced water snake (*Cerberus rhynchops*, specimen No. CAS-222662). Note that the first longitudinal row of scales is smooth.

coroniform around the shield scale, which is in turn surrounded by triangular patches of granular scales, thereby forming a repeating hexagonal star pattern reminiscent of a trihexagonal tiling, would be considered a uniform repeating pattern (Figure 10.6). The first scale row of snakes is usually very different from the ventral scutes, but it is similar in size and shape to the other body scales. In many snake species, the first row or two of scales next to the ventral scutes

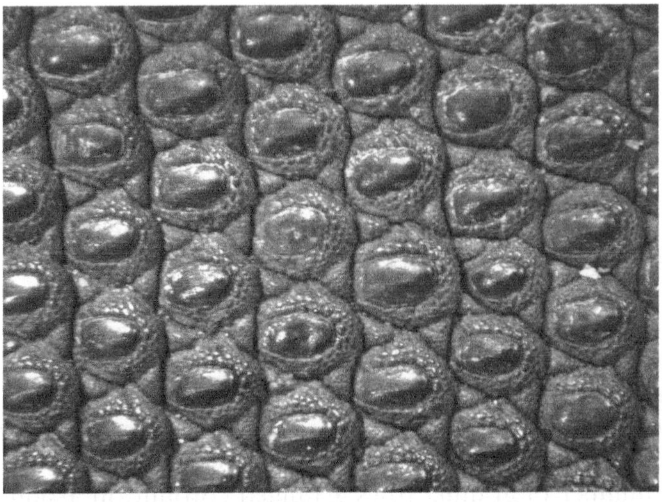

Figure 10.6 Trihexagonal tiling arrangement of the dorsal shield and granula scales of a Bengal monitor (*Varanus bengalensis*, specimen No. CAS-14960).

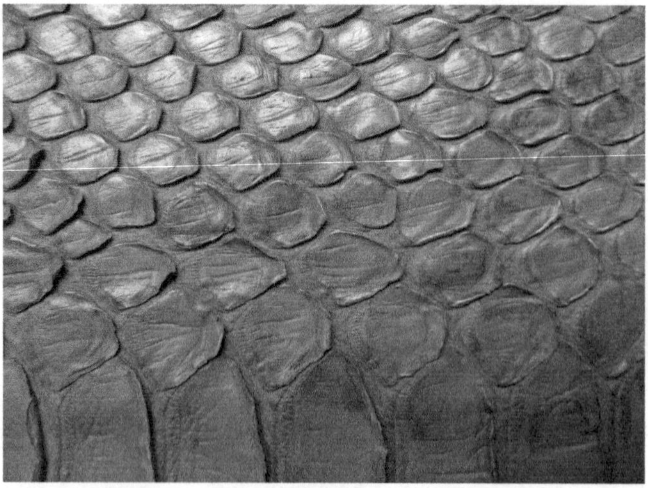

Figure 10.7 Transition between the enlarged belly scutes (bottom), and the lanceolate lateral scales of a green anaconda (*Eunectes murinus*). Note that the first and second longitudinal scale rows are enlarged and more rhomboidal than the lanceolate lateral scales above.

are very different from the other body scales. This difference is noted as the row position of the variable scales followed by a description as to how the lateral body scales are different. For example, the first two rows of body scales next to the scutes of the green anaconda (*Eunectes murinus*) are larger than the rest of the body scales (Figure 10.7), so the position of the rows is recorded followed by a description as to how those scales are different, which is in this case that the scales are about as wide as they are long (1-2nd Enlarged W=L).

Scale topography and micro-structure

The topography of the scale is simply a description of the surface structure of the scale. Scales can be smooth or plate-like, keeled or have any number of spines, or tubercles, protruding from the surface. These features can be quite distinctive as are those of the *Lapemis hardwickii* in Figure 10.4. The micro-topography of reptile scales has great promise for use in species identification. Several recent studies have shown unique micro- and macro-structures on the scale surfaces of several different reptile species (Ananjeva *et al.*, 1991; Hazel *et al.*, 1999; Gower, 2003; Avolio *et al.*, 2006; Berthe *et al.*, 2009; Rocha-Barbosa and Moraes e Silva, 2009; Klein *et al.*, 2010). Fuchs and Fuchs (2003) have suggested that the number and arrangement of the small granula scales found on monitor lizard skin may be very diagnostic of species. The description notation scheme used here is the range of the number of granula rows arranged coroniform around each shield scale on each region of the body followed by the number of granula rows that may be found on the distal convex fringe of the ventral scales. The character table (Table 10.2) provides this second set of values for the convex fringe, or CF, after the CF symbol under the ventral scale column of the granular scale row section. For instance, for *Varanus flavescens*, the table reads 1-2 CF 1-3, which translates to 1 to 2 granula rows coroniform around each ventral scale, and the convex fringe of the belly scales should have an additional 1 to 3 rows of granula along the posterior edge. If this observation holds up under further scrutiny, and especially after the nomenclatural problems with the taxonomy have been worked out and the data adjusted appropriately, this could be a very useful tool for reptile species identification. Further, some of the snake scales photographed during this research show a surprising amount of microstructure even under the relatively low power being used for this research thus far (Figure 10.8).

Scale arrangement

The scales of reptiles can be arranged with an imbricate pattern (Figure 10.8) where the scales alternate and overlap like roof tiles, a juxtaposed pattern (Figure 10.4) where the scales are placed side by side, or in an oblique collar-like arrangement as is found with cobras (*Naja sp.*) (Figure 10.9). The table of snake characteristics (Table 10.3) lists the arrangement of the scales on the ventral, lateral and dorsal surface of each of the species examined during this study.

Scale projection

The percentage of the projecting part of the scale in relation to the total length of the scale as reported by Fuchs and Fuchs (2003) is provided in Table 10.3 as an addendum to the information collected for this study. In hindsight, this morphological characteristic appears to be helpful in distinguishing between some snake species, so scale projection data will be collected as part of this study in the future.

Scale transition

The pattern of scale transition from ventral scale or scute to lateral body scales is recorded in the last column of both the lizard table (Table 10.2) and the snake table (Table 10.3). On the lizard table, the transition is recorded as a ratio of the number of dorsal transverse scale rows emerging from a single ventral scale row. The transition information collected for snake species is a little more complicated as it records the number of scale rows illustrating a configuration change in size, shape and number of longitudinal scale rows impacted by this change.

Table 10.2 Scale morphology of lizard species commonly occurring in the international reptile skin trade.

		CITES	Scale (Shield) Outline				Scale Size Shape Uniformity			
Species	Common Name	App.	Vent.	Lat.	Dorsal	Tail	Vent.	Lat.	Dorsal	Tail
Family Iguanidae	Iguanas									
Iguana iguana	Common Green		OP	OP	OP	OP	UN	UN	UN	UN
Family Teiida	Tegus									
Dracaena guianensis	Guyana Caiman Lizard	II	RT	O/IG	O/IG	RT	UN	Med /Sm	Lg/ Med	V
Dracaena paraguayensis	Paraguay Caiman Lizard	II	RT	O/IG	O/IG	RT	UN	Med /Sm	Lg/ Med	V
Tupinambis merianae	Black & White	II	RT	R	R-O	R-RT	UN	UN	UN	UN
Tupinambis rufescens	Red	II	RT	R	R-O	R-RT	UN	UN	UN	UN
Tupinambis teguixin (=nigropunctatus)	Golden	II	RT	R	R-O	R-RT	UN	UN	UN	UN
Family Helodermatidae	Gila Monsters									
Heloderma horridum	Beaded Lizard	I&II	R-S	R-O	R		UN	UN	UN	
Heloderma suspectum	Gila Monster	II	R-S	R-O	R	R-S	UN	UN	UN	UN
Family Varanidae	Monitor Lizards									
Varanus albigularis	White-throated	II	U	O	O		RP	RP	RP	
Varanus bengalensis	Bengal	I*	U	O	O	U	RP	RP	RP	RP
Varanus exanthematicus	Savannah	II	U	O	O	O-U	RP	RP	RP	RP
Varanus flavescens	Yellow	I*	U	O	E-O	U	RP	RP	RP	RP
Varanus griseus	Desert	I*	U	O	O-G	O-U	RP	RP	RP	RP
Varanus indicus	Mangrove	II	R-U	R	R	U	RP	RP	RP	RP
Varanus niloticus	Nile	II	U	O	O	U	RP	RP	RP	RP
Varanus salvator	Water	II	U	O	O-E	U	RP	RP	RP	RP

Data sources: ‡Fuchs and Fuchs, 2003
*Listed as Endangered under US ESA.
CF-Convex Fringe, D-Domed, E-Elongated, IG-Irregular, IMB-Imbricate, JUX-Juxtaposed, K-Keel, Lat.-Lateral, O-Oval, OP-Oblique Parallelogram, OV-Overlap, PL-Plate, PRE-Posterior Row Edge, R-Round, RP-Repeated Pattern, RT-Rectangle, S-Square, ST-Strongly, TH-Trihexagonal, WK-Weakly, U-U-Shaped, UN-Uniform, V-Variable, Vent.-Ventral.

Scale Topography		Scale Topography		Granular Scale Rows			Scale Gland Pores				Scale Arrangement				Scale Trans.
Vent.	Lat.	Dorsal	Tail	Vent.	Lat.	Dorsal	Vent.	Lat.	Dorsal	Tail	Vent.	Lat.	Dorsal	Tail	
Raised Edge	Raised Edge	Raised Edge	K	0	0	0	0-4 V	0-4 V	0-1 V	1-3 V	JUX	JUX	JUX		Gradual
Faint-K	Faint-K	K	K	PRE	PRE	PRE	0	0	0	0	JUX	JUX	JUX	JUX	1:0-3
Faint-K	Faint-K	K	K	PRE	PRE	PRE	0	0	0	0	JUX	JUX	JUX	JUX	1:0-3
PL	PL	D		PRE	0	0	0	0	0	0	JUX	JUX	JUX	OV	1:3-4
PL	PL	D	K	PRE	0	0	0	0	0	0	JUX	JUX	JUX	OV	1:3-5
PL	PL	D	K	PRE	0	0	0	0	0	0	JUX	JUX	JUX	OV	1:3-5
PL	D	Dimpled		0	0	0	0				Slight IMB	JUX	JUX		
PL	D	D	D	0	0	0	0				Slight IMB	JUX	JUX	Slight-OV	
PL	PL	PL		1-2 CF 1-3‡	3-5‡	2-5‡	1‡	1‡	1‡		JUX	WK-TH	WK-TH		1:1-2
WK-K	WK-K	7-10 K	WK-K	0 CF 2-3‡	3-5‡	3-5‡	1-3‡	1-2 V‡	1-2 V‡	1	JUX	TH	TH	RP	1:1-2
PL	Faint-K	WK-K	K	1 CF 3-4‡	3-4‡	3-5‡	1‡	1‡	1‡	1	JUX	TH	TH	RP	1:1-2
Faint-K	WK-K	K	K	1-2 CF 1-3‡	3-5‡	3-5‡	1-2 V‡	1-2 V‡	1-3‡	1-3	JUX	WK-TH	WK-TH	JUX	1:1-2
Faint-K	WK-K	K	K	0-1 CF 1-3‡	3-4‡	2-4‡	1-2‡	1-3 V‡	1-2 V‡	1-4	JUX	TH	TH	JUX	1:1-3
Faint-K	WK-K	WK-K	K	0-1 CF 1-3	1-3	2-5	1-2	1-2	1-4 V	0-11	JUX	JUX	RP	JUX	1:1
ST-K	K	ST-K	K	0 CF 2-4‡	2-4‡	3-4‡	1-3‡	1-5 V‡	1-3‡	0-4V	JUX	TH	TH	JUX	1:1-2
WK-K	Faint-K	ST-K	K	0 CF 1-3‡	3-6‡	3-6‡	1-2‡	1-3‡	1-4‡	1-2	JUX	TH	TH	JUX	1:1-2

Figure 10.8 Keeled dorsal scale of a dog-faced water snake (*Cerberus rhynchops*, specimen No. CAS-222662) showing the micro-structure of the scale surface.

Identifying Features of Major Reptile Groups

Sea turtles: Cheloniidae

Tortoise shell The visual appeal of the speckled amber and brown scutes of Hawksbill sea turtles (*Eretmochelys imbricata*), and more recently the scutes of the green sea turtle (*Chelonia mydas*), coupled with the utilitarian properties of this natural plastic-like material has resulted in the commercial

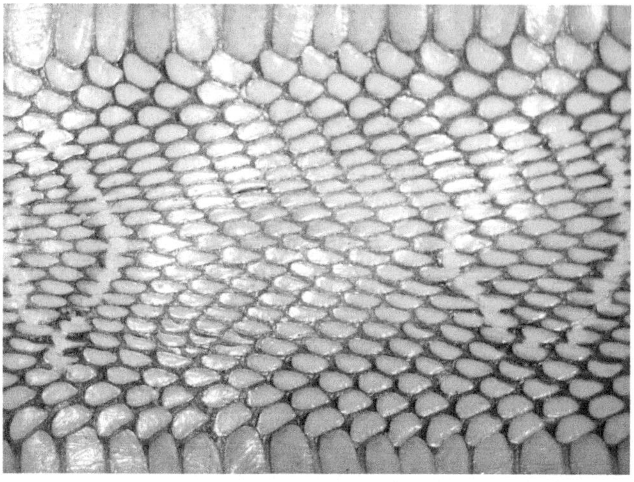

Figure 10.9 Guttiform scales of a cobra (*Naja* spp.) arranged in a collar-like chevron. Note how the scales become more oblique and elongated toward the vertebral line.

exploitation of this species for centuries (Espinoza *et al.*, 2007). Tortoise shell has a unique appearance and can be easily differentiated from other reptile products even when worked into relatively small products (Figure 10.10) because there are only two reptile species that are suitable for the manufacturing of such products, and the products manufactured from these two species are very different in color from one another. The increasing rarity and subsequent restriction of trade in this Endangered and CITES-listed species have led to the replacement of "tortoise shell" products with various natural and man-made materials such as horn sheaths, celluloids and in the past few decades, plastics that superficially appear quite similar to sea turtle scutes. However, products manufactured from sea turtle scutes persist in the wildlife trade, thereby requiring forensic methods to differentiate between natural "tortoise shell," horn sheaths and other man-made replacement materials such as petroleum-based plastics. Morphological methods for distinguishing these materials have been known for some time (O'Connor, 1987; Colbert *et al.*, 1999; Hainschwang and Leggio, 2006), but recent advancements in the use of spectroscopy and discriminant analysis have provided a powerful quantitative tool for differentiating tortoise shell from other biological and non-biological substances with similar properties (Espinoza *et al.*, 2007).

Leather Glossy sea turtle leather is often sold as, or mistaken for, crocodile skin, but the difference between crocodile skin and sea turtle leather, which generally comes from the flipper skin of *Eretmochelys imbricate* and/or *Lepidochelys olivacea*, is that sea turtle leather has randomly shaped angular scales of various sizes in close proximity to one another and areas of skin displaying a spider web type pattern (Figure 10.11; Bour, 1985). Crocodile or alligator skin, on the other hand, has a pattern of regularly arranged square, rectangular or round-oval scales.

Lizards: Sauria

Lizard skin leather can be distinguished from that of the other major reptile groups based on the relatively large number of small dorsal and ventral scales, with the ventral scales arranged in transverse rows of predominantly juxtaposed scales. The single enlarged ventral scutes coupled with the imbricate arrangement of the dorsal scales of most snake species provide a clear way of differentiating most members of these two groups. Lizard skin can be differentiated from crocodilian skin based on the relative size difference between both scale and skin sizes. Further, the scales of crocodilians are mostly square or rectangular, interspersed with round or oval scales of various sizes on the lateral and dorsal surfaces of some crocodilian species. The only lizard to come close to this configuration is the aptly named caiman lizard (*Dracaena* sp.) that is much smaller in overall scale and body size than most commercially produced crocodilian skins. Differentiating between the major lizard groups occurring in the international

Table 10.3 Scale morphology of snake species commonly occurring in the international reptile skin trade.

Species	Common Name	CITES App.	No. Scale Rows	Scale Outline		
				Vent.	Lat.	Dorsal
Family Acrochordidae	File Snakes					
Acrochordus granulatus	Wart Snake		93-112+	Fold Only	O	Arbelos
Acrochordus javanicus	File Snake or Karung		119-153‡	Fold Only	O	Arbelos
Family Xenopeltidae	Sunbeam Snakes					
Xenopeltis unicolor	Sunbeam Snake		13-15‡	W	ROM	QDA
Family Pythonidae	Pythons					
Broghammerus (=Python) reticulatus	Reticulated	II	69-83‡	W	ROM	DIM
Python curtus	Blood	II	51-58‡	Med	R-ROB	QDA
Python (molurus) bivittatus	Burmese	II	60-76‡	W	LAN	QDA
Python molurus (molurus)	Indian	I*	60-76‡	W	LAN	QDA
Python regius	Ball or Royal	II	51-56‡	Med	LAN	QDA
Python sebae	African Rock	II	71-93‡	W	LAN	LAN
Family Boidae	Boas					
Boa constrictor constrictor	Common	II	79-95‡	W	LAN	QDA
Boa constrictor occidentalis	Argentine	I	65-87‡	W	LAN	QDA
Eunectes murinus	Green Anaconda	II	56-86‡	Med	LAN	QDA
Eunectes notaeus	Yellow Anaconda	II	45-52‡	Med	LAN	QDA
Family Colubridae						
Subfamily Colubrinae	Colubrids					
Boiga dendrophila	Mangrove Snake		21-23‡	W	LAN-TRP	CNT-HEX
Dinodon rufozonatum	Red-banded Snake		15-17‡	W	LAN	LAN-DIM
Elaphe (=Coelognathus) radiatus (=radiata)	Radiated Ratsnake		17-19‡	W	LAN	LAN
Euprepiophis (=Elaphe) mandarinus	Mandarin Ratsnake		19-25‡	W	LAN	LAN
Orthriophis (=Elaphe) taeniurus (=taeniura)	Beauty Snake		23-25‡	W	E-LAN	LAN
Ptyas carinata (=carinatus)	Keeled Rat Snake		16-18‡	W	E-LAN	E-LAN

Scale Size Shape Uniformity			Scale Topography			Scale Arrangement			Scale Projection‡		Scale Transition
Vent.	Lat.	Dorsal	Vent.	Lat.	Dorsal	Vent.	Lat.	Dorsal	Lat.	Dorsal	
UN	UN	UN	Spinous	Spinous-K	Anchor-Shaped K		JUX	JUX		none	Lat<Dorsal
UN	UN	UN	Spinous	Spinous-K	Anchor-Shaped K		JUX	JUX		none	Lat<Dorsal
UN	1st W>L	Lat.> Dorsal	SM	SM	SM	OV	JUX	JUX		13-17%	1st EN-ROB
UN	1-3rd W>L	Lat.> Dorsal	SM	SM	SM	OV	IMB	IMB		15-20%	1st Cycloid ≫2>3
UN	1-3rd W>L	Lat.> Dorsal	SM	SM	SM	OV	IMB	IMB		19-21%	1st Cycloid ≫2>3
UN	1-3rd W>L	Lat.> Dorsal	SM	SM	SM	OV	IMB	IMB		14-20%	1st Semicircular >2>3
UN	1-3rd W>L	Lat.> Dorsal	SM	SM	SM	OV	IMB	IMB		14-20%	1st Semicircular >2>3
UN	1-3rd W>L	Lat.> Dorsal	SM	SM	SM	OV	IMB	IMB		6.5-8.5%	1st Semicircular ≫2>3
UN	1-3rd W>L	Lat.> Dorsal	SM	SM	SM	OV	IMB	IMB		12-17%	1st Cycloid >2>3
UN	1-2nd EN, W=L	Lat.> Dorsal	SM	SM	SM	OV	IMB	IMB		6.3-13.5%	1st TRP>2
UN	1-2nd EN, W=L	Lat.> Dorsal	SM	SM	SM	OV	IMB	IMB		7.1-13.9%	1st TRP>2
UN	1-2nd EN, W=L	Lat.≥ Dorsal	SM	SM	SM	OV	IMB	IMB		25-30%	1st ROM>2 LAN
UN	1-2nd EN, W=L	Lat.≥ Dorsal	SM	SM	SM	OV	IMB	IMB		10-24%	1st ROM≥ 2 ROM
UN	UN	Lat.≥ Dorsal	SM	SM	SM	OV	IMB	Vert. JUX	4-8%	1-4%	1=2=3
UN	UN	UN	SM	SM	SM	OV	IMB	IMB		7-14.2%	1=2=3
UN	UN	UN	SM	Post. WK-K	4-6 Vert. K	OV	IMB	IMB	11-15%	5-7%	1=2=3
UN	UN	UN	SM	SM	SM	OV	IMB	IMB	11.5-16.5	5.1-5.9%	1=2=3
UN	UN	UN	SM	1-3rd SM	Ant-SM Post-K	OV	IMB	IMB		7.8-12.8%	1=2=3
UN	1-2nd EN	UN	SM	ST K	ST-K	OV	IMB	IMB		10-14.5%	1≥2=3

(Continued)

Table 10.3 (*Continued*)

Species	Common Name	CITES App.	No. Scale Rows	Scale Outline		
				Vent.	Lat.	Dorsal
Ptyas (=Zaocys) dhumnades	Big-Eye Snake		14-16‡	W	LAN	LAN
Ptyas korros	Indo-Chinese Rat Snake		13-15‡	W	1-2nd R-LAN	LAN
Ptyas mucosus	Oriental Ratsnake	II	16-17‡	W	Ant.-G Post.- QDA	Ant.-G Post.-DIM
Rhadinophis (=Elaphe) prasina (=prasinus)	Green Trinket Snake					
Subfamily Dipsadinae						
Hydrodynastes (=Cyclagras) gigas	False Water Cobra	II	18-20‡	W	O-LAN	LAN
Subfamily Natricinae	Water Snakes					
Atretium schistosum	Olive keelback wart snake				Not Studied	
Rhabdophis (=Natrix) subminiatus (=subminiata)	Red-necked Keelback				Not Studied	
Sinonatrix annularis	Ringed		17-19‡	W	R ROB	LAN
Xenochrophis (=Natrix) piscator	Asiatic	III	17-19‡	W	R ROM	LAN
Family Elapidae						
Subfamily Elapinae	Cobras, Coral Snakes					
Bungarus candidus	Blue Krait				Not Studied	
Bungarus fasciatus	Banded Krait		15‡	W	LAN-TRP	LAN, Vert.-HEX
Bungarus multicinctus	Many-banded Krait		15‡	W	LAN, 1-2nd W=L	LAN, Vert.-HEX
Naja spp.	Chinese Cobra	II	20-26‡	W	G	G to E
Ophiophagus hannah	King Cobra	II	17-19‡	W	G	G to E
Subfamily Hydrophiinae	Sea Snakes					
Acalyptophis peronii	Spiny-headed		21-31+	Narrow	ROM-QDA	QDA
Aipysurus duboisii	Reef shallows		19‡	Med, Post Notch	ROM-QDA	QDA
Aipysurus eydouxii	Spine-tailed		17‡	Med	LAN≥R	LAN≥R

Scale Size Shape Uniformity			Scale Topography			Scale Arrangement			Scale Projection‡		Scale Transition
Vent.	Lat.	Dorsal	Vent.	Lat.	Dorsal	Vent.	Lat.	Dorsal	Lat.	Dorsal	
UN	1st EN	UN	SM	SM	2 Vert. ST-K	OV	IMB	IMB		8-13%	1>2=3
UN	1st EN	UN	SM	1-2nd SM	SM	OV	IMB	IMB		6-10%	1≥2=3
UN	1st Slightly EN	UN	SM	SM	Ant-SM Post-K	OV	IMB	IMB		4.8-8.6%	1≥2=3
UN	UN	Lat.> Dorsal	SM	SM	SM	OV	IMB	IMB		16.8-24.6%	1>2≥3=4
UN	1-2nd EN	UN	SM	1-2nd SM	10-12 Vert. ST-K, Rest WK-K	OV	IMB	IMB		9-14%	1>2>3≥4
UN	1-2nd EN	UN	SM	1-2nd SM	Slightly K	OV	IMB	IMB	17-20%	7-12%	1>2>3=4
UN	W> Spine=E & askew	Vert. row HEX, W>L	SM	SM	SM but Vert. Ridged	OV	IMB	Vert. OV		7.3-9.2%	1>2≥3=4
UN	W> Spine=E & slight-askew	Vert. row HEX, W>L	SM	SM	SM	OV	IMB	Vert. OV		6.9-8.8%	1>2≥ 3=4
UN	1st base PRD	W> Spine =E	SM	SM	SM	OV	OB	OB		4-7%	W 1>2>3>4, L~=
UN	1st base PRD	W> Spine =E	SM	SM	SM	OV	OB	OB	2.6-6.8%	7.5-10.8%	W 1> 2>3>4, L~=
UN	UN	UN	Semi-Divided	Short CNT Spinous-K	Short CNT Spinous-K		Ant-WK-IMB, Post-JUX	Ant-WK-IMB, Post-JUX		6.7-12.8%	1=2=3
UN	UN	UN	SM	SM	Slight K or Series of TUBs	OV	IMB	IMB		8.5-18%	1=2=3
UN	UN	UN	WK CNT-K	SM	SM	OV	IMB	IMB		12.5-19.5%	1≥2=3

(Continued)

Table 10.3 (*Continued*)

Species	Common Name	CITES App.	No. Scale Rows	Scale Outline Vent.	Scale Outline Lat.	Scale Outline Dorsal
Aipysurus laevis	Olive-brown		21-25‡	Med	QDA	QDA-ROM
Chitulia (=Hydrophis) belcheri	Faint-banded		34+	Not Studied		
Chitulia (=Hydrophis) inornata (=inornatus)	Plain		35-48+	Sm-HEX	LAN	LAN
Chitulia (=Hydrophis) ornata (=ornatus)	Ornate Reef		39-59+	Sm-2XW Body	HEX	HEX
Disteira (=Hydrophis) major	Olive-headed		37-43‡	Narrow	LAN	LAN
Disteira (=Astrotia) stokesii	Stoke's		46-63+	Paired-E	LAN≥R	LAN≥R
Lapemis hardwickii	Hardwicke's spine-bellied		23-45+	Narrow-HEX	HEX	HEX Muffin
Leioselasma (=Hydrophis) cyanocincta (=cyanocinctus)	Annulated		35-43‡	Narrow-HEX	QDA	HEX
Leioselasma (=Hydrophis) elegans	Elegant or bar-bellied		37-49‡	Narrow-HEX	DIM	DIM
Pseudolaticauda (=Laticauda) semifasciata	Chinese		21-23‡	Med	QDA	QDA
Subfamily Laticaudinae	Sea Kraits					
Laticauda colubrina	yellow-lipped		21-25‡	W	QDA	LAN
Laticauda laticaudata	blue-lipped		19‡	W	QDA	QDA
Family Homalopsidae	Water Snakes					
Cerberus rhynchops	Dog-faced	III	23-25+	W	LAN	LAN
Enhydris bocourti	Bocourt's		27-29‡	W	QDA	LAN
Enhydris chinensis	Chinese		19-23‡	W	QDA	LAN
Enhydris enhydris	Rainbow			Not Studied		
Homalopsis buccata	Puff-faced		43-47‡	W	LAN	LAN-E
Family Viperidae						
Subfamily Crotalinae	Pit Vipers					
Calloselasma (=Agkistrodon) rhodostoma	Malayan			Not Studied		
Crotalus durissus	Cascabel Rattlesnake	III	27-29‡	W	LAN	E
Rhinocerophis (=Bothrops) alternatus	Urutu		29-35‡	W	LAN	E
Subfamily Viperinae	Vipers					
Daboia (=Vipera) russelii	Russel's	III	27-33‡	W	LAN	E

Data sources: ‡Fuchs and Fuchs, 2003; +Cogger, 1992.
*Listed as Endangered under US ESA
Ant.-Anterior, CNT-Central, DIM-Diamond, E-Elongated, EN-Enlarged, G-Guttiform, HEX- Hexagonal, IMB-Imbricate, JUX-Juxtaposed, K-Keel, L-Long, LAN-Lanceolate, Lat-Lateral, O-Oval, OB-Obliquely, OV-Overlap, Post.-Posterior, PRD-Protrude toward scute, QDA-Quadrangular, R-Round, ROB-Rhombus, ROM-Rhomboidal, SM-Smooth, ST-Strongly, TRP-Trapezium, TUB-Tubercle, UN-Uniform, Vent-Ventral, Vert-Vertebral, W-Wide, WK-Weakly.

Scale Size Shape Uniformity			Scale Topography			Scale Arrangement			Scale Projection‡		Scale Transition
Vent.	Lat.	Dorsal	Vent.	Lat.	Dorsal	Vent.	Lat.	Dorsal	Lat.	Dorsal	
UN	UN	UN	WK CNT-K, Post-notch	SM	SM	OV	IMB	IMB		11.5-16.5%	1=2=3
UN	1st Narrow	UN	Paired Short K	1-2 Short K	CNT TUB	Barely OV	SubIMB	SubIMB			1<2=3
UN	UN	UN	SM	CNT TUB	Short K/TUB	Barely OV	SubIMB	JUX		2.5-3.5%	1=2=3
UN	UN	UN	SM	SM	WK-K	OV	WK-IMB	WK-IMB		7-15%	1=2=3
UN	UN	UN	K	1-2 Spines =K	1-2 Spines =K	OV, K	ST-IMB	ST-IMB		17-29%	1<2=3
UN	UN	Lat.> Dorsal	1-2 Short TUBs	CNT Spine	CNT TUB	JUX	JUX	JUX		none	1≥2≥3
UN	UN	UN	Paired Spines	SM-WK Med. Spine	17 Vert., 1-2 Spines ea=K	OV	JUX	IMB		10-15%	1=2=3
UN	UN	UN	SM	SM	Short K	OV	WK-IMB	WK-IMB	3.8-4.7%	8.5-9.8%	1=2=3
UN	UN	UN	SM	SM	SM	OV	IMB	IMB		16-24%	1=2=3
UN	UN	UN	SM	Pitted, CNT Depressed	Pitted, CNT De-pressed	OV	IMB	IMB		13-18%	1=2=3
UN	UN	UN	SM	SM	SM	OV	IMB	IMB		16-20%	1=2=3
UN	UN	UN	SM	1st SM, rest WK-Med K	ST-K	OV	IMB	IMB	15.5-26.5%	5.5-12.5%	1≥2=3
UN	UN	Lat.> Dorsal	SM	SM	SM	SubIMB	JUX	JUX	13.2-16.3%	9.8-11.4%	1=2=3
UN	1 Row W=L	Lat.> Dorsal	SM	SM	SM	OV	WK-IMB	WK-IMB		7-13.5%	1≥2=3
UN	1 Row W=L	Lat.> Dorsal	SM	1-4th SM	WK-ST K	OV	IMB	IMB		7-11.5%	1≥2=3
UN	1 Row W=L	Lat.> Dorsal	SM	1st SM, 2-3rd WK K	ST-K	OV	IMB	IMB	15.7-28.8%	7.9-12.7%	1>2≥ 3=4
UN	1 Row W=L	Lat.> Dorsal	SM	1st SM, Rest K	ST-K	OV	IMB	IMB		21.5-46.5%	1>2≥ 3=4
UN	1 Row W=L	Lat.> Dorsal	SM	1st SM, 2nd WK-K, Rest K	ST-K	OV		IMB	17-28%		1>2≥ 3=4

Figure 10.10 "Tortoise shell" hair comb carved from the carapace scale of a hawksbill sea turtle (*Eretmochelys imbricata*).

reptile skin trade can be accomplished by comparing the ventral to dorsal scale transition ratios in the last column of Table 10.2.

Iguanidae The Iguanids are a relatively poorly represented group in the reptile skin trade owing largely to the poor quality products that are produced from the inferior leather manufactured from their skin (Jenkins and Broad, 1994).

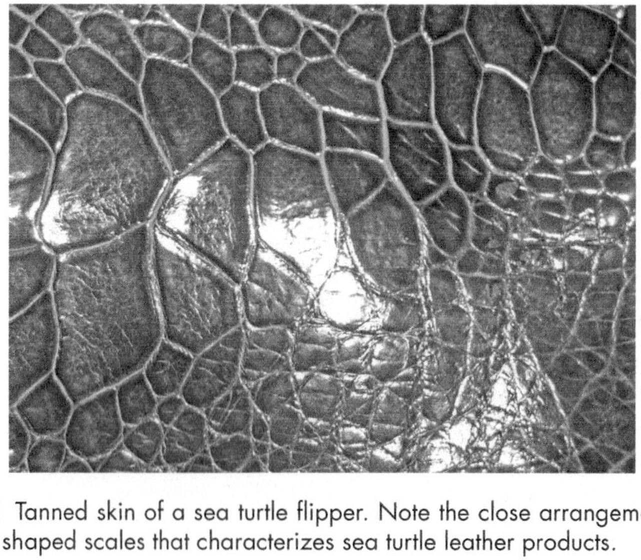

Figure 10.11 Tanned skin of a sea turtle flipper. Note the close arrangement of variously sized irregular shaped scales that characterizes sea turtle leather products.

Figure 10.12 Oblique parallelogram shaped scales of the common green iguana (*Iguana iguana,* specimen No. CAS-97996). Note the upturned distal edge that gives the skin a sandpaper-like feel when rubbed.

The scales of the dorsal, lateral and ventral skin surfaces of Iguanids is largely covered with small oblique-parallelogram scales with a posterior lifted edge that give the feel of sandpaper when rubbed (Figure 10.12). The combination of scale shape and texture is unique among the reptiles commonly exploited in the reptile skin trade.

Teiidae There are two Teiid genera that feature prominently in the reptile skin trade, and they are the caiman lizards (*Dracaena* sp.) and the tegus (*Tupinambis* sp). The dorsal surface of *Dracaena* has unique oval keeled scales on the dorsal surface whereas the dorsal surface of *Tupinambis* is dominated by uniform, small plate-like scales. The ventral surface of both genera are superficially similar, but a closer examination of the transition zone between ventral and dorsal scales reveals each ventral scale row of *Tupinambis* gives rise to three to five dorsal scale rows in a zone where the ventral scales taper to a point and the resulting space is taken up by the dorsal scale rows in a step-like fashion (Figure 10.13). The transition of *Dracaena*, on the other hand, results in an inconsistent pattern where ventral scale rows give rise to two to three dorsal scale rows or alternatively are cut off by adjacent scale rows thereby halting the transition from ventral to dorsal transverse scale rows (Figure 10.14).

Helodermatidae The Helodermatids are only rarely seen in the reptile leather trade as native craft items from Mexico. The skin is characterized by highly domed scales that appear to be dimpled in older individuals (Figure 10.15). The background surrounding each of these scales gives the appearance of skin as opposed to the granular scales observed in Varanids.

Figure 10.13 Transition zone between the rectangular plate-like belly scales and the round lateral scales of a red tegu (*Tupinambis rufescens*, specimen No. CAS-49410). Note how each transverse belly scale row gives rise to three to five dorsal scale rows in a tapering step-like transition.

Varanidae The Varanid lizards are quite a diverse group that, within the 26 species examined thus far, all share a basic scale structure of shield scales surrounded by smaller granular scales represented in Table 10.2. The Varanids can be distinguished from the Teiids by the transition from a ventral transverse scale row into one or two dorsal scale rows without tapering or cutting off the row

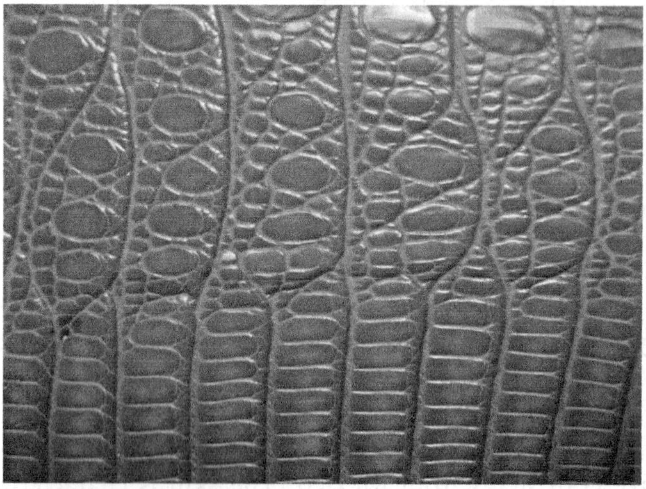

Figure 10.14 Transition zone between the rectangular plate-like belly scales and the irregular and oval scales of the lateral surface of a caiman lizard (*Dracaena* spp.). Note how each transverse belly scale row is either cut off or gives rise to one to three dorsal scale rows.

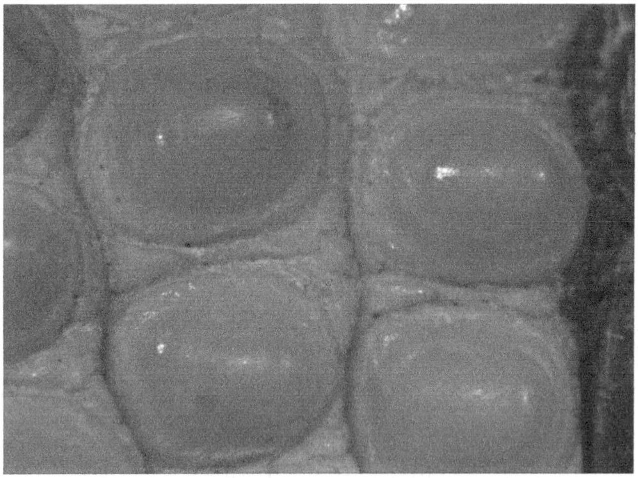

Figure 10.15 Highly domed dorsal scales of a gila monster (*Heloderma suspectum*, specimen No. CAS-115886).

as seen in the other two major lizard groups (Figure 10.16). Differentiation of Varanid species may be possible based on the macro- and micro-morphology of Varanid skin (see Andres *et al.*, 1999; Fuchs and Fuchs, 2003) at some point in the near future, but some technical challenges concerning the variation between stretched hide products and most natural history specimens preserved in a more natural state, which have known locality data and verifiable taxonomic status, will need to be addressed before real progress can be made.

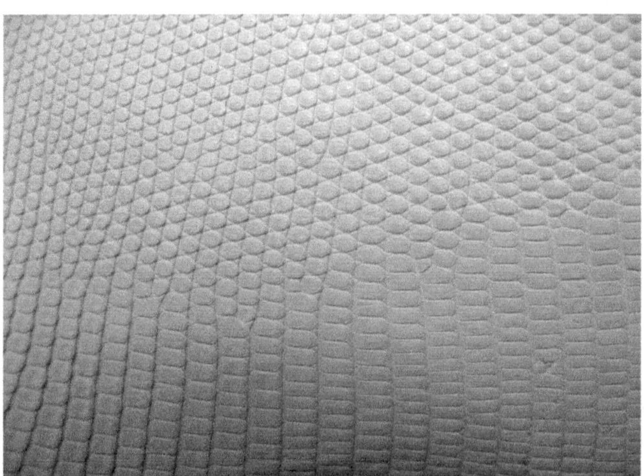

Figure 10.16 Transition zone between the rectangular belly scales and the trihexagonal arrangement of the dorsal scales of a desert monitor (*Varanus griseus*). Note how each transverse belly scale row gives rise to one to three dorsal scale rows by division.

Snakes: Ophidia

As already pointed out, most snake groups can be easily differentiated from lizards based on their general scale morphology, but the not-so-similar differences in scale morphology between snake families can also be used to easily differentiate between snake families, genera and in some cases even species without the use of skin color patterns or scale counts.

Acrochordidae The file snakes are easily differentiated from all other snake families examined thus far based on the arbelos shape of the dorsal scales combined with the raised distal edge of the scale and the central tuberculate keel forming an anchor-shaped structure on the surface of the scale (Figure 10.17).

Xenopeltidae This snake genus can be distinguished by the relatively large smooth quadrangular scales that tend to retain some portion of their iridescence even when tanned (Figure 10.18).

Pythonidae The Pythonids can be distinguished from the Boids of similar appearance based on the shape and relative width of the scales in the first three longitudinal scale rows on either side of the ventral scutes (Figure 10.19). The first scale row is much larger than the enlarged second and third scale rows, but the first row is much wider than long, and all three rows are semicircular or cycloid in shape. The reticulated python (*Broghammerus reticulates*) stands out within the group based on the diamond-shaped imbricate to nearly juxtaposed

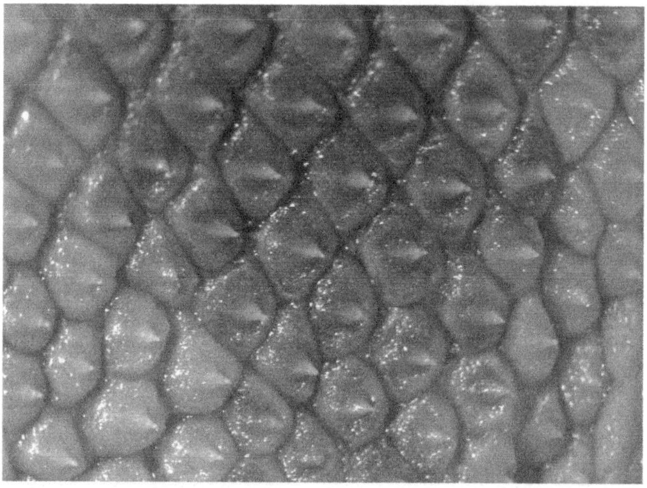

Figure 10.17 Arbelos shaped dorsal scales of a wart snake (*Acrochordus granulates*, specimen No. CAS-23691). The raised distal edge of the scale combined with the central turberculate keel appear as an anchor shape in tanned skins.

Figure 10.18 Purse panel manufactured from the tanned skin of a sunbeam snake (*Xenopeltis unicolor*). Note the quadrangular shape of the dorsal scales.

dorsal scales. There are indications that several of the Python species may be able to be differentiated once a larger sample size can be studied.

Boidae The Boids can be differentiated from the Pythonids based on the relative size and shape of the first three longitudinal scale rows on either side of the ventral scutes (Figure 10.20). The enlarged first scale row in Boids is in the shape of a

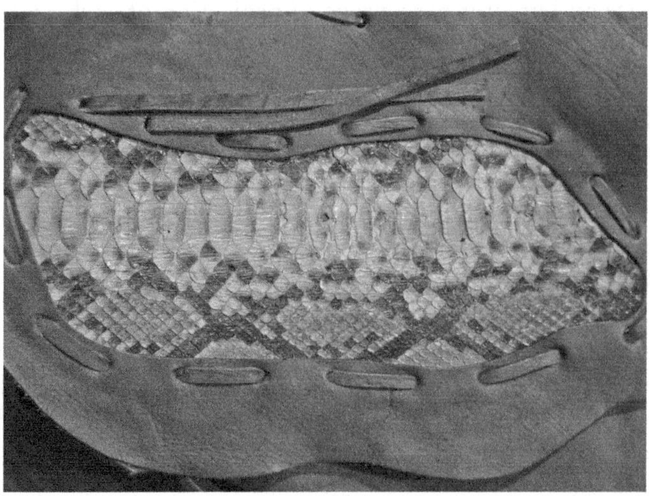

Figure 10.19 Purse panel manufactured from the tanned skin of a reticulated python (*Broghammerus reticulates*). Note the first three transverse scale rows are enlarged and cycloid-shaped relative to the more lanceolate scales of the lateral surface.

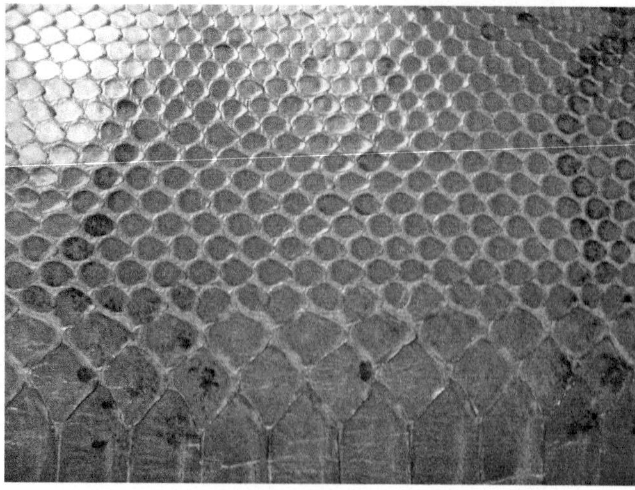

Figure 10.20 Transition zone between the belly scutes and the lanceolate lateral scales of the common boa constrictor (*Boa constrictor*). Note the trapezium shape of the enlarged first and second longitudinal scale rows.

trapezium and as wide or slightly wider than it is long, whereas the first scale row of Pythonids is cycloid or semicircular and much wider than long. Further, the second scale row in Boids is enlarged and lanceolate in shape, but the third row is comparable to the size and shape of the rest of the body scales, whereas in Pythonids the second and third rows are markedly wider and more rounded than the body scales. The Anacondas (*Eunectes* sp.) can be differentiated from the Boas (*Boa* sp.) based on the rhomboidal shape of the first scale row, larger overall scale size and greater percentage of projection of each scale.

Colubridae The Colubrids are a very diverse group of snakes, but they are distinctive by their lack of distinction. As a group the Colubrids have mostly ordinary lanceolate scales with largely unremarkable smooth or simple keeled topography. The lateral scale rows are generally not greatly enlarged as in many other snakes (Figure 10.21). There are, however, notable exceptions to the general appearance of the Colubrids, which means that at least some species may be able to be differentiated in the future based on scale morphology alone.

Homalopsidae The Homalopsids are also a fairly unremarkable family of snakes, but their unique color patterns seem to be preferred by fashion designers, so most of these skins retain at least some of their natural dorsal pattern (Figure 10.22).

Elapidae The Elapids are quite a large and diverse group of snakes ranging from the drop or guttiform scales of the cobras arranged in collar-like rows (Figure 10.9) to the enlarged hexagonal dorsal vertebral scales of the

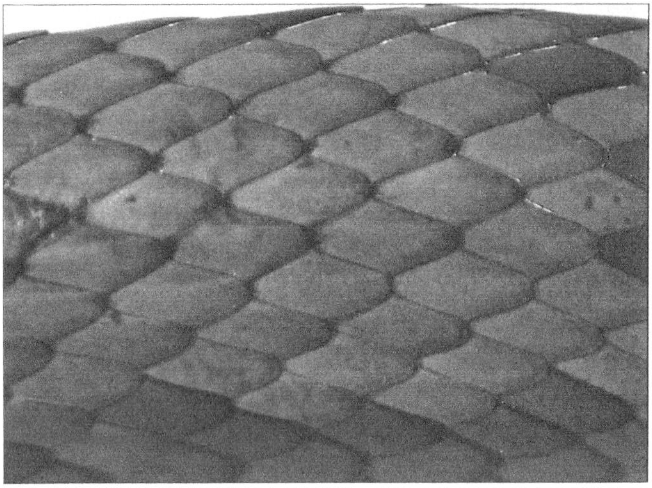

Figure 10.21 Imbricate arrangement of smooth lanceolate scales on the dorsal surface of the Indo-Chinese rat snake (*Ptyas korros*, specimen No. CAS-224645).

Kraits (Figure 10.23). The sea snakes are a particularly interesting and easily distinguishable group of species within this family whereas the Asiatic cobras (*Naja* sp.) are difficult to differentiate between species within the genus.

Viperidae The Viperids are another very diverse family of snakes that seem to share strongly keeled and imbricate dorsal scales and enlarged but smooth first, second and sometimes third ventral scale rows. It appears that this group

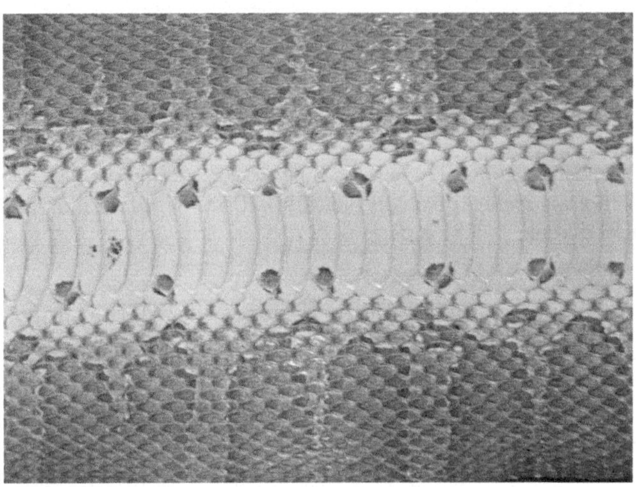

Figure 10.22 Tanned skin of a puff-faced water snake (*Homalopsis buccata*). The skins of this species are often left with the natural color pattern.

Figure 10.23 Enlarged hexagonal vertebral scale (top) and smooth lanceolate dorsal scales of a many-banded krait (*Bungarus multicinctus*, specimen No. CAS-234267).

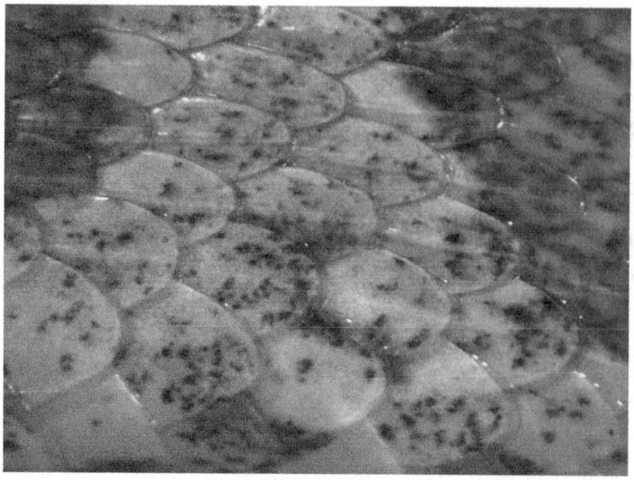

Figure 10.24 Transition zone between the belly scutes and the keeled lateral scales of the Russel's viper (*Daboia russelii*, specimen No. CAS-206671). Note that the first longitudinal row of scales lacks a keel.

has a lot of scale micro-morphology (Figure 10.24) that may be useful for distinguishing species.

Conclusion

This preliminary study demonstrates the large market value and large number of reptiles being killed every year for the international commercial trade in reptile skin and reptile skin products. The US market for products manufactured from reptile skins is large and getting larger, thereby making the US a major market for the international reptile skin trade.

One of the tools needed to enforce international and national wildlife laws aimed at reducing the environmental and species specific impact of this international trade is the ability to identify reptile skins and skin products to the species level. Unfortunately, traditional methods of identifying reptile species often fail when they are applied to reptile skins or skin products that are missing diagnostic features or component parts, and/or have been altered during the tanning and product manufacturing process. This study suggests that there is a high probability that macro- and possibly micro-morphology of reptile scales can be used in the identification of reptile species when more traditional methods of identification fail.

Acknowledgements

I would like to thank Jens Vindum and Robert Drews from the California Academy of Sciences, Department of Herpetology, for access to the CAS collections and for space to work. I thank Bernadette Atencio and Doni Sprague from the USF&WS National Wildlife Repository for access to seized reptile skins and reptile skin products. For their previous hard work in this field, the sharing of information and the many discussions regarding the forensic identification of reptile skin products, without which this study would not have been possible, I thank Peter Brazaitis, Ken McCloud and Barry Baker. I thank my wife Sara for her support and patience with my using our kitchen table as a laboratory to study tanned skins. Finally, Jane Huffman, for her invitation to write this chapter, and for her encouragement and support throughout the production of this chapter.

References

Ananjeva, N.B., Dilmuchamedov, M.E., and Matveyeva, T.N. (1991) The skin sense organs of some iguanian lizards. *Journal of Herpetology*, **25**(2), 186–199.

Andres, K.H., von Düring, M., and Horn, H.G. (1999) Fine structure of scale glands and preanal glands of monitors *Varanidae*. *Mertensiella*, **11**, 277–290.

Anon (1987) The making of a Kundu Drum. *Bikmaus*, **7**(3), 51–61.

Arroyo-Quiroz, I., Perez-Gil, R. and Leader-Willams, N. (2006) Mexico in the international reptile skin trade: a case study. *Biodiversity and Conservation*, **16**, 931–952.

Auliya, M. (2010) *Conservation Status and Impact of Trade on the Oriental Rat Snake* Ptyas mucosa *in Java, Indonesia*, Petaling Jaya, Selangor, Malaysia: TRAFFIC Southeast Asia.

Avolio, C., Shine, R. and Pile, A.J. (2006) The adaptive significance of sexually dimorphic scale rugosity in sea snakes. *American Naturalist*, **167**(5), 728–738.

Baker, B.W. (2006) Forensic implications of dorsal scale row counts on puff-faced water snakes (Colubridae: Homalopsinae: *Homalopsis buccata*). *Herpetological Review*, **37**(2), 171–173.

Baker, B.W. (2008) A brief overview of forensic herpetology. *Applied Herpetology*, **5**(4), 307–318.

Baker, B.W., Reinholz, A.D. and Espinoza, E.O. (under review) Digital near-infrared photography as a tool in forensic snake skin identification. *Herpetological Journal*.

Barber-Meyer, S.M. (2010) Dealing with the clandestine nature of wildlife-trade market surveys. *Conservation Biology*, **24**(4): 918–923.

Berthé, R.A., Westhoff, G., Bleckmann, H. and Gorb, S.N. (2009) Surface structure and frictional properties of the skin of the Amazon tree boa *Corallus hortulanus* (Squamata, Boidae). *Journal of Comparative Physiology*, **195**(3), 311–318.

Bour, R. (1985) Identification aid to sea turtle skins. In *CITES Identification Manual*, Vol. 5; parts and derivatives. Geneva: CITES.

Branch, B. (1998) *Field Guide to Snakes and Other Reptiles of Southern Africa*. Cape Town, South Africa: Struik Publishers, Pty. Ltd.

Brazaitis, P. (1973) Identification of living crocodilians. *Zoologica*, **58**(3–4), 59–101.

Brazaitis, P. (1984) Problems in the identification of commercial crocodilian hides and products, and the effect upon law enforcement. In *Proceedings of the 6th Working Meeting of the IUCN/SSC Crocodile Specialist Group*. Gland, Switzerland: IUCN, pp. 110–116.

Brazaitis, P. (1986a) Biochemical techniques: new tools for the forensic identification of crocodilian hides and products. In *Proceedings of the 7th Working Meeting of the IUCN/SSC Crocodile Specialist Group*, Gland, Switzerland: IUCN, pp. 384–388.

Brazaitis, P. (1986b) Reptile leather trade: the forensic science examiner's role in litigation and wildlife law enforcement. *Journal of Forensic Science*, **31**(2), 621–629.

Brazaitis, P. (1987) Identification of crocodilian skins and products. In G.J.W Webb, S.C. Manolis and P.J. Whitehead (eds.) *Wildlife Management: Crocodiles and Alligators*. Chipping North, NSW, Australia: Surrey Beatty & Sons Pty Ltd in association with The Conservation Commission of the Northern Territory, pp. 373–386.

Brazaitis, P. (1989) The forensic identification of crocodilian hides and products. In *Crocodiles: Their Ecology, Management, and Conservation*. Gland, Switzerland: IUCN/SSC, pp. 17–43.

Broad, S., Mulliken, T. and Roe, D. (2003) The nature and extent of legal and illegal trade in wildlife. In S. Oldfield (ed.), *The Trade in Wildlife: Regulation for Conservation*. London: Earthscan Publishers Ltd.

Busack, S.D. and Pandya, S. (2001) Geographic variation in *Caiman crocodilus* and *Caiman yacare* (Crocodylia: Alligatoridae): systematic and legal implications. *Herpetologica*, **57**(3), 294–312.

Caldwell, J. (2004) *World Trade in Crocodilian Skins, 2000–2002*. Cambridge: UNEP-WCMC.

Caldwell, J. (2007) *World Trade in Crocodilian Skins, 2003–2005*. Cambridge: UNEP-WCMC.

Caldwell, J. (2010) *World Trade in Crocodilian Skins, 2006–2008*. Cambridge: UNEP-WCMC.

Charette, R. (1995) *CITES Identification Guide: Crocodilians*. Ontario, Canada: Environment Canada.

Charette, R. (1999) *CITES Identification Guide : Turtles and Tortoises*. Ontario, Canada: Environment Canada.

CITES (2010) *CITES Species Database*. Available at: http://www.cites.org/eng/resources/species.html (accessed 27 October 2010).

Cogger, H.G. (1992) *Reptiles and Amphibians of Australia*. Chatswood, NSW, Australia: Reed Books.

Colbert, A.A., Woodley, C.M., Seaborn, G.T., Moore, M.K. and Galloway, S.B. (1999) Forensic aspects. In K. L. Eckert and K. A. Bjorndal (eds.) *Research Management Techniques for the Conservation of Sea Turtles*. IUCN/SSC Marine Turtle Specialist Group Publication No. 4, Blanchard, PA: Consolidated Graphic Communications, pp. 232–235.

Cook, D., Roberts, M. and Lowther, J. (2002) *The International Wildlife Trade and Organized Crime: A Review of the Evidence and the Role of the UK*. Godalming: World Wildlife Fund-UK.

Cooper, M.E. (2008) Forensics in herpetology: legal aspects. *Applied Herpetology*, **5**, 319–338.

Engler, M. (2008) The value of international wildlife trade. *TRAFFIC Bulletin*, **22**(1), 4–5.

Ernst, C.H. and Barbour, R.W. (1989) *Turtles of the World*. Washington, DC: Smithsonian Institution Press.

Espinoza, E.O., Baker, B.W. and Berry, C.A. (2007) The analysis of sea turtle and bovid keratin artifacts using DRIFT spectroscopy and discriminant analysis. *Archaeometry*, **49**(4), 685–698.

Fernandez, C. and Luxmoore, R. (1997) The value of the wildlife trade. In T.M. Swanson and R.A. Luxmoore (eds.) *Industrial Reliance on Biodiversity*. A Darwin Initiative Project, WCMC Biodiversity Series No. 7. Cambridge: World Conservation Press, pp. 13–56.

Ferrer, Y. (1995) Colombia-Environment: animal smuggling second only to drug trade. *International Press Service, English News Wire*, July 22.

Fuchs, K. (2006) *The Crocodile Skin: Important Characteristics in Identifying Crocodilian Species*. Frankfurt am Main: Edition Chimaira.

Fuchs, K, and Fuchs M. (2003) *The Reptile Skin*. Frankfurt am Main: Edition Chimaira.

Gibbons, J.W., Scott, D.E., Ryan, T.J., *et al.* (2000) The global decline of reptiles, déjà vu amphibians. *BioScience*, **50**, 653–666.

Gower, D.J. (2003) Scale microornamentation of uropeltid snakes. *Journal of Morphology*, **258**(2), 249–268.

Grismer, L.L. (2002) *Amphibians and Reptiles of Baja California: Including Its Pacific Islands and the Islands in the Sea of Cortez*. Berkeley, CA: University of California Press.

Groombridge, B. and Luxmoore, R. (1991) Pythons in south-east Asia: a review of distribution, status and trade in three selected species: *Python curtus, P. molurus bivittatus* and *P. reticulates*: a report to the CITES Secretariat, World Conservation Monitoring Centre, Cambridge, UK.

Hainschwang, T., and Leggio, L. (2006) The characterization of tortoise shell and its imitations. *Gems and Gemology*, **42**(1), 36–52.

Hazel, J., Stone, M., Grace, M.S. and Tsukruk, V.V. (1999) Nanoscale design of snake skin for reptation locomotions via friction anisotropy. *Journal of Biomechanics*, **32**(5), 477–484.

Holden, J. (1998) *By Hook or by Crook: A Reference Manual on Illegal Wildlife Trade and Prosecutions in the United Kingdom*. Cambridge: The Royal Society for the Protection of Birds, The World Wide Fund for Nature, TRAFFIC International.

IUCN (2010) *IUCN Red List of Threatened Species*, Version 2010.4. Available at: http://www.iucnredlist.org (accessed 27 November 2010).

Jenkins, M. and Broad, S. (1994) *Trade in Reptile Skins: A Review and Analysis of the Main Consumer Markets*, 1983–1991. Cambridge: TRAFFIC International.

King, F.W. and Brazaitis, P. (1971) Species identification of commercial crocodilian skins. *Zoologica*, **56**, 15–70.

Klein, M.C., Deuschle, J.K. and Gorb, S.N. (2010) Material properties of the skin of the Kenyan sand boa *Gongylophis colubrinus* (Squamata, Boidae). *Journal of Comparative Physiology A*, **196**(9), 659–668.

Lin, J. (2005) Tackling Southeast Asia's illegal wildlife trade. *Singapore Year Book of International Law*, **9**, 191–208.

Luxmoore, R. and Groombridge, B. (1990) *Asian Monitor Lizards: A Review of Distribution, Status, Exploitation and Trade in Four Selected Species:* Varanus bengalensis, V. griseus, V. flavescens *and* V. salvator. Lausanne, Switzerland: CITES Secretariat.

Mace, G.M. (2004) The role of taxonomy in species conservation. *Philos Trans R Soc Lond B Biol Sci.*, **358**(1444), 711–719.

Martin, D.L. (2010 abstract) Catalog of monitor lizard skin morphology for use in species identification: A progress report. Society for Wildlife Forensic Science, Inaugural Meeting 2010, Ashland, Oregon.

McCloud, K. (2008) *A Photographic Identification Guide to Star-Patterned Tortoises*. Identification Guides for Wildlife Law Enforcement No. 12. Ashland, OR: USF&WS, National Fish and Wildlife Forensics Laboratory.

Nijman, V. (2009) An overview of the international wildlife trade from Southeast Asia. *Biodiversity and Conservation*, **19**, 1101–1114.

O'Connor, S. (1987) The identification of osseous and keratinaceous materials at York. In K. Starling and D. Watkinson (eds.) *Archaeological Bone, Antler and Ivory*, Occasional Paper No. 5. London: The United Kingdom Institute for Conservation of Historic and Artistic Works of Art, pp. 9–21.

Parker, H.W. (1933) The collection of reptile skins for commercial purposes with reference to the possibilities in Empire Countries. Report by the Advisory Committee on Hides and Skins, Imperial Institute. *Bulletin of the Imperial Institute*, **31**(2), 160.

Perez, B.A. (2008) Poaching American security: impacts to illegal wildlife trade. Testimony before the U.S. House of Representatives Committee on Natural Resources, March 5, 2008. Available at: http://www.fws.gov/laws/TESTIMONY/110th/2008/PerezIllegalWildlifeTrade.html (accessed 22 December 2010).

Pernetta, A.P. (2009) Monitoring the trade: using the CITES database to examine the global trade in live monitor lizards (Varanus spp.). *Biawak*, **3**(2), 37–45.

Pianka, E.R., King, D.R. and Allen King, R. (2004) *Varanoid Lizards of the World*. Bloomington, IN: Indiana University Press.

Rice, S.M. and More, M.K. (2008) Trade secrets: a ten year overview of the illegal import of sea turtle products into the United States. *Marine Turtle Newsletter*, **121**, 1–5.

Rocha-Barbosa, O. and Moraes e Silva, R.B. (2009) Analysis of the microstructure of Xenodontinae snake scales associated with different habitat occupation strategies. *Brazilian Journal of Biology*, **69**(3), 919–923.

Roe, D. (2008) *Trading Nature: A Report, with Case Studies, on the Contribution of Wildlife Trade Management to Sustainable Livelihoods and the Millennium Development Goals*. Cambridge, and Gland, Switzerland: TRAFFIC International and WWF International.

Roe, D.T., Mulliken, T., Milledge, S., Mremi, J., Mosha, S. and Grieg-Gram, M. (2002) *Making a Killing or Making a Living? Wildlife Trade, Trade Controls and Rural Livelihoods*. Biodiversity and Livelihoods Issues No. 6. London: International Institute for Environmental and Development, Earthprint.

Rosen, G.E. and Smith, K.F. (2010) Summarizing the evidence on the international trade in illegal wildlife. *EcoHealth*, 7(1), 24–32.

Roth, H. and Merz, G. (1997) *Wildlife Resources: A Global Account of Economic Use*. Berlin: Springer Verlag.

Schlaepfer, M.A., Hoover, C. and Dodd Jr., K. (2005) Challenges in evaluating the impact of the trade in amphibians and reptiles on wild populations. *BioScience*, **55**, 256–264.

Shinawatra, T. (2004) Opening address. CITES, Thirteenth Meeting of the Conference of the Parties, Bangkok, Thailand, 2–14 October 2004. Available at: http://www.cites.org/eng/news/meetings/cop13/Thai_PM_open.shtml.

Shine, R., Ambariyanto, Harlow, P.S. and Mumpuni (1998) Ecological traits of commercially harvested water monitors, *Varanus salvator*, in northern Sumatra. *Wildlife Research*, **25**, 437–447.

Stuart, B.L., Rhodin, A.G., Grismer, L.L. and Hansel, T. (2006) Scientific description can imperil species. *Science*, **312**, 1137.

Thiele, K. and Yeates, D. (2002) Tension arises from duality at the heart of taxonomy. *Nature*, **419**, 337.

Uetz, P., Hoesk, J., Baker, B., *et al.* (2010) *The Reptile Database*. Available at: http://www.reptile-database.org (accessed 23 December 2010).

UNEP (1998) *Policy Effectiveness and Multilateral Environmental Agreements*. Environment and Trade Series. Geneva, Switzerland: UNEP Economics, Trade and Environment Unit.

USA and China (2010) *Snake Trade and Conservation Management*. Interpretation and implementation of the Convention: Species trade and conservation, CoP15 Doc. 48. CITES 15th meeting of the Conference of the Parties, Doha, Qatar.

USFWS (2010) *Endangered Species Database*. Available at: http://ecos.fws.gov (accessed 27 October 2010).

Vince, G. (2002) Organized gangs target wildlife trade. *New Scientist*, June 17.

Weijola, V.S-A., Sweet, S.S. (2010) A new melanistic species of monitor lizard (Reptilia: Squamata: Varanidae) from Sana Island, Indonesia. *Zootaxa*, **2434**, 17–32.

Wilcove, D.S., Rothstein, D., Dubow, J., Phillips, A. and Losos, E. (1998) Quantifying threats to imperiled species in the United States. *BioScience*, **48**, 607–615.

Wyler, L.S. and Sheikh, P.A. (2008) *International Illegal Trade in Wildlife: Threats and U.S. Policy*. Congressional Research Service Report for Congress, RL34395, 22 Aug 2008, Washington, DC: The Library of Congress.

Zhou, Z. and Jiang, Z. (2004) International trade status and crisis for snake species in China. *Conservation Biology*, **18**(5), 1386–1394.

Zimmerman, M. (2003) The black market for wildlife: combating transnational organized crime in the illegal wildlife trade. *Vanderbilt Journal of Transnational Law*, **36**, 1657–1689.

11

Best Practices in Wildlife Forensic DNA

M. Katherine Moore and Irving L. Kornfield

Introduction

At the time of writing, the forensic science community is undergoing unprecedented change. In 2009, the National Academy of Sciences (NAS) released their critical report, *Strengthening Forensic Science in the United States: a Path Forward*. While the report focused its ire (and some praise) entirely on the world of human forensics,[1] its call for increased scientific rigor, standardization, accreditation of forensic labs and certification of practitioners will doubtless reach to encompass non-traditional disciplines like Wildlife Forensics (WF).

Fortunately, WF practitioners had already set out on the path towards increasing stringency years earlier, with the establishment of an American Society of Crime Laboratory Directors/Laboratory Accreditation Board (ASCLD/LAB)-approved proficiency testing program. The NAS report spurred us as a community to quicken our pace along the same path towards greater trust in and acceptance of WF as a discipline, both in the court system and in the larger community of forensic scientists. In the past several years, WF practitioners have

[1] In this chapter, "wildlife forensics" includes forensic analyses focusing on non-human organisms, including plants and domesticated animals. "Human forensics" means forensics aimed at solving crimes against people or their property.

Wildlife Forensics: Methods and Applications, First Edition. Edited by Jane E. Huffman and John R. Wallace.

benefitted from establishment of key elements of a formal framework for best practices, including:

- Representation by the Society for Wildlife Forensic Sciences (SWFS; see Hawk, 2011, Chapter 2), an international society with a common focus.
- A dedicated website (http://www.wildlifeforensicscience.org/) to facilitate information sharing.
- A Code of Ethics, formalized within the Society for Wildlife Forensic Sciences, that complements several agency documents that address scientific ethics (Salazar, 2009: Office of Science and Technology Policy, 2010; Department of Interior, 2011).
- A Proficiency Testing Program to assess the quality of analysts' work and a Review Committee to oversee the process and review aberrant findings, an important step for accreditation and admissibility in court. The Proficiency Testing Program, initially focused on several terrestrial game species and administered by the US Fish and Wildlife Service (USFWS) National Forensic Lab, is now managed by SWFS and is expanding to include aquatic taxa. One of the main reasons for the change in Proficiency Testing Program administration was to insure that participants' errors would result in administrative notification and substantive consequences for failure or a non-consensus result(s).
- The Scientific Working Group for Wildlife Forensics. SWGWILD, the only forensic SWG with a non-human focus, joins about 18 human forensic SWGs focused on establishing and promulgating relevant standards of practice for their respective disciplines (e.g. ballistics, fingerprints, questioned documents). Though the SWG system is not without its flaws (NAS, 2009; Edwards, 2010), many SWGs provide elements of best practices the WF community can emulate in drafting standards for the unique aspects of our discipline.

All of these elements are part of an extensive system of quality assurance (QA) and quality control (QC). QA and QC so commonly go hand in hand that they are popularly referred to as QA/QC, separated only by a sliver of punctuation. Yet, as Budowle *et al.* (2005) pointed out, they are complementary but different:

> *QA is the monitoring of activities that are intended to verify whether practices and test results are providing reliable information. QC is a mechanism or activity(ies) intended to verify whether test conditions are functioning appropriately to yield defined accurate and reproducible results.*

Rigorous QA and QC set forensic labs apart from research labs, and rightly so – a defendant's reputation, possessions, business, freedom, even life, can hinge on the outcome of forensic analysis.

There have been several publications to date on best practices for WF which have largely been a recasting of the guidelines for human DNA work (Budowle *et al.*, 2005; Cassidy and Gonzales, 2005; Linacre, 2009; Linacre *et al.*, 2011; Pereira *et al.*, 2010). In the development of principles of best practice for forensic wildlife DNA analysis, we exploit our experience as practitioners and incorporate the work of previous authors (Budowle *et al.*, 2005; Cassidy and Gonzales, 2005; Linacre, 2009; Linacre *et al.*, 2011; Ogden *et al.*, 2009; Ogden, 2010; Pereira *et al.*, 2010). Additionally, many *principles* articulated by SWGDAM, the Scientific Working Group for DNA Analysis Methods (in humans), are applicable to most wildlife analogs. However, we do not agree with Linacre *et al.*, (2011) that "Ideally, the recommendations concerning forensic genetic investigations of non-human DNA are identical to those of investigations of human DNA." Clearly some recommendations are inappropriate for laboratories that work with non-human taxa. For example, contamination with human DNA, a rightfully obsessive concern in human forensics, is less problematic in WF since many methods are specifically designed so that they do not work with human DNA. Additional WF standards also need to be considered for voucher specimens on which species identifications hinge. Regardless, the general principles of population genetics (polymorphism and genetic variation; molecular evolution and patterns of inheritance; mutation, migration, and genetic drift; natural selection; phylogenetics (Hedrick, 2000)), DNA probability calculations (estimating heterozygosity; effective population size; Hardy-Weinberg equilibrium; probability of identity; maximum likelihood probabilities; estimation of confidence and statistical power (Butler, 2010)), and validation procedures (sensitivity and repeatability studies; cross-species testing (Linacre, 2009)) are applicable to DNA analyses in all taxonomic groups. Poor implementation of best practices, erroneous lab results, and ethical violations should all bear consequences and all should have plans for corrective actions.

The Need for Appropriate Standards

Like the other forensic disciplines, WF uses science to help resolve legal disputes. But unlike the other forensic disciplines, the victims in wildlife crimes are not human, but are among the multitude of species protected by state, national and international laws. Animal evidence can be probative in human crimes and has been used to help convict and to exculpate (Savolainen and Lundeberg, 1999; Halverson and Lyons, 2004). However, the question WF scientists are most often asked to resolve is not who perpetrated the crime, but whether or not a crime occurred.

In the late 1980s, the first laboratory in the world wholly dedicated to WF was constructed in Ashland, Oregon. The USFWS's mission was to marry modern molecular techniques and traditional criminalistics, such as ballistics and fingerprint analysis, for the purpose of solving wildlife crimes. Despite USFWS's efforts to establish a dedicated forensic facility, much of the analyses conducted in WF science remains in the halls of academia or in the research facilities of other government agencies where high-quality science is conducted, but forensic standards are variably implemented (Ogden, 2010).

While forensic science uses many of the same techniques as those in academic science, it differs in many ways. In this chapter, we highlight differences between research and forensic science and advance fundamental elements of best practices for the wildlife forensic sciences. We use analysis of wildlife DNA as an exemplar because it has matured into a specialty discipline with easily identifiable parallels in forensic analysis of human DNA. Even within the genetics sub-discipline of WF, however, there are large differences between casework conducted in federal and state-level laboratories. State wildlife forensics labs' cases deal largely with common species that, for the most part, can be legally hunted, and whose management is under the control of the individual states. Because hunting of these species is allowed and generally encouraged for management objectives, they are relatively easily sampled and genetically well characterized; the allele frequency databases upon which the state labs rely can be large. Species identifications constitute a portion of their work, and often rest on matching evidence to known DNA haplotypes. However, most of their work is individualization, e.g. matching a gut pile in the woods to a steak in a hunter's freezer, or matching an orphaned bear cub to its illegally killed mother. The surety of individualization relies on short tandem repeat (STR) allele frequency databases for local populations.

In contrast, federal labs are much more likely to work with a broad array of endangered, highly migratory, and imported species that are relatively poorly characterized. In addition, the condition of materials submitted as evidence is often compromised due to the fact that many items in question are crafted, carved, cooked, or manipulated in ways that make morphological and genetic identification a challenge. Difficulties in compiling large databases for endangered species include not only their relative rarity, prohibition against lethal sampling, and sometimes habitat inaccessibility, but also the need for permits. Permits must be obtained in the US to conduct sampling and to receive or maintain archived samples. For countries that have signed the Convention on International Trade in Endangered Species (CITES), additional permits must be obtained for samples that are to cross international borders – from both the exporting and importing country. For some species groups, importation and transport are controlled or prohibited because of disease issues. Because of the difficulty of obtaining and transporting samples, some of the databases on which federal labs rely are small and the species poorly characterized compared to common game species. Additionally, the geographic origin may be unknown, presenting further challenges for narrowing the field of possible source species. The nature of STR databases is species-specific, and, for the few species where STR databases exist, calculating match probabilities using appropriate allele frequencies requires substantial effort to insure that all putative populations of origin are included in the analysis. Because the federally protected species are often not hunted legally under any circumstance, a much larger percentage of the federal labs' work is species ID, not individualization. The result of having smaller databases, a large number of candidate species, and incomplete taxon sampling, is that species identifications often rely on phylogenetic reconstruction instead of haplotype matching.

One of the major differences between WF and human forensics is that the breadth of the field leads to an inability to concentrate all relevant taxonomic expertise in a few specialized forensic laboratories. Human forensic scientists enjoy extensive knowledge of their organism, *Homo sapiens*, whose entire genome has been sequenced multiple times (International Human Genome Sequencing Consortium, 2004; Levy *et al.*, 2007; Bentley *et al.*, 2008; Wang *et al.*, 2008; Wheeler *et al.*, 2008). Because of such intensive focus, the loci used in human forensics are meticulously mapped, validated, and standardized, with industry accomplishing the vast majority of the necessary research and validation to produce easy-to-use "kits" for human identity testing. Conversely, there is little commercial interest in developing WF "kits" as it is not cost-effective for the wide variety of potential target species. Those kits that do exist are targeted for domesticated species of substantial commercial interest, such as cattle, domestic dogs, and horses (Invitrogen MapPairs® Canine Markers, and ABI StockMarks® and FinnZymes Diagnostics kits for dogs, cattle, and horses), and many are based on marker panels suggested by the International Society of Animal Genetics (http://www.isag.us/). WF practitioners often have to perfect their own methods of analysis for the taxa in which they specialize, either by adapting markers and data from publications in population genetics and phylogeny (Bowen *et al.*, 1993; Pouyaud *et al.*, 2000; Anderson *et al.*, 2002; Bellis *et al.*, 2003; Moore *et al.*, 2003; Purcell *et al.*, 2004; Hyde *et al.*, 2005; Dawnay *et al.*, 2007, 2008; Viricel and Rosel, 2011), or by developing their own markers in-house (Braddon *et al.*, 1982; Fain and LeMay, 1995; Straughan *et al.*, 2002; Greig *et al.*, 2005; Espinoza and Baker, 2007; Yates and Sims, 2010) and conducting their own developmental and internal validations. Hence, laboratories will often use different loci for the same task, such as performing individualization on the same deer species with STRs (Anderson *et al.*, 2002; DenDanto *et al.*, 2002) or for shark species detection (Shivji *et al.*, 2002) or identification (Heist and Gold, 1999; Greig *et al.*, 2005; Blanco *et al.*, 2008; Wong *et al.*, 2009).

Because of broad differences in necessary expertise and types of analysis, our recommendations are not as detailed as those laid down by SWGDAM for human ID labs (e.g, FBI, 2009, 2010). Instead, our goal is to detail good laboratory practices and catalyze our maturing discipline's response to the NAS report. To facilitate this task, we identify fundamental elements of best practices that are applicable to forensic science in general, and specific aspects of best practices applicable to DNA analysis of wildlife species. In concentrating on DNA, we acknowledge that we will not cover critical sister disciplines such as morphology, which is newly represented by SWGWILD. To help achieve our objectives, we acknowledge the work of authors who have preceded us in this endeavor (Budowle *et al.*, 2005; Cassidy and Gonzales, 2005; Linacre *et al.*, 2011; Ogden, 2010), seconding or modifying their recommendations and adding new ones based on our experience and extant state, federal and international protocols. Discussions at the first SWGWILD meeting guided our list of topic areas and helped us flesh out many ideas – for that, the participants are gratefully acknowledged. We hope that the ideas put forward here will provide a foundation for further development of guidelines and standards for the Society for Wildlife Forensics and the nascent SWGWILD.

Wildlife Forensic DNA Best Practices

It is important to distinguish two classes of practices generically associated with QA and QC: Standards and Guidelines.

- *Standards* are mandatory minimum practices necessary to ensure that accurate, precise analytical findings are obtained and that results are conveyed in an unbiased, objective manner. Standards are often accompanied by some method of evaluating accuracy and objectivity, either by tracking performance of reagents or equipment, or through technical review of analytical products and reports. Standards are non-negotiable, and every conscientious practitioner, whether in a research laboratory or a dedicated forensic facility, should abide by them.
- *Guidelines* are additional suggestions to optimize the accuracy and precision of methods. Guidelines are not mandatory, but represent a best-case-scenario for practitioners and laboratories which have the means to achieve them. Though those who only encounter forensic casework occasionally may not be able to implement all guidelines, dedicated WF laboratories should implement them. Guidelines often have a wider tolerance in operational parameters within which the accuracy and precision of analyses is assured. In general, both standards and guidelines are dynamic; components should evolve over time in response to new information, innovations, and perspectives.

Standards and Guidelines for Wildlife Forensics

Ethics

The ethical framework for wildlife forensics is central to every aspect of the discipline. Ethics are obligatory for all personnel involved since trust and truth are at the foundation of the judicial system. The NAS Report recommended the establishment of a national code of ethics for forensic practitioners (2009, pp. 7–17 to 7–18), and one of the Education, Ethics and Terminology Interagency Working

Group's goals is to "Identify a code of ethics or professional responsibility that can serve as a uniform code, and recommend a process for implementing and enforcing such a code" (http://www.forensicscience.gov/iwg_ethics.html). The Society of Wildlife Forensic Sciences has established a Code of Ethics which is formally acknowledged by all members. As with most professional codes, there are few established mechanisms for enforcing the Code's provisions. Unlike attorneys, few forensic science practitioners face the threat of official sanctions or loss of certification for serious ethical violations.

In addition to SWFS' code, models of ethical codes in the forensic sciences are readily available from many sources including ASCLD/LAB (http://www.ascld-lab.org/about_us/guidingprinciples.html), the American Academy of Forensic Science (AAFS: http://www.aafs.org/), and the California Association of Criminalists (CAC, http://www.cacnews.org/membership/handbook.shtml.

Standard

Each laboratory that conducts wildlife forensic analyses should have an ethical code which all practitioners must acknowledge and abide by. As the old adage states, "law without enforcement is simply advice," so infraction of the ethical code should result in some meaningful disciplinary action.

One ethical concern is minimization of non-essential information associated with specific cases, particularly when the data require some subjective interpretation by the analyst (Dror *et al.*, 2006). There is substantial debate about whether examiner bias could be influential, and if so, what to do about it (Krane *et al.*, 2008; Ostrum, 2009; Wells, 2009; Krane *et al.*, 2010; Thornton, 2010; Thompson *et al.*, 2011). For example, explicit identification of suspect(s) should be avoided since this is generally of no relevance to the testing being performed. Similarly, when initiating laboratory work on a case, the analyst should not seek to know the explicit hypothesis advanced by the submitting agent/agency, since all testing should be neutral with regard to outcome. Class characterization of most common terrestrial mammals, i.e. species identification via DNA sequencing, does not involve subjectivity. However, for very closely related taxa, discrimination of species must be approached cautiously, particularly with respect to high intraspecific relative to interspecific variation (Ross *et al.*, 2008; Lou and Golding, 2010). There are times when more information is needed from the investigator to define the question s/he is asking and thereby determine what type of analysis is needed and to allow separation of reference and probative evidence. In these instances, it is best to ask for clarification as needed to complete the analysis, but stop judiciously at the point where need-to-know ends and curiosity begins. It can be advantageous to the analyst to know little about the case, as there is less likelihood that opposing counsel will be able to introduce arguments about bias.

Standard

All analysts and supervisors should be knowledgeable about intrinsic bias (Krane *et al.*, 2010). Since the nature of our judicial system is "innocent until proven guilty," analysts and supervisors should make explicit efforts to conduct casework in an unbiased manner. Neutral identification of individual items submitted for analysis should be part of a QA/QC process for evidence submission and documentation.

Training

Training in the application of DNA methodologies to WF spans an enormous range depending upon the jurisdiction (federal versus state), venue (academic lab versus devoted forensic facility), and caseload (continuous versus occasional). In all instances, the scientist or analyst is responsible for understanding the unique QA/QC aspects demanded of forensic investigations. While errors in scientific studies can impact research by other investigators and potentially result in loss of time and funds, errors in forensic practice can potentially have profound impacts on an individual's life and personal circumstance. The WF practitioner must insure that all work minimizes potential for error and fully appreciate the importance of his/her findings and their interpretations.

Experienced individuals from population genetics research labs can easily transition to forensic work since the theories and laboratory techniques are identical (Ogden, 2010). However, while the individual may be technically proficient, s/he must fully understand that WF demands a different perspective, one that has established standards to help insure the integrity of the process. A technically proficient individual should receive sufficient training to strictly adhere to all forensic standard operating protocols (SOPs) they will be expected to perform or review. For such an individual, the nature of training is established by the lab, but should minimally include shadowing an analyst for multiple cases, conducting all standard work on a series of case-like materials that have previously been processed by the lab, and processing a series of new cases under the direct supervision of an experienced analyst at all stages. In addition, the competence of the trainee should be explicitly evaluated. One method is to provide the trainee with case reports that contain errors, and instruct him/her to review the report for accuracy. An SOP for training should include a procedure for correcting errors during training and specify under what circumstances a trainee will not be permitted to undertake casework.

Individuals who are inexperienced in lab work present special concerns. As with any scientific discipline, individuals learning techniques for the first time are expected to make errors. The extent of training necessary to reduce the error rate to zero (or near zero) should be specified in advance. A trainee who continues to make errors after re-training should not be permitted to undertake casework.

Guideline

An SOP should be developed for training both experienced and inexperienced workers. The document should specify the minimal training required before the individual is permitted to independently undertake casework and should include a mechanism to evaluate competency.

Case File

All aspects of wildlife forensic analysis must be scientifically neutral and transparent. All documentation relevant to a case should be available to defense counsel on request.

A file should contain all documentation pertaining to the specific case. Case files should include bench notes, shipping/receiving documentation, copies of email communications, documentation of relevant telephone conversations (participants, date, time, summary of salient points), data files, images, documentation of technical and administrative reviews, chain-of-custody, and final reports. Notes on different cases should be kept separate from each other and from unrelated research notes. If information related to a specific case is requested through discovery, it is preferable that only the relevant notes are produced and notes for unrelated cases and research are not included. Records of email communications, which are particularly susceptible to misinterpretation without the proper context, can take considerable time to maintain, transfer, and review; labs should consider minimizing the amount of communications or material that is not genuinely pertinent to the case in order to assist the court. The actual case file can be electronic, paper, or a mixture of the two. The case file serves to document that all procedures were followed, that all scientific methods were performed according to stated protocols, and that reasonable conclusions were drawn. The case file should also contain a record of any "unanticipated events" related to analysis in the case, such as contamination or instrument problems; such occurrences should additionally be documented in an independent laboratory log. The case file also acts as an information repository to remind the analyst of the details of the case in the event that court testimony is required, often years down the road.

Standard

All relevant information should be included in the case file, including (but not limited to) bench notes, shipping/receiving documentation, copies of emails, documentation of relevant telephone conversations (participants, date, time, summary of salient points), data files, images, documentation of technical and administrative reviews, chain-of-custody, any "unanticipated events," and the final report. Details in bench notes should be sufficient to enable a trained analyst to repeat the analysis conducted.

Security and evidence handling

Sample security is just as much of a concern in WF as in human forensics, and differs markedly from standard sample handling practice in most research laboratories (see ASTM International Standards E1492-05, E860-07 for detailed evidence handling protocols; http://www.astm.org/). Some SOPs are straightforward, for example, the required protocols for receiving, logging, and tracking evidence samples. Chain-of-custody forms document the who/where/how of evidence collection and are used to track each evidence item and when and how the item was transferred between custodians and storage locations. Variations in the format of these documents are immaterial if they contain the requisite information (Figure 11.1). The law enforcement agent should provide an external chain of custody to track the sample from collection to the laboratory's doorstep. An internal chain of custody is used to track the sample's movement from the time it leaves secured storage or possession by an evidence custodian until it is returned after analysis. Since testimony about the responsibility for and control over the evidence may be required at trial, minimizing the number of individuals in the chain-of-custody is advisable.

Standard hasps and padlocks can be inexpensively added to refrigerators, freezers, lockers, incubators and thermal cyclers for security. Evidence containers should be numbered and this identification should be noted in the case file to minimize the possibility of confusing samples. If evidence items contain multiple samples that need to be analyzed individually, those items should be assigned unique identifiers that maintain the connection to the original evidence submission. Chemical reagents designated as "critical reagents" as well as other materials and components of analytical protocols, e.g. polymerase chain reaction (PCR) reagents and controls, should be secured as appropriate to maintain the integrity of the analytical procedure. Security accommodations can be developed if it is necessary to share instrumentation for forensic work in a research setting. For example, forensic specimens submitted to a common sequencer can be spiked with additional DNA to provide a unique signature (Figure 11.2).

Security must extend beyond the analytical lab to computer servers, which should likewise have limited access. Reference databases used for forensic comparisons should be maintained by a limited number of individuals with appropriate knowledge and training. Data collected during forensic analyses should be scrupulously protected and backed up. The use of flash drives and other portable media for sensitive information should be limited so that confidential details are protected in the event of loss or theft of media. Encryption should be automatic if such storage devices are employed to store or transfer documents

STATE OF MAINE

MAINE WARDEN SERVICE FORENSIC LABORATORY

EVIDENCE TRANSFER/RETURN RECEIPT

Lab Case #

Date

Submitting Warden:
Warden Case Number
Arraignment date

OFFENSE:	DATE:
LOCATION:	ARRAIGNMENT STATUS:
DISPOSITION OF EVIDENCE:	OWNER OF PROPERTY:

Send Report to:

Name:
Address:

Phone #:
Pager*:

ITEM#	DESCRIPTION OF EVIDENCE	EXAMINATION REQUESTED

Evidence Relinquished By:	Evidence Received By:
SIGN________________________	SIGN________________________
DATE: __/___/_____	DATE: __/___/_____

Figure 11.1 Evidence Transfer record (Chain-of-Custody). The original is given to the submitting warden, one copy is attached to the Case File, and one copy accompanies the evidence. Pages for additional evidence items and/or signatures are typically added to this record.

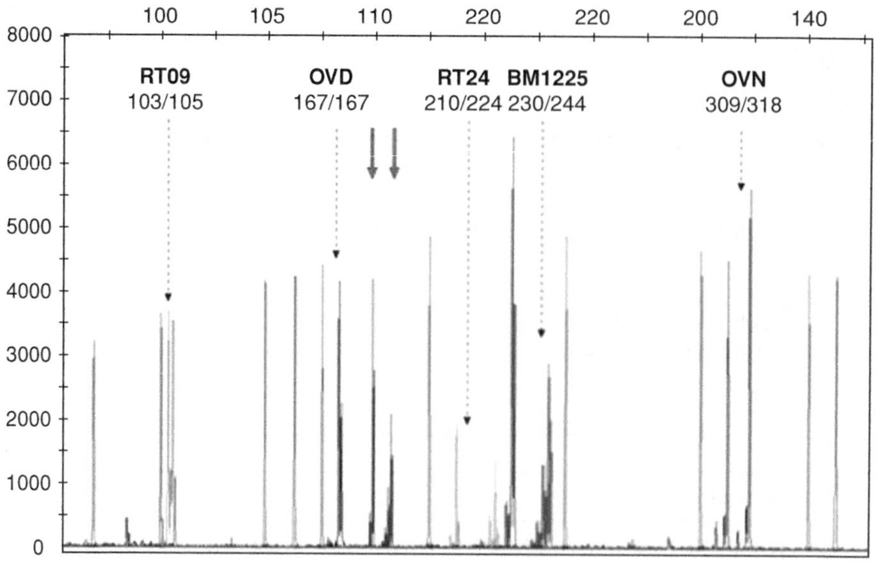

Figure 11.2 STR chromotrogram for white-tailed deer. Prior to sending the sample to a common sequencing facility, the five locus multiplexed reaction was spiked with two PCR amplimers (solid arrows) to provide a unique signature.

that could disclose private information, such as the names of the parties involved (defendant, analyst, agent) or other information specific to the alleged crime.

Standard

Each laboratory should ensure sample security and tracking. Evidence should be stored securely when not being actively examined. Evidence should be maintained in locked storage. Laboratories that do not routinely analyze evidence can, at minimum, use tamper-evident tape for security. Evidence tape used to seal a container should be initialed and dated by the person who has custody of the evidence in a manner in which tampering or removal would be obvious. Evidence containers should be numbered and this identification should be recorded in the case file to minimize the possibility of confusing samples. All evidence should have an associated chain-of-custody record.

Guideline

All analyses should be conducted in a limited-access facility with a round-the-clock system to record lab entry by individual personnel. Access by unauthorized individuals should be under supervision at all times. Such security systems ease concerns about unauthorized access to evidentiary material, but may not be feasible in mixed-use laboratories (Ogden, 2010).

Laboratory Facility (QA)

The subject of the set-up of wildlife forensics facilities under several different support/funding scenarios has been admirably detailed by Ogden (2010). A critical element in analysis of DNA is the potential for contamination. Human DNA contamination is of less concern with WF, where many primers do not amplify human DNA, and any human DNA amplicons are immediately recognized as non-target. Still, design and operation of the facilities should be done in such a manner to minimize contamination by any exogenous DNA. The DNA Advisory Board's Quality Assurance Standards (DAB QAS) for Forensic DNA Testing Laboratories (FBI, 2009) offer a starting place, but many of the standards mirror requirements for accreditation or are FBI- or human-specific (such as a "Quality system," a casework Combined DNA Index System administrator, and a requirement that analysts have a minimum of six months' experience in a human DNA lab). While we agree with Linacre *et al.*'s (2011) recommendation that labs that routinely conduct analysis consider undergoing accreditation, we intend to focus on practices that result in good forensic science without accreditation's high monetary and personnel cost. Normal procedures to both protect the analyst from chemical hazards and protect the evidence from contamination should be employed, such as frequently changing gloves (particularly between evidence items when subsampling requires touching the item), subsampling under the surface of the evidence using disposable forceps/blades whenever possible, decontaminating benches/hoods/equipment with bleach, separation of pre-PCR and post-PCR activities, and following basic good laboratory practice.

Standard

Samples, equipment, lab coats, and supplies should not be transferred from post-PCR to pre-PCR areas unless decontaminated.

Guideline

Following DAB QAS 6.1.5, "The laboratory shall have and follow written procedures for cleaning and decontaminating facilities and equipment" (FBI, 2009).

Standard

Extraction of DNA from archive or voucher specimens for comparison should be physically or temporally separated from extraction of DNA from evidence. Trace evidence should also be processed separately from evidence with high amounts of DNA. When possible, trace samples should be extracted and amplified before high-copy DNA samples, and evidence samples should be extracted before voucher and reference samples.

Standard

When multiple evidence items are to be compared to each other (e.g. questioned vs. known evidence), the items should be processed at different times and/or places.

Standard

Care should be taken to prevent consumption or alteration of all of the evidence whenever possible. A portion of each evidence sample should be archived in the event that the opposing counsel wishes to conduct an independent examination. If it is not possible to retain a sample of the evidence, the agent or counsel should be notified. In any event, a sample of DNA should be retained to enable independent analysis.

Validation

There are two types of validation required for scientific methods applied to forensics: "developmental validation" is a set of experiments that characterize the limits of a "new or novel" technology; "internal validation" refers to experiments performed to confirm that a method that has already been developmentally validated works as expected under the conditions in a specific laboratory (FBI, 2009). In human forensics, most developmental validation is done by commercial entities developing kits or instrumentation for sale, and individual laboratories usually only need to do internal validation. WF scientists must do much of their own developmental as well as internal validation. Despite the fact that validation standards have been written and followed for some time, there is much debate even within the human forensics community about what constitutes "enough" validation (Butler, 2006). Much of WF DNA analysis involves mitochondrial DNA (mtDNA) sequencing, and fortunately it has been well validated (Wilson *et al.*, 1995; Holland and Parsons, 1999; Branicki *et al.*, 2003; Dawnay *et al.*, 2007). Wilson *et al.* (1995) state that:

> A general principle of PCR-based analysis can now be put forward. Through numerous validation studies ... it has become obvious that PCR-based DNA-typing methods are robust and reliable ... provided proper quality assurance procedures have been designed and implemented,

> PCR-based DNA typing, to include mtDNA analysis, should be embraced by the forensic science and legal community without the necessity for repetitive, lengthy validation studies for each new genetic locus.

This is good news, indeed, and significantly lightens the load on WF labs that may have primer sets for many different mtDNA regions. Some validation concerns remain, though, such as how certain primers respond to species mixtures, variable template concentrations, etc. Here, we agree with Linacre *et al.*'s (2011) recommendations 5 and 6 for validation of both mtDNA sequencing and fragment size-based analysis. A more complete discussion of validation of STR loci for wildlife forensics can be found in Dawnay *et al.* (2008).

Standard

New primers should be validated by testing them on a wide variety of likely species to determine specificity. They should likewise be tested with varying dilutions of template, reagent concentrations, annealing temperatures, and cycle numbers to delimit the range of acceptable PCR conditions and to evaluate the likelihood of encountering false positives (Type I error) and false negatives (Type II error).

Standard

New instruments should be validated by analyzing representative samples (vouchers, case-type samples, positive controls) and assessing whether the expected results are achieved.

Standard

Methods expected to be used routinely in casework should be validated. The following validation criteria must be considered, though they may not all be applicable to every method:

- Literature review of the relevant issue.
- Accuracy of the analysis.
- Specificity of the analysis.
- Precision and reproducibility of the analysis.
- Limit and range of detection (upper and lower limits).
- Linearity (analyte response at varying concentrations).
- Robustness.

Standard

Use of analytical methods derived from procedures validated at other laboratories or from methods published in the peer-reviewed literature should undergo an internal validation of sufficient detail to confirm that the expected results of the analysis can be achieved at the testing laboratory with minimal modifications. Substantial modifications to published protocols should be validated appropriately.

Guideline

The number of samples needed to provide sufficient validation of a reagent or method will vary according to the specific test or reagent, and the range of analytical procedures a laboratory conducts. The validation should be sufficient to adequately address the likelihood of Type I or Type II data interpretation errors.

Laboratory Protocols

One of the things that sets a forensic laboratory apart from an academic one is the use of many positive and negative controls. The positive controls provide support for the success of the reaction and the negative controls provide a means by which contamination is detected. Each DNA extraction should include at least one negative control consisting of reagents only. If the DNA is being extracted from fluids or tissues on a substrate (swab or fabric), a substrate negative control may be extracted as well.

At the polymerase chain reaction (PCR) stage, both an appropriate positive and additional amplification negative control should be introduced. If possible, the positive control should produce a result which will make it easy to determine if it is the source of any contamination, for example, a closely related species known to be rarely seen in forensic analyses. In sea turtle cases run at the NOAA Center for Coastal Environmental Health and Biomolecular Research Marine Forensics Program (MFP), for instance, the positive control is *Natator depressus*, the Australian flatback turtle. We have never seen this species in trade, as it is endemic to the region around Australia, but it amplifies well with the primers we use. Should *N. depressus* sequence show up in the negative controls or evidence samples, we know to suspect the positive control as the culprit. For analyses that involve highly specific primers, the positive control may be limited to the species of interest by necessity. In this instance, it is prudent to make use of multiple negative amplification controls. Positive and negative controls should be carried through sequencing, even when there are no negative control PCR products visible on the gel – the detection limit for capillary sequencers is below that of an agarose gel. Bovine serum albumin (BSA), a commonly-used agent for overcoming PCR inhibition, should be used with extreme caution when amplifying DNA with either mammalian or universal primers, as it can be a source of contamination with bovine DNA (Hilgers and Herr, 1993; Hummel, 2007, p. 659). An additional positive control should be included in the sequencing reaction step to demonstrate the efficacy of the reagents; pGEM plasmid DNA is a commonly used sequencing positive control that is sequenced with the standard M13 primer. If amplification primers are designed with the M13 tag, pGEM is an appropriate sequence reaction control. Alternatively, a positive control sample may be sequenced with the same primers used in the original PCR reaction.

Standard

Each DNA extraction should include at least one reagent negative control.

Standard

Each PCR should include the reagent negative control from the extraction, a PCR negative control, and a positive control.

Guideline

Positive and negative controls from PCR reactions must be analyzed alongside evidence samples through the final step (sequencing or fragment size determination).

Dedicated forensic laboratories and researchers who expect to do occasional forensic work should have comprehensive SOPs for all aspects of operations from initial receipt of samples through processing, analysis, review, and dissemination. Analytical SOPs should be the result of careful validation studies defining the limits of optimal assay performance (e.g. minimum/maximum amount of template, annealing temperature, or PCR cycle number). SOPs should be reviewed on a scheduled basis (at the current pace of discovery for DNA, we suggest every three years at minimum), and updated where necessary. Those who normally limit their activities to research and are unexpectedly called upon to do forensic work may not have such extensive formal documentation in hand, but have probably satisfied many of the requirements of validation during the course of their research (for validation guidelines, see Validation section). These scientists should be prepared to assemble and produce such documentation at discovery if necessary.

Guideline

In a dedicated forensic lab or one where forensic analyses are not unexpected, there should be SOPs for:

- Evidence receipt, tracking, storage, transfer, and post-analysis disposition.
- Routine methods such as:
  - DNA extraction, quantification, and visualization;
  - PCR;
  - sequencing.
- Routine methods should be fully validated. If methods are non-routine, they should be science-based and extensively documented (i.e. based on peer-reviewed literature and methods).
- Data analysis and interpretation, including:
  - mixture interpretation;
  - detection of contamination and subsequent action;
  - minimum cut-offs for acceptable data quality (phred scores or signal intensity for sequences or peak height for STRs);
  - records/plans of action for unexpected results.
- Data analysis methods should also incorporate procedures for handling low copy number DNA samples during analysis and data interpretation.
- Management of reference sample collections and reference databases.
- Acceptance criteria, storage conditions, and methods for validation, documentation and tracking of critical reagents or standards whose activity directly influences the success of a reaction or test.
- Case file contents/assembly.
- Reporting (see "Reporting" section).
- Technical and Administrative reviews.

Data Analysis

Analysis of sequence or fragment data should be conducted in accordance with widely accepted population genetic procedures. For mtDNA sequence analysis, comparisons to determine species identity should incorporate knowledge of the genetic variability of the locus of interest at a taxonomic level that is relevant to the species identification. For common, widely distributed species, published literature often contains information about genetic diversity at the species, genus, and family levels. The most precise analysis of mtDNA sequence data will incorporate as comprehensive a collection as possible of closely related species and genera. Highly variable loci and species groups need to incorporate a larger number of individuals; more conservative loci or species groups with fewer members will need fewer comparisons.

An appropriate diagnostic marker for species identification is chosen based upon several factors, including the condition of the evidence from which DNA was extracted, and knowledge of the species group to which the evidence is hypothesized to belong. Published phylogenetic analyses can serve as the basis for marker and primer choice. Identifications that only require a call at the family or genus level can use more conservative loci and universal primers (though be aware that universal primers may be more likely to amplify nuclear copies of mtDNA; Arctander, 1995). Among very closely related species, knowledge of diversity is essential for accurate identifications. WF practitioners must have a working knowledge of phylogenetic theory and molecular evolutionary processes for the species with which they work (Rubinoff *et al.*, 2006; Ross *et al.*, 2008; Austerlitz *et al.*, 2009).

Choice of analytical methodology is as important as the choice of the genetic locus when making species determinations. Phylogenetic tree construction can be performed using clustering algorithms, maximum likelihood, or parsimony algorithms, the choice of which will depend on the characteristics of the data and the locus of interest. The literature on phylogenetic reconstruction is vast, with constant development of new methodologies and critical analyses of extant procedures (Ross *et al.*, 2008; Hall, 2011).

With respect to STR analyses used for individual matching and population assignment tests, data analyses are primarily concerned with appropriate choice of loci and construction of reference databases. The characteristics of STR loci make them suitable for individual matching and population assignment, but their inherent specificity usually requires that different species use different sets of loci and associated primers. Loci that demonstrate high variability at the individual level and limited stutter provide the best analytical framework. Reference databases should be constructed relevant to the analyses that each lab conducts, and encompass the appropriate geographic range for the species of interest. WF STR data analyses should follow general guidelines expressed for human STR data (Budowle *et al.*, 2005). Since many wildlife taxa have limited dispersal, it is essential that probability estimates correct for population structure. In whitetail deer from northern New England, for instance, θ (Weir and Hill, 2002) is approximately 0.04 (Kornfield *et al.*, unpublished data). The appropriate adjustment for genotypic probabilities incorporating this estimate is provided by the National Research Council (1996).

Standard

Where appropriate, all estimates of individualization probabilities should incorporate an adjustment for population structure. When θ is not known for a particular species, a conservative adjustment should be incorporated, e.g., ≥ 0.1.

Guideline

For taxa with limited mobility or species with non-panmictic breeding, estimates of population structure should be acquired.

Interpretation Guidelines

Conclusions drawn from the results of forensic analyses are the highlight of the analytical report. Interpretation of those results must be reported clearly and concisely because the recipients are most often legal professionals and not scientists. The goal of interpretation guidelines is to insure that the conclusions drawn from scientific analyses are supported by the data, that those conclusions are reported objectively, and that they are reported in a manner that is clearly understood by the target audience.

For species identification analyses, a sequence obtained from an unknown sample is usually aligned and compared with reference sequences from known reference material or from public databases. The benefits and pitfalls of the use of public databases are discussed in the following "Public Databases" section.

Key to making accurate species identification of unknown samples is the evaluation of the positive and negative controls. If control reactions yield expected results, the probability of a Type I or Type II error is minimized. Comparison of the evidentiary sequence with known reference samples (samples that are collected and analyzed by the testing laboratory, and maintained in a curated reference database) is the ideal method by which species comparisons and interpretations are made. However, wildlife parts and products originate from a multitude of countries and include species for which little is known about phylogenetic history; acquisition of reference samples for such species is difficult, if not impossible due to permitting and disease control regulations. In those cases, WF practitioners must rely on public databases for making data interpretations.

The results of individual matching and population assignment tests are evaluated using virtually the same criteria as those used in human forensic identification. The main differences between the human and wildlife STR tests are primarily in the sets of loci used and the lack of allelic ladders. Though WF would benefit from development of allelic ladders (Linacre *et al.*, 2011), the research effort and financial investment necessary to produce them for wildlife forensic applications are prohibitive for existing practitioners. Few non-human allelic ladders exist (LaHood *et al.*, 2002; Lim *et al.*, 2011), and we know of none that are commercially available. The salmon population genetics research community provides a good model for standardization of allele calls and data sets without the expense of allelic ladder development (Stephenson *et al.*, 2009). For other taxa, current WF practitioners must rely on locally constructed allelic bin sets, and share data with those practitioners who need to analyze similar data for making accurate interpretations and drawing appropriate conclusions. The technical aspects of data interpretation (relative fluorescence unit intensity limits, reporting of mixtures, statistical analysis) are identical to those of human forensic STR data interpretation (Budowle *et al.*, 2005; FBI, 2010).

Vouchers/Reference Samples

In-house databases

One of the difficulties unique to WF is the need for known voucher specimens from species that are often protected by national and international laws, and may be critically endangered (Ryder *et al.*, 2000). A WF laboratory's voucher collection often delimits their ability to identify species and individuals much more than a lack of instrumentation and technical expertise or familiarity with population genetics theory. This, in turn, hampers enforcement efforts (GAO, 2009). Voucher specimens should be collected whole or, in the case of large species or non-lethal sampling, photographed or imaged when possible (Kalous *et al.*, 2010); species identity should be confirmed by a taxonomic expert. There are few good published models for documentation of voucher specimens (Carter *et al.*, 2007; Ratnasingham and Hebert, 2007). Vouchers should be accompanied by metadata such as collector, identifying authority, collection location and time, life history stage, relevant morphological measurements, etc. It can be difficult to amass sufficient vouchers for comparison because WF scientists often depend on the kindness of field researchers with taxonomic expertise for collection. Sharks, for example, are an extremely speciose group with distribution worldwide, from the bathyal depths to the littoral zone and freshwater rivers. Not only are there approximately 500 species of sharks, but many of them are difficult to identify correctly even when they are whole (much less when they've been reduced to stacks of dried fins destined for a bowl of soup). Collection of vouchers and characterization of genetic markers for such taxa could easily represent a lifetime's work. Additionally, it can be quite time-consuming to obtain CITES, ESA, and/or MMPA permits for collection, transport, or possession of protected species and their directly-derived DNA (Bowen and Avise, 1994; Jones, 1994).

Public databases

While an extensive in-house database of vouchers is desirable, as one can more easily identify and track sources of error and fully control data analysis, the lure of public databases like GenBank (http://www.ncbi.nlm.nih.gov/genbank/), Barcode of Life (BOL; http://www.barcodeoflife.org/), FishPopTrace (http://fishpoptrace.jrc.ec.europa.eu/), FishTrace (http://www.fishtrace.org/), and DNA Surveillance (http://www.cebl.auckland.ac.nz:9000/) is significant. These databases compile the work of many scientists and taxonomic experts into diverse collections of taxa and sequences that no one laboratory could achieve. Still, these databases are limited by what is or is not in them: text returned with a BOL-based species identification rightly cautions that "This identification is solid unless there is a very closely allied congeneric species that has not yet been analyzed. Such cases are rare." This is the difficulty with any collection of samples, whether an in-house archive of vouchers or a public database that does not include all closest relatives – there's always a chance that an evidence sequence's closest match could be the wrong species if the true species has yet to be sampled.

GenBank is well-known to harbor errors (Forster, 2003; Harris, 2003; Longo *et al.*, 2011), whether they be from organisms mis-identified upon collection, tubes mislabeled or swapped in the lab, PCR contamination, base-call errors, or mistakes made in uploading sequences to populate the database. We recommend that species identifications not be based on a single high-similarity GenBank hit alone, but identification is possible if a BLAST search of the evidence sequence at an informative locus returns more than one identical sequence from more than one independent laboratory. Published GenBank sequences can also be used to "fill out" phylogenetic trees based on voucher sequences and, in instances where species identity is suggested by single GenBank sequences, these "hits" can guide collection of voucher specimens of the species and missing congenerics in question. In the MFP, we often use a GenBank BLAST search for fast preliminary identifications. These preliminary identifications then direct further inquiry: high-similarity "hits" that corroborate our initial suspicion of species identity (on which our initial choice of primers rested) result in continuation of data analysis using phylogenetic reconstruction with in-house reference sequences to definitively determine species identity. If the "hits" reveal the evidence in question may belong to a species we did not initially suspect, we may amplify and sequence a different gene region that is more appropriate for the taxon in question. DNA Surveillance, FishTrace, FishPopTrace and Barcode of Life offer curated databases to address problems with misidentifications in the field, lessening, but not eliminating the chance that sequence data housed there is erroneous (Buhay, 2009).

DNA Surveillance, which bases identification on phylogenetic reconstructions, offers databases for whales, Brazilian parrots, rats, and seahorses. Though the database contributors have vetted the sample collection and genetic data before adding sequences to the database, the sample and sequence metadata (such as geographic origin, sequence quality) for each individual animal in the dataset is only available for review on request and with the submitter's permission. For whales, the tree produced from an analysis shows only the common name of the reference whales (see "Nomenclature" section). Still, the whale database is quite useful because it assembles an extensive collection of cetacean species, including several that are critically endangered or known from only a few specimens.

The Barcode of Life (Hebert *et al.*, 2003) offers a large database intended to allay many of the concerns that go along with an uncurated database. "Gene sequences must derive from a designated gene region, they must meet quality standards and they must derive from a specimen whose taxonomic assignment can be reviewed" (Hanner *et al.*, 2007, as referenced in Ratnasingham and Hebert, 2007). One set of barcode primers has been fully validated to forensic standards (Dawnay *et al.*, 2007). Though sequences granted "full barcode status" must meet minimum standards for metadata, data quality, etc. (Ratnasingham and Hebert, 2007), researchers can still upload less-well-documented sequences, and much of the database was originally populated with available GenBank sequences. And again, presumably because of data ownership concerns, much of the information required to confer full barcode status on a sequence is not publicly available, though a relatively small subset of sequences have full documentation that includes photos of the organism, sequence traces, and phred scores so end users can assess specimen identifications and sequence quality independently (Buhay, 2009). The main strength – and weakness – of BOL is that it has identified one locus, the mitochondrial cytochrome oxidase I (COI), as the one "barcode" region that researchers should sequence to build the database for animals (other loci are used for fungi and plants). Advantages to this approach are obvious – everything from butterflies to buffalo are sequenced for the same region. When faced with a chunk of bushmeat of unknown origin, one does not have to have prior knowledge of the evidence's suspected identity in order to know what gene to sequence, as was previously the case – published phylogenies of different taxa often rely on different genes. The main weakness of barcoding is that COI does not provide adequate resolution in many closely-related taxa (Moritz and Cicero, 2004; Meyer and Paulay, 2005; Viricel and Rosel, 2011), including such commercially important species as some tunas (Ward *et al.*, 2005; Viñas and Tudela, 2009), and rockfish (Schwenke, pers. comm.). Identifications usually rest on distance-based measures, but modified assignment methodologies such as Bayesian methods (Lou and Golding, 2010), and nucleotide diagnostic sites (Wong *et al.*, 2009) work on some taxa that are too close to sort out using distance, but still fail to resolve some species pairs (ibid.). Many additional criticisms of barcoding and other single locus approaches are addressed in Rubinoff *et al.* (2006). Additionally, universal use of one region for forensics makes the technique more vulnerable to intentional genetic "mislabeling" of highly valuable products like caviar (Wuertz *et al.*, 2007).

Standard

The provenance and taxonomic identity of reference specimens or sequences used for comparison to unknown evidence items should be well documented. Documentation should include catch/sampling location details, life history stage (if relevant), and basis for species identification.

Standard

Sequences from public databases should be used with caution, and species identifications should not rest on single sequences from uncurated databases.

Species Identification

The possibility of forensic application requires a sound knowledge of the molecular systematics of the involved taxa. For instance, bone carvings suspected to be of marine mammal origin were recently submitted to the MFP. The cytochrome *b* sequence obtained from the bone carvings was identical to several independently-submitted GenBank sequences for banteng (*Bos javanicus*), and the next nearest *Bos* species was a comfortable distance away. Cattle, however, are known to show hybridization and introgression in the mitochondrial genome (Nijman *et al.*, 2003), so the sample was identified only to genus.

Standard

Percent sequence similarity and/or methods based on genetic distances or phylogenetic reconstruction should not be used to infer species identity unless considered within a framework of the completeness of the reference collection and the organism's life history and taxonomy.

Reporting

Nomenclature

Scientific names should be used on reports. Species are officially designated by their scientific names in laws and regulations such as the ESA and CITES. Common names of organisms vary regionally, and of course are different in each language. For example, the popular fish *Coryphaena hippurus* is known as mahi-mahi in Hawaiian, dolphin-fish in English, and dorado in Spanish. Though scientific names do occasionally undergo revision and such revisions can have legal fallout, these changes in formal taxonomy are documented through publication, and the provenance of names can be tracked, for example, through the US federal Integrated Taxonomic Information System (ITIS; www.itis.gov).

In fisheries, nomenclature confusion is compounded by labeling guidelines in the US. The FDA encourages, but in most case does not require, labeling of seafood with "market names" which often encompass several species, and expressly discourages use of unambiguous scientific names (http://www.fda.gov/Food/GuidanceComplianceRegulatoryInformation/GuidanceDocuments/Seafood/ucm113260.htm). This can make it difficult to determine if species are fraudulently labeled, and can lead to ambiguity in reporting or interpreting results (Wong and Hanner, 2008). For example, there are 62 species from two genera (*Sebastes* and *Scorpaena*) allowed to be traded under the market name "rockfish." There are an additional two species from the main "rockfish" family *Scorpaenidae* and seven species from the two other families within the order *Perciformes* whose common name contains "rockfish," but the trade names for these fish are either thornyhead, bass, grouper, or gag, not "rockfish." "Bass" can be any of 15 species from four genera; "sea bass" encompasses a different set of 19 species from 12 genera, while there are an additional 12 species whose market names do not contain "bass," though the vernacular name does contain the word "bass." Similar, though perhaps less extreme, examples can be found from most other groups of vertebrates. The problems of inconsistent and variable common names are if anything even more severe among plants.

Standard

To reduce confusion caused by regional and vernacular differences, and to facilitate reference to lists of legally-protected organisms, species identification reports should always report scientific names. They may additionally report common names.

Contents of the Case Report

The NAS Report (2009) clearly calls for transparency in forensic science, a move away from the historical tendency to say as little as possible about the analyses. If your forensic science is sound, then you should not fear making your methods and findings available for scrutiny by any scientist, including those consulting for the opposing side. Indeed, if an opposing expert agrees your methodology is unassailable, then perhaps council will stipulate to your testimony and choose to argue the case on other grounds. To that end, the NAS recommendations call for reports to include: "methods and materials," "procedures," "results," and "conclusions" (see Figure 11.3 for a sample report). As long as bench notes are comprehensive and reference appropriate SOPs, it is not necessary to provide extensive protocol details in a formal report. "Results" should state the findings; "conclusions" are an opinion statement by the reporting expert, interpreting the results. Vouchers used for comparison should be referenced in either the report or the bench notes. Sources and magnitudes of uncertainty should be clearly identified in the procedures and conclusions; conclusions should not over-state the findings. If, for instance, a genetic analysis identifies the species of a questioned fish fillet as *Oncorhynchus mykiss*, if appropriate, the report should clearly state that the test did not discriminate whether the fish was a freshwater rainbow trout or a protected anadromous steelhead, as these species are genetically identical. Likewise, an STR analysis linking a gut pile in the woods to an elk steak in the freezer should not state that the samples unequivocally came from the same animal, but should present the probability that the match occurred by chance, and an explanation of how this probability was calculated. Clearly, match probabilities can be defined for individualization with STR data, but error and uncertainty are much more difficult to quantify for class characterization such as species identification. Terms should be well defined – what do "match" and "consistent with" mean? A mtDNA evidence sequence might be identical to a voucher sequence, allowing species identification, but it would only "fail to exclude" in the context of individualization. Some labs' reports have a glossary on the back, explaining in plain language the meaning of terms.

Standard

Reports should include information on the provenance of the evidence, methods and materials, procedures, results, and conclusions. The report should contain enough detail for another expert to be able to ascertain how the analysis was accomplished and conclusions were drawn.

Standard

Terms such as "match," "consistent with," etc. should be defined, and known sources of error should be reported.

Review

Case files, including reports and bench notes, should go through technical and administrative reviews before case reports are issued. Technical review by a second party with appropriate knowledge of the theory and limits of the methodology employed will identify errors and ensure that the analyst draws appropriate

UNITED STATES DEPARTMENT OF COMMERCE
National Oceanic and Atmospheric Administration
NATIONAL OCEAN SERVICE
Center for Coastal Environmental Health and Biomolecular Research
219 Fort Johnson Road
Charleston, South Carolina 29412-9110

EVIDENCE EXAMINATION REPORT –DNA ANALYSIS

A. SAMPLE INFORMATION

Identification number: The eggs received as NOAA number C1234567 were assigned Charleston Reference Numbers 2010-045-1 through 2010-045-3. See Sample Analysis Table for further detail.

Date Transferred to NOS Charleston Laboratory: Samples were received on 08/30/2010 via FedEx (tracking number 0123 4567 8910).

Transferred by: Special Agent Pat Rolling, NOAA/NMFS Office for Law Enforcement, 123 Ocean Drive, Miami, FL 33408.

Received by: M. Katherine Moore, National Ocean Service Charleston Laboratory, 219 Ft. Johnson Rd., Charleston, SC 29412.

Comments: The eggs were frozen upon arrival and were stored in a secure freezer.

B. SAMPLE EXAMINATION

Methods and materials:

DNA was extracted from the samples using a Qiagen DNeasy kit. DNA was amplified via polymerase chain reaction (PCR) using universal primers for cytochrome *b*. This region of mitochondrial DNA is informative for species identification of sea turtles (Moore *et al.*, 2003). Amplicons were cycle sequenced using ABI Prism® Big Dye™ Terminator v1.1. Sequence data was collected on an ABI Prism® 3130 automated sequencer. Species identification was determined by phylogenetic reconstruction of evidence and reference standard sequences using *MEGA* version 4.0 (Tamura *et al.*, 2007).

Results: The samples yielded one mitochondrial haplotype with a consensus sequence of 833 base pairs. The evidence consensus sequence was identical to haplotype Cm1, a Marine Forensics internal reference haplotype for *Chelonia mydas* (green sea turtle). (See the Sample Analysis Table).

In phylogenetic reconstruction, all CRN2010-045 samples clustered with the green turtle (*Chelonia mydas*) clade in 100% of the bootstrap replicates

Conclusions: I identified samples CRN 2010-045-1 through -3 as green sea turtle, *Chelonia mydas*. See the Sample Analysis Table for details.

CRN 2010-045/Page 1 of 2

Figure 11.3 Example species identification report produced by the NOAA Marine Forensics Program.

UNITED STATES DEPARTMENT OF COMMERCE
National Oceanic and Atmospheric Administration
NATIONAL OCEAN SERVICE
Center for Coastal Environmental Health and Biomolecular Research
219 Fort Johnson Road
Charleston, South Carolina 29412-9110

EVIDENCE EXAMINATION REPORT –DNA ANALYSIS

Standard species used for comparison: loggerhead (*Caretta caretta*), Atlantic green (*Chelonia mydas*), Pacific green (*Chelonia mydas*), hawksbill (*Eretmochelys imbricata*), leatherback (*Dermochelys coriacea*), olive ridley (*Lepidochelys olivacea*), Kemp's ridley (*Lepidochelys kempii*), flatback (*Natator depressa*), common snapping turtle (*Chelydra serpentina*) and alligator snapping turtle (*Macroclemys temminckii*).

References:

Moore, M. K., Bemiss, J. A., Rice, S. M., *et al.* (2003) Use of restriction fragment length polymorphisms to identify sea turtle eggs and cooked meats to species. *Conservation Genetics,* **4,** 95-103.

Tamura, K., Dudley, J., Nei, M. and Kumar, S. (2007) MEGA4: Molecular Evolutionary Genetics Analysis (MEGA) software version 4.0. *Molecular Biology and Evolution,* **24,** 1596-1599.

C. SAMPLE ANALYSIS TABLE

Description and species identification of CRN 2010-045 samples.

CRN	NOAA case #	Item #	Description	Species ID
2010-045-1	C1234567	1	egg	*Chelonia mydas* (green turtle)
2010-045-2	C1234567	2	egg	*C. mydas* (green turtle)
2010-045-3	C1234567	3	egg	*C. mydas* (green turtle)

Date of report: 10/04/10

Documented by: ____________________

M. Katherine Moore
Forensic Analyst

Figure 11.3 (*Continued*)

conclusions from the results. Such reviews also provide opportunities for co-workers to cross-train and generate ideas for future improvements to laboratory processes or methodology. Administrative review provides an additional chance to catch typographical, formatting, or other errors, and ensures that policies have been properly followed.

Standard

Each case file and report should be technically and administratively reviewed by a qualified second party before reports are issued. Results of the reviews should be documented in the case file.

Guideline

Administrative review should be carried out by a third person, offering a different perspective than those of the analyst and technical reviewer.

Court Testimony

When called to testify about their results, forensic scientists serve as expert witnesses. Expert witnesses are the only witnesses allowed to offer their opinions to the court – others are required to stick only to the facts. Because expert witnesses are assumed to be more knowledgeable about their field than other members of the court, and are allowed opinions in interpreting their results, they must qualify as experts in the matter at hand, demonstrating their expertise through knowledge, experience, publications, participation in professional societies, etc. The recent ruling in *Melendez-Diaz v. Massachusetts* [129 S.Ct. 2527, 2532 (2009)] clarified and reaffirmed a defendant's right to question forensic results presented as evidence against them. The fallout from *Melendez-Diaz* remains to be seen, but prior to the ruling it was quite common for a bench scientist or technician to conduct a forensic analysis, then pass the results to a supervisor for him/her to interpret the results, sign the report, and, if called, testify about the analysis in court. The scientist performing the testing was not the one to testify about the results. In the world of human forensics, this division of labor is enabled by tightly written protocols with no deviation left to the discretion of the bench scientist. If modification of the protocol is necessary, the supervisor must sign off on it, so in any case, the supervisor knows exactly how the analysis was performed and can testify about the analysis as well as interpretation of the results. In wildlife labs, there is seldom such a division of labor because there are fewer personnel. Also, with a wide array of taxa to analyze that are not as well-characterized as humans and no standardized commercial kits available, wildlife forensic protocols are often written with a range of acceptable conditions defined, so the analyst is allowed some discretion in the execution of the protocol. All analysts, therefore, should perform their analyses and sign their reports with the expectation of being called to testify. Expert witness testimony training is recommended for all personnel likely to be called to testify.

Standard

All reports should include the name(s) and signature(s) of all who were involved in generation and interpretation of forensic data.

Guideline

All members of the laboratory who handle evidence should receive expert witness training.

The Way Forward

We intend for this chapter to provide guidance for continual improvement among WF DNA practitioners, and a road map to follow for those researchers who are unexpectedly called upon to provide analyses for the courts. Our aim was to strike a balance between pragmatism necessary when dealing with such a diversity of species and the rigor required for the courts. Ideally, laboratories will use these standards and guidelines in conjunction with third-party administered proficiency testing and certification of practitioners (a certification program is in the planning stages). SWGWILD will continue to build upon these ideas in drafting consensus standards for SWFS' review and adoption to raise the bar for WF practice and spur the discipline to further maturity. Lastly, we acknowledge that the larger forensic community's rapid movement towards universal accreditation of laboratories and certification of practitioners will likely overtake specialty disciplines like WF, and we hope that this chapter will assist accrediting bodies in preparing auditors for the unique task of assessing wildlife laboratories.

Acknowledgements

The authors are the Chair (MKM) and Vice-Chair (ILK) of the newly-formed SWGWILD. Though these recommendations do not represent final work product of the entire SWG, we gratefully acknowledge the remaining members and subject matter experts (SMEs) for fruitful discussions on best practices at and subsequent to the first meeting: Lara Adams, Mary Burnham-Curtis, Carolyn Ferrel, Kim Frazier, DeeDee Hawk, John Paul Jones (SME), Robin Jones (SME),

Trey P. Knott (SME), Christina Lindquist, Piper Schwenke, and Paul Wilson. Ed Espinoza and Rob Ogden also contributed positively to many a debate. Mary Burnham Curtis provided extensive and welcome input on data analysis and interpretation guidelines as well as a detailed and constructive review. Maggie Broadwater, Trey P. Knott, Lawrence E. Moore, Nancy P. Moore, and Jessica Tiedeken also provided helpful reviews. ILK thanks Maryhaven for continued support. MKM thanks Tom Ognibene for his patience and support. This work was partially funded by the National Oceanic and Atmospheric Administration/National Ocean Service (NOAA/NOS).The National Ocean Service (NOS) does not approve, recommend, or endorse any proprietary product or material mentioned in this publication. No reference shall be made to NOS, or to this publication furnished by NOS, in any advertising or sales promotion which would indicate or imply that NOS approves, recommends, or endorses any proprietary product or proprietary material mentioned herein or which has as its purpose any intent to cause directly or indirectly the advertised product to be used or purchased because of NOS publication. The authors declare they have no competing financial interests.

References

Anderson, J.D., Honeycutt, R.L., Gonzales, R.A., *et al.* (2002) Development of microsatellite DNA markers for the automated genetic characterization of white-tailed deer populations. *Journal of Wildlife Management*, **66**, 67–74.

Arctander, P. (1995) Comparison of a mitochondrial gene and a corresponding nuclear pseudogene. *Proceedings of the Royal Society of London Series B-Biological Sciences*, **262**, 13–19.

Austerlitz, F., David, O., Schaeffer, B., *et al.* (2009) DNA barcode analysis: a comparison of phylogenetic and statistical classification methods. *BMC Bioinformatics*, **10 Suppl 14**, S10.

Bellis, C., Ashton, K. J., Freney, L., *et al.* (2003) A molecular genetic approach for forensic animal species identification. *Forensic Science International*, **134**, 99–108.

Bentley, D. R., Balasubramanian, S., Swerdlow, H.P., *et al.* (2008) Accurate whole human genome sequencing using reversible terminator chemistry. *Nature*, **456**, 53–59.

Blanco, M., Pérez-Martín, R. I. and Sotelo, C. G. (2008) Identification of shark species in seafood products by Forensically Informative Nucleotide Sequencing (FINS). *Journal of Agricultural and Food Chemistry*, **56**, 9868–9874.

Bowen, B.W. and Avise, J.C. (1994) Conservation research and the legal status of PCR products. *Science*, **266**, 713.

Bowen, B.W., Nelson, W.S. and Avise, J.C. (1993) A molecular phylogeny for marine turtles: trait mapping, rate assessment, and conservation relevance. *Proceedings of the National Academy of Sciences, USA*, **90**, 5574–5577.

Braddon, S.A., Caffrey, B.B. and Pike, J.R. (1982) Identification of suspect sea turtle meat samples and determination of species, a law enforcement problem. NOAA Technical Memorandum NMFS-SEFC-TM-105.

Branicki, W., Kupiec, T. and Pawlowski, R. (2003) Validation of cytochrome b sequence analysis as a method of species identification. *Journal of Forensic Sciences*, **48**, 83–87.

Budowle, B., Garofano, P., Hellman, A., *et al.* (2005) Recommendations for animal DNA forensic and identity testing. *International Journal of Legal Medicine*, **119**, 295–302.

Buhay, J.E. (2009) "COI-like" sequences are becoming problematic in molecular systematic and DNA barcoding studies. *Journal of Crustacean Biology*, **29**, 96–110.

Butler, J. (2006) Debunking some urban legends surrounding validation within the forensic DNA community. *Profiles In DNA*, **9**, 3–6.

Butler, J. (2010) *Fundamentals of Forensic DNA Typing*. San Diego, CA, Academic Press.

Carter, R., Bryson, C.T. and Darbyshire, S.J. (2007) Preparation and use of voucher specimens for documenting research in weed science. *Weed Technology*, **21**, 1101–1108.

Cassidy, B.G. and Gonzales, R.A. (2005) DNA testing in animal forensics. *Journal of Wildlife Management*, **69**, 1454–1462.

Dawnay, N., Ogden, R., McEwing, R., *et al.* (2007) Validation of the barcoding gene COI for use in forensic genetic species identification. *Forensic Science International*, **173**, 1–6.

Dawnay, N., Ogden, R., Thorpe, R.S., *et al.* (2008) A forensic STR profiling system for the Eurasian badger: a framework for developing profiling systems for wildlife species. *Forensic Science International: Genetics* **2**, 47–53.

DenDanto, D., Palman, D., Kornfield, I., *et al.* (2002) Allele frequencies for three STR loci RT24, RT09, and BM1225 in northern New England white-tailed deer. *Journal of Forensic Sciences*, **47**, 673–675.

Department of Interior (2011) Integrity of scientific and scholarly activities. In *Departmental Manual, Part 305*, Chapter 3. Available at: http://elips.doi.gov/app_dm/act_getfiles.cfm?relnum=3889.

Dror, I.E., Charlton, D. and Péron, A.E. (2006) Contextual information renders experts vulnerable to making erroneous identifications. *Forensic Science International*, **156**, 74–78.

Edwards, H.T. (2010) The National Academy of Sciences report on forensic sciences: what it means for the bench and bar. Paper presented at Conference on the Role of the Court in an Age of Developing Science and Technology. Superior Court of the District of Columbia, Washington, D.C.

Espinoza, E.O. and Baker, B.W. (2007) The analysis of sea turtle and bovid keratin artefacts using drift spectroscopy and discriminant analysis. *Archaeometry*, **4**, 685–698.

Fain, S.R. and LeMay, J.P. (1995) Gender identification of humans and mammalian wildlife species from PCR amplified sex linked genes. In *Proceedings of the American Academy of Forensic Science (February 13–18, 1995)*, 34.

FBI (2009) Quality assurance standards for forensic DNA testing laboratories. Available at: http://www.cstl.nist.gov/strbase/QAS/Final-FBI-Director-Forensic-Standards.pdf (accessed March 21 2011).

FBI (2010) SWGDAM Interpretation Guidelines for Autosomal STR Typing by Forensic DNA Testing Laboratories. Available at: http://www.fbi.gov/about-us/lab/codis/swgdam-interpretation-guidelines (accessed March 21 2011).

Forster, P. (2003) To err is human. *Annals of Human Genetics*, **67**, 2–4.

GAO (2009) *Seafood Fraud: FDA Program Changes and Better Collaboration among Key Federal Agencies Could Improve Detection and Prevention.* Washington, DC: GAO.

Greig, T. W., Moore, M. K., Woodley, C. M. and Quattro, J. M. (2005) Mitochondrial gene sequences useful for species identification of commercially regulated Atlantic Ocean sharks. *Fishery Bulletin*, **103**, 516-523.

Hall, B.G. (2011) *Phylogenetic Trees Made Easy: A How-To Manual*. Sunderland, MA, Sinauer.

Halverson, J.L. and Lyons, L.A. (2004) Forensic DNA identification of feline hairs: casework and a mitochondrial database. *Proceedings of the American Academy of Forensic Sciences*, **X**, B150.

Harris, D. J. (2003) Can you bank on GenBank? *Trends in Ecology and Evolution*, **18**, 317–319.

Hebert, P. D. N., Cywinska, A., Ball, S.L. and deWaard, J. R. (2003) Biological identifications through DNA barcodes. *Proceedings of the Royal Society of London Series B*, **270**, 313–321.

Hedrick, P. (2009) *Genetics of Populations*. Sudbury, MA: Jones and Bartlett Publishers.

Heist, E.J. and Gold, J.R. (1999) Genetic identification of sharks in the U.S. Atlantic large coastal shark fishery. *Fishery Bulletin*, **97**, 53–61.

Hilgers, L.J. and Herr, C. (1993) DNA contamination of reagents used in embryo transfer and culture. *Theriogenology*, **40**, 923–932.

Holland, M.M. and Parsons, T.J. (1999) Mitochondrial DNA sequence analysis – validation and use for forensic casework. *Forensic Science Review*, **11**, 21–50.

Hummel, S. (2007) Ancient DNA. In W. Henke and I. Tattersall (eds.) *Handbook of Paleoanthropology*. Berlin: Springer, pp. 643–672.

Hyde, J.R., Lynn, E., Humphreys Jr., R., *et al.* (2005) Shipboard identification of fish eggs and larvae by multiplex PCR, and description of fertilized eggs of blue marlin, shortbill spearfish, and wahoo. *Marine Ecology Progress Series*, **286**, 269–277.

International Human Genome Sequencing Consortium (2004) Finishing the euchromatic sequence of the human genome. *Nature*, **431**, 931–945.

Jones, M. (1994) PCR products and CITES. *Science*, **266**, 1930.

Kalous, L., Šlechtová, V., Petrtýl, M., *et al.* (2010) Do small fish mean no voucher? Using a flatbed desktop scanner to document larval and small specimens before destructive analyses. *Journal of Applied Ichthyology*, **26**, 614–617.

Krane, D.E., Ford, S., Gilder, J.R., *et al.* (2008) Sequential unmasking: a means of minimizing observer effects in forensic DNA interpretation. *Journal of Forensic Sciences*, **53**, 1006–1007.

Krane, D.E., Ford, S., Gilder, J.R., *et al.* (2010) Commentary on: Budowle B, Bottrell MC, Bunch SG, Fram R, Harrison D, Meagher S, Oien CT, Peterson PE, Seiger DP,Smith MB, Smrz MA, Soltis GL, Stacey RB. A perspective on errors, bias, and interpretation in the forensic sciences and direction for continuing advancement. *Journal of Forensic Sciences*, **55**, 273–274.

LaHood, E.S., Moran, P., Olsen, J., *et al.* (2002) Microsatellite allele ladders in two species of Pacific salmon: preparation and field-test results. *Molecular Ecology Notes*, **2**, 187–190.

Levy, S., Sutton, G., Ng, P.C., *et al.* (2007) The diploid genome sequence of an individual human. *PLoS Biology*, **5**, e254.

Lim, H.T., Kim, B.W., Yoon, D., *et al.* (2011) An allelic ladder for eleven short tandem repeat loci for use in the cattle identity test. *Animal Genetics*, **42**, 226–227.

Linacre, A. (ed.) (2009) *Forensic Science in Wildlife Investigations*. Boca Raton, FL: CRC Press.

Linacre, A., Gusmão, L., Hecht, W., *et al.* (2011) ISFG: Recommendations regarding the use of non-human (animal) DNA in forensic genetic investigations. *Forensic Science International: Genetics*, **5**, 501–505.

Longo, M.S., O'Neill, M.J. and O'Neill, R.J. (2011) Abundant human DNA contamination identified in non-primate genome databases. *PLoS One*, **6**, e16410.

Lou, M. and Golding, G.B. (2010) Assigning sequences to species in the absence of large interspecific differences. *Molecular Phylogenetics and Evolution*, **56**, 187–194.

Meyer, C.P. and Paulay, G. (2005) DNA barcoding: error rates based on comprehensive sampling. *PLoS Biology*, **3**, e422.

Moore, M.K., Bemiss, J.A., Rice, S.M., *et al.* (2003) Use of restriction fragment length polymorphisms to identify sea turtle eggs and cooked meats to species. *Conservation Genetics*, **4**, 95–103.

Moritz, C. and Cicero, C. (2004) DNA barcoding: promise and pitfalls. *PLoS Biology*, **2**, e354.

National Academy of Sciences (2009) *Strengthening Forensic Science in the United States: A Path Forward*. Washington, DC: National Research Council.

National Research Council (1996) *NRC I: The Evaluation of Forensic DNA Evidence*. Washington, DC: National Academy Press.

Nijman, I.J., Otsen, M., Verkaar, E.L.C., *et al.* (2003) Hybridization of banteng (*Bos javanicus*) and zebu (*Bos indicus*) revealed by mitochondrial DNA, satellite DNA, AFLP and microsatellites. *Heredity*, **90**, 10–16.

Office of Science and Technology Policy (2010) Memorandum for the Heads of Executive Departments and Agencies: Scientific Integrity. Available at: http://www.whitehouse.gov/sites/default/files/microsites/ostp/scientific-integrity-memo-12172010.pdf.

Ogden, R. (2010) Forensic science, genetics and wildlife biology: getting the right mix for a wildlife DNA forensics lab. *Forensic Science, Medicine, and Pathology*, **6**, 172–179.

Ogden, R., Dawnay, N. and McEwing, R. (2009) Wildlife DNA forensics – bridging the gap between conservation genetics and law enforcement. *Endangered Species Research*, **9**, 179–195.

Ostrum, B. (2009) Commentary on: Authors' response [J Forensic Sci 2009;54(2):501] to Wells' comments [J Forensic Sci 2009;54(2):500] regarding Krane DE, Ford S, Gilder JR, Inman K, Jamieson A, Koppl R, Kornfield IL, Risinger DM, Rudin N, Taylor MS, Thompson WC. Sequential unmasking: a means of minimizing observer effects in forensic DNA interpretation. *Journal of Forensic Sciences*, **54**, 1498–1499; author reply 1500–1501.

Pereira, F., Carneiro, J. and van Asch, B. (2010) A guide for mitochondrial DNA analysis in non-human forensic investigations. *The Open Access Forensic Science Journal*, **3**, 33–44.

Pouyaud, L., Teugels, G.G., Gustiano, R. and Legendre, M. (2000) Contribution to the phylogeny of pangasiid catfishes based on allozymes and mitochondrial DNA. *Journal of Fish Biology*, **56**, 1509–1538.

Purcell, M., Mackey, G., LaHood, E., *et al.* (2004) Molecular methods for the genetic identification of salmonid prey from Pacific harbor seal (*Phoca vitulina richardsi*) scat. *Fishery Bulletin*, **102**, 213–220.

Ratnasingham, S. and Hebert, P.D.N. (2007) BOLD: The Barcode of Life Data System (www.barcodinglife.org). *Molecular Ecology Notes*, **7**, 355–364.

Ross, H.A., Murugan, S. and Li, W.L.S. (2008) Testing the reliability of genetic methods of species identification via simulation. *Systematic Biology*, **57**, 216–230.

Rubinoff, D., Cameron, S. and Kipling, W. (2006) A genomic perspective on the shortcomings of mitochondrial DNA for "barcoding" identification. *Heredity*, **97**, 581–594.

Ryder, O.A., McLaren, A., Brenner, S., *et al.* (2000) DNA banks for endangered animal species. *Science*, **288**, 275–277.

Salazar, K. (2009) Enhancing and promoting an ethical culture within the Department of the Interior. In Department of Interior (ed.) *Secretarial Order 3288*. Washington, DC: U.S. Government Printing Office.

Savolainen, P. and Lundeberg, J. (1999) Forensic evidence based on mtDNA from dog and wolf hairs. *Journal of Forensic Sciences*, **44**, 77–81.

Shivji, M., Clarke, S., Pank, M., *et al.* (2002) Genetic identification of pelagic shark body parts for conservation and trade monitoring. *Conservation Biology*, **16**, 1036–1047.

Stephenson, J.J., Campbell, M.R., Hess, J.E., *et al.* (2009) A centralized model for creating shared, standardized, microsatellite data that simplifies inter-laboratory collaboration. *Conservation Genetics*, **10**, 1145–1149.

Straughan, D.J., Burnham-Curtis, M.K. and Fain, S.R. (2002) Experimental search for forensically useful markers in the genus *Scaphirhynchus*. *Journal of Applied Ichthyology*, **18**, 621–628.

Thompson, W.C., Ford, S., Gilder, J.R., *et al.* (2011) Commentary on: Thornton JI. Letter to the editor – a rejection of "working blind" as a cure for contextual bias, J Forensic Sci (2010) **55**,1663. *Journal of Forensic Sciences*, **56**, 562–563.

Thornton, J.I. (2010) Letter to the editor – A rejection of "working blind" as a cure for contextual bias. *Journal of Forensic Sciences*, **55**, 1663.

Viñas, J. and Tudela, S. (2009) A validated methodology for genetic identification of tuna species (genus *Thunnus*). *PLoS One*, **4**, e7606.

Viricel, A. and Rosel, P.E. (2011) Evaluating the utility of *cox1* for cetacean species identification. *Marine Mammal Science*, ePub ahead of print.

Wang, J., Wang, W., Li, R., *et al.* (2008) The diploid genome sequence of an Asian individual. *Nature*, **456**, 60–65.

Ward, R.D., Zemlak, T.S., Innes, B.H., *et al.* (2005) DNA barcoding Australia's fish species. *Philosophical Transactions of the Royal Society, Part B*, **360**, 1847–1857.

Weir, B.S. and Hill, W.G. (2002) Estimating F-statistics. *Annual Review of Genetics*, **36**, 721–750.

Wells, J. D. (2009) Commentary on: Krane DE, Ford S, Gilder JR, Inman K, Jamieson A, Koppl R, Kornfield IL, Risinger DM, Rudin N, Taylor MS, Thompson WC. Sequential unmasking: a means of minimizing observer effects in forensic DNA interpretation. *J Forensic Sci* (2008), **53**(4), 1006–1007. *Journal of Forensic Sciences*, **54**, 500; author reply 501.

Wheeler, D. A., Srinivasan, M., Egholm, M., *et al.* (2008) The complete genome of an individual by massively parallel DNA sequencing. *Nature*, **452**, 872–876.

Wilson, M. R., DiZinno, J. A., Polanskey, D., *et al.* (1995) Validation of mitochondrial DNA sequencing for forensic casework analysis. *International Journal of Legal Medicine*, **108**, 68–74.

Wong, E. H.-K. and Hanner, R.H. (2008) DNA barcoding detects market substitution in North American seafood. *Food Research International*, **41**, 828–837.

Wong, E. H.-K., Shivji, M.S. and Hanner, R.H. (2009) Identifying sharks with DNA barcodes: assessing the utility of a nucleotide diagnostic approach. *Molecular Ecology Resources*, **9**, 243–256.

Wuertz, S., Belay, M. and Kirschbaum, F. (2007) On the risk of criminal manipulation in caviar trade by intended contamination of caviar with PCR products. *Aquaculture*, **269**, 130–134.

Yates, B.C. and Sims, M.E. (2010) Tupilak transformations: traditional ivory objects as modern souvenirs. In D. Campana, P. Crabtree, S.D. deFrance, J. Lev-Tov, and A. Choyke (eds) *Anthropological Approaches to Zooarcheology: Colonialism, Complexity, and Animal Transformations*. Oakville, CT: Oxbow Books, pp. 230–234.

12

Statistics for Wildlife Forensic DNA

B.S. Weir

Introduction

DNA evidence has been used to great effect in human forensic science for over 20 years, and it is also having a substantial impact on wildlife forensic science. Although many of the issues of interpretation are the same in the human and non-human situations, there are also differences. Identifying the species or population of origin of the animal that was the source of a biological sample is a major concern in the wildlife setting, as is the need to account for inbreeding and relatedness to a much greater extent than in the human setting. Wildlife forensic scientists often have to work with much smaller reference databases than do their colleagues working with human samples. Nevertheless, the statistical underpinnings for the interpretation of DNA profiles are general, and they will be treated here. Chapter 13 in this volume by McGraw, Keeler and Huffman provides information about the genetic typing systems used in wildlife forensics.

This chapter reviews the statistical underpinnings of DNA profile interpretation with two principal themes: first, DNA profiles are genetic and so have been shaped by evolutionary history. An understanding of the variation introduced by evolutionary forces is necessary. Second, there is uncertainty attached to any quantity that is estimated with data on a sample from a population, as opposed to a complete census of the population. Fortunately, there are well-established procedures in place for incorporating both these sources of variation: the "genetic" and the "statistical."

Wildlife Forensics: Methods and Applications, First Edition. Edited by Jane E. Huffman and John R. Wallace.

The Central Problem

Suppose a biological sample from some animal C is to be used as evidence. This sample may be from the carcass of an endangered animal or from a hair on the clothing of a murder victim. Another sample, from animal S, may link a suspect to a crime. This sample may be from meat in the suspect's freezer or from a cat in the suspect's house. The two samples are typed and found to have matching DNA profiles: does that provide strong evidence against the suspect? There are competing hypotheses:

H_p: The two profiles match because S and C are the same animal.

H_d: The match is coincidental: S and C are not the same animal.

A good way of quantifying the strength of the evidence is to compare the probabilities of the two profiles under each hypothesis:

$$\text{LR} = \frac{\text{Probability of the profiles of } S \text{ and } C \text{ if } H_p \text{ is true}}{\text{Probability of the profiles of } S \text{ and } C \text{ if } H_d \text{ is true}}$$

This equation allows us to address complexities such as inbreeding, relatedness, population structure, and mixtures.

Forensic STR markers often have 10 or more alleles, so there are 55 or more genotypes per diploid marker. With 10 markers, there are at least $55^{10} > 10^{17}$ possible profiles – more than there are individuals of that species. It is not very helpful, therefore, to say the matching profile is rare because all profiles are rare. The important question is: once we have seen the profile from animal S, how likely is it that we will see the profile again in animal C if S and C are different animals?

Profile and match probabilities

Suppose that the matching profiles both have the genotype A_1A_2 at an autosomal locus. The probability that a randomly chosen individual has this profile, the "profile probability," is written as $\Pr(A_1A_2)$. The probability that an unknown individual C will be found to have profile A_1A_2 given that a different individual S has been found to have that profile, the "match probability," is written as $\Pr(A_1A_2|A_1A_2)$. In general, as we will see below, $\Pr(A_1A_2|A_1A_2)$ is greater than $\Pr(A_1A_2)$ and the actual difference between the two depends on inbreeding, relatedness, population structure and so on. The chance of seeing a profile increases once the profile has already been seen – having seen a profile once, we know that it is one of the vast number of possible profiles that actually exists. The evolutionary processes that led to this profile may well have done so more than once.

The exception to this difference between match and profile probabilities arises when all individuals in a population are independent, so knowing the profile of one individual provides no information about that of another. Such independence could be assumed for very large populations mating at random and when there are no related individuals within the population. These conditions do not hold in any real population, although they may lead to useful approximate results.

If the observed match is just what is expected under the proposition H_p, so the evidence probability under H_p is 1, then the likelihood ratio is the reciprocal of the match probability:

$$\text{LR} = \frac{1}{\Pr(A_1A_2|A_1A_2)}$$

Large likelihood ratios are obtained when the match probabilities are small. Large values indicate strong evidence: the evidence of a match is much more likely under H_p than it is under H_d.

Statistical sampling

We can estimate profile and match probabilities by seeing how often the constituent alleles occur in a sample of individuals of that species. For autosomal markers, we generally assume Hardy-Weinberg equilibrium in the population so that profile probabilities are

$$\begin{aligned}\Pr(A_1A_1) &= p_1^2, \quad \text{for homozygotes}\\ \Pr(A_1A_2) &= 2p_1p_2, \quad \text{for heterozygotes}\end{aligned}$$

If the allele A_1 has a frequency of $\tilde{p}_1$ in a sample from the population, then we can estimate:

$$\Pr(A_1A_1)$$

for example, by $\tilde{p}_1^2$. If a sample of n individuals is taken at random from a population, then the number of copies of allele A_1 in the sample has a binomial distribution and the sample allele frequency $\tilde{p}_1$ has an expected or average value over all samples equal to the population frequency p_1, and a variance over samples of $p_1(1 - p_1)/2n$.

The quality of estimated profile probabilities increases as the sample size increases, meaning that both bias and variance decrease. If a sample of n individuals was used, then in the random mating situation, the expected values of estimated homozygote and heterozygote frequencies follow from the binomial distribution as:

$$E\left(\tilde{p}_1^2\right) = p_1^2 + \frac{p_1(1-p_1)}{2n}$$

$$E\left(2\tilde{p}_1\tilde{p}_2\right) = 2p_1p_2 - \frac{2p_1p_2}{2n}$$

The terms with n in the denominator are the biases and these become small for moderately large values of n. Still assuming random mating, the variances of estimated genotype frequencies are:

$$\mathrm{Var}\left(\tilde{p}_1^2\right) \approx \frac{4p_1^3(1-p_1)}{2n}$$

$$\mathrm{Var}\left(2\tilde{p}_1\tilde{p}_2\right) \approx \frac{4p_1p_2(p_1+p_2-4p_1p_2)}{2n}$$

and these also decrease as the sample size n increases.

For unlinked markers, we may assume independence over loci and multiply the estimates together to get an overall profile probability estimate for the profile probability P:

$$\text{If } \hat{P}_l \text{ is the estimate for locus } l, \text{ then } \hat{P} \text{ is } \prod_l \hat{P}_l$$

where $\prod$ indicates a product. The product is approximately normally distributed *on the log scale* and this gives rise to confidence intervals of the form $(\hat{P}/C, \hat{P}C)$. Beecham and Weir (2011) show that, for a 95% confidence interval, C is e raised to the power of $1.96\sqrt{\mathrm{Var}(\ln \hat{P})}$. The quantity C typically is in the range of 10 to 100. If $C = 10$, a profile probability of 1 in a million would have a 95% confidence interval of 1 in 10 million to 1 in a hundred thousand. The DNAMIX3 software to perform calculations is available online (at http://biostat.washington.edu/~bsweir/DNAMIX3). As an example, consider the Polymarker™ profile in Table 12.1 with numerical results based on data

Table 12.1 A Polymarker™ profile.

Locus	Genotype	$\hat{P}$	$\ln(\hat{P})$	$\mathrm{Var}(\ln \hat{P})$
LDLR	AB	0.4921	−0.7092	0.0003
GYPA	BB	0.2125	−1.5487	0.0227
HBGG	BC	0.0044	−5.4330	0.9626
D7S8	AB	0.4961	−0.7009	0.0002
Gc	BC	0.2185	−1.5210	0.0138
Profile		Product 0.000,050	Sum −9.9128	Sum 0.9996

published by the FBI. Thus, the interval becomes (0.000,007 to 0.000,352) on the original scale – a factor 7 in each direction from the estimate.

95% CI on the log scale is $-9.9128 \pm 1.96\sqrt{0.9996}$ or $(-11.8724, -7.9532)$.

Genetic Sampling

A major difficulty with forensic DNA calculations lies in knowing what allele frequencies to use. The previous section referred to "population" and "sample" allele frequencies without further detail. Wildlife populations are likely to exist as a series of subpopulations, only one of which may be relevant for a particular forensic situation. We write the frequency for allele A_1 in such a subpopulation as p_1^*, and invoke a population genetic framework in which the average, or expectation, over all subpopulations of this quantity is the population frequency p_1: $E(p_1^*) = p_1$. We are especially interested in the variation of the p^*'s among subpopulations, and so we introduce the population structure parameter θ, or F_{ST}, by the result

$$\mathrm{Var}\left(p_1^*\right) = p_1(1 - p_1)\theta$$

When a sample of n individuals is taken from the whole population, there is statistical variation because of the particular individuals in the sample as well as genetic variation because of the particular subpopulations represented in the sample. Following the discussion given by Beecham and Weir (2011) we find that the variation of a allele frequency in a sample from a single subpopulation changes from the binomial variance of $p_1(1 - p_1)/2n$ to

$$\mathrm{Var}\left(\tilde{p}_1\right) = p_1(1 - p_1)\left(\theta + \frac{1-\theta}{2n}\right)$$

It is more likely that a sample of n individuals contains individuals from an unknown number of subpopulations, and we will use this same expression as an upper bound on the variance of the allele frequency for a sample from the whole population. This expression shows that there is variation attached to sample allele frequencies, and hence to estimated genotypic frequencies and likelihood ratios, even when the sample size becomes very large. The variation reflects the differences in allele frequencies among subpopulations.

Match probabilities

The genetic sampling process that gives rise to variation among subpopulations also causes dependencies among individuals within subpopulations. An intuitive explanation of these dependencies follows from imagining it is possible to trace the pedigree of any two individuals back in time. Simply because natural populations are finite, there will be a time in the past when there is an ancestor common to both individuals. This relatedness due to common ancestors will increase over time and the resulting similarities within subpopulations leads to divergence among subpopulations. The population structure parameter θ serves to measure both this divergence among subpopulations and the convergence within subpopulations. The following development can be regarded as addressing the issue of population structure and it is necessary as soon as we consider events that took place in previous generations, as we must also do when considering inbreeding and relatedness.

There is wide class of evolutionary scenarios for which the distribution of allele frequencies p^* over subpopulations has a form known as the Dirichlet (Balding and Nichols, 1994). A very useful consequence of this distribution is that it is possible to give expressions for the probabilities of any set of alleles. The probability of allele A_1 if a set of n alleles already seen includes n_1 of type A_1 is:

$$\Pr(A_1|n_1 \text{ among } n \text{ alleles}) = \frac{n_1\theta + (1-\theta)p_1}{1+(n-1)\theta}$$

Setting $n_1 = n = 0$ gives the probability p_1 of a single allele being of type A_1. Then, setting $n_1 = n = 1$ gives the probability of an A_1 following an A_1: $\Pr(A_1|A_1) = [\theta + (1-\theta)p_1]$. The laws of probability then lead to the joint probability of two A_1's, i.e. the genotype probability of A_1A_1,

$$\begin{aligned}\Pr(A_1A_1) &= \Pr(A_1)\Pr(A_1|A_1) = p_1[\theta + (1-\theta)p_1] \\ &= p_1^2 + p_1(1-p_1)\theta\end{aligned}$$

The probability of an A_1 allele after an A_2 is found by setting $n_1 = 0$, $n = 1$: $\Pr(A_1|A_2) = (1-\theta)p_2$. Allowing for both orders, $A_1|A_2$ and $A_2|A_1$, leads to the heterozygote probability

$$\begin{aligned}\Pr(A_1A_2) &= \Pr(A_1)\Pr(A_2|A_1) + \Pr(A_2)\Pr(A_1|A_2) \\ &= 2(1-\theta)p_1p_2\end{aligned}$$

Extending this argument gives the match probabilities for A_1A_1 homozygotes

$$\Pr(A_1A_1|A_1A_1) = \frac{[3\theta + (1-\theta)p_1][2\theta + (1-\theta)p_1]}{(1+\theta)(1+2\theta)}$$

and this is greater than the profile probability $\Pr(A_1A_1)$. For A_1A_2 heterozygotes

$$\Pr(A_1A_2|A_1A_2) = \frac{2[\theta + (1-\theta)p_1][\theta + (1-\theta)p_2]}{(1+\theta)(1+2\theta)}$$

which is greater than the profile probability $\Pr(A_1A_2)$. A realistic value of θ for wildlife populations may be 0.05. If allele frequencies are about 0.10, the Hardy-Weinberg profile probabilities for homozygotes and heterozygotes, p_1^2 and $2p_1p_2$, are 0.01 and 0.02. Adding in the θ terms changes the profile probabilities to 0.0145 and 0.0190. The match probabilities are larger at 0.0414 and 0.0364, respectively.

Substituting sample allele frequencies leads to estimates of the match probabilities, and hence to likelihood ratios. The approach of Beecham and Weir (2011) constructs variances of these quantities and then confidence intervals for the likelihood ratios. Providing θ is greater than zero, the variances remain non-zero no matter how large the sample size n becomes.

What value of θ should be used? Because it refers to variation among subpopulations, we would need data from those subpopulations to estimate θ – but if we could sample the subpopulations we would not need the "theta correction" as we would already have estimates of allele frequencies for the subpopulation and we would not need to use population-wide sample values. For estimation of θ we have to rely on variation among the populations we can sample. We do know that, under certain assumptions, $\theta = 1/(1 + 4N\mu)$ where N is the number of individuals in the population and μ is the mutation rate. There is a similar result, $\theta = 1/(1 + 4Nm)$ that relates population structure to migration rate m but this assumes an infinite number of islands with equal migration rates among them all and this may be too far from reality to be useful.

Lineage Markers

Especially for degraded samples, mitochondrial and Y-chromosome markers offer a useful addition to autosomal STR markers. An individual has contributions from only one parent for these lineage markers and so is haploid. The lack of recombination on the mitochondrion or Y chromosome means that forensic calculations usually refer to multi-site haplotypes rather than individual markers. Simply reporting the frequency with which a particular haplotype occurs in a database does not seem satisfactory if that frequency is zero since the same result would hold if the haplotype was extended to include more matching markers. Intuition would suggest a strengthening of evidence with longer matching haplotypes.

The same general approach as for autosomal markers can be adopted as a starting point, as shown by Krawczak *et al.* (2011). For an mtDNA or Y-chromosome haplotype of type A_1 the match and profile probabilities for a specific subpopulation are both equal to p_1^*, the profile frequency in that subpopulation. If there was a sample available from that subpopulation, it would furnish an estimate of this quantity. When there is population structure, match and profile probabilities are no longer the same and the previous discussion of variation in allele frequencies across subpopulations provides the match probability:

$$\Pr(A_1|A_1) = \theta + (1 - \theta)p_1$$

This can be given a numerical value if reasonable estimates of p_1 and θ are available. Notice that the match probability within a particular subpopulation is also greater than the haplotype frequency in the whole population since $\theta + (1-\theta)p_1 > p_1$. Two haplotypes are more likely to be the same when they are taken from the same subpopulation than when they are taken randomly from the whole population.

Statistical sampling only

If a sample from the relevant subpopulation is available, the sample haplotype frequency $\tilde{p}_1$ is a reasonable estimate of the actual haplotype frequency p_1^* and therefore can be used to estimate p_1 for the match probability. If haplotype A_1 is seen x times in a sample of n haplotypes, $\tilde{p}_1 = x/n$. An exact confidence interval based on the binomial distribution was described by Clopper and Pearson (1934). An upper $100(1-\alpha)\%$ one-sided confidence limit p_0 is found by solving:

$$\sum_{k=0}^{x} \binom{n}{k} p_0^k (1-p_0)^{n-k} = \alpha$$

If the sample does not contain any copies of A_1, $x = 0$, then $p_0 = 1 - \alpha^{1/n}$ and for a 95% confidence limit, this is approximately $3/n$ once n is 100 or more. These confidence limits do not, however, address variation of p_1^* over subpopulations.

Statistical and genetic sampling

If there is population structure it is still possible to account for the effect of sampling variation on the relevant expression $\theta + (1-\theta)\tilde{p}_1$. Different samples will provide different values of $\tilde{p}_1$ and the variation among these values will decrease as the sample size increases. Use of the match probability equation incorporating θ, however, explicitly acknowledges variation among subpopulations and this variation, in turn, inflates the variance of $\tilde{p}_1$. For a sample taken from the whole population, with contributions from an unknown number of subpopulations

$$\text{Var}[\theta + (1-\theta)\tilde{p}_1] \approx p_1(1-p_1)\frac{(1-\theta)^3}{n}$$

What value of θ should be used for lineage markers? We do know that, under certain assumptions, $\theta = 1/(1+2N\mu)$ where N is the number of haplotypes in the population and μ is the mutation rate. As the number of markers in a haplotype increases, μ becomes larger and θ becomes smaller. The match probability $\Pr(A_1|A_1)$ tends towards the profile probability p_1 which decreases with the number of markers. For a large number of markers, the profile is quite likely not to be seen in the database – leading us back to the $3/n$ upper confidence limit.

Recently, Amorim (2008) has raised the issue whether likelihood ratios calculated from lineage and autosomal markers may be multiplied in order to obtain a single measure of the genetic evidence in a given case. Amorim challenged the practice of LR multiplication mainly on the grounds that lineage markers are not individual-specific but are instead shared by the suspect's whole lineage. Amorim's criticism was partly motivated by his perception of a common practice of sampling human lineages rather than sampling at random. Under such regimes, people with the same surname would be deliberately avoided when constructing a frequency database which, in turn, would lead to biased haplotype frequency estimates. With proper sampling of wildlife populations, it is appropriate to multiply autosomal and lineage likelihood ratios together, recognizing that they might well have different values of θ.

Relatedness

A common situation is where animals S and C, if not the same, may be related. The alternative hypotheses are:

H_p: The two profiles match because S and C are the same animal.

H_d: The two profiles match because S and C are related (to a specified degree).

If there is no inbreeding, relatedness can be described by three quantities that add to one: k_0, k_1, k_2 are the probabilities that the two individuals share 0, 1, 2 alleles *identical by descent*. The match probabilities change to:

$$\Pr(A_1A_1|A_1A_1) = k_0p_1^2 + k_1p_1 + k_2$$
$$\Pr(A_1A_2|A_1A_2) = 2k_0p_1p_2 + \frac{1}{2}k_1(p_1 + p_2) + k_2$$

For full siblings, $k_0 = 0.25$, $k_1 = 0.5$, $k_2 = 0.25$ and $\Pr(A_1A_1|A_1A_1) = (1 + p_1)^2/4$ instead of p_1^2 in the unrelated case. If $p_1 = 0.1$, the change is from 0.01 to 0.30. The strength of the evidence is reduced by a factor of 30 for each such locus. For heterozygotes the effect is similar. The sibling match probability is $(1 + p_1 + p_2 + 2p_1p_2)/4$, or 0.305 when $p_1 = p_2 = 0.1$ instead of $2p_1p_2 = 0.020$ for unrelated heterozygotes. Values of the k's for other pairs of relatives are given in Table 12.2.

It is straightforward to combine the effects of population structure and relatedness in non-inbred randomly mating populations. Some of the alleles carried by two relatives are identical by descent because they have descended from the same allele(s) in a recent generation for which the structure parameter is θ. With probabilities k_0, k_1, k_2 the four alleles carried by the relatives at one

Table 12.2 Identity coefficients for common relationships.

Relationship	k_2	k_1	k_0
Identical twins	1	0	0
Full sibs	$\frac{1}{4}$	$\frac{1}{2}$	$\frac{1}{4}$
Parent–child	0	1	0
Double first cousins	$\frac{1}{16}$	$\frac{3}{8}$	$\frac{9}{16}$
Half sibs*	0	$\frac{1}{2}$	$\frac{1}{2}$
First cousins	0	$\frac{1}{4}$	$\frac{3}{4}$
Unrelated	0	0	1

*Also grandparent–grandchild and avuncular (e.g. uncle–niece).

autosomal locus descend from four, three or two alleles respectively in the recent past and the probabilities for those sets of ancestral alleles follow from the Dirichlet assumption:

$$\begin{aligned}
\Pr(A_1A_1|A_1A_1) &= k_0\frac{[3\theta+(1-\theta)p_1][2\theta+(1-\theta)p_1]}{(1+\theta)(1+2\theta)} \\
&\quad + k_1\frac{2\theta+(1-\theta)p_1}{1+\theta} + k_2 \\
\Pr(A_1A_2|A_1A_2) &= k_0\frac{2[\theta+(1-\theta)p_1][\theta+(1-\theta)p_2]}{(1+\theta)(1+2\theta)} \\
&\quad + k_1\frac{2\theta+(1-\theta)(p_1+p_2)}{1+\theta} + k_2
\end{aligned}$$

Different pairs of alternative hypotheses may of interest in a wildlife forensic setting. For example, do two carcasses belong to members of the same family? The hypotheses may be:

H_p: S and C are related (to a specified degree).
H_d: S and C are not related.

The numerator is calculated with k_0, k_1, k_2 for the specified relationship and the denominator is calculated with $k_0 = 1$, $k_1 = k_2 = 0$. Suppose two samples have genotypes A_1A_1 and A_1A_2 at a locus, the strength of the evidence favoring full-siblingship versus unrelated is:

$$\begin{aligned}
\text{LR} &= \frac{\Pr(A_1A_1, A_1A_2|\text{Full sibs})}{\Pr(A_1A_1, A_1A_2|\text{Unrelated})} \\
&= \frac{1+p_1}{4p_1}
\end{aligned}$$

The likelihood ratios for each locus are multiplied together to give the overall strength of the evidence for one degree of relatedness versus another.

A much more difficult task is to estimate the degree of relatedness of two animals from their genetic profiles. The number of markers used in forensic science is too small to allow for good estimates: several hundred STRs or several thousand SNPs would be needed and even then distinguishing between estimates for, say, half-siblings and first cousins can be difficult.

Inbreeding

Matings between related pairs of individuals may be common in wildlife populations and it leads to inbreeding. Within a subpopulation, the effects of inbreeding can be described with the "within-population" inbreeding coefficient f or F_{IS}. Technically this is a correlation coefficient and can be negative but it is generally regarded as being a positive quantity. For a subpopulation to which f applies, genotype probabilities are:

$$\Pr(A_1A_1)^* = (p_1^*)^2 + f p_1^*(1 - p_1^*), \text{ homozygote}$$
$$\Pr(A_1A_2)^* = 2(1 - f)p_1^* p_2^*, \text{ heterozygote}$$

We shall see below that non-zero f values are detected by tests for Hardy-Weinberg equilibrium. If these genotype equations are averaged over subpopulations, we can relate whole-population genotype frequencies to the whole-population allele frequencies:

$$\begin{aligned}\Pr(A_1A_1) = E[\Pr(A_1A_1)^*] &= E[(p_1^*)^2] + f\varepsilon[p_1^*(1 - p_1^*)] \\ &= [p_1^2 + p_1(1 - p_1)\theta] + f[p_1 - p_1^2 - p_1(1 - p_1)\theta] \\ &= p_1^2 + p_1(1 - p_1)F \\ \Pr(A_1A_2) = E[\Pr(A_1A_2)^*] &= 2(1 - F)p_1p_2\end{aligned}$$

Here, F or F_{IT}, is the "total" inbreeding coefficient and $f = (F - \theta)/(1 - \theta)$. F can be regarded as the probability that the two alleles carried by an individual are identical by descent because they are both copies of the same allele in the (recent) past. There is an explicit concept of looking back in time to determine the value of F. An individual with full siblings as parents is inbred to an extent $F = 0.25$.

Match probabilities

Ayres and Overall (1999) allowed for both inbreeding and population structure effects on match probabilities. Unrelated (i.e. independent) individuals in the same subpopulation each have probability $\Pr(A_1A_1)^*$ of being homozygous A_1A_1. Taking the expected value of $[\Pr(A_1A_1)^*]^2$ over subpopulations gives their joint probability in terms of the whole-population allele frequency p_1:

$$\Pr(A_1A_1, A_1A_1) = E[(p_1^*)^2 + fp_1^*(1 - p_1^*)]^2$$

Using the Dirichlet distribution results and dividing by the profile probability $\Pr(A_1A_1) = p_1[F + (1 - F)p_1]$ gives the match probability

$$\Pr(A_1A_1|A_1A_1) = \frac{\theta + (1-\theta)p_1}{F + (1-F)p_1}\left\{(1-f)^2\frac{[2\theta + (1-\theta)p_1][3\theta + (1-\theta)p_1]}{(1+\theta)(1+2\theta)}\right.$$
$$\left. + 2f(1-f)\frac{[2\theta + (1-\theta)p_1]}{(1+\theta)} + f^2\right\}$$

It is not immediately obvious from this expression, but the probability of matching increases with f. The corresponding expression for matching heterozygotes is:

$$\Pr(A_1A_2|A_1A_2) = 2(1-f)\frac{[\theta + (1-\theta)p_1][\theta + (1-\theta)p_2]}{(1+\theta)(1+2\theta)}$$

showing that the chance of a match decreases as inbreeding increases.

Testing for Allele Independence

Much of the methodology reviewed here has assumed independence of alleles within and between the loci within a DNA profile. Independence of alleles at a single locus is referred to as Hardy-Weinberg equilibrium (HWE), and departures from HWE are indicated by non-zero values of the within-population inbreeding coefficient f. HWE at the subpopulation level was assumed in all the previous sections except the one labeled "Inbreeding."

Note that HWE within a subpopulation can lead to departures from HWE at the whole-population level if there are allele frequency differences among subpopulations – these departures are measured by the total inbreeding coefficient F. If $f = 0$, then the total inbreeding and population structure parameters, F and θ are equal. There may be local (subpopulation) HWE but departures from HWE detected with data collected from the whole population. If we adopt the "theta correction" for match probabilities as acknowledgment of population structure, there is little point in testing for HWE since it is assumed not to hold. Nevertheless, conducting a test may reveal genotyping errors at a particular locus.

Hardy-Weinberg testing

The best test for HWE, especially in small samples, is the exact test where "exact" refers to the method of calculating the p-value of the observed genotypic data. If a sample of size n contains n_g animals with genotype g, H animals that are heterozygous, and n_A alleles of type A, then the test statistic is the probability of the genotype counts conditional on the allele counts if HWE holds:

$$\Pr(\{n_g\}|\{n_A\}, \text{HWE}) = \frac{n!}{\prod_g n_g!} \frac{2^H \prod_A n_A!}{(2n)!}$$

This probability is added to the probabilities for all other sets of genotype counts that give the same set of allele counts but that are not larger than this probability. This sum is called the p-value and if that is small, say, less than 0.05, HWE is rejected.

For STR loci, even in samples of 100 or so, there is too much computation to enumerate all sets of genotype counts with the same allele counts. Instead, a permutation approach is used: the entire collection of $2n$ alleles in the sample are shuffled and re-sorted into n genotypic pairs. The proportion of such permuted data sets that have a probability no bigger than that for the observed data is the p-value. Typically, 10,000 such permutations will be performed using software such as GDA (http://www.eeb.uconn.edu/people/plewis/software.php).

Multi-locus testing

Profile or match probabilities are usually multiplied over loci for autosomal loci under the assumption of independence among loci. A lack of independence is often called (gametic) linkage disequilibrium although that is something of a misnomer here as what is required is independence of genotypes rather than independence of alleles within gametes. Forensic data sets, human or wildlife, are not large enough to allow adequate statistical testing for independence at more than two or three loci.

A demonstration that independence is a reasonable assumption makes use of observed and expected match probabilities. If a database of n profiles is available, all possible $n(n-1)/2$ pairs of profiles may be compared and the proportion that match at a specified number of loci can be taken as the observed match probability. This proportion can be compared to the product of match probabilities obtained by multiplying the appropriate single-locus values. For human forensic databases, good agreement is generally found, especially when θ is set to some value greater than zero. This procedure should be regarded as a reasonable demonstration of independence of match probabilities rather than a rigorous statistical test, but its utility was demonstrated by Menotti-Raymond *et al.* (2011) for a feline database. For a set of 10 STR markers, those authors compared the numbers of pairs of profiles that matched at $x = 0, 1, \ldots, 10$ loci, partially matched at $y = 0, 1, \ldots 10 - x$ loci and mismatched at $10 - x - y$ loci to the numbers expected under independence among loci.

Expected matching (both alleles matching at a locus), partial matching (one allele matching) or mismatching (no alleles matching) probabilities, written as P_2, P_1, P_0 respectively, were given by Weir (2007) as:

$$P_2 = \frac{1}{D}\left[6\theta^3 + \theta^2(1-\theta)(2+9S_2) + 2\theta(1-\theta)^2(2S_2+S_3) + (1-\theta)^3\left(2S_2^2 - S_4\right)\right]$$

$$P_1 = \frac{1}{D}\left[8\theta^2(1-\theta)(1-S_2) + 4\theta(1-\theta)^2(1-S_3) + 4(1-\theta)^3\left(S_2 - S_3 - S_2^2 + S_4\right)\right]$$

$$P_0 = \frac{1}{D}\left[\theta^2(1-\theta)(1-S_2) + 2\theta(1-\theta)^2(1-2S_2+S_3) + (1-\theta)^3\left(1 - 4S_2 + 4S_3 + 2S_2^2 - 3S_4\right)\right]$$

where S_i is the sum of the ith powers of all the allele frequencies at the locus and $D = (1+\theta)(1+2\theta)$. The Dirichlet distribution has been assumed.

These matching probabilities can be modified for non-inbred relatives:

$$\begin{aligned}
\Pr(\text{Match}) &= k_2 + k_1[\theta + (1-\theta)S_2] + k_0P_2 \\
\Pr(\text{Partial Match}) &= k_1(1-\theta)(1-S_2) + k_0P_1 \\
\Pr(\text{Mismatch}) &= k_0P_0
\end{aligned}$$

Assignment Testing

So far we have used likelihood ratios to quantify the evidence of matching DNA profiles and to compare alternative statements about relatedness of the animals represented by profiles. We now consider using the same approach to help determine the population from which an animal was drawn. This approach uses the allele frequencies for alternative populations to calculate the probabilities of the observed profile if the animal was drawn from either population. The alternative hypotheses for animal S are

H_p: Animal S is from population A.

H_d: Animal S is from population B.

Suppose the allele frequencies for A_1, A_2 are a_1, a_2 in population A and b_1, b_2 in population B. Then the likelihood ratio if S has genotype A_1A_1 is a_1^2/b_1^2, and if the genotype is A_1A_2 it is

$$2a_1a_2/2b_1b_2.$$

If the product of these likelihood ratios over all loci in the profile is greater than one, then the evidence favors A as the population of origin. Alternatively, a series of possible populations could be ranked according to the probabilities of the profile given each one. This general approach was introduced by Paetkau *et al.* (1995) and the DOH software is available at www2.biology.ualberta.ca/jbrzusto/Doh.php. Population assignment will be easier when there are greater allele frequency differences between populations, meaning greater values of θ for these populations.

The likelihood ratio approach is straightforward but has given way to methods based on Bayesian reasoning, as reviewed by Pearse and Crandall (2004). A simple motivation for this reasoning can be given by supposing that genotypic data D are available to make statements about H, the hypothesized population of origin. The likelihood ratio makes use of probabilities $\Pr(D|H)$ of the data given the hypothesis whereas what is really wanted is the transposed probability $\Pr(H|D)$ of the hypothesis given the data. The translation from one probability to the other is given by Bayes' Theorem:

$$\Pr(H|D) = \frac{\Pr(D|H)\Pr(H)}{\Pr(D)}$$

This formulation updates the prior probability $\Pr(H)$ of the population of origin to the posterior probability $\Pr(H|D)$ given the data. Clearly there must be some measure of prior belief in H. Determining the denominator probability $\Pr(D)$ may be difficult as it requires priors for all possible populations. If there were only two possible populations

$$\Pr(D) = \Pr(D|A)\Pr(A) + \Pr(D|B)\Pr(B)$$

Pritchard *et al.* (2000) introduced another Bayesian approach that does not require distinct populations to be identified and sampled before assignment. Instead, all individuals sampled are assigned to groups that are defined on the basis of genetic profiles. Simplifying assumptions such as the groups represent random-mating subpopulations can be made but the number of groups is not known prior to the analysis. The STRUCTURE software developed by Pritchard *et al.* (2000) is available at pritch.bsd.uchicago.edu/software.html.

Conclusion

DNA profiles used for wildlife forensic purposes are genetic and have been shaped by the evolutionary history of the sampled populations. This history leads to variation among populations for a species that cannot be eliminated by increasing sample sizes, but can be accounted for by the population structure parameter θ. A consequence of a shared history of individuals within populations is that their genetic profiles are not independent, so forensic match probabilities (statements about two animals) are larger than profile probabilities (statements about one animal). The differences between these quantities depend on θ.

The interpretation of matching forensic profiles can be approached through the use of likelihood ratios that compare the probabilities of the profiles under alternative hypotheses. This approach can accommodate the complexities of inbreeding and relatedness and it offers a means of population assignment. If it is desired to make probability statements about a hypothesis, as opposed to statements about the profiles, it is necessary to use Bayesian analyses.

References

Amorim, A. (2008) A cautionary note on the evaluation of genetic evidence from uniparentally transmitted markers. *Forensic Science International: Genetics*, **2**, 376–378.

Ayres, K.L. and Overall, A.D.J. (1999) Allowing for within-population inbreeding in forensic match probabilities. *Forensic Science International*, **103**, 207–216.

Balding, D.J. and Nichols, R.A. (1994) DNA match probability calculation: how to allow for population stratification, relatedness, database selection and single bands. *Forensic Science International*, **64**, 125–140.

Beecham, G.W. and Weir, B.S. (2011) Confidence intervals for DNA evidence likelihood ratios. *Journal of Forensic Sciences*, **S1**, S166–S171.

Buckleton, J.S., Krawczak, M. and Weir, B.S. (2011). The interpretation of lineage markers in forensic DNA testing. *Forensic Science International: Genetics*, **5**, 78–83.

Clopper, C.J. and Pearson, E.S. (1934) The use of confidence or fiducial intervals illustrated in the case of the binomial. *Biometrika*, **26**, 404–413.

Menotti-Raymond, M., David, V., Weir, B.S. and O'Brien, S. (2011) A population genetic database of cat breeds developed in coordination with a domestic cat STR multiplex. *Journal of Forensic Sciences* (in press).

Paetkau, D., Celvert, W., Sterling, I. and Strobeck, C. (1995) Microsatellite analysis of population structure in Canadian polar bears. *Molecular Ecology*, **4**, 347–354.

Pearse, D.E. and Crandall, K.A. (2004) Beyond FST : Analysis of population genetic data for conservation. *Conservation Genetics*, **5**, 585–602.

Pritchard, J.K., Stephens, M. and Donnelly, P. (2000) Inference of population structure using multilocus genotype data. *Genetics*, **155**, 945–959.

Weir, B.S. (2007) The rarity of DNA profiles. *Annals of Applied Statistics*, **1**, 358–370.

13

Forensic DNA Analysis of Wildlife Evidence

Sabrina N. McGraw, Shamus P. Keeler, and Jane E. Huffman

Introduction

The advent of forensic DNA analysis revolutionized human criminal investigations when it was introduced in the mid-1980s. These techniques allowed law enforcement to unequivocally connect individuals to crime scenes using trace amounts of biological material deposited during the commission of a crime. Today, forensic DNA analysis is an indispensable tool in most criminal investigations and has led to the arrest of hundreds of perpetrators who otherwise might have gone free and has allowed for the exoneration of many individuals who were wrongly convicted. Since the introduction of DNA profiling, forensic DNA analysis techniques have continued to improve thus increasing the utility of these techniques, and reducing the cost of this technology. These technological improvements have resulted in a greater availability of these technologies for applications outside of human criminal investigations. One emerging application for forensic DNA analysis is for investigation of wildlife-related crimes and wildlife conservation.

Wildlife and their products constitute the third most illegally traded commodity worldwide after arms and drugs (Manel *et al.*, 2002; Karlsson and Holmlund, 2007). Global efforts to protect species through trade and harvest regulations rely heavily on enforcement for future success (Peppin *et al.*, 2010; Ogden, 2011). In the past 25 years, genetics-based analyses of forensic evidence have become increasingly important in human legal cases, and have captured the public imagination thanks to high profile defendants and prime-time courtroom drama.

Wildlife Forensics: Methods and Applications, First Edition. Edited by Jane E. Huffman and John R. Wallace.

Although the reality of genetic evidence has perhaps far greater limitations than fiction would have us believe, its potential remains staggering. As forensic science continues to make leaps and bounds in strictly human casework, advances in animal forensics have followed close behind (Jeffreys *et al.*, 1985). In 1995, feline microsatellite markers were used in the first documented United States court case involving animal genetics as evidence (Cassidy and Gonzales, 2005), and while this case employed an animal as a "silent witness" to a human crime scene, animal genetics have begun to play a far more pivotal role in the international justice system. Genetic forensic tools have been used in the prosecution of cases involving the illegal trade of such diverse products as ivory, olive oil, rice, timber, and traditional medicines (Ogden, 2008). The rapidly growing field of wildlife forensics is striving continuously to identify improved techniques and more stringent controls in the presentation of evidentiary support for the prosecution of smuggling, poaching, and laundering of wildlife and their products. In the following sections we will outline the numerous molecular markers and analytical techniques identified for use in answering the myriad of questions posed by during the investigation of wildlife related crimes.

DNA Isolation and Handling

Deoxyribonucleic acid (DNA) and ribonucleic acid (RNA) are stable hereditary molecules present in the cells of animals and plants. While cellular RNA rapidly degrades, DNA is present for longer periods in post-mortal tissues allowing for extraction, purification, and use in diagnostic assays (Kashyap *et al.*, 2004). Genetic material can be extracted from almost every tissue imaginable, from bear bile (Peppin *et al.*, 2008) and snake venom (Ogden *et al.*, 2009) to rhinoceros horn (Peppin *et al.*, 2010) and molted feathers (Rojas *et al.*, 2011). The scientific literature contains peer-reviewed protocols for methods used for most tissues and extraction conditions.

No matter the tissue or material to be extracted, it is essential that a basic set of standard sample handing rules, or standard operating procedures (SOPs) be identified and strictly adhered to for forensic samples. Consistency, careful documentation, and a strict chain of custody are just a few of the hallmarks of a forensics laboratory. The final sections of this chapter address concerns over method validation and court admissibility of genetic evidence, and references are provided for further reading.

All samples to be considered for DNA analysis should be carefully labeled with applicable identifying information and stored using techniques to prevent contamination, and further degradation. Personnel handling DNA evidence should wear full personal protection equipment (PPE) as part of good general laboratory practices, including clean lab coats and gloves (Wobeser, 1996). Long hair should be bound, and if necessary, hair nets may be used to prevent contamination with human tissue. Samples should be stored in sealed containers or bags where they cannot come into contact with other biological materials, dust, or sunlight. Dust, which contains skin particles, is also laden with ubiquitous

DNases (DNA nucleases) which degrade DNA. Prior to purification, evidence for DNA analysis should be stored at −20°C or lower (Endler and Slavka, 2010).

Complex biological samples should be processed as soon as possible to remove the anticipated source of DNA from other materials in the sample. Many bodily fluids and molecules can inhibit polymerase chain reactions (PCR) through various chemical interactions with reaction reagents. In many wildlife forensic samples, inhibitors are difficult to avoid. Inhibitors common in biological samples include hemoglobin and heparin in blood, urea in urine, bile salts in feces, and collagen in tissues. The best way to avoid inhibition is to prevent processing of the inhibitor with the sample. In the mentioned samples, however, this can often be difficult to impossible. In these instances, specialized commercial DNA extraction kits should be used for extraction to ensure the cleanest possible sample and optimal PCR conditions should be used including selecting a polymerase that is less sensitive to inhibition (ibid.).

Typical wildlife forensic samples are not procured prior to the death of the animal but are instead autolyzed and may be partially degraded. The degradation of DNA in samples is variable tissue to tissue. Hard tissues, like bone and teeth, may have the least DNA of body tissues, but typically have the longest preserved sample. Likewise, soft parenchymal tissues have copious amounts of DNA that is rapidly degraded (Ogden *et al.*, 2009). In order to obtain the best diagnostic DNA sample, it may be necessary to sample several parts of the tissue, including the interior or the exterior of the samples (especially if there are intact hair roots or feather shafts that may be collected). Sampling should be done using sterile laboratory techniques to prevent cross-contamination of genetic material (Rojas *et al.*, 2011). Samples may appear to consist of a single animal, but genetic material may be present from human perpetrators or law enforcement and laboratory personnel at the crime scene, environmental contaminants, or other sources (Cassidy and Gonzales, 2005). Where possible, always limit the potential for contamination by other materials, even if they are derived from the same sample.

Commercial DNA extraction kits are available from various manufacturers. For labs where such kits may be cost-prohibitive, extraction protocols using chloroform/phenol/isopropanol precipitation and purifications techniques are frequently described (Jones *et al.*, 2002). Purified DNA may be stored in Tris-EDTA buffer at room temperature for 6 months or at 2–8°C for 1 year in the absence of DNases. DNases may be inactivated by depletion of Mg^{2+} and Ca^{2+} ions by added a chelating agent (e.g. ethylenediaminetetraacetic acid (EDTA)) to the sample, adjusting the pH to 7.5, cold storage (<−20°C), or drying the sample. Storage of these samples may be extended to 7 years at −20°C and even longer at lower temperatures (Endler and Slavka, 2010).

Polymerase Chain Reaction (PCR)

Polymerase chain reaction has become an invaluable tool in molecular biology since its original description in 1983 (Mullis and Faloona, 1987; Schneider, 2007; Ogden, 2011). This procedure revolutionized how we work with genetic markers, allowing for the amplification of target sequences by thousands to millions of copies. This not only allows for the use of biological samples containing only trace amounts of DNA, it can also make use of partially degraded nucleic acid and facilitates downstream genotyping and sundry other protocols.

PCR is capable of amplifying DNA at very low concentrations, which means that any contamination of genetic material may become a significant problem during PCR analyses of samples. It is vital that good laboratory practices be followed stringently to avoid erroneous amplification of non-sample DNA. Negative water controls should be used at each step of DNA handling, from extraction through PCR, and these controls should be handled in the exact same manner as biological samples. For further control measures regarding the proper handling of PCR products and DNA samples, please refer to the final section of this chapter for information on published guidelines.

Sample Speciation

Perhaps the most central challenge faced in wildlife forensics revolves around the question of species identification. In cases of decomposed carcasses or processed wildlife products, morphologic species characteristics may be lacking, and ancillary testing are necessary to prove species identity (Thommasen *et al.*, 1989; Verma *et al.*, 2003). Early species identification of biological samples involved macromolecular analyses (e.g. high performance liquid chromatography (HPLC) of hemoglobin, fatty acid discrimination) and immunological techniques, which could potentially differentiate species as far as the family level (Thommasen *et al.*, 1989; Bellis *et al.*, 2003). While this can certainly be very helpful for exclusionary purposes, for most wildlife forensic applications, prosecution requires species-level identification.

Today the DNA-based techniques utilized most often to identify species include restriction fragment length polymorphism (RFLP) analysis and direct sequencing of mitochondrial DNA (mtDNA) markers. However, other methods have also been utilized to detect, if not identify, species in unknown forensic samples (Ogden, 2011).

Minisatellites (VNTRs)

The earliest use of genetics to identify animal remains followed shortly behind human techniques (Jeffreys *et al.*, 1985; Ogden *et al.*, 2009). Initially, largely intact genomic DNA was screened for variable nucleotide tandem repeats (VNTRs), also known as 'minisatellites', which are not localized to a known chromosomal locus. These repeats consist of hundreds to thousands of base pairs (0.5–30kb), with repeat motifs of 8–80bp (Kashyap *et al.*, 2004; Cassidy and Gonzales, 2005). The method used to identify VNTR alleles prior to PCR techniques involved fragmentation of the genome using restriction enzymes, and Southern blot hybridization of core "multi-locus probes (MLPs)" which were specific to the core repeat portion of the VNTRs (Cassidy and Gonzales, 2005). This resulted in visualization of variably sized DNA fragments. This method of fragmenting the genome and assessing the patterns of fragment sizes is known as restriction fragment length polymorphism (RFLP) analysis, and is still used today in a variety of assays.

There are limitations to use of these genetic techniques in wildlife cases. Analysis of VNTRs (minisatellites) requires relatively non-degraded nuclear DNA, which is not typical of forensic wildlife samples (Verma *et al.*, 2003; Gupta *et al.*, 2005). Multi-locus probes also provide a challenge as hybridization techniques are best performed by experienced technical staff and are not efficient for high throughput analysis. Multi-locus probes were therefore soon replaced with single-locus probes (SLP) based on the conserved regions flanking tandem repeats, which provided greater specificity for genotype profiling since these alleles could now be localized to a specific chromosomal marker. Large minisatellites were outshone by smaller short tandem repeats (STRs) which consist of repeating motifs of 2–6bp, with overall size ranges easily amplified by PCR.

Mitochondrial Markers (mtDNA)

The most common means of species identification today include sequencing of mitochondrial gene markers including portions of the cytochrome b (*cyt b*), cytochrome c oxidase 1 (COI), and the mitochondrial D-loop control region (D-loop) (Dawnay *et al.*, 2007; Dalton and Kotze, 2011; Ogden, 2011). Additional mitochondrial markers, including rRNA subunits, have also been extensively used (Bellis *et al.*, 2003; Sahajpal and Goyal, 2010; Rojas *et al.*, 2011).

Mitochondrial DNA is especially useful in wildlife forensics techniques for several reasons. The mitochondrial genome is small relative to the somatic genome, consisting of only 16,569bp of double-stranded circular DNA in humans (Karlsson and Holmlund, 2007). Unlike nuclear DNA, which exists as only one set of diploid copies per cell, mitochondrial DNA is present in each of potentially thousands of cytoplasmic mitochondria per cell (the actual number varies with the cell type). This abundance makes successful DNA extraction possible in highly degraded or processed samples, which are the mainstay of wildlife forensics (Amorim, 2010). Mitochondrial haplotypes are also of value in species identification because they do not undergo recombination and are inherited in a uniparental manner. This tends to result in reduced within-species diversity as species become reproductively isolated, and therefore makes mitochondrial markers well suited for species determination (Dawnay *et al.*, 2007; Rojas *et al.*, 2011).

Cytochrome b (*cyt b*)

Universal and species-specific primers for *cyt* b have been used extensively for species identification. The Genbank sequence database contains sequence data for many non-model species thanks to research publications, and thus *cyt b* is a commonly utilized marker for a wide variety of species (Wan and Fang, 2003; Gupta *et al.*, 2005; Kyle and Wilson, 2007). Direct sequencing of the *cyt b* gene is a comprehensive means of providing species information in an individual (Verma and Singh, 2003; Ogden, 2008), and when direct sequencing is not feasible, RFLP analysis of *cyt b* amplicons may be used for speciation (see below). The *cyt b* gene is also used to identify species of birds (An *et al.*, 2007). Cytochrome *b* data may be used in conjunction with non-genetic forensic analyses, such as hair examination (Sahajpal and Goyal, 2010). The use of degenerate primers can allow for the amplification of DNA from several species within a single sample. This allows for amplification that is not quite species-specific, but not universal, either. Degenerate primers are actually mixes of primers that differ at certain loci, allowing for binding on sites that may vary slightly (Kyle and Wilson, 2007).

Cytochrome C Oxidase 1 (COI)

The COI marker has been billed as the species "barcode," and extensive databases of molecular species data derived from this region are continuously growing thanks to support from natural history museums, herbaria, wildlife researchers and other organizations (Dawnay *et al.*, 2007; Ratnasingham and Hebert, 2007; Dalton and Kotze, 2011). The central concept of species barcoding is to compare an unknown sample to a broad database of sequences and identify the species of origin. This marker has been shown to be diagnostic over shorter sequences, with as few as 100–210bp (Dawnay *et al.*, 2007). This technique does not work in samples of mixed DNA origins, as the primers are universal and will amplify all mtDNA present in the sample. Also, to be effective, this technique requires extensive reference data, with numerous authenticated haplotypes reported for every species. Until sufficient sequences are submitted and authenticated, these techniques work best for well-studied commercial species for which multiple haplotypes are known, and in the growing number of non-model species with adequate numbers of reported haplotypes (ibid.).

Mitochondrial D-loop control region

Relative to the remaining mitochondrial genome, the mitochondrial D-loop control region is hyper-variable, mutating up to five times faster (Wu *et al.*, 2005). For this reason, this region is often used to delineate between populations that are have recently separated, such as in the case of subspecies. Subspecies do not tend to differ significantly at the *cyt b* gene, and thus this marker is not typically used in subspecies descriptions. An example of a practical application of the D-loop control region is its use in monitoring the population of origin of Chinese sika deer (*Cervus nippon*) products. While the species is reportedly overabundant in Japan, these deer have been nearly extirpated in mainland

China. Several subspecies have been kept domestically, bred for medicinal products for centuries. There now exist four subspecies in China, two being farmed (*C. n. hotrulorm* and *C. n. nippon*), and the other two (*C. n. sinchuanicus* and *C. n. kopschi*) free-ranging on the Chinese mainland. The D-loop control region is sequenced to identify subspecies identity and therefore identify products illegally obtained from free-ranging animals (ibid.). The successful use of this marker in this situation is likely due to the isolated, fragmented nature of the populations, which contributes to inter-population diversity.

Pyrosequencing techniques

Another technique which has been used with increasing regularity in wildlife research is DNA pyrosequencing. This technique allows for direct sequencing of thousands of small DNA fragments (either PCR amplicons or digested genomic DNA) in a single run. Resultant sequences are analyzed and reconstructed using bioinformatics methods. Pyrosequencing techniques have been used to prescreen samples prior to more fine-tuned individual typing in cases where no prior knowledge of species identity is known (Karlsson and Holmlund, 2007). Pyrosequencing is rapid, accurate, flexible, and allows for parallel processing and easy automation.

Additional Genetic Speciation Methods

Mitochondrial DNA can be analyzed without sequencing, which can be very useful in laboratory settings where direct sequencing is cost prohibitive. Bataille *et al.* (1999) developed a method by which human and non-human DNA could be differentiated without direct nucleotide sequencing. In this method, they amplified two gene products in a single duplexed reaction. The first pair of primers were universal, and amplified the *cyt b* gene while the second pair of primers were human-specific, and amplified the hyper-variable mitochondrial D-loop control region. When visualized on gel electrophoresis, human samples would generate two bands, one for each primer set, while non-humans would generate only one, from the universal *cyt b* primers (ibid.). Another similar assay involves PCR amplification of *cyt b* in cases where the species of origin of a forensic sample must be differentiated between a domestic pig and wild boar. Following amplification of *cyt b* using porcine specific primers, the products are digested using the restriction enzyme *Ava*II. In wild boar, but not domestic swine, there is a single base pair deletion in the second restriction site for this enzyme. Gel electrophoresis and staining of the resultant fragments reveal a single band in wild boar, and two bands in domestic swine. It should be noted that this assay will identify a domestic swine/wild boar hybrid as wild boar if the mother was a wild boar, since mitochondrial DNA follows a matrilineal inheritance (Lorenzini, 2005). Additional RFLP analyses were developed by Dubey *et al.* and Meganathan *et al.* for the speciation of three Indian snake species and three Indian crocodile species, respectively, using RFLP patterns in digested *cyt b* products (Meganathan *et al.*, 2009; Dubey *et al.*, 2010).

Singh *et al.* (2004) published results using a single novel microsatellite for speciation of the three large felid species present in India. According to the authors, this assay does not require sequencing, with each species differing significantly in the number of repeats at this locus, a valuable tool for use in rapid identification of forensic samples.

Limitations of Genetic Speciation

While innumerable studies have found success in species identification using the markers described here, it should be noted that species determination using genetic techniques is by no means a finite and absolute rule. Taxonomists have long based species identification on morphologic characteristics, which may or may not be able to be directly linked to genetic changes in commonly used markers. The selection that drives speciation does not necessarily drive changes in observed markers, and thus changes across species should not be considered to be linear in terms of changes elsewhere in the genome or cytoplasm (Humphries and Winker, 2011). There are no set guidelines that state an individual may be determined to be a member of a given species only if it demonstrates X amount of sequence homology with authenticated reference sequences. In some cases, it may be best to consult with experienced wildlife geneticists or forensic scientists experienced in the species or genera of interest before making a species identification. For mitochondrial markers, it would not be uncommon for an individual sample to express 100% sequence homology with published reference sequences, but they could have as low as 98% sequence homology and still be considered within a threshold of species variability (Kyle and Wilson, 2007). In cases where the degree of homology may be questionable, it may be due to limited reference sequences available for the species, and therefore a phylogenetic tree would be of greater informative value than sequence homology. Phylogenetic trees may be created using several different statistical modalities (neighbor-joining, maximum parsimony, etc.), and allow for the visualization of a query sequence's relation to other similar sequences and their identity. In this way a sample may be visually placed with close relative species, even if the actual species of the sample is not present in the database.

Species detection in mixed-DNA samples

The most common mixed DNA sample encountered that affects endangered species conservation is arguably traditional medicine. These products may claim to contain ingredients derived from endangered or otherwise restricted species.

In order to enforce trade and harvesting laws, an accurate identification of the species present in the sample is needed. Since multiple species may be present, this is an example of a mixed DNA sample. An additional example of a mized-DNA sample that is often encountered during the investigation of wildlife poaching is wild game sausage or other food items prepared by mixing meat collected from multiple games species. In cases such as these, methods involving species-specific primers may be used to detect a species by amplifying DNA only from the selected species (Rojas *et al.*, 2011). It is important to note that assays involving species-specific primers or markers (usually mtDNA of SNPs), are *species detection* assays, not *species identification* assays (Ogden, 2008). Validation of species-specific primers usually involves proving exclusion of a set number of selected species. Assays used to detect a species within a mixed sample are used when the possible species (or likely species) are known or able to be closely estimated. Positive bands on PCR than may be attributed to the species-specific target, and therefore detect the species of interest (Ogden, 2008).

Sample Sexing

A second challenge for individual characterization of a forensic sample is sexing. In some cases, knowledge of the gender of the source of a forensic sample is necessary. In some species or regions, protection laws may be gender specific, and thus enforcement relies on the sexing of specimens that may be too processed or decomposed to be accurately sexed by physical examination (An *et al.*, 2007). Also, in some large animals, including elephants, testes are internal, and the outward appearance of individuals, especially young animals, may not allow for easy sexing by visual examination. In birds, the chromo-helicase-DNA (CHD) binding gene is amplified for sex determination. Avian males are homozygous (ZZ) while females are heterozygous (ZW). The CHD-Z and CHD-W PCR products vary in size due to an intron length polymorphism, and can be differentiated visually using agarose gel electrophoresis techniques (An *et al.*, 2007). In mammalian samples, several markers have been used successfully for sexing forensic samples. Human cases often use the amelogenin gene; however, this marker has been shown to fail to amplify in otherwise normal, fertile males. Another marker used in sexing is the sex determining region (SRY), which is only present on the Y-chromosome. These sequences are highly conserved, making primers broadly available for most samples. Since a failure to produce a band can signify either a female sample or failed PCR, a second, constitutive marker, like β-actin or D-loop control, is often included in a PCR duplex reaction. In this case, a female would have a single band, and a male would have two bands (Gupta *et al.*, 2006). In cases of individualization of an unknown sample, concurrent sexing of the sample is a simple means of providing exclusion for 50% or random sample comparisons, and therefore sexing techniques are valuable tools in a laboratory's repertoire (Manel *et al.*, 2002).

Sample Individualization

There are many instances in wildlife forensics where it may be of great value to identify an individual animal. Examples include cases where a specific carcass can be linked to DNA evidence in a suspect's home, or parts taken as a trophy may be linked to a poached body. Other, less obvious examples include cases where a mix of animal products, for example, a freezer of meat, need to be assayed to determine how many animals were poached (Fajardo *et al.*, 2009). An additional possibility for individualized samples is the localization of a sample to its reproductive population of origin, if certain criteria are met (Manel *et al.*, 2002).

For use in individualization of samples, mitochondrial markers, even the hyper-variable D-loop control region, tend to mutate too slowly to provide sufficient variation. However, microsatellite markers (STRs) and panels of SNPs can provide sufficient data about an individual to allow for individual identification.

Microsatellite markers (STR)

Short tandem repeats (STRs), sequences comprised of short 2–6 bp repeats surrounded by conserved flanking regions, are known to be highly mutable, and are therefore of value in individual identification (Hoff-Olsen *et al.*, 2001; Xu *et al.*, 2005). Identifying the alleles at a series of these marker loci produces a multi-locus genotype for a single individual. If enough markers of sufficient polymorphism are present in the panel, it is very unlikely that the genetic profile of two individuals will be identical. The probability of identity (P_{ID}) is the probability that two samples share the same genotype by chance, and are not from the same individual. For example, a panel of twelve microsatellites developed for forensic use in wild boar in Italy had an estimated P_{ID} of 6.7×10^{-6} (approximately 2 in 150,000 individuals show the same genotype by chance alone), which is a conservative estimate, taking into account the likely presence of siblings in the population (Lorenzini, 2005). Microsatellite marker panels are published for numerous species, but in uncommon and non-model species, it may be necessary to identify markers *de novo*. Microsatellite identification involves the identification of repeat motifs using bead capture technology (Jones *et al.*, 2002). Once microsatellites are identified, they are amplified using primers designed to be complementary to their conserved flanking sequences (Poetsch *et al.*, 2001). Microsatellites are selected and analyzed based on criteria and guidelines discussed in detail in the validation section of this chapter. Unfortunately, these methods can be time-consuming and cost-prohibitive for laboratories with limited facilities. Attempting amplification of DNA using microsatellite loci designed for closely related species frequently results in viable allele data (Hoff-Olsen *et al.*, 2001; Poetsch *et al.*, 2001). It should be noted that use of non-specific markers may increase the number of null and otherwise non-amplifying alleles (Cassidy and Gonzales, 2005). Microsatellites are nuclear in origin, and therefore exist as a single pair of loci in any given cell. For this reason, microsatellite genotyping may not be feasible for highly degraded or processed samples. Studies in human forensics have examined microsatellite stability in decomposed human remains, and have found them to be consistent across intra-individual tissues through late stage decomposition (Hoff-Olsen *et al.*, 2001).

Single-nucleotide polymorphisms (SNP)

In most cases, the differences seen between alleles in genetic markers are due to an array of single base pair changes. These single alterations are known as single-nucleotide polymorphisms (SNPs), and they are becoming of increasing interest to wildlife researchers and forensic scientists alike (Ogden, 2011). A rapid means of identifying large numbers of SNPs has been identified which utilizes 454 pyrosequencing technologies. The production of SNP chips able to test 1536 SNPs simultaneously is currently helping to construct an incredibly ambitious database composed of SNP data from several commercially valuable marine fish. It is the primary hope of this group (discussed below, FishPopTrace) to use SNPs to localize illegally caught fish and therefore provide a means of regulatory enforcement and hopefully future deterrent against overharvesting (Martinsohn and Ogden, 2009; Stokstad, 2010).

Sample Localization

In many cases, non-compliance of regulatory laws involves the harvesting of wildlife from restricted populations. A common example is the enforcement of marine fishing restrictions. A given species may be legal to harvest at X limits in one region, but be banned entirely in another area. Once at shore, the identification of contraband in these cases is problematic, since the legal species is the same as the illegal species; only the point of origin is in question. Localizing a sample to a geographic location using Bayesian statistics in population genetics is the same as identifying its original *reproductive population*. The statistical tests involved are generally termed *assignment* (which assign an individual to a population) and *exclusion* tests (which determine that a sample did *not* originate in a candidate population). These tests use a genotype profile from an individual (usually STR alleles, but SNP panels are being developed for this purpose) and compare it to the allelic data known for the candidate populations (Manel *et al.*, 2002).

Assignment tests require a great deal of reference information from candidate populations for accurate population assignment. This test compares the alleles in the genotyping profile of the sample to the allelic frequencies of the candidate populations, assigning the individual to the population from which it would most likely be derived. The more reference data that is known; the more likely it is that a sample will be correctly assigned to its population of origin. Assignment tests and likelihood-ratio analyses are used most often when the genotype of the parent group is not completely known. Errors can occur with assignments if the sample individual carries an allele that is rare in the source population, or is not among the reference data. Assignment tests work optimally when there are limited candidate populations, which is common in forensic cases. For example, when a suspect claims a sample comes from population A, but authorities suspect it actually comes from population B. Candidate populations should also be diverse, with allelic frequency differences represented by F_{ST} values >0.5, and using genotyping profiles consisting of >20 polymorphic markers (STRs). If there is gene flow between candidate populations, it is generally not worth the effort to attempt assignment testing for the sample (Manel *et al.*, 2002; Renshaw *et al.*, 2006).

In the simplest scenario, all of the potential parent genotypes are known. This situation would not occur in wild populations, but it could occur if the question of origin concerns whether a sample comes from a farm-raised animal or a wild-caught specimen. By comparing the genotype of the sample with the genotypes of the known parent stock, it is possible to *exclude* the sample from the parent population. That is to say, it would be possible to state that is not possible that a given individual's genotype could arise from the genotypes present in the parent stock. A possible source of error is the incorrect exclusion of an individual due to mutation or genotyping errors. Mutation is generally rare in a single generation at a given locus (expected average STR mutation rate to be 0.1–0.5%, (Schneider, 2007)), and ideally the mutation rates would be known for the markers used, but this may not be feasible in wildlife populations. It is possible for germ-line mutations to introduce single base pair mutations (insertions), which can cause inconsistencies in genotyping data (Cassidy and Gonzales, 2005). Genotyping errors include human error and null alleles, where a mutation occurs in the flanking sequence of a marker and amplification fails (Renshaw *et al.*, 2006).

Given that over 60% of global marine fish stocks are reported to be over-exploited or at their maximum sustainable limits, it should not be surprising that there are currently global initiatives to control illegal, unreported, and unregulated (IUU) fishing world-wide. The European Union has recently funded a project to develop a database of SNP markers that will be used globally to profile several commercially important marine species (Martinsohn and Ogden, 2008, 2009; Ogden, 2010). With enough SNP profile data, it is very likely that marine samples from these species may be localized to their reproductive populations of origin, which will assist in regulatory and protection efforts (Martinsohn and Ogden, 2009).

Validation of Wildlife Forensic Techniques

Human forensic laboratories are governed by strict accreditation policies and quality assurance and control (QA and QC) guidelines. No such guidelines are defined for wildlife cases, and thus human standards should be adhered to whenever possible (Dawnay *et al.*, 2007; Ogden *et al.*, 2009; Ogden, 2010). All molecular markers intended for use in legal forensic cases require validation prior to use in diagnostic case work. Validation studies examine reproducibility and heteroplasmy, mixed DNA samples, DNA template concentration variation, chemical treatments, substrate variation, environmental conditions, and thermocycling parameters (Dawnay *et al.*, 2007).

Validation of genetic markers, including microsatellites should include studies to ensure Mendelian inheritance of loci (barring rare silent alleles), assessment of cross-species contamination, validation of case-type samples, development of an allelic ladder, and publication of allelic frequency data (Thommasen *et al.*, 1989; Dawnay *et al.*, 2007; Schneider, 2007). Many molecular markers come directly from research, and may not have been intended for forensic work. However, studies have shown such markers may be used as long as proper guidelines are followed (Dawnay *et al.*, 2007; Dawnay *et al.*, 2008; Dawnay *et al.*, 2009). Marker quality controls should also include accuracy and reproducibility of allele determination. "Stutter bands" are PCR artifacts that appear as products that are <11% of the peak height of a 4bp higher band. These should be excluded even if the peak height is within an acceptable range (Hoff-Olsen *et al.*, 2001). Stutter bands can be more frequent or difficult to discern from actual bands in dinucleotide repeats, where spacing between alleles may be reduced. For this reason, most alleles used in human typing consist of 4–5bp repeat motifs (Cassidy and Gonzales, 2005). Stutter-free markers are best for explaining to courts and jurors, where the less error that must be potentially explained, the better (Jones *et al.*, 2002). Allele ladders are created by pooling all of the known alleles identified in a given data set for comparison with subsequent analyses. These internal controls provide consistent means of comparison of allele sizes from one analysis to another, and aid in reducing variation in allele designations (Cassidy and Gonzales, 2005; Dawnay *et al.*, 2009).

Markers should be selected based on these criteria, which may be found listed in several guidelines, including those provided by the Society of Animal Genetics-Food and Agriculture Organization (ISAG-FAO) Advisory Committee for domestic animals (Lorenzini, 2005), the Scientific Working Group on DNA Analysis Methods (SWGDAM), and others (Dawnay *et al.*, 2008).

Analytical techniques should be selected with care. For example, all electrophoretic systems used to size alleles should be denaturing, so that alleles will be assessed based on sequence length alone, with no affects from secondary structure. Alleles should be designated by their number of repeats, which allows them to be compared to published data (Schneider, 2007). The choice of analytical techniques should be selected to minimize sample handling and human error likelihood. For example, the handling of post-PCR products greatly increases the possibility of contamination with high concentrations of DNA, which can contaminate other laboratory assays. The use of techniques like real-time PCR can reduce post-PCR sample handling and reduce this risk (Rojas *et al.*, 2011).

Court Admissibility

In order to justify the commitment of funding and laborious efforts associated with robust wildlife forensic investigation, coordinating laboratory officials and law enforcement personnel should be well acquainted with the legal requirements for genetic data in their local and regional court systems. In the US, individual states may differ in their requirements for admissibility of genetic data depending on their criteria for scientific rigor. Several standards have been adopted by individual states, including the *Frye* (1923) and *Daubert* (1993) standards for scientific evidence. The *Daubert* standard outlines a requirement for individual judicial review of methods used, and requires that techniques used to provide evidence be thoroughly statistically evaluated, and error rates must be fully described to establish reliability (Cassidy and Gonzales, 2005). Exclusion probability is defined as the probability that variation between DNA samples is sufficient to exclude them as being from the same individual. These probabilities are a common note of contention in legal cases, with any variation in sequence or genotyping results between a suspect and an evidentiary DNA sample intensely scrutinized. Admissible values are well documented in human cases, but not so in wildlife. This may be of particular significance in cases involving animals from small populations or inbreeding groups, where the lack of intra-specific variation increases the homology required before two samples may be declared to be from the same individual (Cassidy and Gonzales, 2005). Overall, it is essential that all techniques used to produces forensic data be outlined in peer-reviewed literature and currently accepted by the scientific community. Evidence must follow a strictly documented chain of custody from crime scene to court room (ibid.).

Conclusion

The number of molecular tools available to investigate wildlife-related crime continues to increase with advancements in human law enforcement and laboratory modalities. However, due to the often prohibitive cost of genetic analysis, the field of wildlife forensics owes much of its success, past and future, to the commitment of the men and women dedicated to this field. It can only be hoped that as the ability to enforce wildlife protection and conservation regulations increases, that a commensurate decrease in non-compliance may be the result, and that we may begin to see the benefits of these initiatives in the rebounding of threatened species worldwide.

Cases Cited

Daubert v. Merrell Dow Pharmaceuticals [1993] 509 U.S. 579.
Frye v. United States [1923] 293 F. 1013.

References

Amorim, A. (2010) Introduction to the Special Issue on Forensic Genetics: non-human DNA. *The Open Forensic Science Journal*, **3**, 6–8.

An, J., Lee, M.-Y., Min, M.-S., Lee M.-H. and Lee, H. (2007) A molecular genetic approach for species identification of mammals and sex determination of birds in a forensic case from South Korea. *Forensic Science International*, **167**, 59–61.

Bataille, M., Crainic, K., Leterreux, M., Durigon, M. and De Mazancourt, P. (1999) Multiplex amplification of mitochondrial DNA for human and species identification in forensic evaluation. *Forensic Science International*, **99**, 165–170.

Bellis, C., Ashton, K.J., Freney, L. Blair, B. and Griffiths, L.R. (2003) A molecular genetic approach for forensic animal species identification. *Forensic Science International*, **134**, 99–108.

Cassidy, B.G. and Gonzales, R.A. (2005) DNA Testing in animal forensics. *Journal of Wildlife Management*, **69**, 1454–1462.

Dalton, D.L. and Kotze, A. (2011) DNA barcoding as a tool for species identification in three forensic wildlife cases in South Africa. *Forensic Science International*, **207**, e51–e54.

Dawnay, N., Ogden, R., McEwing, R., *et al.* (2007) Validation of the barcoding gene Coi for use in forensic genetic species identification. *Forensic Science International*, **173**, 1–6.

Dawnay, N., Ogden, R., Thorpe, R.S., *et al.* (2008) A forensic STR profiling system for the Eurasian badger: a framework for developing profiling systems for wildlife species. *Forensic Science International: Genetics*, **2**, 47–53.

Dawnay, N., Ogden, R., Wetton, J.H., *et al.* (2009) Genetic data from 28 STR loci for forensic individual identification and parentage analysis in 6 bird of prey species. *Forensic Science International: Genetics*, **3**, e63–e69.

Dubey, B., Meganathan, P.R. and Haque, I. (2010) Molecular identification of three Indian snake species using simple Pcr_Rflp Method. *Journal of Forensic Sciences*, **55**, 1065–1067.

Endler, G. and Slavka, G. (2010) Stability of the specimen during preanalytics. In H. Kessler (ed.) *Molecular Diagnostics of Infectious Diseases*. New York: Walter de Gruyter GmBH and Co., pp. 25–34.

Fajardo, V., I. Gonzalez, I. Martin, I., *et al.* (2009) A lightcycler Taqman Pcr assay for quantitative detection of chamois (*Rupricapra Rupricapra*) and Pyrenean Ibex (*Capra Pyrenaica*) in experimental meat mixtures. *Food Science and Technology*, **44**, 1997–2004.

Gupta, S.K., Thangaraj, K., and Singh, L. (2006) A simple and inexpensive molecular method for sexing and identification of the forensic samples of elephant origin. *Journal of Forensic Sciences*, **51**, 805–807.

Gupta, S.K., Verma, S.K. and Singh, L. (2005) Molecular insight into a wildlife crime: the case of a peafowl slaughter. *Forensic Science International*, **154**, 214–217.

Hoff-Olsen, P., Jacobsen, S., Mevag, B., *et al.* (2001) Microsatellite stability in human post-mortem tissues. *Forensic Science International*, **119**, 273–278.

Humphries, E.M. and Winker, K. (2011) Discord reigns among nuclear, mitochondrial and phenotypic estimates of divergence in nine lineages of trans-Beringian birds. *Molecular Ecology*, **20**, 573–583.

Jeffreys, A.J., Wilson, V. and Thein, S.L. (1985) Hypervariable 'minisatellite" regions in human DNA. *Nature*, **314**, 67–73.

Jones, K.C., Levine, K.F. and J.D. Banks, J.D. (2002) Characterization of 11 polymorphic tetranucleotide microsatellites for forensic applications in California elk (*Cervus Elaphus Canadensis*). *Molecular Ecology Notes*, **2**, 425–427.

Karlsson, A.O., and Holmlund, G. (2007) Identification of mammal species using species-specific DNA pyrosequencing. *Forensic Science International*, **173**, 16–20.

Kashyap, V.K., Sitalaximi, T., Chattopadhyay, P. *et al.* (2004) DNA profiling techniques in forensic analysis. *International Journal of Human Genetics*, **4**, 11–30.

Kyle, C.J. and Wilson., C.C. (2007) Mitochondrial DNA identification of game and harvested freshwater fish species. *Forensic Science International*, **166**, 68–76.

Lorenzini, R. 2005. DNA forensics and the poaching of wildlife in Italy: a case study. *Forensic Science International*, **153**, 218–221.

Manel, S., Berthier, P. and Luikart, G. (2002) Detecting wildlife poaching: identifying the origin of individuals with Bayesian assignment tests and multilocus genotypes. *Conservation Biology*, **16**, 650–659.

Martinsohn, J.T., and Ogden, R. (2008) A forensic genetic approach to European fisheries enforcement. *Forensic Science International: Genetics*, **1**, 610–611.

Martinsohn, J.T., and Ogden, R. (2009) Fishpoptrace: developing Snp-based population genetic assignment methods to investigate illegal fishing. *Forensic Science International: Genetics*, **2**, 294–296.

Meganathan, P.R., Dubey, B. and Haque, I. (2009) Molecular identification of Indian crocodile species: Pcr-Rflp method for forensic authentication. *Journal of Forensic Sciences*, **54**, 1042–1045.

Mullis, K.B. and Faloona, F.A. (1987) Specific synthesis of DNA in vitro via a polymerase-catalyzed chain reaction. *Methods in Enzymololgy*, **155**, 335–350.

Ogden, R. (2008) Fisheries forensics: the use of DNA tools for improving compliance, traceability and enforcement in the fishing industry. *Fish and Fisheries*, **9**, 462–472.

Ogden, R. (2010) Forensic science, genetics and wildlife biology: getting the right mix for a wildlife DNA forensics lab. *Forensic Science, Medicine, and Pathology*, **6**, 172–179.

Ogden, R. (2011) Unlocking the potential of genomic technologies for wildlife forensics. *Molecular Ecology Resources*, **11**, (Suppl. 1), 109–116.

Ogden, R., Dawnay, N. and McEwing, R. (2009) Wildlife DNA forensics: bridging the gap between conservation genetics and law enforcement. *Endangered Species Research*, **9**, 179–195.

Peppin, L., McEwing, R., Ogden, R. *et al.* (2010) Molecular sexing of African rhinoceros. *Conservation Genetics*, **11**, 1181–1184.

Peppin, L., McEwing, R., Webster, S. *et al.* (2008) Development of a field test for the detection of illegal bear products. *Endangered Species Research*, **9**, 263–270.

Poetsch, M., Seefeldt, S. Maschke, M. *et al.* (2001) Analysis of microsatellite polymorphism in red deer, roe deer, and fallow deer – possible employment in forensic applications. *Forensic Science International*, **116**, 1–8.

Ratnasingham, S. and Hebert, P.D.N. (2007) BOLD: The barcode of life data system (Www.Barcodinglife.Org). *Molecular Ecology Notes*, **7**, 355–364.

Renshaw, M.A., Saillant, E., Broughton, R.E. *et al.* (2006) Application of hypervariable genetic markers to forensic identification of 'wild' from hatchery-raised red drum, *Sciaenops Ocellatus*. *Forensic Science International*, **156**, 9–15.

Rojas, M., Gonzalez, I., Pavon, M.A. *et al.* (2011) Development of a real-time PCR assay to control the illegal trade of meat from protected capercaillie species (*Tetrao Urogallus*). *Forensic Science International*, **161**.

Sahajpal, V. and Goyal, S.P. (2010) Identification of a forensic case using microscopy and forensically informative nucleotide sequencing (Fins): a case study of small Indian civet (*Viverricula Indica*). *Science and Justice*, **50**, 94–97.

Schneider, P.M. (2007) Scientific standards for studies in forensic genetics. *Forensic Science International*, **165**, 238–243.

Singh, A., Gaur, A., Shailaja, K. *et al.* (2004) A novel microsatellite (STR) marker for forensic identification of big cats in India. *Forensic Science International*, **141**, 143–147.

Stokstad, E. (2010) To fight illegal fishing, forensic DNA gets local. *Science*, **330**, 1468–1469.

Thommasen, H.V.,Thomson, M.J., Shutler, G.G. *et al.* (1989) Development of DNA fingerprints for use in wildlife forensic science. *Wildlife Society Bulletin*, **17**, 321–326.

Verma, S.K., Prasad, K., Nagesh, N. *et al.* (2003) Was elusive carnivore a panther? DNA typing of faeces reveals the mystery. *Forensic Science International*, **137**, 16–20.

Verma, S.K. and Singh, L. (2003) Novel universal primers establish identity of an enormous number of animal species for forensic application. *Molecular Ecology Notes*, **3**, 28–31.

Wan, Q.-H. and Fang, S.-G. (2003) Application of species-specific polymerase chain reaction in the forensic identification of tiger species. *Forensic Science International*, **131**, 75–78.

Wobeser, G. (1996) Forensic (medico-legal) necropsy of wildlife. *Journal of Wildlife Diseases*, **32**, 240–249.

Wu, H., Wan, Q.-H., Fang, S.-G. *et al.* (2005) Application of mitochondrial DNA sequence analysis in the forensic dentification of Chinese sika seer subspecies. *Forensic Science International*, **148**, 101–105.

Xu, Y.C., Li, B., Bai, S.Y., *et al.* (2005) Individualization of tiger using microsatellites. *Forensic Science International*, **151**, 45–51.

14
DNA Applications and Implementation

Robert Ogden

Introduction

The development and application of DNA methods for the identification of evidence are widely considered to be the most important advance in forensic science in the past 50 years. The discovery of DNA fingerprints by Sir Alec Jeffreys, in 1983, first allowed samples of biological material to be matched back to an individual contributor, providing extremely strong evidence to link suspects to crime scenes. The subsequent development of DNA profiling techniques together with national DNA databases now provides investigators around the world with a powerful suite of analytical tools for identifying human DNA. The focus of most forensic scientists has been on human DNA analysis, however, from a biological perspective, there is no reason why these same approaches cannot be used to analyze animal or plant DNA to provide forensic evidence. The passive transfer of non-human DNA may be used to help reconstruct crime scenes; alternatively animals may be actively used to perpetrate crimes; however, the most common use of non-human DNA in forensic analysis is when the animal or plant itself is the subject of criminal activity. The development and application of DNA analysis techniques capable of providing evidence to assist in conservation law enforcement, commonly termed "wildlife DNA forensics" has long been recognized but is now receiving increasing attention as a discipline in its own right.

Wildlife DNA forensics is essentially concerned with the identification of evidence items in order to determine the species, population, relationship or individual identity of a sample. The subject has developed in parallel to human forensic genetics and has benefited from the horizontal transfer of molecular and statistical techniques; however, it remains a highly specialist area with its own

Wildlife Forensics: Methods and Applications, First Edition. Edited by Jane E. Huffman and John R. Wallace.

distinct set of challenges, situated between wildlife conservation research and applied forensic science (Ogden *et al.*, 2009). With the development of national and international legislation to protect ever-diminishing habitat and species diversity, DNA forensics is now becoming a key investigative tool to combat wildlife crime. At the same time, the way in which non-human DNA evidence is generated and presented in court is coming under renewed scrutiny. This chapter highlights the potential advantages and practical requirements surrounding this emerging field, as well as considering likely future developments.

History

The use of genetic analysis to identify non-human evidence began shortly after the first DNA fingerprints were applied to human forensic investigation (Gill *et al.*, 1985). The realization that the same technique could allow familial identification in birds (Burke and Bruford, 1987) rapidly led to the use of these methods to verify captive breeding claims in cases where wild bird theft was suspected (Shorrock, 1998). The development of individual DNA identification systems has since followed that of human methods through the use of multi-locus (Thommasen *et al.*, 1989) and single-locus (Wetton and Parkin 1997) probes and microsatellites (Jones *et al.*, 2002; Singh *et al.*, 2004; Xu *et al.*, 2005). In parallel to this research, DNA also began to be used to identify the species from which trace evidence originated (Cronin *et al.*, 1991; Parson *et al.*, 2000). This application relied on molecular taxonomy rather than human forensic techniques and proved particularly useful for investigating cases of illegal trade (Baker *et al.*, 1996; Baker and Palumbi, 1994) and poaching (Guglich *et al.*, 1994; Sweijd *et al.*, 1998).

Today we can see a wide array of molecular identification techniques applied in many countries to evidence originating from a diverse range of taxa. This expansion offers huge potential for the conservation of endangered species but at the same time presents multiple challenges to those attempting to transfer research methods into forensic analytical tools. Perhaps the most pressing issue of all is the need to find an acceptable balance between the utilization of academic research to drive the development of genetic identification techniques, and the expectations and requirements of the forensic science community to present clear, unequivocal evidence produced using validated, robust methods. In addition to discussing the techniques and applications relevant to wildlife DNA forensics, this chapter will therefore also explore some of the issues relating to the practical implementation of DNA forensic analysis in wildlife crime enforcement.

Questions and Techniques: Wildlife Crime Issues

In recent years the law enforcement community has observed increasing links between wildlife crime and organized crime. The illegal trade in flora and fauna offers financial rewards comparable to those of the narcotics trade with only a fraction of the risk, and thus attracts the attention of international criminal organizations. Such activities clearly threaten the survival of critically endangered target species, for example, tiger, rhinoceros and mahogany; however, they also reduce our ability to sustainably harvest more abundant species, pushing them towards extinction and threatening global economic markets such as the fishing and timber industries. This new understanding has added weight to the long-held position of conservationists regarding the need to legally protect global biological resources.

Legislation for the protection of specific species and the strength with which any such laws are enforced varies widely among countries. Internationally, the Washington Convention on International Trade in Endangered Species of Wild Fauna and Flora (CITES), provides a framework for trade control and monitoring; however, each of the current 173 member states is responsible for implementation of the convention through national law. National laws generally extend beyond CITES to include species conservation within each country, controlling exploitation and trade at a domestic level. For example, in the USA, the Endangered Species Act (ESA) describes federal wildlife laws for both national conservation and international trade. Any application of wildlife DNA forensic analysis must be directly related to the legislation being enforced and, conversely, any new legislation relating to biological identification must be enforceable, making it important to develop a reciprocal understanding between wildlife legislators, law enforcers and forensic scientists.

The purpose of any forensic analysis is to provide information or evaluate hypotheses concerning the evidence available. This means that analysis is driven by the questions asked by casework investigators (Table 14.1). Individual cases generate individual questions; however, in wildlife law enforcement most forensic enquiries can be divided into four main problems: what species is it?, where is it from?, which individual is it from?, and who is it related to? Each of these questions can be considered in wildlife DNA forensics using a variety of different techniques.

Species Identification

The use of genetic analysis to identify the species of an evidence sample is the most common application in wildlife DNA forensics. Species identification may be used in cases of illegal poaching in order to identify trace evidence in the field or from a suspect's possessions (Gupta *et al.*, 2005). It has also been widely applied to the identification of traded products that have lost identifying morphological characters, such as processed wood (Deguilloux *et al.*, 2002), traditional medicines (TMs) (Hsieh *et al.*, 2003; Wetton *et al.*, 2004; Peppin *et al.*, 2008) and shark fins (Shivji *et al.*, 2002; Chapman *et al.*, 2003).

Genetic species identification relies on the isolation and analysis of DNA markers that show variation among species, but are generally conserved within species. In animals, the most commonly used markers are gene regions within

Table 14.1 A summary of the primary investigative questions, their associated scientific questions and the range of genetic tools currently applied to address them in wildlife DNA forensics.

	Evidential/Investigative question			
Considerations	What is it?	Where's it from?	Does it match this individual?	Was it laundered?
Forensic identification	Species ID	Population ID	Individual profile matching	Parentage/batch exclusion
Discrete or continuous unit of identification?	Discrete	Continuous	Discrete	Discrete
Appropriate methods	Identification via diagnostic fixed differences	Identification via allele frequency differences	Identification via profile matching	Exclusion via observed differences
DNA target	mtDNA/cpDNA	mtDNA/cpDNA and nDNA	nDNA	nDNA
DNA markers	Sequences SNPs	Sequences Microsatellites/SNPs	Microsatellites/SNPs	Microsatellites/SNPs

mitochondrial DNA, particularly cytochrome b (Parson *et al.*, 2000) and cytochrome oxidase subunit I (COI) (Herbert *et al.*, 2003a, 2003b), as their mutation rates roughly coincide with the rate of species evolution. In plants, suitable genetic markers are normally found in the chloroplast genome within genes such as matK and trnH-psbA (Kress *et al.*, 2005). Due to the presence of multiple mitochondrion and chloroplast organelles within a single cell, these markers are present in multiple copies. This increases the chance of success when analyzing trace evidence samples that typically contain relatively little cellular material (Butler and Levin, 1998; Budowle *et al.*, 2003).

In practice, there are several techniques used to analyze species informative markers (Figure 14.1). The principal method is DNA nucleotide sequencing, followed by comparison of the resulting sequence with reference sequence data from different species. DNA nucleotide sequencing utilizes all of the information present in the target sequence; however the differences observed among species at a genetic marker are largely due to single base pair changes in the DNA sequence, known as single nucleotide polymorphisms (SNPs) (Figure 14.1). SNPs can be directly utilized to identify species, without the need for full sequencing, using a number of techniques that are either more cost-effective and low-tech, for example PCR-restriction fragment length polymorphism (RFLP) (Figure 14.1) (Tahir *et al.*, 1996; Hold *et al.*, 2001), or enable analysis of shorter DNA sequence regions via SNP genotyping (Figure 14.1). Minimizing the size of the genetic marker targeted is often necessary to obtain results from samples that are either degraded or have been highly processed, fragmenting the DNA (Butler *et al.*, 2003; Hajibabaei *et al.*, 2006). Further information on species identification methods is provided in Chapter 13.

Identification of Geographic Origin

Wildlife legislation usually operates within political boundaries such as national and regional borders or marine fishery zones. Species distributions are governed by biological and environmental factors that rarely coincide with such legislation. This mismatch often leads to wildlife crime investigations asking questions concerning the geographic origin of a sample. For example, to enforce CITES regulations, it may be necessary to demonstrate the geographic source of a specific sample, in addition to identifying the species. Similarly, the effective management of marine protected areas requires methods that enable illegally harvested stocks to be distinguished from those taken legally from elsewhere. Genetic analysis has been employed to infer geographic origin of samples in biological research for many years; however, the number of published studies detailing the application of these tools to forensic casework is low, suggesting this area is in its infancy. Identification of geographic origin is also addressed elsewhere in this issue.

From a forensic genetic perspective, identifying the geographic origin of a sample is usually equivalent to identifying its *reproductive population* of origin.

1. DNA nucleotide sequencing

Sequencing identifies each nucleotide (base) within a specific target region of DNA (the genetic marker). Species identification usually involves sequencing around 500 bases of DNA to provide a species-specific sequence. Sequencing provides data for developing genetic markers such as SNPs microsatellites and InDels, which describe specific areas of sequence variation.

a) Four DNA sequences of 16 bases in length; the three references sequences differ, the unknown sequence matches Ref. 2.

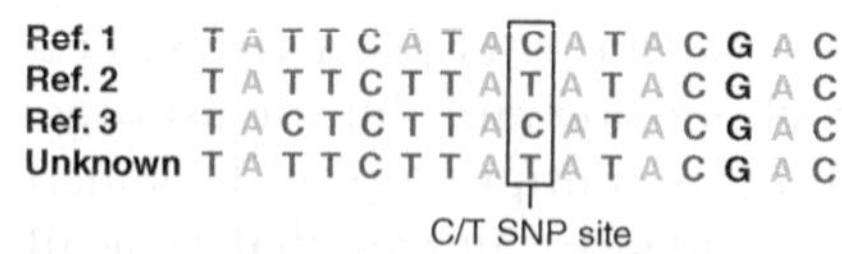

Single base differences are known as single nucleotide polymorphisms (SNPs). Individual variants (e.g. C or T) are referred to as 'alleles'.

2. SNP typing

SNP typing, or genotyping, allows specific variable sites in a DNA sequence to be investigated. Focussing on a SNP site allows faster, cheaper tests to be developed that do not require such long fragments of high quality DNA, however less information is gained in comparison to DNA sequencing. There are multiple methods for typing SNP markers; three examples used in DNA forensics are provided below:

i) PCR-RFLP

PCR-RFLP relies on the ability of enzymes to cut DNA at specific recognition sites. Where these sites coincide with a SNP marker, some sequences will be cut to produce two DNA fragments (S1), others will not (S2), leading to differences in the number and length of DNA fragments between samples. These differences can be resolved under electrophoresis.

b) Enzyme recognition site only present in S1, therefore only S1 DNA is cut.

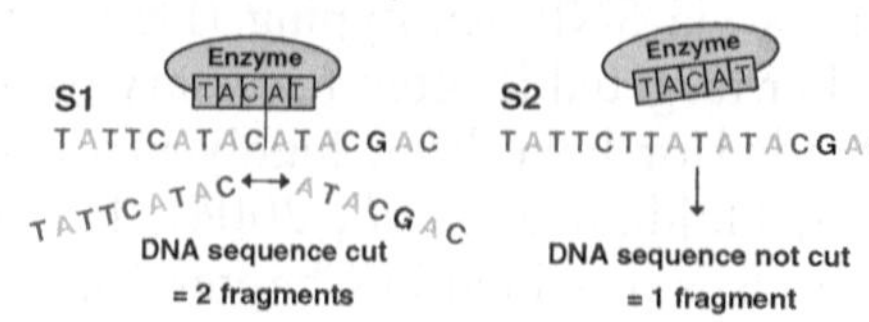

ii) Allele specific PCR

Primers used in PCR for amplifying genetic markers can be designed for conserved regions of DNA (universal primers) or regions where DNA varies between species or populations (allele specific primers). Allele specific primers are designed so that PCR only works when DNA from the target sequence is present in a sample.

c) Complementary primer only binds to target DNA sequence (S1), enabling amplification.

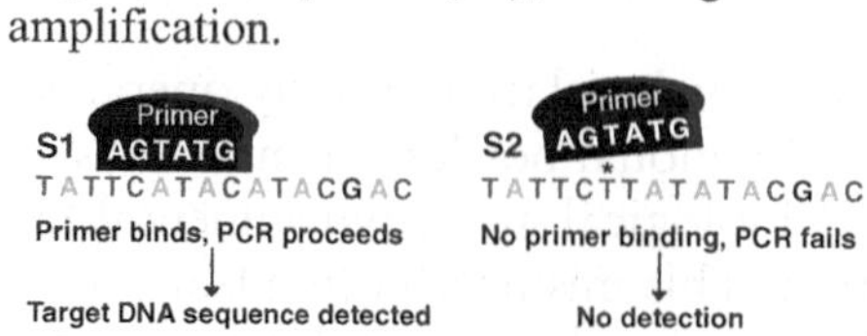

iii) Allele specific probes

An alternative to using specific primers, is to use universal primers in combination with a specific probe. Different probes are designed to attach to different DNA sequence variants (S1 & S2) allowing the base present at a SNP site to be detected.

d) PCR amplification with universal primers (UP). Allele-specific probes detect target SNPs

Figure 14.1 Introduction to the current techniques used in wildlife DNA forensics.

3. Microsatellite genotyping
Microsatellite markers describe differences between DNA sequences due to variation in the number of repetitive units of DNA in a specific region. Changes in the repeat number lead to different sized DNA fragments (alleles) that can be resolved under electrophoresis.

e) The number of repeat units (ACAT) varies between the two samples, altering the length of the DNA fragments (microsatellite alleles).

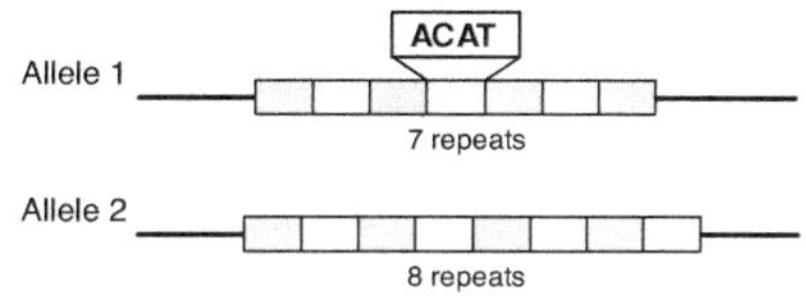

Figure 14.1 *(Continued)*

Biological populations include many different levels of genetic variation, from extended families to subspecies, making them difficult to define. Populations are often capable of sharing genetic material, therefore compared to species identification, DNA markers are less likely to show discrete differences among groups. Geographic origin identification is based on our ability to assign a sample to a particular population, requiring the source population to be sufficiently genetically distinct from other candidate populations and relying on the existence of population data from multiple areas. Despite these limitations, a wealth of existing academic and conservation management research focusing on population assignment is now being transferred to address the urgent need for enforcement techniques capable of identifying geographic origin. The methods employed are largely dictated by the degree of genetic differentiation between populations.

Within some species, populations may be so isolated from one another that there is effectively no exchange of genetic material between them. Genetic differences will gradually accumulate over evolutionary time to a point where members of an isolated region share the same types of genetic marker (alleles) within their population, but exhibit different alleles to that of any other population. Markers that exhibit such *discrete variation* are very useful for identifying populations and therefore for assigning an individual to a geographic region with a high degree of confidence. In highly divergent populations, mitochondrial DNA (mtDNA) can be used to identify populations, similar to species identification. The hypervariable mtDNA control region, or D-loop, is often used as a marker in geographic origin identification, with individual control region sequence types (haplotypes) corresponding to specific populations. Wu *et al.* (2005) applied this technique to the Chinese sika deer *Cervus nippon* that is classified into four subspecies. Following widespread hunting to supply the TM trade, two sub-species were extirpated (lost) from the wild and now exist only in captivity where they are bred in large numbers for medicinal use. The remaining two subspecies that exist in the wild are Critically Endangered and heavily protected by Chinese law. In order to enforce this conservation legislation, a method to discriminate one of the wild subspecies from one of the domesticated subspecies was developed, based on mtDNA control region haplotype variation.

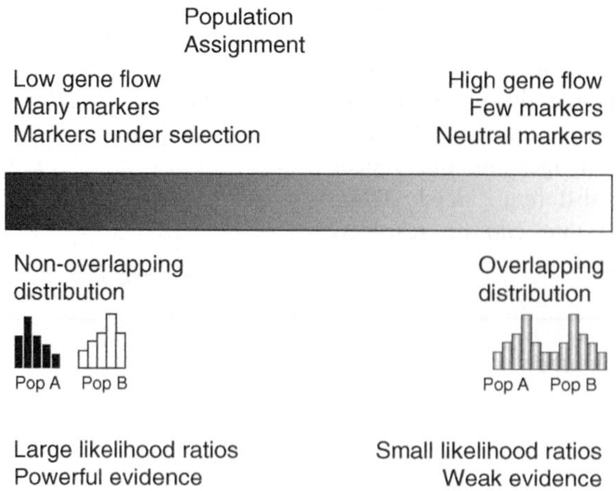

Figure 14.2 The level of genetic diversity between populations exhibits continuous variation, from subspecies (dark end) to extended families (light end). The degree of population (Pop) divergence dictates the selection of genetic markers and subsequent analytical methods used to assign a sample to its geographic origin. Ultimately, highly divergent populations are easier to distinguish and typically enable the provision of stronger forensic evidence.

In the absence of sufficient mitochondrial DNA variation, it is necessary to employ genetic markers from the nuclear genome that show variability among regions. Although some microsatellite and SNP markers (Figure 14.1) do show discrete differences, individual alleles will often be distributed across populations. This means that differentiation can only be achieved on the basis of differing *allele frequencies* (Figure 14.2). The frequency of the alleles observed in a population can be used to characterize its genetic structure and to assess the probability of a sample originating from that area. Such probabilistic approaches have two important implications for wildlife forensic investigations. First, it is necessary to develop large genetic databases to provide representative allele frequencies for all of the potential source populations. Second, it requires the use of statistical analysis to provide quantitative probabilities of assignment for a sample to each of those populations.

In practice, a DNA profile is first generated from a test sample using a panel of genetic markers. The profile is then assigned to a population by comparing the alleles observed in the profile with the allele frequencies observed in the populations. There is a wide range of analytical methods available for assignment (reviewed by Manel *et al.*, 2005) and it is important to understand the statistical basis and underlying assumptions of any that are used. In a forensic context it is necessary to select a method that enables the scientist to evaluate both prosecution and defense hypotheses; that is, one which provides a quantitative estimate of the probability that the sample originated from the source claimed by the defense, rather than simply identifying the most likely genetic geographic origin. Assignment tests are normally implemented in software packages, and a number are freely available for data analysis (reviewed by Hauser *et al.*, 2006). Population assignment is extensively used to prosecute illegal salmon fishing in the NW Pacific (Withler *et al.*, 2004), where large databases have been established (Seeb *et al.*, 2007), but applications are currently limited for endangered species where data are difficult to collect.

In populations that exhibit much larger rates of gene exchange, allele frequencies among different regions may be almost equal at neutral genetic markers, making it impractical to apply this approach to identify the geographic origin of wildlife samples. To address this problem, researchers are now turning to non-neutral genetic markers, or markers that are *under selection*, in order to increase the geographic resolution at which samples may be assigned. For example, work on markers under selection in the European cod has shown that SNP markers associated with functional genes show much higher allele frequency variation at local scales than is seen at neutral SNP markers (Nielsen *et al.*, 2009). By targeting these markers which may be linked to environmental factors such as salinity or temperature, fish forensic scientists are able to pinpoint the geographic origin of fish catches with much greater precision.

Individual Identification

The use of DNA profiling for the individual identification of genetic evidence has revolutionized human forensic analysis over the past twenty years. In contrast, the identification of individual animals and plants has often been less relevant to the protection of endangered species. However, for certain issues such as poaching, where it may be necessary to demonstrate that a horn, tusk, bone or skin has originated from a specific individual, DNA profiling techniques can provide key evidence to wildlife crime investigations. Other applications include the identification of stolen animals and the authentication of legally traded wildlife products.

DNA profiling works by targeting genetic markers that are highly variable within species and are therefore likely to show differences among individuals. As with geographic origin identification, multiple microsatellite or SNP markers are used to create a profile that consists of a series of alleles (Figure 14.1). The greater the number of markers used, the less likely it is that another individual in the species will be found with the same series of alleles (same profile). If two samples produce different DNA profiles, the possibility that they originate from the same individual can be *excluded*. If two samples share the same profile, it suggests that they may come from the same individual and it is then necessary to calculate the probability that two individuals have the same profile by chance. This probability is affected by the number and variability of markers in the profile, how common the alleles are in the species (their frequency), and how closely related individuals are in the population where the samples were taken. Evaluating these factors requires a representative sample of DNA profiles from the population.

The development of individual profiling techniques for wildlife DNA forensic investigation has been limited by the need to generate reference data; however, examples of successful applications do exist. In Canada, DNA profiling systems have been developed and are regularly applied to support investigations into the poaching of mule deer *Odocoileus heimonus*, white-tailed deer *O. virginianus*, elk *Cervus canadiensis*, moose *Alces alces*, caribou *Rangifer tarandus* and black bear *Ursus americanus* (www.forensicdna.ca/dnadatabases.html). The illegal trade in rhinoceros horn is also being investigated using DNA profiling techniques to link smuggled horns back to poached rhino carcasses. In response to a sharp rise in poaching in southern Africa in 2010, wildlife forensic scientists are identifying individual rhinoceros to help investigators determine crime scenes and trade routes involved in the illegal harvest and trade of horn.

Individual DNA profiles can also be used to regulate the legal trade in species that are protected in only part of their range, or are subject to strict quotas. Wildlife DNA registers in which legally traded specimens can be individually recognized through a DNA profile provide a method of authenticating wildlife products. This has been demonstrated in principle for the minke whale *Balaenoptera acutorostrata* by comparing samples obtained from markets to an existing Norwegian genetic register of legally caught whales (Palsbøll *et al*., 2006). However, DNA registers are not without controversy. The ability to individually identify tigers using DNA profiles has been used to support the argument for tiger farms in China, by demonstrating that animal bones and skins originate from captive sources. In such species, any level of legal trade may threaten the survival of those remaining in the wild.

Exclusion

In DNA forensics, demonstrating that biological samples come from different source individuals (exclusion) is easier than demonstrating that samples come from the same individual (identification). This is because with identification it is always theoretically possible, by chance, to have the same profile in different individuals. The forensic scientist must therefore use relevant background genetic data to evaluate the statistical probability of observing this chance event, before commenting on the strength of a DNA profile match. Establishing background genetic data sets is time-consuming, expensive, and, in the case of very rare species, may be practically impossible, so wildlife forensic scientists often attempt to make use of exclusion approaches to support wildlife crime investigations.

Supply chain verification

Supply chain verification takes the concept of a DNA register and turns it around, so that instead of identifying which individual a sample has come from, an exclusion approach is used to demonstrate that a sample could not have come from a batch. This approach is applied in South-east Asia to verify the source of merbau *Intsia spp.*, a tropical hardwood traded under quota. DNA profiles are produced for each tree stump in a concession and stored on a database. Logs and timber products originating from that concession are subsequently resampled throughout shipment and processing. Wood that has been illegally laundered into the supply chain wood can be identified via DNA profile exclusion from the original tree stumps (Lawson, 2007). This type of innovative approach can provide forensic evidence for enforcing trade controls, but importantly also offers a method for self-regulation, allowing limited enforcement resources to be more efficiently deployed elsewhere.

Parentage testing

The ability to verify or refute familial relatedness is the fourth principal application of wildlife DNA forensic techniques. Establishing levels of relatedness is important for many aspects of conservation genetics, but for forensic investigation the focus lies primarily on the differentiation of captive-bred from wild-caught animals. Captive breeding programs are now commonplace throughout the world and focus on either sustaining global populations of highly endangered species, or the production of animals and plants of commercial value. Problems arise when the two drivers cross-over, as they often do, and rare species become highly prized commodities with large profits to be made from their commercial trade. This situation may lead to unscrupulous "breeders" laundering animals or plants taken from the wild and re-selling them as captive bred individuals. Examples of current issues include the trade in parrots, birds of prey, tortoises and orchids.

The fact that genetic markers are inherited from one generation to the next allows DNA profiles to be used to verify parent–offspring relationships. The alleles present in the DNA profile of an individual must also be present in its putative parents, one allele per marker in each parent. If alleles are observed that do not correspond to those in the putative parental profiles, then the possibility of the individual being their offspring can be excluded. This method of profile *exclusion* to refute parentage claims, like supply chain verification, does not require profile data from the wider population and is therefore relatively simple to apply. However, the results of parental exclusion are not as definitive as those for individual profile exclusion and require more interpretation. The basis of variability at a genetic marker is the occurrence of heritable mutation events, where one allele changes to another between generations. Although such events rarely occur, they do create the possibility that disagreement between parent and offspring profiles may be due to mutation rather than false parentage. Ideally, as in human genetics, the mutation rate at each marker should be incorporated into parentage analysis; however, this is rarely possible for wildlife species, and profile interpretation therefore requires caution.

A number of forensic DNA profiling systems have been developed specifically for parentage verification. In the UK, where the theft of chicks from wild nest sites persists, genetic tools have been used to investigate captive breeding claims in a number of predatory bird species for the past 20 years (Wetton and Parkin, 1997; reviewed by Shorrock, 1998). The techniques used have evolved in parallel to human forensic genetic techniques, resulting in the development of microsatellite DNA profiling systems for six different species (Dawnay *et al.*, 2008b). Similar systems are employed throughout Europe and Australia to verify captive bird breeding, while in Russia, parentage analysis is used to authenticate caviar produced from captive sturgeon (S. Rastorguev, pers. comm.). Wildlife DNA forensic approaches offer a powerful way to investigate wild animal laundering and are set to become more widely used as conservation enforcement increases.

Practical Applications

The diverse range of questions that can be addressed using genetic methods offers great potential to forensic investigation and wildlife law enforcement. All of the techniques discussed so far, while sometimes originally developed for forensic use, are readily available to university scientists working in academic fields such as molecular ecology and evolutionary genetics. To move from academic analysis to the generation of forensic evidence requires the laboratory process and environment to be controlled and for the analytical techniques and reference data to be suitably validated. In this section, the practical implications of performing forensic DNA testing are considered, highlighting the differences and similarities between wildlife DNA forensics, human DNA forensics and academic research. To begin with, though, we consider the different types of biological material that can be examined as sources of DNA.

Sample Types for DNA Analysis

The successful recovery of DNA from biological evidence is the most important stage in any forensic genetic investigation. The diversity of DNA sources available to human forensic scientists has been well publicized and includes soft body tissues, bones, teeth, hair, saliva, sweat, urine and feces. The methods used to extract DNA from these sample types can often be transferred to other species; however, wildlife forensic geneticists may be faced with quite different sample types such as fish scales, feathers, fruits or processed timber. Scientists have developed techniques for recovering DNA from a remarkable array of sample types (e.g. snake venom, Pook and McEwing, 2005; moulted feathers; Horvath *et al.*, 2005; fish scales, Kumar *et al.*, 2007; porcupine quills, Oliveira *et al.*, 2007; historic eggs, Lee and Prys-Jones, 2008), enabling genetic information to be recovered from almost any biological material.

Laboratory Models: Individual Facilities

Wildlife DNA forensics combines human DNA forensic rigor with wildlife genetic expertise. In practice, bringing these aspects together is not simple, particularly given the lack of money typically available for such applications. The facilities available for performing wildlife DNA forensic analysis may range from a dedicated wildlife forensics unit through to a university research laboratory; the type of facility used will dictate the levels of security and quality assurance that can be supported which in turn will ultimately affect the robustness of the forensic evidence (Figure 14.3). As an example, four different types of facility are considered here, reflecting the diversity of laboratories currently in use:

1. *Government-funded dedicated wildlife DNA forensics facilities.* Core facilities for processing all casework together with the capacity to undertake validation studies. The implementation of a rigorous Quality Assurance (QA) system is not compromised by the demand for profit, or alternate uses of the same laboratory space. A pool of forensic expertise can be developed able to address a very wide range of questions.
2. *Commercial forensic genetic facility offering wildlife DNA services.* Organizations operating for profit (or at least full cost recovery) may provide services, however, financial controls will limit the available methods to those used frequently. QA systems are likely to be available, however, the associated cost is likely make the per sample analysis fee very high. In most countries,

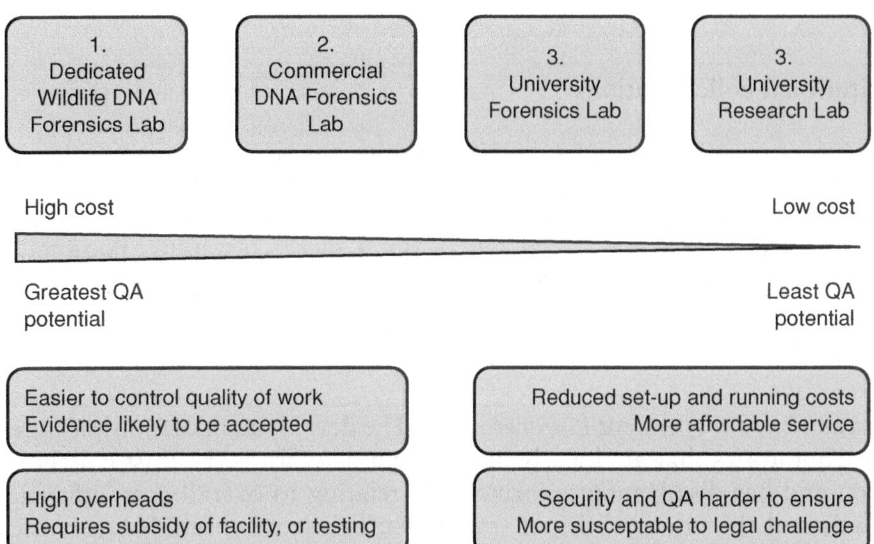

Figure 14.3 Summary of four possible laboratory models for undertaking wildlife DNA forensic analysis, describing their key characteristics.

such a model will only function if the enforcement agencies receive specific additional support to fund forensic analysis.

3. *University or institutional research facility with dedicated forensic laboratory space*. This model encompasses a broad range of institutional laboratory facilities, from correctly designed, properly controlled, professional forensic units situated in a research institute to academic experts in their field with little understanding of forensic processes who are, for a variety of reasons, offering a forensic service. There is no doubt that at one extreme, a number of universities have dedicated sufficient laboratory space, staff and resources to provide first class forensic genetic services; at the other extreme, the risk of evidence being rubbished, or worse still being wrong, rapidly increases.
4. *Multi-use research laboratory*. Research laboratories typically operate with low levels of security, equipment is rarely fully calibrated, quality systems are not in place. Neither staff nor students have undergone any forensic training.

Comparing these four model systems it is easy to conclude that the fully-funded government model is the ideal and that a research laboratory model is not acceptable (Figure 14.3). In reality, many countries already using wildlife DNA forensic analysis, or that are seeking to develop capacity, are restricted to operating under the second and third models due the cost and/or prioritization of wildlife crime. In order for these models to work, it is essential to have the correct resources in place, not only in terms of laboratory facilities, but also in relation to personnel (Ogden, 2010). An alternative to compromising on the quality of an individual facility is to pool resources with a neighboring region, or even another country, and share wildlife forensic DNA facilities.

Institutional collaborations

As with many other types of resource, the prospect of sharing wildlife DNA forensic capacity among stakeholders will doubtless be problematic and may appear impractical. However, it may also be the only viable option. Three possible models for a collaborative approach to the delivery of wildlife DNA forensic services are considered here: (A) a network of independent laboratories; (B) a single core laboratory; and (C) a single central laboratory with regional satellite laboratories (Figure 14.4).

A Network of Independent Laboratories The development of multiple independent laboratories that are loosely linked via a network is the least collaborative option and has disadvantages, principally relating to overall cost, efficiency of analysis and the practicalities of training sufficient wildlife DNA forensic scientists; however in some regions, it is the only politically acceptable solution. The benefits of establishing a strong network among independent laboratories include sharing novel techniques and reference data, establishing partnerships

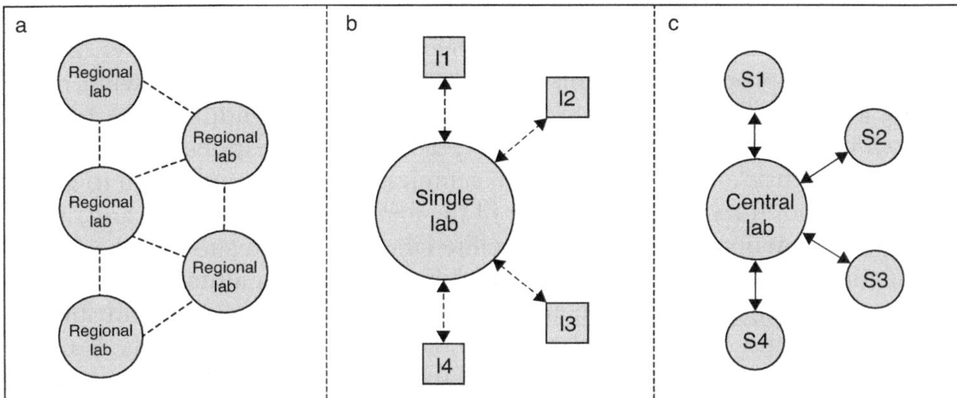

Independent regional laboratories	Single core laobratory	Central Laboratory & local satellite laboratories
Each region runs and operates its own wildlife DNA forensics lab. Collaboration among labs as part of existing or novel networks.	Investigations from multiple regions (I1-I4) send all evidence to one facility Coordinated analysis, one QA system Analytical results supplied back to individual regions	Core lab: Casework DNA analysis and reporting Performance of validation studies Satellite labs (S1-S4): Examination, Sampling, extraction, R&D, retention of reference materials
High set-up & per sample costs Institutional independence Maximum capacity building	Low set-up & per sample costs Institutional dependence Minimal capacity building	Medium set-up & per sample costs Institutional dependence Targeted capacity building

Figure 14.4 Three models for providing wildlife DNA forensic laboratory services across a number of regions or countries. Model a describes a loosely linked system of independent laboratories, Model b describes a single laboratory system and Model c describes an intermediate solution, incorporating one central laboratory and multiple satellite laboratories.

for inter-laboratory studies and, importantly for investigations of international illegal trade, communicating with neighboring forensic scientists in relation to emerging issues. The Association of South-East Asian Nations (ASEAN) is developing such a wildlife forensics network to help support wildlife forensic capacity in individual countries.

A Single Core Laboratory The opposite approach to a system of independent laboratories is to have a single, quality assured, internationally recognized laboratory offering affordable services to all (Figure 14.4b). The single lab model should be the most cost-effective solution, providing analysis to a very high standard across a broad range of investigative questions. This is what the US Fish and Wildlife Service's Forensic Laboratory (USFWS-FL) offers in relation to CITES investigations worldwide, with some notable success on large-scale multinational investigations. However, at least at an international level, this model is restricted by issues of data sharing and the negative perception of stakeholders concerning reliance on third countries for forensic support.

A Central Laboratory with Regional Satellite Laboratories In situations where collaboration among parties is highly developed and legislation allows, a third model has been proposed that aims to rationalize the use of resources while maintaining local involvement in casework and ownership of wildlife DNA forensic research (Figure 14.4c). Under this model, each region is responsible for coordinating the forensic analysis of their own samples, including submission to a local "satellite" laboratory for examination of the item, evidence recovery and, as appropriate, extraction of DNA. The satellite laboratory then submits the sample to a single central wildlife DNA forensic laboratory that maintains a full range analytical tests operating under an accredited quality system. The advantages and disadvantages of this model relate to those described for models A and B; the intention being to mitigate the disadvantages and retain the advantages of each. It is envisaged that this approach may be suitable at a European level, or within a single large country.

These three different models for implementing coordinated wildlife DNA forensic analysis will be appropriate in different situations and other solutions are likely to exist. The key point is that wildlife DNA forensics is unlikely to ever attract the level of resources and investment afforded to its human equivalent and it will probably always be necessary to work harder and think more laterally to ensure that access to high quality wildlife DNA forensic services is available to those that need it most.

Taken together, the practical issues of validation and quality assurance, discussed elsewhere in this volume and the laboratory models discussed in this section characterize the applied nature of the wildlife DNA forensics. These factors, together with the science of wildlife genetic identification, have combined in recent years to establish wildlife DNA forensics as an applied discipline in its own right. With an increasing amount of pressure being placed on a wider range of species, wildlife DNA forensics will need to continue to develop, responding to the needs of law enforcement agencies worldwide. The next section discusses some of the current limitations and highlights what might be expected to emerge in the field over the coming years.

Technical challenges and opportunities

From a scientific perspective, the techniques presented in this chapter have been heavily researched and demonstrated to be reliable methods for the analysis of genetic material. The outstanding issues in relation to DNA identification relate mostly to reference data. For species identification, the availability of comprehensive, accurate sequence data against which to compare unknown samples and develop new tests is of utmost importance. The largest source of comparative data, the NCBI/EMBL/DDBJ database collaboration, contains a significant number of errors, both in terms of the DNA sequence data itself and the labeling of DNA sequences. The majority of the errors are obvious to an experienced scientist and can be accounted for; however the use of such data sources for forensic identification is certainly compromised to some extent. At the opposite extreme, many wildlife forensic laboratories hold their own reference sample and data collections that have been authenticated for forensic use; the limitation here is the range of reference materials required to identify the thousands of species that may pass through a laboratory over time. The BOLD (Barcoding of Life) database offers a solution to these problems by aiming to make authenticated reference sequence data available for all species. By employing strict criteria for the generation and submission of sequence information, the BOLD system should in time represent the best solution to the need for authenticated sequence data.

In contrast, identification below the species level will probably always be limited by the availability of reference population data. Individual datasets have been developed for forensic use in some flagship species (e.g. rhinoceros and tiger) or species of commercial value (e.g. salmon, cod, herring, hake and sole); however, the inherent difficulty in sampling from endangered populations, combined with a lack of agreed data quality standards, or a cooperative basis for data sharing, remain significant challenges to the widespread application of forensic genetic methods. A move towards the use of SNP markers in wildlife forensics should help with both the speed of data generation and exchange of data among groups (Ogden, 2011); nevertheless it is inevitable that the development of techniques for individual and geographic origin identification will need to be heavily prioritized.

While there are practical limits to the resources available for developing species-specific tests, the post-genomic era does now offer a huge opportunity for the development of DNA markers capable of identifying individuals and geographic origin with increasing precision. Genome sequencing is becoming faster and less expensive, and is being applied to an ever greater number of taxa. While novel technologies are invariably focused on human and model species systems, horizontal transfer is now bringing genomic methods within reach of the endangered species researcher community. This offers great promise the development of novel markers for forensic identification and the subsequent production of reference data. Increased genomic data is not only providing larger numbers of traditional genetic markers used for identification, such as neutral SNP and microsatellite markers, but is also enabling the discovery and application of markers associated with adaptive traits, allowing increasingly fine levels of geographic assignment.

Future Developments

Coordination and integration

The future development of wildlife DNA forensics is not only dependent on the continued development and transfer of technologies to address new enforcement issues. In many respects it is more reliant on the continued development of government policies to formulate new conservation legislation and enforce existing regulations. While specific issues in individual countries are currently approached using forensic genetic tools to support enforcement investigations, the full potential of these techniques will only be achieved through the more widespread development of an integrated forensic framework for tackling crime against endangered species.

The use of forensic genetics in wildlife law enforcement requires a multi-agency approach that include field officers, investigation agencies and prosecution authorities often from a range of organizations, such as customs, police, national parks, government departments and non-governmental organizations; in addition to forensic scientists. Communication and cooperation among all elements is essential to enable forensic evidence to be successfully collected, stored, transferred, analyzed and presented in court. This requirement is now recognized by many stakeholders and examples of coordinated national strategies for wildlife crime investigation exist (UK: Partnership for Action against Wildlife Crime [PAW], www.defra.gov.uk/paw; US: Fish and Wildlife Service, www.fws.gov/le/). International resources for helping to improve forensic capacity are also being developed (e.g. TRACE, www.tracenetwork.org/; SWFS, www.wildlifeforensicscience.org; Interpol, www.interpol.int/; the Australasian region, www.anzpaa.org.au; the ASEAN region, www.asean-wfn.org); however, much more work is needed if benefits from technological progress in wildlife DNA forensics are to be fully realized.

Summary

- The use of DNA forensics to support conservation began over twenty years ago and has gradually developed alongside human forensic genetic techniques, conservation genetic applications and strengthening wildlife legislation.
- Forensic genetic methods are now used to address questions relating to the identification of species, geographic origin, family relatedness and individual identity, offering a large number of possible investigative tools to enforcement officers worldwide.
- Wildlife DNA forensics is heavily dependent on academic research for the development of novel techniques and production of reference datasets; however, it is vital that a distinction is made between applied conservation genetics and any extension to forensic genetic investigation.
- A number of laboratory models exist for the development of wildlife DNA forensic services; the most appropriate solution will vary with the situation, but basic forensic requirements cannot be compromised.
- In addition to the development and application of novel tools, the continued growth of wildlife DNA forensics requires cooperation and coordination among all members of the wildlife law enforcement community.

References

Altschul, S.F., Madden, T.L., Schaffer, A.A. *et al.* (1997) Gapped BLAST and PSI-BLAST: a new generation of protein database search programs. *Nucleic Acids Research*, **25**, 3389–3402.

Baker, C.S., Cipriano, F. and Palumbi, S.R. (1996) Molecular genetic identification of whale and dolphin products from commercial markets in Korea and Japan. *Molecular Ecology*, **5**, 671–685.

Baker, C.S. and Palumbi, S.R. (1994) Which whales are hunted – a molecular genetic approach to monitoring whaling. *Science*, **265**, 1538–1539.

Balding, D.J. (2005) *Weight of Evidence for DNA Profiles*. Chichester: John Wiley & Sons, Ltd.

Branicki, W., Kupiec, T. and Pawlowski, R. (2003) Validation of cytochrome b sequence analysis as a method of species identification. *Journal of Forensic Science*, **48**, 83–87.

Budowle, B., Allard, M.W., Wilson, M.R. *et al.* (2003) Forensics and mitochondrial DNA: applications, debates, and foundations. *Annual Review of Genomics and Human Genetics*, **4**, 119–141.

Burke, T., and Bruford, M.W. (1987) DNA fingerprinting in birds. *Nature*, **327**, 149–152.

Butler, J.M. and Levin, B.C. (1998) Forensic applications of mitochondrial DNA. *Trends in Biotechnolology* **16**, 158–162.

Butler, J.M., Shen, Y. and McCord, B.R. (2003) The development of reduced size STR amplicons as tools for analysis of degraded DNA. *Journal of Forensic Science* **48**, 1054–1064.

Chapman, D.D., Abercrombie, D.L., Douady, C.J., *et al.* (2003) A streamlined, biorganelle, multiplex PCR approach to species identification: application to global conservation and trade monitoring of the great white shark, *Carcharodon carcharias*. *Conservation Genetics* **4**, 415–425.

Cronin, M.A., Palmisciano, D.A., Vyse, E.R. *et al.* (1991) Mitochondrial-DNA in wildlife forensic-science: species identification of tissues. *Wildlife Society Bulletin*, **19**, 94–105.

Dawnay, N., Ogden, R., McEwing, R. *et al.* (2007) Validation of the barcoding gene COI for use in forensic genetic species identification. *Forensic Science International*, **173**, 1–6.

Dawnay, N., Ogden, R., Thorpe, R.S. *et al.* (2008a) A forensic STR profiling system for the Eurasian badger: a framework for developing profiling systems for wildlife species. *Forensic Science International: Genetics*, **2**, 47–53.

Dawnay, N., Ogden, R., Wetton, J.H. *et al.* (2008b) Genetic data from 28 STR loci for forensic individual identification and parentage analyses in six bird of prey species. *Forensic Science International: Genetics*, **3**, e63–e69.

Deguilloux, M.F., Pemonge, M.H. and Petit, R.J. (2002) Novel perspectives in wood certification and forensics: dry wood as a source of chloroplast, mitochondrial and nuclear DNA. *Proceedings of the Royal Society B: Biological Sciences*, **269**, 1039–1046.

Evett, I.W., and Weir, B.S. (1998) *Interpreting DNA Evidence: Statistical Genetics for Forensic Scientists*. Sunderland, MA: Sinauer Associates.

Gill, P., Jeffreys, A.J. and Werrett, D.J. (1985) Forensic applications of DNA "fingerprints," *Nature*, **318**, 577–579.

Guglich, E.A., Wilson, P.J. and White, B.N. (1994) Forensic application of repetitive DNA markers to the species identification of animal tissues. *Journal of Forensic Science*, **39**, 353–361.

Gupta, S.D., Verma, S.K. and Singh, L. (2005) Molecular insight into a wildlife crime: the case of a peafowl slaughter. *Forensic Science International*, **154**, 214–217.

Hauser, L., Seamons, T.R., Dauer, M. *et al.* (2006) An empirical verification of population assignment methods by marking and parentage data: hatchery and wild steelhead (*Oncorhynchus mykiss*) in Forks Creek, Washington, USA. *Molecular Ecology*, **15**, 3157–3173.

Hajibabaei, M., Smith, M.A., Janzen, D.H. *et al.* (2006) A minimalist barcode can identify a specimen whose DNA is degraded. *Molecular Ecology Notes*, **6**, 959–964.

Hebert, P.D.N., Ratnasingham, S. and deWaard, J.R. (2003a) Barcoding animal life: cytochrome *c* oxidase subunit 1 divergences among closely related species. *Proceedings Royal Society of London Series B Biological Sciences* **270**(Suppl 1), 96–99.

Hebert, P.D.N., Cywinska, A., Ball, S.L., *et al.* (2003b) Biological identifications through DNA barcodes. *Proceedings Royal Society of London Series B Biological Sciences* **270**, 313–321.

Hold, G.L., Russell, V.J., Pryde, S.E. *et al.* (2001) Validation of a PCR-RFLP based method for the identification of salmon species in food products. *European Food and Research Technology*, **212**, 385–389.

Horvath, M.B., Martinez-Cruz, B., Negro, J.J. *et al.* (2005) An overlooked DNA source for non-invasive genetic analysis in birds. *Journal of Avian Biology*, **36**, 84–88.

Hsieh, H.M., Huang, L.H., Tsai, L.C. *et al.* (2003) Species identification of rhinoceros horns using the cytochrome b gene. *Forensic Science International*, **136**, 1–11.

Jones, K.C., Levine, K.F. and Banks, J.D. (2002) Characterization of 11 polymorphic tetranucleotide microsatellites for forensic applications in California elk (*Cervus elaphus canadensis*). *Molecular Ecology Notes*, **2**, 425–427.

Koumi, P., Green, H.E., Hartley, S. *et al.* (2004) Evaluation and validation of the ABI 3700, ABI 3100, and the MegaBACE 1000 capillary array electrophoresis instruments for use with short tandem repeat microsatellite typing in a forensic environment. *Electrophoresis*, **25**, 2227–2241.

Kress, W.J., Wurdack, K.J., Zimmer, E.A. *et al.* (2005) Use of DNA barcodes to identify flowering plants. *Proceedings of the National Academy of Science USA*, **102**, 8369–8374.

Kumar, R., Singh, P.J., Nagpure, N.S., Kushwaha, B., Srivastava, S.K. and Lakra, W.S. (2007) A non-invasive technique for rapid extraction of DNA from fish scales. *Indian Journal of Experimental Biology*, **45**, 992–997.

Lawson, S. (2007) Certisource DNA legality assurance system: independent assessment. Available at: www.certisource.net/data+downloads/02_Independent_Certisource_Report_Summary_09-2007.pdf (accessed 26 May 2008).

Lee, P.L.M. and Prys-Jones, R.P. (2008) Extracting DNA from museum bird eggs, and whole genome amplification of archive DNA. *Molecular Ecology Resources*, **8**, 551–560.

Lygo, J.E., Johnson, P.E., Holdaway, D.J. *et al.* (1994) The validation of short tandem repeat (STR) loci for use in forensic casework. *International Journal of Legal Medicine*, **107**, 77–89.

Manel, S., Gaggiotti, O.E. and Waples, R.S. (2005) Assignment methods: matching biological questions with appropriate techniques. *Trends in Ecology & Evolution*, **20**, 136–142.

Nielsen, E.E., Hemmer-Hansen, J., Poulsen, N.A. *et al.* (2009) Genomic signatures of local directional selection in a high gene flow marine organism; the Atlantic cod (*Gadus morhua*). *BMC Evolutionary Biology* **9**, 276.

Ogden, R. (2010) Forensic science, genetics and wildlife biology: getting the right mix for a wildlife DNA forensics lab. *Forensic Science Medicine and Pathology*, **6**, 172–179.

Ogden, R. (2011) Unlocking the potential for genomic technologies for wildlife forensics. *Molecular Ecology Research*, **11**(Suppl 1), 109–116.

Ogden, R., Dawnay, N. and McEwing, R. (2009) Wildlife DNA forensics: bridging the gap between conservation genetics and law enforcement. *Endangered Species Research*, **9**, 179–195.

Oliveira, C.G., Martinez, R.A. and Gaiotto, F.A. (2007) DNA extraction from bristles and quills of Chaetomys subspinosus (Rodentia: Erethizontidae) using a novel protocol. *Genetics and Molecular Research*, **6**, 657–666.

Palsbøll, P.J., Bérubé, M., Skaug, H.J., *et al.* (2006) DNA registers of legally obtained wildlife and derived products as means to identify illegal takes. *Conservation Biology*, **20**, 1284–1293.

Parson, W., Brandstatter, A., Alonso, A. *et al.* (2004) The EDNAP mitochondrial DNA population database (EMPOP) collaborative exercises: organization, results and perspectives. *Forensic Science International*, **139**, 215–226.

Parson, W., Pegoraro, K., Niederstatter, H. *et al.* (2000) Species identification by means of the cytochrome b gene. *International Journal of Legal Medicine*, **114**, 23–28.

Peppin, L., McEwing, R., Carvalho, G.R. *et al.* (2008) A DNA based approach for the forensic identification of Asiatic black bear (*Ursus thibetanus*) in a traditional Asian medicine. *Journal of Forensic Science*, **53**, 1358–1362.

Pook, C.E. and McEwing, R. (2005) Mitochondrial DNA sequences from dried snake venom: a DNA barcoding approach to the identification of venom samples. *Toxicon*, **46**, 711–715.

Ratnasingham, S. and Hebert, P.D.N. (2007) BOLD: The Barcode of Life Data System (http://www.barcodinglife.org). *Molecular Ecology Notes*, **7**, 355–364.

Seeb, L.W., Antonovich A., Banks, A.A. *et al.* (2007) Development of a standardized DNA database for Chinook salmon. *Fisheries*, **32**, 540–552.

Shivji, M., Clarke, S., Pank, M. *et al.* (2002) Genetic identification of pelagic shark body parts for conservation and trade monitoring. *Conservation Biology*, **16**, 1036–1047.

Shorrock, G. (1998) The success of DNA profiling in wildlife law enforcement. *International Journal of Bioscience and the Law*, **1**, 327–341.

Singh, A., Gaur, A., Shailaja, K. *et al.* (2004) Novel microsatellite (STR) marker for forensic identification of big cats in India. *Forensic Science International*, **141**, 143–147.

Sweijd, N.A., Bowie, R.C.K., Lopata, A.L. *et al.* (1998) A PCR technique for forensic, species-level identification of abalone tissue. *The Journal of Shellfish Research*, **17**, 889–895.

Tahir, M.A., Caruso, J.F., Hamby, P.P. *et al.* (1996) Deoxyribonucleic acid profiling by restriction fragment length polymorphism analysis – a compilation of validation studies. *Science Justice*, **36**, 173–182.

Thommasen, H.V., Thomson, M.J., Shutler, G.G. *et al.* (1989) Development of DNA fingerprints for use in wildlife forensic science. *Wildlife Society Bulletin*, **17**, 321–326.

Wetton, J.H., and Parkin, D.T. (1997) A suite of falcon single-locus minisatellite probes: a powerful alternative to DNA fingerprinting. *Molecular Ecology*, **6**, 119–128.

Wetton, J.H., Tsang, C.F.S., Roney, C.A. *et al.* (2004) An extremely sensitive species-specific ARMs PCR test for the presence of tiger bone DNA. *Forensic Science International*, **140**, 139–145.

Withler, R.E., Candy, J.R., Beacham, T.D. *et al.* (2004) Forensic DNA analysis of Pacific salmonid samples for species and stock identification. *Environmental Biology of Fishes*, **69**, 275–285.

Wu, H., Wan, Q.H., Fang, S.G. *et al.* (2005) Application of mitochondrial DNA sequence analysis in the forensic identification of Chinese sika deer subspecies. *Forensic Science International*, **148**, 101–105.

Xu, Y.C., Li, B., Li, W.S. *et al.* (2005) Individualization of tiger by using microsatellites. *Forensic Science International*, **151**, 45–51.

15 Conservation Genetics and Wildlife Forensics of Birds

Rebecca N. Johnson

Introduction

Birds are a high profile and significant part of the global fauna. They are, however, like many other animal and plant groups, facing an increasing rate of extinction (Butchart *et al.*, 2010; Hoffmann *et al.*, 2010) largely due to anthropogenic-induced changes. The most significant impact is habitat loss, but other factors such as introduced exotic competitors/predators, diseases and the illegal wildlife trade also have a major impact.

The ongoing destruction of habitat is a direct threat to biodiversity, which then through reduced population size and fragmentation, detrimentally impacts the key requirements for genetically healthy populations (Frankham, 1999). The second biggest threat to global biodiversity after habitat destruction is the unregulated or illegal wildlife trade (Sellar, 2009). This is a major threat to threatened species, because those in low numbers are often specifically targeted since they are more desirable on the illegal market and fetch higher prices. Individuals targeted for trafficking are often removed from already diminished and declining wild populations, further reducing their chances of persistence through additional negative impacts on their demography (e.g. sex ratio) and genetic diversity.

In order to assess the genetic health of a population, it is necessary to establish some solid foundations upon which to apply the principles of conservation genetics. There are a number of important key areas to consider for any 'unit' being managed for conservation purposes (a 'unit' can be a population, but can also be a species in other circumstances). This applies especially in the field of

Wildlife Forensics: Methods and Applications, First Edition. Edited by Jane E. Huffman and John R. Wallace.

conservation genetics (DeSalle and Amato, 2004; Mace, 2004) where it is important to gather knowledge for consideration in the following key areas:

1. *Systematics*: the study of the diversity of life (major components are taxonomy and phylogenetics):
   a. *Taxonomy*: the scientific practice of classification of organisms into groups based on similarities of structure. Taxonomic classification groups living things into a hierarchy according to their relatedness to one another. The basic 'unit' under consideration in taxonomy is species.
   b. *Phylogenetics*: the study of evolutionary relatedness, determined via molecular and morphological data.
2. *Population biology*: study of populations of organisms that can interbreed, including population size, number of offspring, age of reproduction, habitat, introgression, hybridization, etc.
3. *Population genetics*: the study of allele/gene frequency under the influence of evolutionary processes of natural selection, gene flow, genetic drift, and mutation.
4. *Genetics/genomics*: molecular genetics tools ranging from single loci/gene regions to analysis of the entire genome of an organism.

The aim of conservation genetics is to maximize genetic diversity and therefore the genetic health and likelihood of persistent remaining individuals and populations. Maximizing genetic diversity is important as it represents evolutionary potential which enables a population or species to evolve. Typically conservation genetics requires careful management of the challenges that come with small population size: inbreeding depression, loss of genetic diversity, isolation, fragmentation, accumulation of deleterious mutations, genetic adaptation to captivity and outbreeding depression (Frankham, 1995, 1999). If these factors are not adequately managed, the consequences can include reduced reproductive fitness and ability to adapt to environmental change, reduction in migration and adverse effects on captive breeding and reintroductions (Frankham, 1995, 1999). The rate of mainly human-mediated extinctions we are currently observing is comparable to that of the previous mass extinctions observed in the geological record and has been described as the "sixth extinction" (Pimm *et al.*, 1995; Butchart *et al.*, 2010; Frankham *et al.*, 2010). Conservation genetics is often described as a "crisis discipline" because new technologies are rapidly adopted and quick management decisions need to be made often with limited information to help conserve the ever-growing list of threatened species (DeSalle and Amato, 2004).

To adequately address all of the major issues, and considerations in conservation genetics would require an entire book and so I refer the reader to Frankham, Ballou and Briscoe (2010) for an excellent and comprehensive treatment of this topic. The aim of this chapter is to give an introduction into avian conservation genetics with a particular focus on avian wildlife forensics. While there is much overlap in the genetic techniques utilized in these fields, forensics requires quite distinct and specific practices.

Avian Genetics

Avian genetics is a field with a long history. Molecular techniques were adapted to the study of birds early after their development in humans. For example, some of the earliest major systematic revisions in birds were conducted using data from DNA-DNA hybridization. Molecular techniques such as allozymes, DNA-DNA hybridization, Restriction Fragment Length Polymorphisms, the Polymerase Chain Reaction and DNA sequencing were adopted readily to better understand the genetic relationships among individuals, populations and species. In combination with ecological and demographic data modern molecular methods are now routinely applied in a conservation genetics context (Haig, 1998; Tuinen *et al.*, 2000; Hedrick, 2001; Ouborg, *et al.*, 2010). A brief description of the most commonly used molecular methods from the recent past and present are included in Table 15.1.

Molecular genetic techniques have long been used to investigate avian systematics with the early attempts using DNA-DNA hybridization (Sibley and Ahlquist, 1982, 1990; Sibley, *et al.*, 1988) but they proved to be highly controversial and were not fully accepted by the field (Springer and Krajewski, 1989; Sarich *et al.*, 1989). Subsequently avian systematics was conducted more routinely using mtDNA and nuclear DNA sequences (Tuinen *et al.*, 2000, reviewed in Edwards *et al.* 2005). Early molecular work resulted in somewhat controversial reassessments of evolutionary relationships of many families within the avian phylogeny (Sibley *et al.*, 1988) but also resulted in resolving potential species status and direct conservation efforts, for example, towards the threatened Hawaiian Honeycreepers status (Sibley and Ahlquist, 1982), which was later confirmed by mtDNA sequencing (Tarr and Fleischer, 1993), a further early example of molecular contributions to conservation.

Early genetic methods, especially allozymes, and subsequently microsatellites and DNA sequencing, revealed introgression (or introgressive hybridization) was surprisingly common among avian species (Grant and Grant, 1992). It was first discovered among the mallard ducks (genus *Anas*) (Gillespie, 1985; Rhymer *et al.*, 1994; Rhymer and Simberloff, 1996) but later found in other bird species (reviewed in Randler, 2006). Genetic analysis has also revealed hybridization in other species and subspecies such as owls (genus *Strix*) (Hamer *et al.*, 1994; Kelly *et al.*, 2004; Haig *et al.*, 2004; Barrowclough *et al.*, 2005; Gutiérrez *et al.*, 2007; Hamer *et al.*, 2007) which was proposed to have been exacerbated by alteration/loss of habitat allowing one species to encroach on the other. This is likely to be a phenomenon observed in increasing frequency as the habitat of many endemic species is increasingly encroached upon by urbanization.

Molecular markers play a very important role in assessing population structure (i.e., genetic diversity, effective size, inbreeding). Allozymes were some of

Table 15.1 Brief description of molecular methods used in conservation genetics and wildlife forensic analyses, past and present.

Method	Description	Technique pros	Technique cons
Allozymes	Co-dominant protein loci (with multiple alleles) that can be visualized by differing mobility on a charged gel – Nuclear DNA markers	Inexpensive, can be extremely informative, no prior knowledge required	Large amount of tissue required, proteins degrade if not stored adequately
Antigen/Antibody reactions	Antibody/antigen reaction between blood serum protein and antiserum. Antibodies and antigens from the same species will bind while those from different species will not	No prior knowledge required of species being analysed	Antibody must first be produced and isolated; Requires high quantity and quality sample (often not possible in wildlife forensics cases), some uncertainty due to cross-reactivity between similar species
DNA-DNA hybridization	Measures the degree of genetic similarity between genomes by mixing and incubating to allow DNA strands to dissociate and re-anneal, forming hybrid double-stranded DNA. Hybridized sequences with a high degree of similarity will bind more firmly, and require more energy to separate them: i.e. they separate when heated at a higher temperature than dissimilar sequences	No prior knowledge required of species being analysed	Non-specific hybridization between closely related species. Repeatability
Minisatellites sometimes called variable number tandem repeats (VNTRs)	Minisatellites consist of tandemly repeated regions of DNA where repeats range in length from 10 to over 100 bp. Tandem arrays can be 0.5 to 30 kb in length and are not distributed evenly throughout the genome but rather on the proterminal ends of chromosomes and at nucleolar organizing regions	Often highly variable	Repeatability
RFLPs – Restriction Fragment Length Polymorphisms (non-PCR based) also known as DNA fingerprinting	Whole genome is cut into fragments using restriction enzymes which cleave at specific enzyme recognition sites, followed by southern blot analysis using specific probes. This technique exploits different restriction recognition sites between individual genomes	More sensitive than allozymes, detect more differences at DNA sequence level	Reliance on a relatively high quality template, issues with reproducibility of results, little possibility of producing a reference database.

PCR-based methods			
RAPDs – Random amplification of polymorphic DNA	DNA markers (usually dominant) that are generated via PCR from a whole genomic DNA sample using random short oligonucleotide primers	No prior knowledge required of species being analysed	Some issues with replicating results between different machines and laboratories
AFLPs – Amplified fragment length polymorphisms	Detects polymorphisms via use of restriction enzymes to digest genomic DNA followed by ligation of adapters and amplification via selective PCR	No prior knowledge required of species being analysed, can analyse a large cross section of the genome simultaneously	Methodologically time consuming and costly. Determining DNA sequence of polymorphic regions can sometimes be difficult.
RFLPs – Restriction Fragment Length Polymorphisms (PCR-based)	Specific PCR products are amplified then cut into fragments using restriction enzymes which cleave at specific enzyme recognition sites	Relatively inexpensive, high repeatability	Not all polymorphisms are detected. Only short regions amplified via PCR are able to be analysed at a time
Microsatellites – also called Short Tandem Repeats (STRs), or Simple sequence repeat (SSR)	Microsatellites are short repeated regions (typically di- tri- or tetra-nucleotide) that occur frequently and randomly throughout most eukaryotic genomes	Nuclear markers, highly informative for population genetics	Markers must be developed per species as required. Cross species utility can be limited
DNA sequencing – mtDNA or nuclear DNA	PCR amplification of specific gene regions: these can be Sanger sequenced using fluorescently labelled dideoxy nucleotides, used in Real-Time PCR, used in a microarray etc.	Highly informative, accurate and replicable, can be nuclear or mitochondrial	Reasonable amount of knowledge required about the genome of the animal being analysed, materials/equipment can be relatively costly
SNP (or Single nucleotide polymorphism) typing	PCR based technique that exploits single nucleotide differences as part of the PCR primer design	Get large amount of info rapidly from across genome	Need good knowledge of genome to identify informative SNPs

the earliest genetic techniques used for assessing population structure (Avise and Hamrick, 1995), however, these techniques often found minimal variation in birds (Barrowclough, 1983) and they were not found to be particularly adequate markers in conservation applications, such as a severely bottlenecked populations or species (Haig, 1998). Molecular methods have also been used extensively to assess avian population structure, allowing direct application to population management by enabling monitoring of movements, gene flow and population mixing. This level of investigation can provide valuable information for all species, regardless of their conservation status, but has been used especially for endangered species. Some high profile examples include conservation and planning to preserve genetic diversity in the highly endangered Peregrine Falcon (*Falco peregrinus*) (Wetton and Parkin, 1997; Nesje *et al.*, 2000a, 2000b; Brown *et al.*, 2007) and molecular tools such as minisatellite DNA, RAPDs, allozymes and, more recently microsatellites, to assess the possibility of translocation for species such as the endangered Red-cockaded Woodpecker (*Picoides borealis*) which is rapidly experiencing habitat fragmentation (Haig *et al.*, 1993; Haig, *et al.*, 1994a; Haig, *et al.*, 1994b; Haig *et al.*, 1996; Fike *et al.*, 2009).

Early molecular markers (RAPD markers) were used to demonstrate the surprising route and distance of migration in shorebirds (Haig *et al.*, 1997). More recently, the discovery and development of hypervariable markers like microsatellites has transformed the field of conservation genetics. This technique allows accurate assessment of population genetics structure both temporarily and spatially and can be applied to populations (for example, population analysis of captive populations of Guam Rails (*Rallus owsoni*), Haig and Ballou, 1995) or to investigate gene flow and population structure, such as of the endangered Hyacinth Macaw, *Anodorhynchus hyacinthinus*, and to establish if apprehended specimens could be genetically assigned to a population (Faria *et al.*, 2008).

Next-generation sequencing (NGS) technologies are being rapidly adopted by the field of avian conservation genetics (Lerner and Fleischer, 2010). These new platforms are increasingly being used to analyze large portions of entire species genomes for conservation applications (Kohn *et al.*, 2006; Primmer, 2009; Allendorf *et al.*, 2010). NGS has recently been used to give insight into the diet of captive little penguins (*Eudyptula minor*) where faeces were sequenced to analyse diet and found the unexpected result that the proportion of species fed did not closely correlate with the proportion of species detected in the faeces, possibly due to differences in prey digestibility (Deagle *et al.*, 2011). Genomic tools have also been used to identify candidate loci for heritable embryonic conditions that have become prominent in critically endangered species due to extremely small effective population size. For example, Quantitative Trait Loci (QTLs) are now being mapped for debilitating heritable genetic disorders in critically endangered California condors (*Gymnogyps californianus*) (Ralls and Ballou, 2004; Romanov *et al.*, 2009). Next generation technologies are even being used to analyze extremely low template samples such as ancient DNA and museum DNA samples (Lee and Prys-Jones, 2008; Oskam *et al.*, 2010).

As outlined briefly above, genetics has been used successfully to aid avian conservation efforts, wildlife forensics and learn new things about bird phylogeny and behavior. As new techniques are developed, the level of genetic analysis will only increase, thereby enhancing conservation genetic efforts.

Avian Taxonomy, Legislation and Conservation

Avian taxonomic classification

Taxonomy and conservation go hand-in-hand. As outlined above, in order to conserve, we must first understand the taxonomy and the proposed taxonomic unit of conservation (Goldstein *et al.*, 2000; Mace, 2004; Zink, 2004). Avian classification follows standard nomenclature established by Carolus Linnaeus (also known as Carl von Linné) in his 1735 work *Systema Naturae*. Often referred to as the "father of taxonomy" Linnaeus was the first to propose the concept of "binomial nomenclature" – establishing universally recognized categories that imply taxonomic hierarchy between organisms. As the name implies, binomial nomenclature is a two-name system, the first indicating the genus (or related group) to which it belongs, while the second gives the species (or its specific name) within the genus.

What is now known as the Linnean system of classification was for a long time based on an organism's morphology – their external characters (such as shape, structure, size, color, pattern) and internal structures (such as skeleton and internal organs). In recent decades classification now often includes molecular data in addition to traditional morphological data in concordance with internationally recognized standards (ICZN, 2011).

Birds are classified into levels (highest to lowest), starting with the Kingdom Animalia; Phylum Chordata; Class Aves, then Order, Family, Genus and Species. An example showing the classification for the Blue-fronted Amazon parrot can be seen in Table 15.2. Avian taxonomy at the lower levels (Order and below) is frequently and hotly debated in the scientific literature and there are several

Table 15.2 Example classification for the Blue-fronted Amazon parrot. Kingdom divides plants from animals. Animals are then grouped into Phyla (singular: Phylum). These groups are then successively divided into Class, Order, Family, Genus and Species.

Classification level	Scientific Latin name	Description
Kingdom	Animalia	Animals
Phylum	Chordata	Animals with backbones
Class	Aves	Animals called Birds
Order	PSITTACIFORMES	Parrots
Family	Pssittacidae	True parrots
Genus	*Amazona*	Amazon parrots
Species	*Amazona aestiva*	Blue-fronted Amazon

proposed lists with variations mainly at the classification levels of Order and Family (Morony *et al.*, 1975; Dickinson, 2003). There are 25–40 bird Orders, 233–234 Families and over 10,000 species of birds currently recognized (Gill *et al.*, 2010; Roberson, 2011; Bird Life International, 2011). The order Passeriformes contains the 'perching birds' which comprises around half (>5,000) the bird species. Taxonomy is of particular importance because species are the category often used for management, legislation and regulation.

Aves and CITES (Convention on International Trade in Endangered Species of Wild Fauna and Flora)

Many threatened bird species are protected under the Convention on International Trade in Endangered Species of Wild Fauna and Flora (CITES) which regulates the international trade of both flora and fauna based on a list, reviewed annually, which reflects species' vulnerability and subsequent need for protection (CITES, 2011). The level of protection under CITES can be to species, subspecies or even specific populations of a species.

Currently there are 175 Parties (approximately corresponding to countries but may fluctuate due to geopolitical changes) that have ratified the convention, which came into force on 1 July 1975. All countries that have ratified CITES are expected to adopt their own domestic legislation that legally enforces this international agreement.

CITES categorizes floral and faunal species into one of three Appendices, depending on the levels or types of protection needed to protect them from overexploitation. Trade can be authorized in these different categories and is only permitted after the issuing of specific permits or certificates:

- *Appendix I* lists the most endangered animal and plant species. They are threatened with extinction and international trade in these species is prohibited except under exceptional circumstances, for example, when the purpose of the import is not commercial, but for scientific research.
- *Appendix II* lists species that are not necessarily threatened currently with extinction but may become so unless their trade is closely controlled. Appendix II also includes so-called "look-alike species," i.e. including species that may be in trade that look like those of species listed for the purposes of conservation.
- *Appendix III* lists species included at the request of a particular Party to help control trade in that species to prevent unsustainable exploitation in that country.

The CITES appendices are updated annually and many avian species are listed (see Table 15.3). In many cases entire families are listed in Appendix II with more highly endangered species listed in Appendix I (ibid.). The Appendices can include entire groups, such as primates, cetaceans, sea turtles, parrots, corals,

Table 15.3 Approximate number of species, subspecies and populations from Class Aves that are restricted or prohibited from trade under the three CITES Appendices* at 14 October 2010 using agreed taxonomic names.

Birds species, subspecies and populations*	Appendix I	Appendix II	Appendix III
*At October 2010	153 species 11 subspecies 14 populations	1301 species 36 subspecies	1 species and 28 populations (from 24 species)

Note that these numbers are approximate because there are no agreed lists for some of the higher taxa (Zink, 2004).

cacti and orchids, but in some cases only a subspecies or geographically separate population of a species (for example the population of just one country) is listed.

The occurrence of hybrids (inter-specific or inter-subspecific hybrids), either human-created or in the wild, does not exclude them from protection under CITES (for example, Sturgeon caviar and Macaw hybrids). Where at least one of the animals in the previous four generations is of a species included in Appendix I, hybrids shall be treated as specimens of species included in Appendix I; where at least one of the animals in the previous four generations is of a species included in Appendix II, and there are no specimens of an Appendix I species in such lineage, hybrids shall be treated as specimens of species included in Appendix II; and where at least one of the animals in the previous four generations is of a species included in Appendix III, and there are no specimens of an Appendix I or Appendix II species in such lineage, hybrids shall be treated as specimens of species included in Appendix III (CITES, 1997).

Aves and the International Union for Conservation of Nature (IUCN)

The aim of the International Union for Conservation of Nature (IUCN) is to regularly assess and monitor species at a global level and to highlight their risk of extinction, therefore promoting their conservation. They do this by producing a regular list, the *IUCN Red List of Threatened Species*, of species most at risk of extinction. The IUCN Red List has been adopted by the Parties to the Convention on Biological Diversity to monitor the world's progress in reducing biodiversity loss (CBD, 2011; IUCN, 2011). The IUCN Red List has nine risk categories ranging from "extinct" to "not evaluated," representing highest to lower extinction risk (IUCN, 2011) (Figure 15.1).

The IUCN, via expert committees, has assessed the majority of the over 10,000 described bird species. Each assessment record contains information regarding geographic range, population, habitat and ecology. At present* >12% of bird species are in the threatened category globally (*current at December 2010, see red boxed region in Figure 15.1, based on threatened categories).

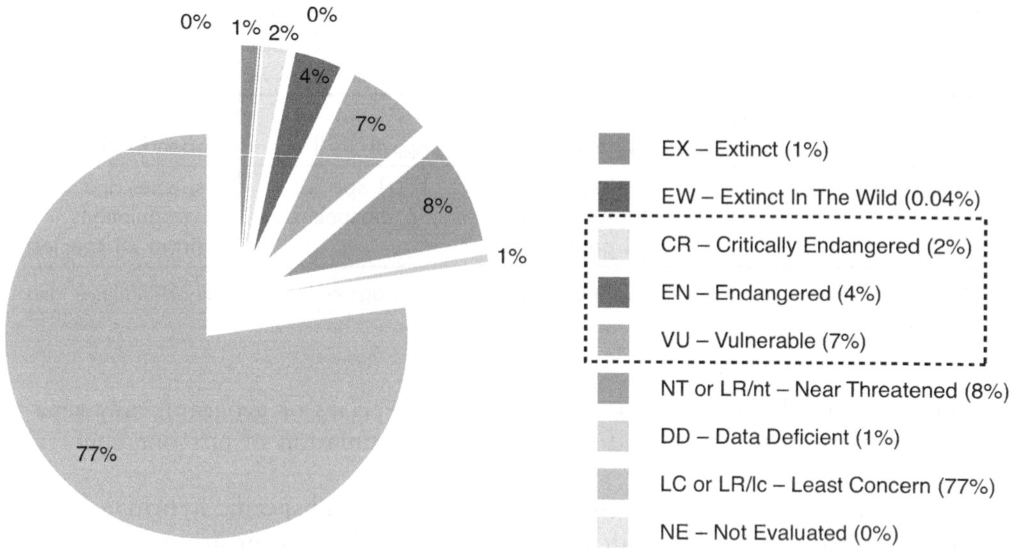

Figure 15.1 Relative proportions of bird species assessments for each IUCN Red List Category.

Note: Dashed line encompasses what the IUCN consider 'Threatened Categories' *current at December 2010.

Avian Wildlife Forensics: A Range of Applications

Background: illegal wildlife trade

Conservation genetics is a highly applied and useful science. Wildlife forensics takes this application yet further, to where it becomes a discipline heavily intermeshed with the legal system, and situated at the interface between laws that protect species and the evidence required to enforce those laws.

Forensic analysis is now used widely in many applications concerning suspected wildlife crime. Wildlife trafficking is an illegal multi-billion dollar industry worldwide (Ferrier, 2009; Interpol, 2010). Wildlife smuggling is an extremely lucrative business with relatively minor penalties and it can involve illegal trafficking of animals or plant species. Illegal wildlife trafficking typically involves a very high mortality rate for the wildlife individuals concerned, as well as threatening the survival of entire species because the rarer a species (i.e. the higher on the CITES appendices), the more likely it will be targeted by the illegal trade. Serious environmental consequences are often associated with illegal wildlife trafficking, including disruption of ecosystem processes, introduction of exotic pest species and spread of wildlife diseases.

Illegal wildlife trade is perpetrated through two broad avenues: smuggling or via fraud and there is evidence of organized crime involvement in wildlife smuggling (Sellar, 2009), with relatively low detection rate and lucrative crime with relatively low penalties if caught.

Wildlife forensics applications to the illegal wildlife trade

Wildlife forensics is now a science that frequently assists in prosecuting cases of wildlife crime. It is a young discipline that is complex and multifaceted, potentially involving both flora and fauna, which straddles the legal system at a different level from traditional conservation genetics. The type of questions that wildlife forensic biologists are asked to answer includes:

- What species does this sample come from?
- Does this sample come from this individual?
- Does this individual have the pedigree that agrees with what is claimed?
- Does this individual come from this specific geographic population?
- Can this sample be dated/geographically located (i.e. ivory taken before the 1986 ban)?

Wildlife forensics has even been used as important evidence in murder cases. The most famous early case involved genetic analysis of hair from Snowball the cat, the pet of a prime suspect and whose hair was one of the few pieces of evidence recovered with the dead body of the suspect's wife (Menotti-Raymond *et al.*, 1997). In another case, genetics revealed fraudulently submitted fish in a hotly contested fishing competition (Primmer *et al.*, 2000). The 5.5 kg salmon submitted to the competition was able to be excluded as originating from the fishing competition location ($p < 0.0001$) and the suspect later confessed to purchasing the fish at a local shop. There are also many avian examples involving the application of wildlife forensics in cases of illegal smuggling, poaching and trading of birds.

Wildlife trafficking of birds

Avian species are often targeted for illegal wildlife trafficking (Herrera and Hennessey, 2007) and there appears to be an unfortunately strong relationship between demand on the illegal market and the rarity of the bird species concerned, presumably because they attract higher prices (Rosen and Smith, 2010).

Frequently targeted are birds of the Orders:

- Psittaciformes (Families: Catatuidae – Cockatoos; Loriidae – lories, lorikeets; and Psittacidae – Amazons, Macaws, parakeets, parrots);
- Falconiformes (Families: Accipitridae – Hawks, eagles; Cathartidae – New World Vultures; Falconidae – Falcons);
- Strigiformes (Families: Strigidae – Owls; Tytonidae – Barn Owls).

In an attempt to control trade, CITES has listed the entire Order PSITTACIFORMES as a minimum of Appendix II (with few exceptions of very common species). Similarly the order FALCONIFORMES are all listed under Appendices I, II or III (with the exception of some species in the vulture family Cathartidae, which are not listed) and the entire order STRIGIFORMES are listed under CITES.

Bird wildlife trafficking can involve live adults or juveniles that are tightly packed and/or drugged to prevent them moving or attempting to escape (ibid.). In addition to the live trade, whole animal specimens, body parts including feathers, feet, bones, and skins are also commonly transported. Live eggs are a common method of illegal wildlife trafficking. These are typically smuggled inside specially designed clothing worn close to the body as the eggs require constant rotation and warmth to remain viable during transport. Eggs of many non-Passerine birds are white, and nondescript and it is not uncommon for them to be smashed by a smuggler upon detection to presumably avoid determination of species (Alacs and Georges, 2008). Species determination is now possible even from remnants of smashed eggs, irradiated, or extremely undeveloped eggs using molecular technology (Johnson, 2010), see also Box 15.1.

Box 15.1: Bird smuggling the case of the irradiated eggs

In August 2006, a passenger arriving at Sydney International airport from Bangkok Thailand was questioned by Australian Customs and Australian Quarantine officers. Before long it was discovered he had illegally transported something into the country strapped to his body. Further investigation revealed that it was not drugs he was carrying illegally on his body but rather he was wearing a specially designed vest which contained 23 white eggs.

The eggs were suspected to be bird eggs. At the time, Thailand was a high risk country for H5N1 (Avian Influenza) so there was a direction by the Australian Quarantine Inspection Service to euthanize and gamma-irradiate the eggs. An avian expert from Taronga Zoo, Sydney candled (using a specialty light source) the eggs, to determine the presence of blood vessels, which were then measured and weighed. Each egg was photographed by the Australian Federal Police, the egg was then opened to reveal a wide range of developmental stages (from small blastoderm to large embryo close to hatching).

A small subsample (–25 mg) of tissue was then taken from each egg for genomic DNA extraction, PCR for genes appropriate for species identification, followed by DNA sequencing. Because of the gamma-irradiation treatment, there was a risk the DNA would be too damaged to amplify for the target mitochondrial genes (Cytochrome b and Cytochrome Oxidase I). Fortunately mitochondrial DNA is robust and can withstand damage better than other parts of the genome (due to its high quantity and circular configuration) and DNA sequences were successfully obtained from the 23 eggs.

Sequences were checked for quality, assembled, and analysed against a selection of avian reference sequences derived from validated reference specimens. The bird eggs were identified to be from seven bird species from two families: Psittacidae (six different species of Conure, Macaws, Eclectus Parrot and Grey Parrot), and Cacatuidae (two birds of the single species: Salmon-crested Cockatoo).

The majority of the species involved in this seizure are in CITES Appendix II, however, two individuals seized were Appendix I species. These birds were brought into Australia illegally without appropriate permits for CITES listed live animals. Due to the severity of the crime – illegal trafficking of CITES Appendix I and II listed wildlife – charges were laid for contravening the Commonwealth Environment Protection and Biodiversity Act 1999, the Convention on International Trade in Endangered Species (CITES), the Australian Customs Act 1901 and the Australian Quarantine Act 1908, to which the defendant pleaded guilty. Evidence was submitted that the birds would have fetched almost AUD$250,000 on the illegal market. The defendant was fined AUD$10,000 and sentenced to 2 years imprisonment. He was deported upon release from jail.

Birdstrike: an example of applied wildlife forensics

Wildlife forensics finds regular application in some unusual or unexpected arenas. One such example could be in the aviation industry in the analysis of wildlife strike. Aviation wildlife strike is the occurrence of animal–aircraft collisions. This is commonly termed 'birdstrike' as birds in flight are most often involved in this event, however; flying mammals, terrestrial mammals, reptiles and even some flightless birds are recorded to have been involved in aviation wildlife strike events.

Wildlife forensics provides an important service by identifying species so that the risk they pose to the aviation industry and ultimately to passenger safety can be assessed. For the purposes of this chapter, which focuses on birds, the term birdstrike will be used. Like other wildlife forensic applications, this is a use of genetics that interfaces with the legal system as it is generally accepted there is an onus on the providers of airport space to assess potential risks and have procedures in place to minimize them (Allan, 2006).

Birdstrike is a serious safety hazard to the aviation industry and these events can also lead to expensive damage to aircraft along with costly flight delays. More than 200 aircraft (civilian and military) and over 200 human lives have been lost directly to birdstrike (Allan, 2006; Dolbeer *et al.*, 2009). The cost of birdstrike is substantial, roughly estimated to cost the industry several billion dollars annually at approximately $US100,000–150,000 per serious incident (Dolbeer *et al.*, 2009) and the instance of birdstrike is increasing (Transport Canada, 2004; Dolbeer *et al.*, 2009; ATSB, 2010) largely due to increased aircraft movements and improved reporting of birdstrikes. Most birdstrike incidents occur during landing and takeoff (over 90% at $\leq$ 3000 feet). In order to manage the risk of birdstrike, individual airfields must be aware of the species present in their local areas and manage them accordingly.

The most serious aspect is that air crashes due to birdstrike have caused considerable loss of human life (Allan, 2006) with the most notable 'near miss' being US Airways Flight 1549 emergency landing into the Hudson River after a double engine failure due to significant birdstrike on January 15, 2009 (Marra *et al.* 2009).

Birdstrike is of significant interest in both civil and military aviation safety due to the collision impact force between bird and aircraft (this includes impact speed, bird weight, density, dimensions and configuration, as well as angle of impact) meaning that impact force is proportional to bird mass and the square of impact speed (Transport Canada, 2004). To give a real example, a single 4 lb (or 1.8 kg) bird (such as an Ibis) that strikes an aircraft flying at an airspeed of 250 kts will deliver an impact force of approximately 38,000 lbs (or approximately 17 Tonnes). A collision with that same bird at an airspeed of 400 kts, increases to 1000,000 lbs (or approximately 45 Tonnes). The most common damage is from animals striking the nose/radome, wing and/or engine of the aircraft (ibid.). Of particular concern is when the bird is ingested into the engine – as happened above in the recent high profile incident resulting in an emergency landing in the Hudson River (Marra *et al.*, 2009).

Until quite recently approximately 50% of recorded birdstrikes in many countries were not able to be identified (Transport Canada, 2004; ATSB, 2010). Accurate identification of species after a birdstrike is important for a number of reasons:

1. Knowledge of the approximate weight and size of the birds will allow incident investigators to assess the impact the bird had on an aircraft part even if there is no visible damage.
2. Depending on the species, investigators can gauge the likelihood that more than one individual was involved in the strike (based on whether it is a solitary species or a flocking species).
3. Prevention of birdstrike is obviously the most beneficial measure, therefore, if investigators know more accurately which bird species are most commonly involved in birdstrikes they can better design bird avoidance models and manage the areas surrounding an aerodrome by targeting known problem species.
4. Instances of birdstrike appear to be increasing worldwide (for example, Australia, Canada, New Zealand, the United Kingdom and the United States of America), therefore it is important to constantly monitor the different species present and monitor for changes in species representation over time that may be due to seasonal or climactic changes.
5. Knowledge of high risk species is used in new designs of aircraft parts such as engines, and windscreens.

Identification of birdstrike remains using feather morphology was pioneered by the Smithsonian Feather Identification Laboratory starting as early as the 1960s. Species identification using feather morphology is a highly specialist skill and is not always conclusive, even for experts, due to a range of factors such as feather damage, feather type, or lack of reference feathers for comparison. More recently, many birdstrike identification laboratories are moving toward DNA analysis as a potentially valuable tool for identifying remains from a birdstrike, particularly if there are no visual clues as to its identity.

Some innovative analysis was recently used in the Hudson River near-miss incident where isotope analysis was used to help determine the Canada Geese involved were from a migrant population rather than the resident population of geese (Marra *et al.*, 2009). More often though, DNA is being routinely used in instances of birdstrike to identify species and even estimate number of individuals involved in a strike. One initiative, the Barcode of Life (Ratnasingham and Hebert, 2007) has been applied widely in the identification of birdstrikes. The DNA bar-coding project is a collaborative worldwide initiative to create a DNA database of all known species, which could enable identification of most animals based on a sample of their DNA (Hebert *et al.*, 2004). DNA barcoding has been shown to be particularly effective in identifying a wide range of northern hemisphere bird species (Yoo *et al.*, 2006; Kerr *et al.*, 2007; Dove *et al.*, 2008) and DNA barcodes from bird species from other countries are being added increasingly to the publicly available database (Waugh *et al.*, 2011).

Conservation Genetics and Wildlife Forensics: Identification Using DNA

The limits of morphology

Identification using morphology of reptiles is discussed at length in Chapter 10 and briefly here. If morphological characters are lacking from a specimen (or specimen part), an identification (to species, population or individual) can be difficult or even impossible. Accurate identification is often critical to a successful prosecution in cases of wildlife crime (for example, those involving CITES species) or to ensure accurate management of key species (aviation birdstrike). As discussed previously, illegally trafficked items may include whole animal specimens (live or dead), whole or partial skins, eggs (live or dead), body parts including: feathers, feet, bones, hair, powder, internal organs etc. Conclusive identification using morphology is either not possible or very difficult in a range of circumstances, for example:

- Species cannot be determined morphologically if:
  - body parts have been removed from the individual and altered, for example, it has been filleted, minced or mutilated in some other manner;
  - body parts have been removed from the individual intact but making morphological species identification of those parts extremely difficult, for example, gall bladders, shark fins, bones;

  - the animal is a juvenile or immature, for example, bird embryo, insect larvae or pupae, young mammal.
- Determination of gender is difficult in some avian species where both males and females are sexually monomorphic. For these species, gender identification can only be determined conclusively using invasive internal examination if the animal is alive. If the animal is dead and has had its reproductive organs removed, gender may still be inconclusive.
- The use of morphology can be extremely limited in circumstances requiring analysis at the population or individual level:
  - there is a requirement to assign an individual to a particular population or group;
  - assessment of genetic viability of a population for management purposes;
  - individualization and determination of pedigree (in cases of disputed parentage).

Use of molecular techniques in wildlife forensics

Prior to the introduction of the polymerase chain reaction (PCR), time-consuming and less conclusive techniques requiring large amounts of starting material – such as whole genome, protein or antibody/antigen reactions – were used for analysis. PCR revolutionized the field of molecular biology after its discovery in the early 1980s (Mullis and Faloona, 1987). Over the past ~30 years, a range of PCR-based methods have come to dominate the field of conservation genetics, and more recently wildlife forensics. PCR-based techniques typically require a small amount of starting template, are usually highly accurate and replicable, characteristics that are essential in any forensic tool.

DNA becomes a valuable tool in wildlife forensics applications to answer questions in cases such as 1–3 below:

1. species identification;
2. population genetics and genetic individualization
   a. individual identification;
   b. assigning an individual to a specific population;
   c. pedigree assignment;
3. gender identification.

Throughout the short history of DNA-based wildlife forensics, a number of molecular markers have been used to answer questions such as 1–3 above using techniques outlined in Table 15.1. Original techniques did not hold the statistical power, compared to those used at present, but were still able to identify species and populations to some extent (Shorrock, 2005). Table 15.4 summarizes the most common molecular methods that have been used or are still being used in current wildlife forensics and the applications they can be used for.

Table 15.4 Applicability of different methods used in wildlife forensic analyses past and present.

Method	Wildlife forensic applications: Species ID	Population genetic/ individual ID	Gender ID	Reference
Allozymes	yes – limited	limited	no	Kim and Shelef, 1986; Skarpeid *et al.*, 1998; Wallman and Adams, 2001; Kento *et al.*, 2003
Antigen/Antibody reactions	yes – limited	no	no	Whitehead and Brech, 1974; Whitehead *et al.*, 1974; Macedo-Silva *et al.*, 2000
DNA-DNA hybridization	yes – limited	no	unlikely	Sibley and Ahlquist, 1984; Sibley and Ahlquist, 1990; Chikuni *et al.*, 1990, Ebbehøj and Thomsen, 1991
PCR-based methods				
RAPDs	yes – limited	yes – limited	possible	Lee and Chang, 1994; Lessells and Mateman, 1998; Calvo *et al.*, 2001; Hsu *et al.*, 2009
AFLPs	yes – including interspecific hybrids	possible	possible	Griffiths and Orr, 1999; Congiu *et al.*, 2001; Congiu *et al.*, 2002; Wuertz *et al.*, 2006
RFLPs (PCR-based)	yes	yes – limited	possible	Pfeiffer *et al.*, 2004; Rojas *et al.*, 2009; El-Sayed *et al.*, 2010; Singh and Neelam, 2011
Microsatellites	yes	yes	possible	Shorrock, 1998; Frantz *et al.*, 2006; Dawnay *et al.*, 2009; Marin *et al.*, 2009; Leite *et al.*, 2008
DNA sequencing – mtDNA or nuclear DNA	yes	yes – some applications limited	yes – specific regions	Parson *et al.*, 2000; Hsieh *et al.*, 2003; Dawnay *et al.*, 2007; Lee *et al.*, 2008; Lee *et al.*, 2009; Lowenstein, *et al.*, 2009; Johnson, 2010; Tobe *et al.*, 2010
Single Nucleotide Polymorphisms or Size Polymorphism	yes	yes – limited	yes – specific regions	Verma and Singh, 2003; Clarke *et al.*, 2006; Berry and Sarre, 2007; Lee *et al.*, 2010
Microarray	yes	possible	possible	Teletchea *et al.*, 2008

Species identification using mitochondrial DNA

Table 15.4 indicates the range of molecular techniques used to identify species. As the field of DNA-based wildlife forensics has grown, two of these that have been phased out of common use for species identification purposes are antibody/antigen reactions between blood serum proteins from different species and DNA-DNA hybridization. More recently, DNA sequencing of phylogenetically informative regions amplified via PCR has been commonly used for species identification in wildlife forensics cases (see Table 15.4). To date, mitochondrial DNA is most commonly used in wildlife forensics cases requiring species identification with different mitochondrial genes employed depending on the class or group requiring identification. The mitochondrial genome is encoded in the mitochondria – important organelles in the cellular cytoplasm responsible for generating energy in the form of adenosine triphosphate (ATP) through the process of oxidative phosphorylation via an electron transport chain in the inner membrane of the mitochondria. Box 15.2 outlines the benefits of using mitochondrial sequence data for wildlife forensics analysis and also the limitations. A schematic diagram of the avian mitochondrial genome is shown in Figure 15.2.

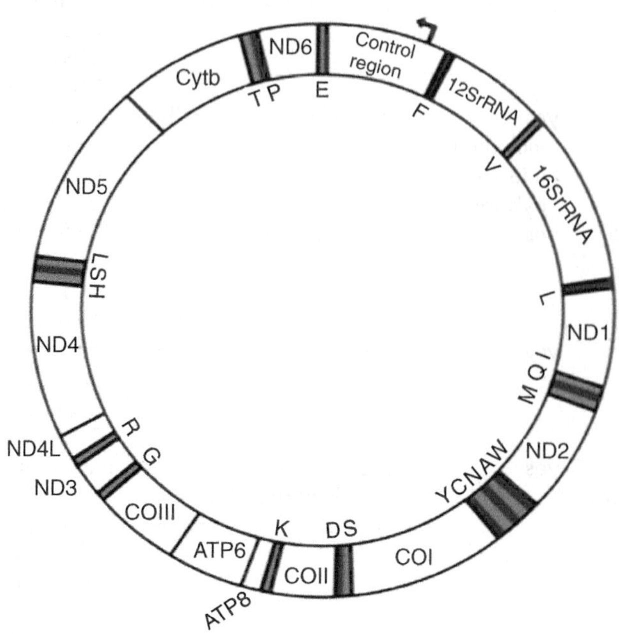

Figure 15.2 Representation of the gene order in the avian mitochondria. Genes are represented by the white open boxes. Transfer RNAs between genes are represented by grey shaded boxes. The origin of replication is designated by the right-angled arrow. Mitochondrial DNA is most commonly used in wildlife forensics cases requiring species identification with different mitochondrial genes employed depending on the class or group requiring identification, those include Cytb, COI, 16SrRNA, 12SrRNA, and Control Region (D loop).

Box 15.2: Mitochondrial DNA pros and cons for species identification

Mitochondrial DNA sequence analysis is well suited for many wildlife forensics applications because:

1. Mitochondria have their own circular genomes, which are present in high copy number (1–15 copies per mitochondrion) compared to nuclear DNA (two copies per nucleus for a diploid genome), in addition, there can be many mitochondria per cell depending on the tissue type.
2. This high copy number combined with the robustness of its circular genome (Figure 15.2) has meant that mitochondrial DNA has been used in many wildlife forensics analyses, particularly those involving degraded or damaged samples.
3. Finally, the mitochondrial genome is thought to evolve up to 10 times faster than the rate of the nuclear genome (Brown *et al.*, 1979; Brown, 1981; Brown and Simpson, 1982; Wolstenholme, 1992; García-Moreno, 2004; Zink and Barrowclough, 2008), hence allowing for the level of phylogenetic variability essential to distinguish even closely related species.

Mitochondrial DNA is not the perfect solution for species identification, however, limitations of mtDNA sequence analysis for wildlife forensics applications include:

1. The rate of mtDNA evolution is relatively slow in birds (Mindel *et al.*, 1996; Livezey and Zusi, 2007).
2. mtDNA typically does not recombine and only shows maternal inheritance (Pereira and Baker, 2006) making analysis of hybrids impossible as only the female contribution is inherited and available for analysis (i.e. sturgeon caviar, and macaw hybrids).
3. mtDNA is useful for population genetic studies and phylogenetic studies of closely related species due to its relatively rapid rate of substitution, however, for older divergences, those same rapid rates of substitution lead to saturation of base pair changes that cause homoplasy (similarity not through descent) because phylogenetic signal is diminished (Ballard and Whitlock, 2004; Rubinoff, 2006).

In recent years there have been initiatives to standardize the gene region in use such as the Barcode of Life Initiative (Ratnasingham and Hebert, 2007) which uses a 500–600bp fragment at the 5' end of Cytochrome oxidase 1 (CO1) mitochondrial gene. The intention of BOLD is to identify the 95% of species that are able to be uniquely identified via the sequencing of this short region of DNA. This has been extremely successful in groups such as Lepidopterans (deWaard *et al.*, 2010; Dincaf *et al.*, 2011), Arthropods (Hendrich *et al.*, 2010), and even for some vertebrate applications (Hebert *et al.*, 2004; Kerr *et al.*, 2007). However, other studies have shown that CO1 has limitations in some groups and still recommend using it in combination with other genetic data such as mtDNA genes Cytochrome b, ND2, ND4 or in addition to other nuclear genes (Tobe *et al.*, 2010; Wilson-Wilde *et al.*, 2010).

Gender identification using DNA

In birds, the heterogametic sex (i.e. the gender with two different sex chromosomes allowing production of two types of gametes) is the female, with both W and Z chromosomes, whereas male birds have two Z chromosomes, making them the homogametic sex. Molecular determination of gender in birds has been used increasingly over the past 15 years (Ellegren, 1996; Griffiths *et al.*, 1996; Griffiths *et al.*, 1998; Kahn *et al.* 1998' Fridolfsson and Ellegren, 1999; Jensen *et al.*, 2003; Bantock *et al.*, 2008; Lee *et al.*, 2010). Determining gender of bird samples can be challenging for a number of reasons:

- The species may be sexually monomorphic (i.e. anatomy and plumage color of males and females from the same species are indistinguishable as judged by the human eye).
- If the bird is live, from a species that is sexually monomorphic, often the only possibility for determining gender with certainty is an invasive internal examination of the reproductive organs.
- If only a part of the bird remains, it may not be morphologically indicative of species.
- If a bird embryo or nestling has been seized, it will not have enough characters for gender determination.

The chromo-helicase-DNA binding gene (CHD) is present on both the W and Z chromosomes, but in many species the W and Z copies of the CHD gene show size variation. Use of this size polymorphism in the CHD gene is the most commonly used method for gender determination in birds, however, there is not yet a universal method for determining gender in birds leading to a vast amount of literature as different researchers discover techniques or variations that work on specific species (Griffiths and Tiwari, 1995; Ogawa *et al.*, 1998; Duan and Fuerst, 2001; Itoh *et al.*, 2001; Li *et al.*, 2001; Cheng *et al.*, 2006; Huynen *et al.*, 2006; Wu *et al.*, 2007).

Some primer sets are able to be resolved using agarose gel electrophoresis whereas it is now becoming more common to resolve allele sizes for these fragments using capillary electrophoresis (Lee *et al.*, 2010) or using newer techniques such as melt curve analysis, a technique that relies upon the unique melting properties of each specific DNA sequence and can then be compared to a reference melt curve to make extremely accurate predictions of gender (Lyon, 2001;

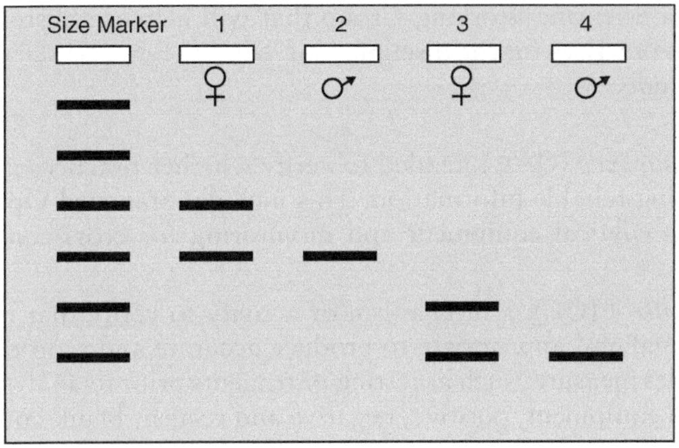

Figure 15.3 A representation electrophoresis of size polymorphic sections of the CHD gene amplified by PCR for both female (ZW) and male (ZZ) birds. There are many different sets of primers reported in the literature that are informative on a wide range of bird families but equally there are some species or genus specific primers available. Lanes 1 and 2 depict one set of primers and lanes 3 and 4 depict a different set. In both examples the fragment amplified from the Z chromosome is the larger fragment and that amplified from the W chromosome is the smaller fragment. If trialing a set of primers on a new species, it is always recommended that several individuals of know gender be used to determine if that particular primer set is informative for gender in species being tested.

Chang *et al.*, 2008) and species (Berry and Sarre, 2007). Figure 15.3 graphically depicts what can be seen when amplifying a region of the CHD gene that is size polymorphic on the Z and W chromosomes enabling assignment of male and female birds.

Validation of methods

Analyses in wildlife forensics cases use essentially the same molecular markers and techniques as population genetics and phylogenetic studies. The primary difference between these two disciplines is the demonstrable level of quality control and accuracy demanded by the legal system for any forensic application (Ogden, 2010). There are externally determined levels of accreditations such as the International Standard: ISO/IEC 17025:2005, which specifies the general requirements for the competence to carry out forensic work, and the Scientific Working Group on DNA Analysis methods (SWGDAM) which is a group of forensic scientists that meet under the guidance of the Federal Bureau of Investigation (FBI). SWGDAM is the body that proposes and recommends revisions to the National Quality Assurance Standards for a range of DNA forensic applications. Compliance with these externally set guidelines help to ensure key measures required for results of a forensic standard are delivered. These key measures are highly recommended for any wildlife forensic investigation (Budowle *et al.*, 2005). Late 2010 the Society for Wildlife Forensic Science formed

SWGWILD, a Scientific Working Group that will help establish standards and prescribe best practices for the disclipline of Wildlife Forensic science. These key measures include:

- *Quality assurance* (QA): intended to verify whether practices and test results are providing reliable information. This includes Standard Operating Procedures for analytical equipment and monitoring for cross-contamination of samples.
- *Quality control* (QC): a mechanism or activity to verify that test conditions are functional and appropriate to produce accurate and reproducible results. This includes measures such as testing of reagents prior to analysis, calibration of essential equipment, positive, negative and reagent blank controls.
- *Methodology validation*: validation of methods and markers prior to forensic application to evaluate efficacy and reliability of a method or procedure. Includes determining the operational limits of the technique and demonstrating that the method is fit for the purpose and produces accurate and reliable results under a range of experimental conditions (Dawnay *et al.*, 2007; Dawnay *et al.*, 2008, Dawnay *et al.*, 2009).
- *Proficiency testing*: should be carried out periodically to demonstrate the quality and performance of work. This is preferably done by an outside agency, or in the case of wildlife forensics, as an exchange program with properly designed and implemented tests.

For wildlife forensics, method validation can be complex due to the number of species involved. Validated independent reference material is particularly important in cases where species identification is required. It is vastly preferable that the sample be identified against a sample that is "vouchered" such as those that exist in museums and herbaria. Other chapters in this book give a comprehensive overview of statistics for wildlife forensics, defining a crime scene and collecting evidence, as well as "Laboratory Standardization and Quality Assurance." These are all essential pillars in any wildlife forensics case and should be read with the information contained in this chapter.

Box 15.3: Wildlife forensic analysis of samples

It is important that chain of custody be strictly maintained at all stages in this process. The sample should have a known location at all times and should be securely held in an access-controlled environment when not undergoing analysis. The following control steps should be performed:

1. Receive sample (document all details, time date location and assign unique tracking number).
2. Record all relevant details and photograph *in situ* in packaging.

3. Photograph samples (with a scale) once taken from package, weigh and measure if applicable to the case.
4. Under sterile conditions, take a small subsample (choose a subsampling location on the sample that has minimal chance of contamination from extraneous sources).
5. Extract DNA from the sample using a method that has been validated for that purpose including a reagent blank control (in order to monitor any results are not due to contaminated reagents).
6. Quantitate gDNA extraction to determine concentration.
7. Conduct PCR amplification of DNA regions appropriate to the question to be answered (see above for discussion of gene regions) including amplification of the DNA reagent blank control and the addition of a negative control for every round of amplification to monitor any interfering contamination that may be present in the reagents.
8. For DNA sequencing (i.e. species identification etc.) follow steps 1–11. For fragment analysis (i.e. individual identification etc. follow steps 1–6 and 12–14).
9. DNA sequencing.
10. Analyze success of the PCR amplification by separating products against a size/concentration standard on an agarose gel using an electric current paying special attention that the reagent blank and negative controls do not show any signs of amplification.
11. Remove unincorporated PCR reagents from successful reactions (via PCR clean-up) then conduct DNA sequencing (typically using fluorescently labeled dideoxy nucleotides) of successful PCR amplifications. Only clear unambiguous bidirectional sequences should be used for subsequent analysis steps.
12. Fragment analysis
13. Highly polymorphic regions for analysis are amplified via PCR using a fluorescently labeled primer.
14. Successful PCRs are then subjected to fragment separation via capillary electrophoresis. When this is done in combination with a known size, standard fragment sizes are able to be accurately determined.

Conclusion

It has been adequately argued in this chapter that good taxonomic knowledge is essential for all facets of conservation genetics and wildlife forensics. This same case can be argued for all flora and fauna and there is much work to be done in the highly skilled disciplines of taxonomy and systematics. Taxonomic knowledge is of particular importance in the groups that fall under CITES, the Convention on Biological Diversity and other local conservation and protection legislations, as species are often the evidence upon which charges for illegal trafficking can or cannot be laid and can also be critical in conservation applications.

The illegal wildlife trade in birds makes up a significant proportion of activity and it may involve live adult or juvenile animals, eggs, whole dead specimens or specimen parts. Identification of species can sometimes be possible using morphology of whole adult animals, but often DNA is the only option for many samples and is commonly used in addition to morphology to answer questions of individualization or determination of gender. DNA is of particular importance for identification of eggs or parts of a specimen or if an attempt is being made to assign an individual to a particular population.

Wildlife forensics is a young discipline and it is important that the quality assurance and quality control standards expected in the discipline of human forensics are applied. It is important that techniques be validated as fit for purpose and laboratory processes are in place to ensure individual samples are tracked and contamination is detected along with many other measures of quality control. Following that, it is important that results are analyzed and interpreted to a standard that is expected for evidence that could be presented in a legal context.

Finally, wildlife forensics is a much broader discipline than human forensics in the sense that the number of species is potentially huge compared with the one species to which human forensics is directed. This presents a challenge to the discipline of wildlife forensics, especially when identifying a specimen of unknown species. In these applications it is highly recommended that high quality reference material be used such as expert-identified specimens held in a museum or herbarium collection. Nowadays it is common for a "voucher" to be held as a skin, skeleton, dried, spirit preserved specimen in a collection along with a tissue and/or DNA sample from that particular specimen stored under ultra-cold or cryogenic conditions. These make the ideal reference material for DNA identifications in wildlife forensics as the source of the tissue sample is held, potentially in perpetuity and available, for inspection by any expert for that particular animal or plant group and can provide the highest quality reference source available for species identification.

Avian biology can only continue to benefit from application of technologies such as next-generation sequencing (Lerner and Fleischer, 2010) in the areas of biology, conservation, systematics and wildlife forensics. The application of avian genomics will see the number of genetic markers, at both the species and individual level, increase at a rate beyond exponential with potentially limitless applications. This could be extremely valuable in assisting conservation genetics efforts of highly endangered species by providing a large amount of genetic data upon which to make assessments. This will only improve current management efforts to minimize things such as inbreeding in small populations or can assist in specifically breeding to avoid deleterious mutations that could be pinpointed in a genome of an endangered species. Similarly the potential applications for wildlife forensics are extremely exciting. Statistical power for analyses will be boosted by simultaneously analyzing large amounts of nuclear and mitochondrial data, even from small or degraded samples. This will hopefully increase the possibility of successfully achieving a species, population or even an individual identification for wildlife forensics practitioners.

Avian genetics has progressed substantially over the past few decades with new technologies being quickly embraced and adopted by the field of avian researchers. Some of the earliest applications were in conservation genetics and were used to make assessments of the genetic health of species at risk including inbreeding depression, loss of genetic diversity, isolation, fragmentation, accumulation of deleterious mutations, genetic adaptation to captivity and outbreeding depression. Illegal wildlife smuggling is one of the major threats to avian biodiversity which is increasingly driving more species towards being threatened or endangered. Increased use of wildlife forensic methods to identify illegally trafficked wildlife along with the large penalties applicable to successful prosecutions will hopefully act as a strong deterrent to potential perpetrators. As a bare minimum, reducing the impact of the illegal wildlife trade in combination with other avian conservation efforts should be strongly encouraged.

References

Alacs, E. and Georges, A. (2008) Wildlife across our borders: a review of the illegal trade in Australia. *Australian Journal of Forensic Sciences*, **40**, 147–160.

Allan, J. (2006) A heuristic risk assessment technique for birdstrike management at airports. *Risk Analysis*, **26**, 723–729.

Allendorf, F. W., Hohenlohe, P. A. and Luikart, G. (2010) Genomics and the future of conservation genetics. *Nat Rev Genet*, **11**, 697–709.

ATSB (2010) Australian aviation wildlife strike statistics: bird and animal strikes, 2002 to 2009. Available at: www.atsvb.gov.au.

Avise, J.C. and Hamrick, J.L. (eds.) (1995) *Conservation Genetics: Case Histories from Nature*. New York: Columbia University Press.

Ballard, J.W.O. and Whitlock, M.C. (2004) The incomplete natural history of mitochondria. *Molecular Ecology*, **13**, 729–744.

Bantock, T.M., Prys-Jones, R.P. and Lee, P.L.M. (2008) New and improved molecular sexing methods for museum bird specimens. *Molecular Ecology Resources*, **8**, 519–528.

Barrowclough, G.F. (1983) Biochemical studies of microevolutionary processes. In A.H. Brush and G.A. Clark Jr (eds.) *Perspectives in Ornithology*. Essays Presented for the Centennial of the American Ornithologists Union. Cambridge: Cambridge University Press.

Barrowclough, G.F., Groth, J.G., Mertz, L.A. and Gutierrez, R.J. (2005) Genetic structure, introgression, and a narrow hybrid zone between northern and California spotted owls (Strix occidentalis). *Molecular Ecology*, **14**, 1109–1120.

Berry, O. and Sarre, S.D. (2007) Gel-free species identification using melt-curve analysis. *Molecular Ecology Notes*, **7**, 1–4.

Bird Life International (2011) Bird Life International. Available at: www.birdlife.org.

Brown, G.G. and Simpson, M.V. (1982) Novel features of animal mtDNA evolution as shown by sequences of two rat cytochrome oxidase subunit II genes. *Proceedings of the National Academy of Sciences of the United States of America*, **79**, 3246–3250.

Brown, J.W., Van Coeverden De Groot, P.J., Birt, T.P., *et al.* (2007) Appraisal of the consequences of the DDT-induced bottleneck on the level and geographic distribution of neutral genetic variation in Canadian peregrine falcons, Falco peregrinus. *Molecular Ecology*, **16**, 327–343.

Brown, W.M. (1981) Mechanisms of evolution in animal mitochondrial DNA. *Annals of the New York Academy of Sciences*, **361**, 119–132.

Brown, W.M., George, M. and Wilson, A.C. (1979) Rapid evolution of animal mitochondrial DNA. *Proceedings of the National Academy of Sciences of the United States of America*, **76**, 1967–1971.

Budowle, B., Garofano, P., Hellman, A., *et al.* (2005) Recommendations for animal DNA forensic and identity testing. *International Journal of Legal Medicine*, **119**, 295–302.

Butchart, S.H.M., Walpole, M., Collen, B. and Al, E. (2010) Global biodiversity: indicators of recent declines. *Science*, **328**, 1164–1168.

Calvo, J. H., Zaragoza, P. and Osta, R. (2001) Random amplified polymorphic DNA fingerprints for identification of species in poultry pate. *Poultry Science*, **80**, 522–524.

CBD (2011) Convention on Biological Diversity. Secretariat of the Convention on Biological Diversity, Montreal, Canada. Available at: www.cbd.int.

Chang, H.-W., Cheng, C.-A., Gu, D.-L., *et al.* (2008) High-throughput avian molecular sexing by SYBR green-based real-time PCR combined with melting curve analysis. *BMC Biotechnology*, 8, 12.

Cheng, Y.H., Kuo, T.F., Lee, D.N. and Weng, C.F. (2006) Sex identification of the black-faced spoonbill (Platalea minor). *Zoological Studies*, **45**, 104–113.

Chikuni, K., Ozutsumi, K., Koishikawa, T. and Kato, S. (1990) Species identification of cooked meats by DNA hybridization assay. *Meat Science*, **27**, 119–128.

CITES (1997) Resolution Conf. 10.17 (Rev. CoP14) Animal hybrids. Geneva: CITES Secretariat.

CITES (2011) Convention on International Trade in Endangered Species of Wild Fauna and Flora. Geneva: CITES Secretariat. Available at: http://www.cites.org/.

Clarke, S.C., Magnussen, J.E., Abercrombie, D.L., *et al.* (2006) Identification of shark species composition and proportion in the Hong Kong shark fin market based on molecular genetics and trade records (Identificación de la Composición y Proporción de Especies de Tiburón en el Mercado de Aletas de Tiburón en Hong Kong con Base en Genética Molecular y Registros Comerciales). *Conservation Biology*, **20**, 201–215.

Congiu, L., Dupanloup, I., Patarnello, T., *et al.* (2001) Identification of interspecific hybrids by amplified fragment length polymorphism: the case of sturgeon. *Molecular Ecology*, **10**, 2355–2359.

Congiu, L., Fontana, F., Patarnello, T., *et al.* (2002) The use of AFLP in sturgeon identification. *Journal of Applied Ichthyology*, **18**, 286–289.

Dawnay, N., Ogden, R., McEwing, R., *et al.* (2007) Validation of the barcoding gene COI for use in forensic genetic species identification. *Forensic Science International*, **173**, 1–6.

Dawnay, N., Ogden, R., Thorpe, R.S., *et al.* (2008) A forensic STR profiling system for the Eurasian badger: a framework for developing profiling systems for wildlife species. *Forensic Science International: Genetics*, **2**, 47–53.

Dawnay, N., Ogden, R., Wetton, J.H., *et al.* (2009) Genetic data from 28 STR loci for forensic individual identification and parentage analyses in 6 bird of prey species. *Forensic Science International: Genetics*, **3**, e63–e69.

Deagle, B., Chiaradia, A., McInnes, J. and Jarman, S. (2011) Pyrosequencing faecal DNA to determine diet of little penguins: is what goes in what comes out? *Conservation Genetics*, **11**, 2039–2048.

Desalle, R. and Amato, G. (2004) The expansion of conservation genetics. *Nature Reviews Genetics*, **5**, 702–712.

Dewaard, J.R., Mitchell, A., Keena, M.A., *et al.* (2010) Towards a global barcode library for Lymantria (Lepidoptera: Lymantriinae) tussock moths of biosecurity concern. *PLoS ONE*, **5**, e14280.

Dickinson, E.C. (ed.) (2003) *The Howard and Moore Complete Checklist of the Birds of the World*. Revised and enlarged 3rd edn. London: Christopher Helm.

Dincaf, V., Zakharov, E.V., Hebert, P.D.N. and Vila, R. (2011) Complete DNA barcode reference library for a country's butterfly fauna reveals high performance for temperate Europe. *Proceedings of the Royal Society B: Biological Sciences*, **278**, 347–355.

Dolbeer, R., Wright, S., Weller, J. and Begier, M. (2009) Wildlife strikes to civil aircraft in the United States 1990–2008. Available at: http://wildlife-mitigation.tc.faa.gov/wildlife/.

Dove, C.J., Rotzel, N.C., Heacker, M. and Weigt, L.A. (2008) Using DNA barcodes to identify bird species involved in birdstrikes. *Journal of Wildlife Management*, **72**, 1231–1236.

Duan, W. and Fuerst, P. A. (2001) Isolation of a sex-linked DNA sequence in cranes. *Journal of Heredity*, **92**, 392–397.

Ebbehoj, K.F. and Thomsen, P.D. (1991) Differentiation of closely related species by DNA hybridization. *Meat Science*, **30**, 359–366.

Edwards, S.V., Bryan Jennings, W. and Shedlock, A.M. (2005) Phylogenetics of modern birds in the era of genomics. *Proceedings of the Royal Society B: Biological Sciences*, **272**, 979–992.

Ellegren, H. (1996) First gene on the avian W chromosome (CHD) provides a tag for universal sexing of non-ratite birds. *Proceedings of the Royal Society of London Series B Biological Sciences*, **263**, 1635–1641.

El-Sayed, Y., Mohamed, O., Ashry, K. and Abd El-Rahman, S. (2010) Using species-specific repeat and PCR–RFLP in typing of DNA derived from blood of human and animal species. *Forensic Science, Medicine, and Pathology*, **6**, 158–164.

Faria, P.J., Guedes, N.M.R., Yamashita, C., *et al.* (2008) Genetic variation and population structure of the endangered hyacinth macaw (Anodorhynchus hyacinthinus): implications for conservation. *Biodiversity and Conservation*, **17**, 765–779.

Ferrier, P. (2009) *The Economics of Agricultural and Wildlife Smuggling*. Economic Research Report No. 81 (September 1, 2009). Available at SSRN: http://ssrn.com/abstract=1492832.

Fike, J.A., Athrey, G., Bowman, R., Leberg, P.L. and Rhodes, O.E., Jr. (2009) Development of twenty-five polymorphic microsatellite markers for the endangered red-cockaded woodpecker (Picoides borealis). *Conservation Genetics*, **10**, 1021–1023.

Frankham, R. (1995) Conservation genetics. *Annual Review of Genetics*, **29**, 305–327.

Frankham, R. (1999) Quantitative genetics in conservation biology. *Genetical Research*, **74**, 237–244.

Frankham, R., Ballou, J.D. and Briscoe, D.A. (2010) *Introduction to Conservation Genetics*, 2nd edn. Cambridge: Cambridge University Press.

Frantz, A.C., Pourtois, J.T., Heuertz, M., *et al.* (2006) Genetic structure and assignment tests demonstrate illegal translocation of red deer (Cervus elaphus) into a continuous population. *Molecular Ecology*, **15**, 3191–3203.

Fridolfsson, A.-K. and Ellegren, H. (1999) A simple and universal method for molecular sexing of non-ratite birds. *Journal of Avian Biology*, **30**, 116–121.

Garcia-Moreno, J. (2004) Is there a universal mtDNA clock for birds? *Journal of Avian Biology*, **35**, 465–468.

Gill, F., Wright, M. and Donsker, D. (2010) IOC World Bird Names (version 2.0). Available at: www.worldbirdnames.org.

Gillespie, G.D. (1985) Hybridization, introgression, and morphometric differentiation between Mallard (Anas platyrhynchos) and Grey Duck (Anas superciliosa) in Otago, New Zealand. *Auk*, **102**, 459–469.

Goldstein, P.Z., Desalle, R., Amato, G. and Vogler, A.P. (2000) Conservation genetics at the species boundary. *Conservation Biology*, **14**, 120–131.

Grant, P.R. and Grant, B.R. (1992) Hybridization of bird species. *Science*, **256**, 193–197.

Griffiths, R., Daan, S. and Dijkstra, C. (1996) Sex identification in birds using two CHD genes. *Proceedings of the Royal Society of London Series B Biological Sciences*, **263**, 1251–1256.

Griffiths, R., Double, M.C., Orr, K. and Dawson, R.J.G. (1998) A DNA test to sex most birds. *Molecular Ecology*, **7**, 1071–1075.

Griffiths, R. and Orr, K. (1999) The use of amplified fragment length polymorphism (AFLP) in the isolation of sex-specific markers. *Molecular Ecology*, **8**, 671–674.

Griffiths, R. and Tiwari, B. (1995) Sex of the last wild Spix's macaw. *Nature*, **375**, 454. doi: 10.1038/375453a0.

Gutierrez, R., Cody, M., Courtney, S. and Franklin, A. (2007) The invasion of barred owls and its potential effect on the spotted owl: a conservation conundrum. *Biological Invasions*, **9**, 181–196.

Haig, S.M. (1998) Molecular contributions to conservation. *Ecology*, **79**, 413–425.

Haig, S.M. and Ballou, J.D. (1995) Genetic diversity in two avian species formerly endemic to Guam. *Auk*, **112**, 445–455.

Haig, S.M., Belthoff, J.R. and Allen, D.H. (1993) Examination of population structure in red-cockaded woodpeckers using DNA profiles. *Evolution*, **47**, 185–194.

Haig, S.M., Bowman, R. and Mullins, T.D. (1996) Population structure of red-cockaded woodpeckers in south Florida: RAPDs revisited. *Molecular Ecology*, **5**, 725–734.

Haig, S.M., Gratto-Trevor, C.L., Mullins, T.D. and Colwell, M.A. (1997) Population identification of western hemisphere shorebirds throughout the annual cycle. *Molecular Ecology*, **6**, 413–427.

Haig, S.M., Mullins, T.D., Forsman, E.D., *et al.* (2004) Genetic identification of spotted owls, barred owls, and their hybrids: legal implications of hybrid identity. *Conservation Biology*, **18**, 1347–1357.

Haig, S.M., Rhymer, J.M. and Heckel, D.G. (1994a) Population differentiation in randomly amplified polymorphic DNA of red-cockaded woodpeckers Picoides borealis. *Molecular Ecology*, **3**, 581–593.

Haig, S.M., Walters, J.R. and Plissner, J.H. (1994b) Genetic evidence for monogamy in the cooperatively breeding red-cockaded woodpecker. *Behavioral Ecology and Sociobiology*, **34**, 295–303.

Hamer, T.E., Forsman, E.D., Fuchs, A.D. and Walters, M.L. (1994) Hybridization between barred and spotted owls. *The Auk*, **111**, 487–492.

Hamer, T.E., Forsman, E.D. and Glenn, E.M. (2007) Home range attributes and habitat selection of barred owls and spotted owls in an area of sympatry. *The Condor*, **109**, 750–768.

Hebert, P.D.N., Stoeckle, M.Y., Zemlak, T.S. and Francis, C.M. (2004) Identification of birds through DNA barcodes. *PLoS Biology*, **2**, e312.

Hedrick, P.W. (2001) Conservation genetics: where are we now? *Trends in Ecology & Evolution*, **16**, 629–636.

Hendrich, L., Pons, J., Ribera, I. and Balke, M. (2010) Mitochondrial sequence data reliably uncover patterns of insect diversity but suffer from high lineage-idiosyncratic error rates. *PLoS ONE*, **5**, e14448.

Herrera, M. and Hennessey, B. (2007) Quantifying the illegal parrot trade in Santa Cruz de la Sierra, Bolivia, with emphasis on threatened species. *Bird Conservation International*, **17**, 295–300.

Hoffmann, M., Hilton-Taylor, C., Angulo, A. and Al, E. (2010) The impact of conservation on the status of the world's vertebrates. *Science*, **330**, 1503–1509.

Hsieh, H.-M., Huang, L.-H., Tsai, L.-C., *et al.* (2003) Species identification of rhinoceros horns using the cytochrome b gene. *Forensic Science International*, **136**, 1–15.

Hsu, H. A., Wang, P.H., Chao, M.C., *et al.* (2009) Use of random amplified polymorphic DNA to identify several novel markers for sex identification in the crested serpent eagle and crested goshawk. *Theriogenology*, **72**, 755–764.

Huynen, L., Miles, J. and Lambert, D. (2006) Unusual electrophoretic mobility of a DNA fragment of the universal "non-ratite" sexing marker CHD allows sexing of New Zealand's endangered kiwi ratite Apteryx spp. *Ibis*, **148**, 167–168.

ICZN (2011) The International Commission on Zoological Nomenclature (ICZN). Available at: http://iczn.org/.

INTERPOL (2010) Wildlife crime. Available at: http://www.interpol.int/Public/EnvironmentalCrime/Wildlife/Default.asp.

Itoh, Y., Suzuki, M., Ogawa, A., *et al.* (2001) Identification of the sex of a wide range of Carinatae birds by PCR using primer sets selected from chicken EE0.6 and its related sequences. *Journal of Heredity*, **92**, 315–321.

IUCN (2011) IUCN Red List of Threatened Species. Version 2010.4. Available at: http://www.iucnredlist.org.

Jensen, T., Pernasetti, F. M. and Durrant, B. (2003) Conditions for rapid sex determination in 47 avian species by PCR of genomic DNA from blood, shell-membrane blood vessels, and feathers. *Zoo Biology*, **22**, 561–571.

Johnson, R.N. (2010) The use of DNA identification in prosecuting wildlife-traffickers in Australia: do the penalties fit the crimes? *Forensic Science, Medicine, and Pathology*, **6**, 211–216.

Kahn, N.W., St. John, J. and Quinn, T.W. (1998) Chromosome-specific intron size differences in the avian CHD gene provide an efficient method for sex identification in birds. *Auk*, **115**, 1074–1078.

Kelly, E.G., Forsman, E.D. and Zink, R.M. (2004) Recent records of hybridization between Barred Owls (Strix varia) and Northern Spotted Owls (S. occidentalis caurina). *The Auk*, **121**, 806–810.

Kento, O., Manabu, S., Keiko, S., *et al.* (2003) Genotyping of cytochrome P450 isoform genes is useful for forensic identification of cadaver. *Legal Medicine (Tokyo, Japan)*, **5**, 132–138.

Kerr, K.C.R., Stoeckle, M.Y., Dove, C.J., *et al.* (2007) Comprehensive DNA barcode coverage of North American birds. *Molecular Ecology Notes*, **7**, 535–543.

Kim, H. and Shelef, L.A. (1986) Characterization and identification of raw beef, pork, chicken and turkey meats by electrophoretic patterns of their sarcoplasmis proteins. *J Food Science*, **51**, 731–741.

Kohn, M.H., Murphy, W.J., Ostrander, E.A. and Wayne, R.K. (2006) Genomics and conservation genetics. *Trends in Ecology & Evolution*, **21**, 629–637.

Lee, J.C.I. and Chang, J.G. (1994) Random amplified polymorphic DNA polymerase chain reaction (RAPD PCR) fingerprints in forensic species identification. *Forensic Science International*, **67**, 103–107.

Lee, J.C.I., Tsai, L.C., Huang, M.T., *et al.* (2008) A novel strategy for avian species identification by cytochrome b gene. *Electrophoresis*, **29**, 2413–2418.

Lee, J.C.I., Tsai, L.C., Liao, S.P., *et al.* (2009) Species identification using the cytochrome b gene of commercial turtle shells. *Forensic Science Investigative Genetics*, **3**, 67–73.

Lee, J.C.I., Tsai, L.C., Hwa, P.Y., *et al.* (2010) A novel strategy for avian species and gender identification using the CHD gene. *Molecular and Cellular Probes*, **24**, 27–31.

Lee, P.L.M. and Prys-Jones, R.P. (2008) Extracting DNA from museum bird eggs, and whole genome amplification of archive DNA. *Molecular Ecology Resources*, **8**, 551–560.

Leite, K.C., Seixas, G.H., Berkunsky, I., *et al.* (2008) Population genetic structure of the blue-fronted Amazon (Amazona aestiva, Psittacidae: Aves) based on nuclear microsatellite loci: implications for conservation. *Genetics and Molecular Research*, **7**, 819–829.

Lerner, H.R.L. and Fleischer, R.C. (2010) Prospects for the use of next-generation sequencing methods in ornithology. *The Auk*, **127**, 4–15.

Lessells, C.M. and Mateman, A.C. (1998) Sexing birds using random amplified polymorphic DNA (RAPD) markers. *Molecular Ecology*, **7**, 187–195.

Li, M., Ding, C., Wei, F., *et al.* (2001) Sex-related gene and sex identification of Crested Ibis; Nipponia; (Ciconiiformes: Threskiornithidae). *Chinese Science Bulletin*, **46**, 669–671.

Livezey, B.C. and Zusi, R.L. (2007) Higher-order phylogeny of modern birds (Theropoda, Aves: Neornithes) based on comparative anatomy. II. Analysis and discussion. *Zoological Journal of the Linnean Society*, **149**, 1–95.

Lowenstein, J.H., Amato, G. and Kolokotronis, S.O. (2009) The real maccoyii: identifying tuna sushi with DNA barcodes; contrasting characteristic attributes and genetic distances. *PLoS ONE*, **4**, e7866.

Lyon, E. (2001) Mutation detection using fluorescent hybridization probes and melting curve analysis. *Expert Review of Molecular Diagnostics*, **1**, 92–101.

Mace, G.M. (2004) The role of taxonomy in species conservation. *Philosophical Transactions of the Royal Society of London. Series B: Biological Sciences*, **359**, 711–719.

Macedo-Silva, A., Barbosa, S.F.C., Alkmin, M.G.A., *et al.* (2000) Hamburger meat identification by dot-ELISA. *Meat Science*, **56**, 189–192.

Marin, J.C., Saucedo, C.E., Corti, P. and Gonzalez, B. A. (2009) Application of DNA forensic techniques for identifying poached guanacos (Lama guanicoe) in Chilean Patagonia. *Journal of Forensic Sciences*, **54**, 1073–1076.

Marra, P.P., Dove, C.J., Dolbeer, R., *et al.* (2009) Migratory Canada geese cause crash of US Airways Flight 1549. *Frontiers in Ecology and the Environment*, **7**, 297–301.

Menotti-Raymond, M.A., David, V.A. and O'Brien, S.J. (1997) Pet cat hair implicates murder suspect. *Nature*, **386**, 774.

Mindel, D.P., Knight, A., Baer, C. and Huddleston, C.J. (1996) Slow rates of molecular evolution in birds and the metabolic rate and body temperature hypotheses. *Molecular Biology and Evolution*, **13**, 422.

Morony, J.J., Bock, W.J. and Farrand J., Jr. (1975) *Reference List of the Birds of the World*. New York: American Museum of Natural History.

Mullis, K. and Faloona, F.A. (1987) Specific synthesis of DNA in vitro via a polymerase catalysed chain reaction. *Methods in Enzymology*, **155**, 335–350.

Nesje, M., Roed, K.H., Bell, D.A., *et al.* (2000a) Microsatellite analysis of population structure and genetic variability in peregrine falcons (Falco peregrinus). *Animal Conservation*, **3**, 267–275.

Nesje, M., Roed, K.H., Lifjeld, J.T., *et al.* (2000b) Genetic relationships in the peregrine falcon (Falco peregrinus) analysed by microsatellite DNA markers. *Molecular Ecology*, **9**, 53–60.

Ogawa, A., Murata, K. and Mizuno, S. (1998) The location of Z- and W-linked marker genes and sequence on the homomorphic sex chromosomes of the ostrich and the emu. *Proceedings of the National Academy of Sciences of the United States of America*, **95**, 4415–4418.

Ogden, R. (2010) Forensic science, genetics and wildlife biology: getting the right mix for a wildlife DNA forensics lab. *Forensic Science, Medicine, and Pathology*, **6**, 172–179.

Oskam, C.L., Haile, J., McLay, E., *et al.* (2010) Fossil avian eggshell preserves ancient DNA. *Proceedings of the Royal Society B: Biological Sciences*, **277**, 1991–2000.

Ouborg, N.J., Pertoldi, C., Loeschcke, V., *et al.* (2010) Conservation genetics in transition to conservation genomics. *Trends in Genetics, TIG*, **26**, 177–187.

Parson, W., Pegoraro, K., Niederstatter, H., *et al.* (2000) Species identification by means of the cytochrome b gene. *International Journal of Legal Medicine*, **114**, 23–28.

Pereira, S.L. and Baker, A.J. (2006) A mitogenomic timescale for birds detects variable phylogenetic rates of molecular evolution and refutes the standard molecular clock. *Molecular Biology and Evolution*, **23**, 1731–1740.

Pfeiffer, I., Burger, J. and Brenig, B. (2004) Diagnostic polymorphisms in the mitochondrial cytochrome b gene allow discrimination between cattle, sheep, goat, roe buck and deer by PCR-RFLP. *BMC Genetics*, **5**, 30.

Pimm, S.L., Russell, G.J., Gittleman, J.L. and Brooks, T.M. (1995) The future of biodiversity. *Science*, **269**, 347–350.

Primmer, C.R. (2009) From conservation genetics to conservation genomics. *Annals of the New York Academy of Sciences*, **1162**, 357–368.

Primmer, C.R., Koskinen, M.T. and Piironen, J. (2000) The one that did not get away: individual assignment using microsatellite data detects a case of fishing competition fraud. *Proceedings of the Royal Society of London*. Series B: Biological Sciences, **267**, 1699–1704.

Ralls, K. and Ballou, J.D. (2004) Genetic status and management of California condors. *The Condor*, **106**, 215–228.

Randler, C. (2006) Extrapair paternity and hybridization in birds. *Journal of Avian Biology*, **37**, 1–5.

Ratnasingham, S. and Hebert, P.D.N. (2007) bold: The Barcode of Life Data System (http://www.barcodinglife.org). *Molecular Ecology Notes*, **7**, 355–364.

Rhymer, J.M. and Simberloff, D. (1996) Exinction by hybridization and introgression. *Annual Review of Ecology and Systematics*, **27**, 83–109.

Rhymer, J.M., Williams, M.J. and Braun, M.J. (1994) Mitochondrial analysis of gene flow between New Zealand mallards (Anas platyrhynchos) and grey ducks (A. superciliosa). *Auk*, **111**, 970.

Roberson, D. (2011) *Bird Families of the World* (10th edn.). Available at: http://creagrus.home.montereybay.com/list.html.

Rojas, M., Gonzalez, I., Fajardo, V., *et al.* (2009) Identification of raw and heat-processed meats from game bird species by polymerase chain reaction-restriction fragment length polymorphism of the mitochondrial D-loop region. *Poultry Science*, **88**, 669–679.

Romanov, M., Tuttle, E., Houck, M., *et al.* (2009) The value of avian genomics to the conservation of wildlife. *BMC Genomics*, **10**, S10.

Rosen, G. and Smith, K. (2010) Summarizing the evidence on the international trade in illegal wildlife. *EcoHealth*, **7**, 24–32.

Rubinoff, D. (2006) Utility of mitochondrial DNA barcodes in species conservation. *Conservation Biology*, **20**, 1026–1033.

Sarich, V.M., Schmid, C.W. and Marks, J. (1989) DNA hybridization as a guide to phylogenies: a critical analysis. *Cladistics*, **5**, 3–32.

Sellar, J.M. (2009) Illegal trade and the Convention on International Trade in Endangered Species of Wild Fauna and Flora (CITES). In A. Linacre (ed.) *Forensic Science in Wildlife Investigations*. Boca Raton, FL: CRC Press.

Shorrock, G. (1998) The success of DNA profiling in wildlife law enforcement. *International Journal of Bioscience Law*, **1**, 327–341.

Shorrock, G. (2005) *Wildlife Crime: A Guide to the Use of Forensic and Specialist Techniques in the Investigation of Wildlife Crime*. London: Defra.

Sibley, C.G. and Ahlquist, J.E. (1982a) The relationships of the Australasian whistlers Pachycephala as indicated by DNA-DNA hybridization. *Emu*, **82**, 199–202.

Sibley, C.G. and Ahlquist, J.E. (1982b) Relationships of the Hawaiian Honeycreepers (Drepaninini) as indicated by DNA-DNA hybridization. *Auk*, **99**, 130–140.

Sibley, C.G. and Ahlquist, J.E. (1984) The phylogeny of the hominoid primates, as indicated by DNA-DNA hybridization. *Journal of Molecular Evolution*, **20**, 2–15.

Sibley, C.G. and Ahlquist, J.E. (1990) *Phylogeny and Classification of Birds: A Study in Molecular Evolution*, New Haven, CT: Yale University Press.

Sibley, C.G., Ahlquist, J. and Monroe Jr., B.L. (1988) A classification of the living birds of the world based on DNA-DNA hybridization studies. *Auk*, **105**, 409–423.

Singh, V.P. and Neelam, S. (2011) Meat species specifications to ensure the quality of meat-a review. *International Journal of Meat Science*, **1**, 15–26.

Skarpeid, H.J., Kvaal, K. and Hildrum, K.I. (1998) Identification of animal species in ground meat mixtures by multivariate analysis of isoelectric focusing protein profiles. *Electrophoresis*, **19**, 3103–3109.

Springer, M. and Krajewski, C. (1989) DNA hybridization in animal taxonomy: a critique from first principles. *Quarterly Review of Biology*, **64**, 291–318.

Tarr, C.L. and Fleischer, R.C. (1993) Mitochondrial-DNA variation and evolutionary relationships in the Amakihi complex. *Auk*, **110**, 825–831.

Teletchea, F., Bernillon, J., Duffraisse, M., *et al.* (2008) Molecular identification of vertebrate species by oligonucleotide microarray in food and forensic samples. *Journal of Applied Ecology*, **45**, 967–975.

Tobe, S.S., Kitchener, A.C. and Linacre, A.M.T. (2010) Reconstructing mammalian phylogenies: a detailed comparison of the cytochrome and cytochrome oxidase subunit I mitochondrial genes. *PLoS ONE*, **5**, e14156.

Transport Canada (2004) *Sharing the Skies: An Aviation Industry Guide to the Management of Wildlife*, 2nd edn. Ottowa: Civil Aviation, Transport Canada.

Tuinen, M.V., Sibley, C.G. and Hedges, S.B. (2000) The early history of modern birds inferred from DNA sequences of nuclear and mitochondrial ribosomal genes. *Molecular Biology and Evolution*, **17**, 451–457.

Verma, S.K. and Singh, L. (2003) Novel universal primers establish identity of an enormous number of animal species for forensic application. *Molecular Ecology Notes*, **3**, 28–31.

Wallman, J. and Adams, M. (2001) The forensic application of allozyme electrophoresis to the identification of blowfly larvae (Diptera: Calliphoridae) in southern Australia. *Journal of Forensic Science*, **46**, 681–684.

Waugh, J., Evans, M.W., Millar, C.D. and Lambert, D.M. (2011) Birdstrikes and barcoding: can DNA methods help make the airways safer? *Molecular Ecology Resources*, **11**, 38–45.

Wetton, J.H. and Parkin, D.T. (1997) A suite of falcon single-locus minisatellite probes: a powerful alternative to DNA fingerprinting. *Molecular Ecology*, **6**, 119–128.

Whitehead, P.H. and Brech, A. (1974) A micro-technique involving species identification and ABO grouping on the same fragment of blood. *Journal of the Forensic Science Society*, **14**, 109–110.

Whitehead, P.H., Brech, A. and Gayzer, I. (1974) The identification of the species origin of bloodstains using sensitized latex. *Journal of the Forensic Science Society*, **14**, 103–107.

Wilson-Wilde, L., Norman J., Robertson, J., *et al.* (2010) Current issues in species identification for forensic science and the validity of using the cytochrome oxidase I (COI) gene. *Forensic Science, Medicine, and Pathology*, **6**, 233–241.

Wolstenholme, D.R. (1992) Animal mitochondrial DNA: structure and evolution. *International Review of Cytology*, **141**, 173–216.

Wu, C.P., Horng, Y.M., Wang, R.T., *et al.* (2007) A novel sex-specific DNA marker in Columbidae birds. *Theriogenology*, **67**, 328–333.

Wuertz, S., Gaillard, S., Barbisan, F., *et al.* (2006) Extensive screening of sturgeon genomes by random screening techniques revealed no sex-specific marker. *Aquaculture*, **258**, 685–688.

Yoo, H.S., Eah, J.Y., Kim, J.S., *et al.* (2006) DNA barcoding Korean birds. *Molecules and Cells*, **22**, 323–7.

Zink, R.M. (2004) The role of subspecies in obscuring avian biological diversity and misleading conservation policy. *Proceedings of the Royal Society of London. Series B: Biological Sciences*, **271**, 561–564.

Zink, R.M. and Barrowclough, G.F. (2008) Mitochondrial DNA under siege in avian phylogeography. *Molecular Ecology*, **17**, 2107–2121.

16

Wildlife Forensics in Thailand:

Utilization of Mitochondrial DNA Sequences

Suchitra Changtragoon

Introduction

Orangutans, tigers, elephants and banteng are all protected and endangered species. In addition, orangutans, tigers, elephants are protected by CITES (Convention of International Trade of Endangered Species of Wild Fauna and Flora). However, some of these species and their products are still poached and illegally traded in developing countries both in Asia and Africa (Singh *et al.*, 2004; Stiles, 2004; Wasser *et al.*, 2008).

In Thailand, there have been a number of confiscated wildlife cases that were investigated for origin, species and subspecies. Four cases were selected as case studies in this chapter. Investigation of the geographic origin of 53 confiscated orangutans, identification of the subspecies of 17 tiger meat and 6 tiger skin confiscated samples; identification of the species of elephants from 7 ivory products; and determining if the confiscated meat is from a banteng (*Bos* spp., also known as tembadau, a species of wild cattle). In order to identify the origin of confiscated orangutans, the subspecies of confiscated tiger samples as well as the species of elephants from ivory products and meat samples which were suspected from banteng, mitochondrial DNA sequencing at control region, NDH dehydrogenase and the cytochrome b gene were used to investigate these four cases.

DNA Extraction and Amplification

Samples were collected from four sets of confiscated case material: blood from 53 orangutans; 17 pieces of confiscated tiger meat samples and six pieces of tiger

---

Wildlife Forensics: Methods and Applications, First Edition. Edited by Jane E. Huffman and John R. Wallace.

skin samples; seven ivory products and one meat sample which is suspected to be from a bantang from Cambodia. DNA of each of these samples was extracted using Qiagen© DNeasy blood and tissue extraction kit. For the ivory products, each sample was ground and calcium was removed using a minimally invasive method before DNA extraction. The PCR product of the control region was amplified from each of the orangutan samples based on Warren *et al.*'s (2001) protocol. The PCR product of NDH dehydrogenase and the cytochrom b gene were amplified from known tiger and ivory samples, and the unknown samples based on Lou *et al.* (2004), Cracraft *et al.* (1998) Lei *et al.* (2008); Xuan *et al.* (2010), respectively, as shown in Table 16.1.

DNA Sequencing

The obtained PCR product of each sample was isolated from the agarose gel and cloned into the pGEM-T Easy vector system (Promega, USA). The reaction was incubated at 16°C overnight. Recombinant vectors were transformed into DH5α competent cells by $CaCl_2$ heat shock transformation and the plasmid inserts were PCR amplified using the universal primers T7 and SP6. Plasmids were extracted using GenElute™ Plasmid Miniperp kit (Sigma) and used as a template for the sequencing reactions. However, in some cases the DNA was directly sequenced. Sequencing of the DNA fragments was performed using BigDye Terminator v3.1 Cycle Sequencing Kit (Applied Biosystems, Foster City, CA) and carried out with an ABI Prism 3100-Avant Genetic Analyzer (Applied Biosystems, Foster City, CA).

Origin Identification

Blood samples from the confiscated orangutans were collected and used for amplification of the fragment of the mitochondrial DNA control region. The obtained 240–304 bp mitochondrial DNA sequences from the unknown origin orangutans were compared with the corresponding published orangutan mtDNA sequences from Warren *et al.* (2001) in the NCBI GenBank (http://www.ncbi.nlm.nih.gov) which included the sequences of orangutans from Sumatra and the four geographic regions in Borneo. Comparing variable sites of mitochondrial DNA sequences at the control region and phylogenetic analysis by constructing neighbor-joining (NJ) trees and the bootstrap test were used to place and identify the origin of unknown orangutans using the following computer programs: BioEdit sequence aligment, DnaSP 4.0 (Rozas *et al.*, 2003) and Mega 3.1 (Kumar, Tamura and Nei, 2004).

Species and Subspecies Identification

To identify subspecies of tigers, the obtained 250–555 bp DNA sequences from the17 pieces of confiscated tiger meat samples and six pieces of tiger skin samples

Table 16.1 Primers used for amplification of mtDNA segments and product size.

Case study	Size (bp)	Mitochondrial DNA segments/ genes	5′⟷3′	References
Orangutan	280–304	D1/D5	CAACATGAATATCACCC TGTGCGGGATATTGATTTCAC	Warren *et al*. (2001)
		D2/D4	ACACAACAATCGCTTAAC GATGGTGAGYAAGGGATT	
Tiger	443	ND6	TCTCCTTCATAATCACCCTGA TGGCTGGTGGTGTTGGTTGCGG	Lou *et al*. (2004)
	555	Cytb1	TTGCCGCGACGTAACCACG GTTGGCGGGGATGTAGTTATC	
	250	CR	TCAAAGCTTACACCAGTCTTGTAAACC CGTGTTGTGTGTTCTGTAT	
	345	ND1	CGAAGCGAGCTCCATTTGATTTA GTGGAATGCTTGCTGTAATGATGGG	
	443	ND2	CTTATAGTCTGAATCGGCTTCG AGCTATGATTTTTCGTACCT	
	517	ND2	GGGGAGTTAACCAAACCGAG CAAGGACGGATAGTATTGGTG	
	425	Cytb2	CGAAGCTTGATATGAAAAACCATCGTTG AAACTGCAGCCCCTCAGAATGATATTTG TCCTCA	Cracraft *et al*. (1998)
Ivory	1,266	Cytb	ATGACCCACAYYCGAAAATCTCA TTACTTAATGAGGTAGTTTTCG	Lei *et al*. (2008)
Suspected banteng	610	Cytb	GAAAAACCATCGTTGTCATTCA TGGATTGGGATTTTGTCTACG	Xuan *et al*. (2010)

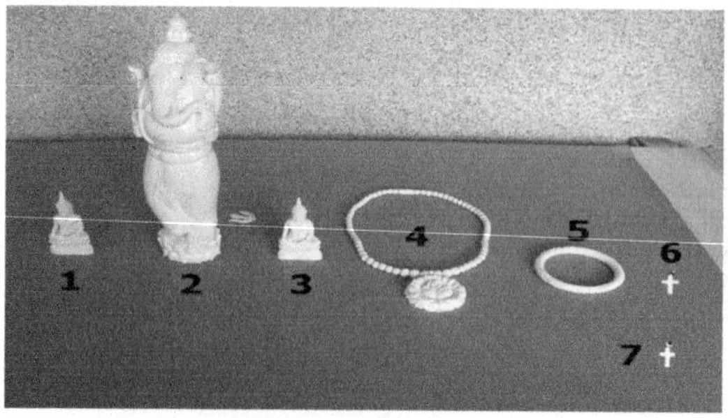

Figure 16.1 Seven confiscated ivory products.

were compared with mitochondrial DNA sequencing in the control region (CR), NDH dehydrogenase (ND) and cytochrome b (cyt b) segments (Table 16.1) and genes with published DNA sequences from Lou *et al.* (2004) and Cracraft *et al.* (1998) in Genbank. This also included the control region, NDH dehydrogenase and cytochrome b sequences of the tiger subspecies.

In order to identify species of elephants from seven ivory products, as shown in Figure 16.1, the obtained 1,266 bp mitochondrial DNA cytochrome b sequences were compared with the published cytochrome b sequences from Lei, Brenneman and Louis Jr. (2008) in GenBank which included cytochrome b sequences from Asian and African species as well as from placenta of wild elephants in Kuiburi National Park, Thailand.

In order to identify that the confiscated meat was from a banteng (*Bos* spp.), the obtained 610 bp mitochrondrial DNA sequences in the cytochrome b gene was compared with published cytochrome b sequences from Xuan *et al.* (2010) in Genbank.

The phylogenetic analysis was done by constructing neighbor-joining (NJ) trees and the bootstrap test was used to place and identify the unknown subspecies and species by using the computer programs: BioEdit sequence aligment, DnaSP 4.0 (Rozas *et al.*, 2003) and Mega 3.1 (Kumar *et al.*, 2004).

Results of the Investigations

Case study 1: Orangutans

The orangutan (*Pongo pygmaeus*) is listed as an endangered species due to habitat destruction and poaching. It is currently restricted to small patches in Borneo and Sumatra. Over forty years ago, Van Bemmel (1968) and Jones (1969) classified orangutans taxonomically into two distinct subspecies: the Bornean (*Pongo pygmaeus pygmaeus*) and the Sumatran (*Pongo pygmaeus abelli*). Some time ago, 53 orangutans were illegally imported to Thailand. They were later confiscated and cared for by the Department of National Park, Wildlife and

Conservation. However, the government of the kingdom of Thailand decided to send the orangutans back to their geographic range of origin.

There have been several genetic studies on orangutan divergence, differentiation and subspecies analysis using isozyme analysis (Janczewski *et al.* 1990), mitochondrial DNA restriction fragment length polymorphisms (Zhi *et al.*, 1996), microsatellite markers (Warren *et al.*, 2000; Zhang *et al.*, 2001; Kanthaswamy and Smith, 2002), nuclear minisatellite (Zhi *et al.*, 1996), as well as mitochondrial DNA sequences (Zhi *et al.*, 1996; Xu and Arnason, 1996; Warren *et al.* 2001; Zhang *et al.*, 2001). Zhang, Ryder and Zhang (2001) estimated from their data that the divergence time between the two subspecies is approximately 2.3 +/− 0.5 million years ago (MYA), which is much earlier than the isolation of their geological distribution. Neither subspecies underwent a recent bottleneck, though the Sumatran subspecies may have experienced expansion approximately 82,000 years ago. However, Warren *et al.* (2001) suggested that the two subspecies have been geographically isolated for 10,000–15,000 years and possess only subtle morphological differentiation. Based on Warren *et al.* (2001), it is estimated that Bornean and Sumatran orangutans diverged approximately 1.1 million years ago and that the four distinct Bornean populations (1. Southwest and Central Kalimantan, 2. Northwest Kalimantan and Sarawak, 3. Sabah and 4. East Kalimantan) diverged 860,000 years ago. These findings have important implications for management, breeding, and reintroduction practices in orangutan conservation and protection efforts.

Based on the results of comparing variable nucleotide sites and phylogenetic analysis (Figure 16.2), it is suggested that that the 53 confiscated orangutans are Bornean subspecies (*P. pygmaeus pygmaeus*). Fifty orangutans possibly came from Southwest and Central Kalimantan, Borneo, Indonesia, and the other three orangutans possibly came from East Kalimantan, Borneo, Indonesia. These results are useful to CITES law enforcement and implemental in sending the orangutans back to their correct geographic origin. If the confiscated orangutans were sent to the wrong geographic origin range, they might not have been welcomed by the other orangutans and could not communicate well with them. They also might not be able to find mates, which consequently may affect the gene pool of the natural orangutan populations. The information obtained in this and other studies is very important for the efficient wildlife forensic research, enforcement of CITES law, as well as ASEAN Wildlife Enforcement Network (ASEAN-WEN).

Case study 2: Tigers (*Panthera* spp.)

The tigers in this investigation had been poached and in route to the northern border of Thailand for illegal trade when they were confiscated by the CITES authority of Thailand. Seventeen tiger meat samples and later six tiger skin samples were sent to the DNA lab of the Department of National Parks, Wildlife and Plant Conservation to identify species and subspecies. Species and

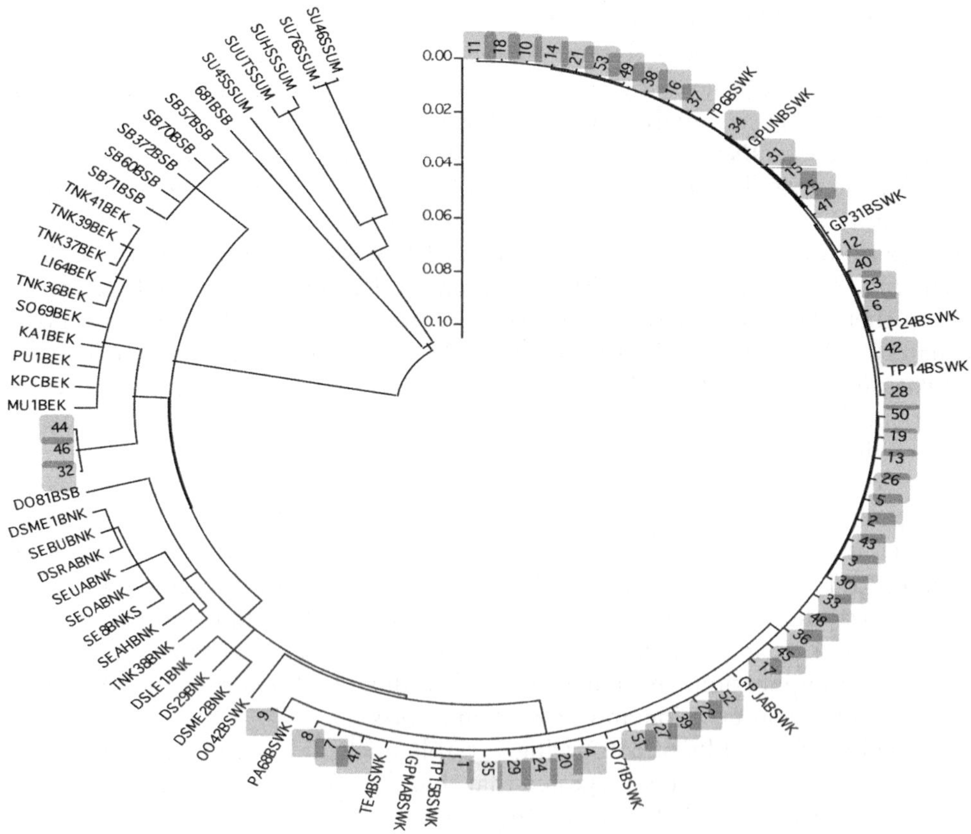

Figure 16.2 Phylogenic relationship using neighbor-joining analysis placing the unknown orangutans (numbers 1–53) to the most genetically related populations.

subspecies of tigers were identified by seven segments of mitochondrial genes as shown in Table 16.1. Comparing variable nucleotide sites and phylogenetic analysis placed samples at the most genetically related species and subspecies. The results showed that out of 17 samples, 12 samples were *Panthera tigris*, consisting of three subspecies namely Indochinese tiger (*P. t. corbetti*), Amur tiger (*P. t. altaica*) and Malayan tiger (*P. t. jacksoni*), as shown in Table 16.2 and Figure 16.3. Of the remaining three samples, one was identified as *P. pardus* and two were identified as *Neofelis nebulosa,* as shown in Figure 16.3. Nucleotide variable specific sites for *Panthara tigris* subspecies were made comparing to Lou *et al.* (2004). In regards to the six pieces of tiger skin samples, it was found that three samples were Indochinese tiger (*P. t. corbetti*) and the other three samples were *P. pardus,* as shown in Table 16.2. The outcome of this investigation could be used to implement CITES laws and to protect and conserve tigers.

Table 16.2 Nucleotide variable specific sites for *Panthara tigris* subspecies comparing to Lou *et al*. (2004).

Sample NO.	Subspecies	Common name	Sub group	Variable site: ND6 C1494F/ T1936R	Cytochome B C2339F/ T1936R	Control Region CR-UPF/ CR-R2B	ND1 C8276F/ T8620R	ND2 T8942F/ C9384R	ND2 C9366F/ T9882R	Additional Variable
	Panthera.tigris.alltaica	Amur	ALT	A(1471)					G(5332)	
Pan6*	*P.t.altaica*	Amur		A(1471)					G(5332)	G
Pan8*	*P.t.altaica*	Amur		A(1471)					G(5332)	G
	Panthera.tigris.amoyensis	South China	AMO1	C(1459), G(1471)	T(1575)		G(4257)	C(5155)	T(5332), C(5349), A(5518), C(5674), A(5728)	
	Panthera.tigris.amoyensis	South China	AMO2	G(1471)	A(1540), (1559)	T(1631)			T(5332)	
	Panthera.tigris.corbetti	Indochinese	COR1	G(1471)	A(1540), (1559)	T(1631)			T(5332)	
	P.t.corbetti	Indochinese	COR2	G(1471)	A(1540), (1559)	T(1631)		G(5186)	T(5332)	
	P.t.corbetti	Indochinese	COR3	G(1471)	A(1540), (1559)	T(1631)	C		T(5332)	
Pan5*	*P.t.corbetti*	Indochinese		G(1471)	A(1540), (1559)	T(1631)	C		T(5332)	G
Pan18**	*P.t.corbetti*	Indochinese		G(1471)	A(1540), (1559)	T(1631)	C		T(5332)	G

(*Continued*)

Table 16.2 *(Continued)*

Sample NO.	Subspecies	Common name	Sub group	Variable site: ND6 C1494F/ T1936R	Cytochome B C2339F/ T1936R	Control Region CR-UPF/ CR-R2B	ND1 C8276F/ T8620R	ND2 T8942F/ C9384R	ND2 C9366F/ T9882R	Additional Variable
Pan4*	*P.t.corbetti*	Indochinese		G(1471)	A(1540), (1559)	T(1631)			T(5332)	G
Pan20**	*P.t.corbetti*	Indochinese		G(1471)	A(1540), (1559)	T(1631)			T(5332)	G
	Panthera.tigris.corbetti	Indochinese	COR4	G(1471)	A(1560), T(1569), (1575)	T(1639)			T(5332)	
Pan1*	*P.t.corbetti*	Indochinese		G(1471)	A(1560), T(1569), (1575)	T(1639)			T(5332)	G
Pan10*	*P.t.corbetti*	Indochinese		G(1471)	A(1560), T(1569), (1575)	T(1639)			T(5332)	G
Pan11*	*P.t.corbetti*	Indochinese		G(1471)	A(1560), T(1569), (1575)	T(1639)			T(5332)	G
Pan19**	*P.t.corbetti*	Indochinese		G(1471)	A(1560), T(1569), (1575)	T(1639)			T(5332)	G
	Panthera.tigris.jacksoni	Malayan	COR5	G(1471)	T(1569), (1575)	T(1639)			T(5332)	
	P.t.jacksoni	Malayan	COR6	G(1471)	T(1575)	C(1631)			T(5332), G(5515)	
	P.t.jacksoni	Malayan	COR7	G(1471), T(1478)	T(1575)	C(1631)			T(5332), G(5515)	

Pan7*	*P.t.jacksoni*	Malayan		G(1471), T(1478)	T(1575)	C(1631)			T(5332), G(5515)	G
pan9*	*P.t.jacksoni*	Malayan		G(1471), T(1478)	T(1575)	C(1631)			T(5332), G(5515)	G
	P.t.jacksoni	Malayan	COR8	G(1471), T(1478)	C(1539), T(1575)	C(1631)			T(5332), G(5515)	
Pan3*	*P.t.jacksoni*	Malayan		G(1471), T(1478)	C(1539), T(1575)	C(1631)			T(5332), G(5515)	G
Pan2*	*P.t.jacksoni*	Malayan		G(1471), T(1478)	C(1539), T(1575)	C(1631)			T(5332), G(5515)	G
Pan12*	*P.t.jacksoni*	Malayan		G(1471), T(1478)	C(1539), T(1575)				T(5332), G(5515)	G
	Panthera.tigris.tigris	Bengal	TIG3	T(1461), G(1471)	T(1575)		C(4442)	T(5050), C(5155)	T(5332), A(5533)	
	P.t.tigris	Bengal	TIG5	T(1461), G(1471)	C(1537), T(1575)		C(4442)	T(5050), C(5155)	T(5332), A(5533)	
	P.t.tigris	Bengal	TIG1	T(1461), G(1471)	C(1537), T(1575)			A(4963), T(5050), C(5155)	T(5332), A(5533), T(5737)	
	P.t.tigris	Bengal	TIG2	T(1461), G(1471)	C(1537), T(1575)		C(4442)	T(5050), C(5155)	T(5332), A(5533)	
	P.t.tigris	Bengal	TIG6	T(1461), G(1471)	C(1537), T(1575)		C(4442)	T(5050), C(5155)	T(5332), A(5533), T(5737)	
	P.t.tigris	Bengal	TIG4	T(1461), G(1471)	C(1537), T(1575)		C(4442)	T(5050), C(5155)	T(5332), A(5533)	
	Panthera.tigris.sumatrae	Sumatran	SUM5	G(1471)	C(1537), G(1574), T(1575)		C(4442)	C(5155)	T(5332), T(5608)	
	P.t.sumatrae	Sumatran	SUM1	G(1471)	G(1574), T(1575)		C(4442)	C(5155)	T(5332), T(5608)	

(Continued)

Table 16.2 (*Continued*)

Sample NO.	Subspecies	Common name	Sub group	Variable site: ND6 C1494F/ T1936R	Variable site: Cytochome B C2339F/ T1936R	Variable site: Control Region CR-UPF/ CR-R2B	Variable site: ND1 C8276F/ T8620R	Variable site: ND2 T8942F/ C9384R	Variable site: ND2 C9366F/ T9882R	Additional Variable
	P.t.sumatrae	Sumatran	SUM4	G(1471)	G(1574), T(1575)		C(4442)	C(5155)	T(5332), T(5608)	
	P.t.sumatrae	Sumatran	SUM2	G(1471)	G(1574), T(1575)		C(4442)	C(5155)	T(5332), T(5608)	
	P.t.sumatrae	Sumatran	SUM3	G(1471)	C(1558), G(1574), T(1575)		C(4442)	C(5155)	T(5332), T(5608)	
	P.t.sumatrae	Sumatran	SUM6	G(1471)	C(1535), G(1574), T(1575)		C(4442)	C(5155)	T(5332), T(5608)	
	P.t.sumatrae	Sumatran	SUM8	G(1471)	C(1535), G(1574), T(1575)		G(4406), C(4442)	C(5155)	T(5332), T(5608)	
	P.t.sumatrae	Sumatran	SUM7	G(1471)	C(1535), G(1574), T(1575)		G(4406), C(4442)	C(5155)	T(5332), T(5608)	

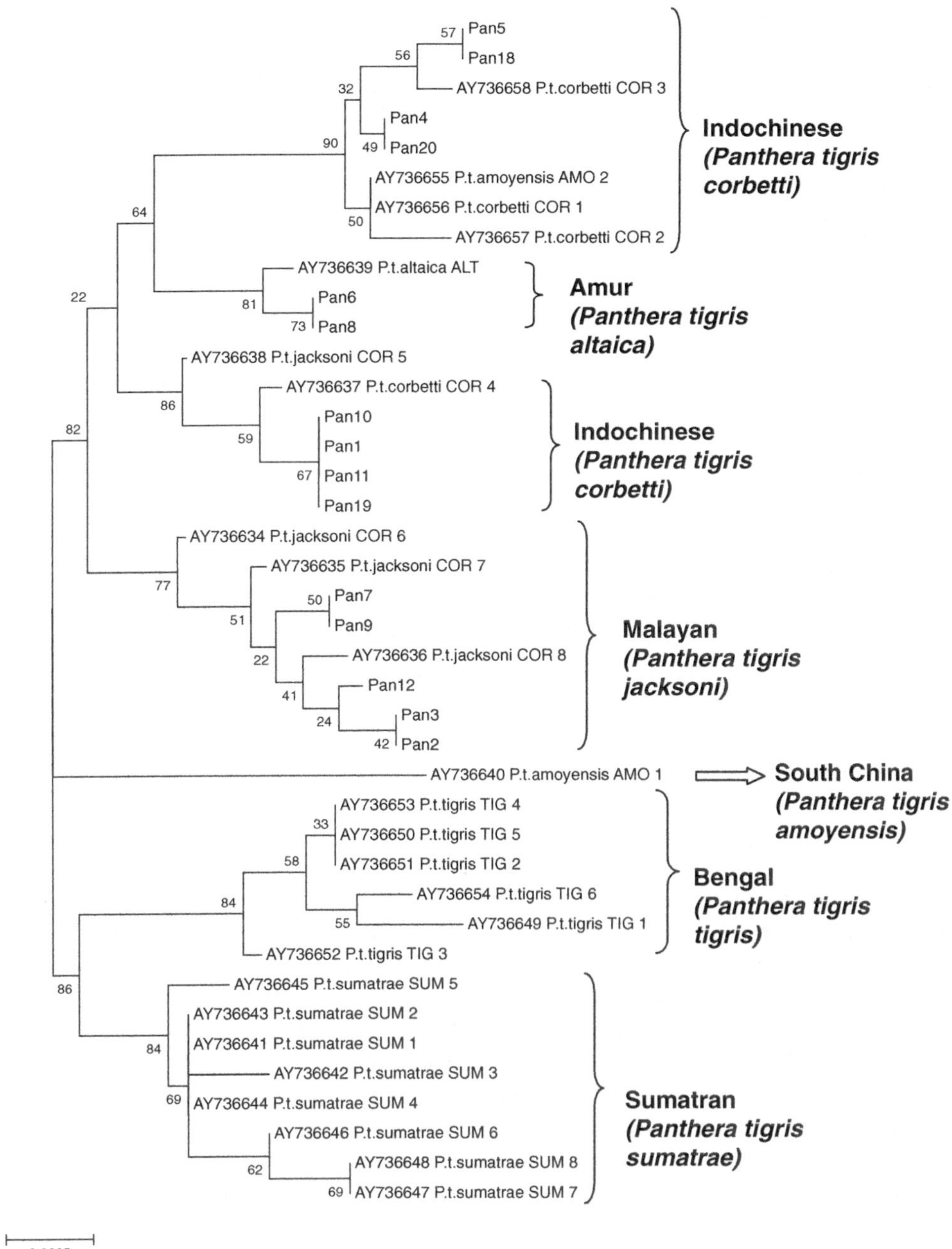

Figure 16.3 Phylogenetic relationship using neighbor-joining analysis at 6 Mt DNA segments and genes placing the unknown subspecies to the most genetically related subspecies based on Lou *et al.* (2004).

Case Study 3: Ivory

The Convention on the International Trade of Endangered Species of Wild Fauna and Flora (CITES) banned the international trade of Asian and African elephant species by listing them on Appendix I in 1973 and 1989, respectively (Stiles, 2004). Therefore, international ivory trading is against the CITES law. In order to charge the suspected ivory trader in Thailand, Freeland Foundation and police pretended to buy seven ivory products from the suspected trader and wanted to prove whether any ivory products were from African elephants. The seven ivory products were sent to the DNA lab of the Department of National Parks, Wildlife and Plant Conservation to identify species by using DNA sequencing.

Based on mitochondrial DNA sequencing analysis at the Cyt b gene, the comparison of variable nucleotide sites and phylogenetic analysis placed the unknown species of ivory product to the most genetically related species. The results show that there were 15 species-specific variable nucleotide sites for Asian elephant (*Elephas maximus*) and 14 species-specific variable nucleotide sites for African elephant. The results suggest that five ivory products are from Asian elephants and two ivory products are from African forest elephants (*Loxodonta africana cyclotis*), as shown in Figure 16.4. The results are useful for strengthening the implementation of law enforcement of CITES and can be used to prevent the illegal trade of ivory in the future.

Case study 4: Suspected Banteng

Banteng (*Bos* spp.) are a protected and endangered species. However, illegal trade of this wildlife still occurs. Confiscated meat was sent from the Management Authority of Cambodia through ASEAN-WEN and CITES authority in Thailand to our lab to identify if it was from banteng (*Bos* spp.). The identification of the suspected species of this confiscated sample was carried out by comparing mitochrondrial DNA sequencing in the cytochrome b gene with published sequences in Genbank, which include sequences from banteng and related species. Based on the species-specific nucleotide sites and phylogenetic analysis, the results suggest that this confiscated meat sample is from water buffalo (*Bulalus bubalis*). Since water buffalo is a domestic species and not a wildlife species, selling of this meat is not against CITES law. The outcome of this analysis was sent to the Management Authority of Cambodia for further review.

Conclusion

The outcome of the identification of origin, species and subspecies of these four cases are summarized in Table 16.3. Genetic tools are powerful and useful for the strengthening of CITES law enforcement. It also shows that collaboration among countries in wildlife forensics is useful and could strengthen the implementation

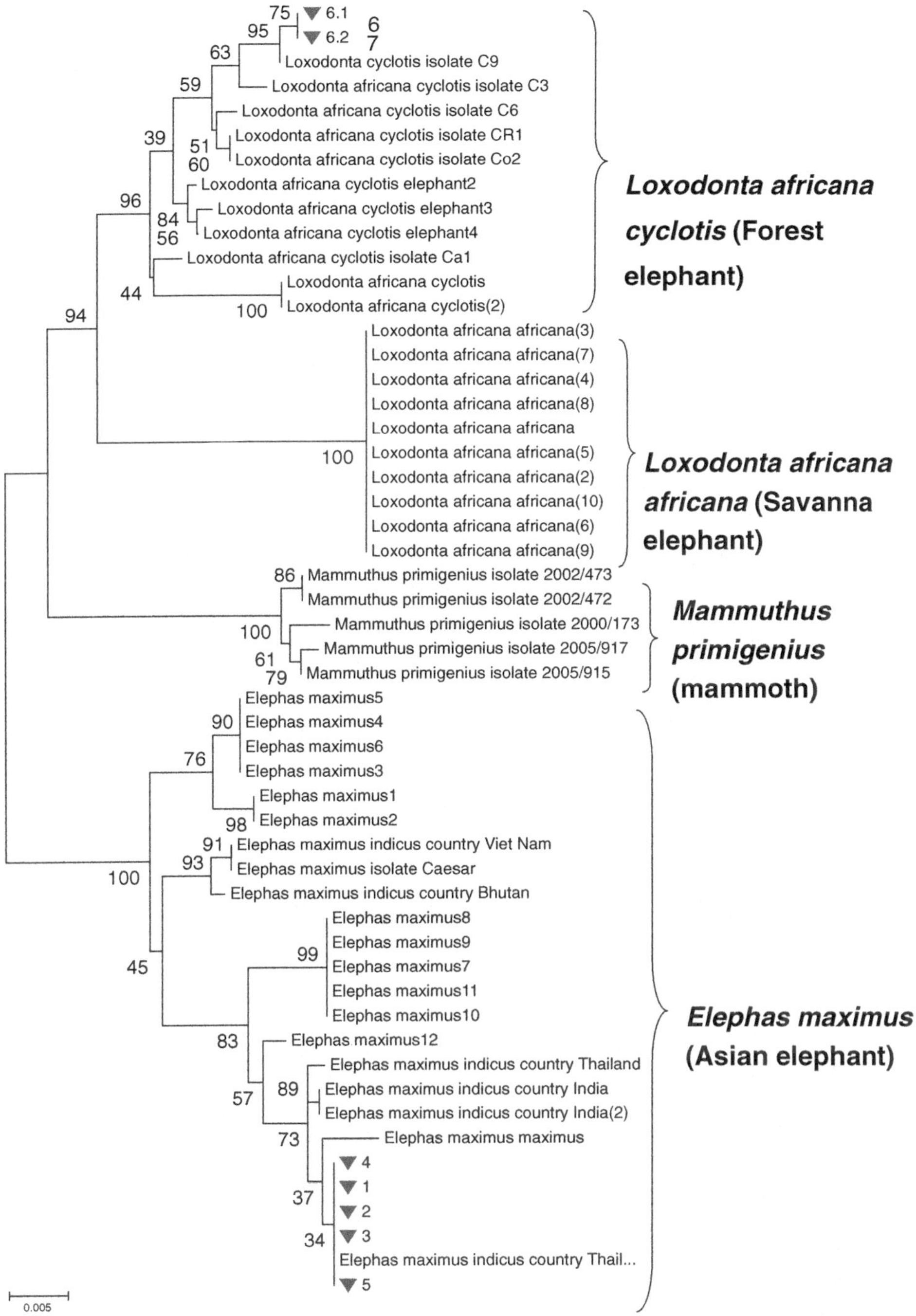

Figure 16.4 Phylogenetic relationship using neighbor-joining analysis at Cyt b gene placing 5 (No. 1–5) ivory products to the same clad as Asian elephant (*Elephas maximus*) and two ivory products (Nos. 6 and 7) to the same clad as African forest elephant (*Loxodonta africana cyclotis*).

Table 16.3 Summary of case studies.

Case study	Genetic tools	Outcome	Implication
Orangutans	mtDNA sequences at control region	53 orangutans possibly came from South-west and Central Kalimanatan, Borneo, Indonesia Three orangutans possibly came from East Kalimatan, Borneo, Indonesia	The confiscated orangutans were sent back to Indonesia
Tigers	mtDNA sequences at cytochrome b gene	Out of 17 samples, 12 samples were *Panthera tigris* consisting of three subspecies namely Indochinese tiger (*P. t. corbetti*), Amur tiger (*P. t. altaica*) and Malayan tiger (*P. t. jacksoni*). Of the remaining three samples one was classified as *P. pardus* and two as *Neofelis nebulosa* In regards to the six pieces of tiger skin samples, it was revealed that three samples were Indochinese tiger (*P. t. corbetti*) and the other 3 samples were *P. pardus*	The results were sent to CITES authorities and police for further investigation
Ivory	mtDNA sequences at cytochrome b gene	Five ivory products are from Asian elephants (*Elephas maximus*) and 2 ivory products are from African forest elephant (*Loxodonta africana cyclotis*)	The results were sent to the police for investigation and the ivory trader was sentenced and fined in court
Suspected banteng meat	mtDNA sequences at cytochrome b gene	The suspected meat was from water buffalo (*Bulalus bubalis*) not from banteng (*Bos* spp.)	The results were sent to the Management Authority of Cambodia through the CITES office in Thailand and ASEAN-WEN for further implementation

of CITES law enforcement in the ASEAN region to conserve and protect endangered species. It could also help police and CITES authorities to sentence and charge illegal wildlife traders and also could protect suspected traders if they are innocent.

Knowledge of the implication of wildlife forensics and public awareness should be distributed to the local people and traders so that it is known that any confiscated wildlife can be investigated and identified by genetic tools. Furthermore, to fulfill and strengthen law enforcement, especially in developing countries, genetic databases derived from research on phylogenetics, phylogeography, population genetics, DNA barcoding, and assignment analysis of wildlife should be carried out. Elephants, tigers, and pangolins should be listed as a priority for the database due to the frequency of cases involving these species. In the case of ivory, the collaboration on assignment analysis should be extended to African regions as well.

Acknowledgements

I would like to express my sincere appreciation to Dr. Shujin Luo, Beijing University (former staff of National Cancer Institute Laboratory of Genomic Diversity, Frederick, MD, USA) for her suggestions, guidance and information on the analysis of orangutan and tiger analysis.

I would like to thank Mr. Arthit Vimoltat, Miss Tantawan Pasawaka, Miss Kittiya Singthong and Miss Chulinna Lapsongphol for their excellent assistance in DNA analysis. Thank you to Dr. Ratthaphon Pattanarangsan, Faculty of Veterinary, Mahidol University, and his staff for helping on blood collection as well as Mr.Pornchai Patumrattanathan, Chief of Khao Prathap Chang Wildlife Breeding Research Station, Wildlife Conservation Office of the Department of National Park Wildlife and Plant Conservation (DNP) and his staff for taking care of the confiscated orangutans. I also thank the Department of National Park Wildlife and Plant Conservation (DNP) for financial support and encouragement.

I also recognize the effort of the CITES office, ASEAN-WEN and Forest and Plant Conservation Office of DNP for the communication and collaboration on this work. Special thanks to the Freeland Foundation (former Wildaid) for their financial support of orangutan analysis.

References

Cracraft, J., Feinstein, J., Vaughn, J. *et al.* (1998) Sorting out tigers (*Panthera tigris*): mitochondrial sequences, nuclear inserts, systematics, and conversation genetics. *Animal Conservation*, **1**, 139–150.

Janczewski, D.N., Goldman, D. and O'Brien, S.J. (1990) Molecular genetic divergence of orangutan *Pongo pygmaeus* subspecies based on isozyme and two-dimensional gel electrophoresis. *Journal of Heredity*, **81**, 375–387.

Jones, M.L. (1969) The geographical races of orangutan. *Proceeding of the 2nd International Congress of Primates*, **2**, 217–223.

Kanthaswamy, S. and Smith, D.G. (2002) Population subdivision and gene flow among wild Orangutans. *Primates*, **43**, 315–327.

Kumar, S., Tamura, K. and Nei, M. (2004) MEGA3: Integrated software for molecular evolutionary genetics analysis and sequence alignment. *Briefings in Bioinformatics*, **5**, 150–163.

Lei, R., Brenneman, R.A. and Louis Jr, E.E. (2008) Genetic diversity in the North American captive African elephant collection. *Journal of Zoology*, **275**, 252–267.

Lou, S., Kim, J., Johnson, W.E. *et al.* (2004) Phylogeography and genetic ancestry of tigers (*Panthera tigris*). *PLoS Biology*, **2**, e442.

Rozas, J., Sanchez-Delbarrio, J.C., Messeguer, X. and Rozas, R. (2003). DnaSP, DNA polymorphism analyses by the coalescent and other methods. *Bioinformatics*, **19**, 2496–2497.

Singh, A., Gaur, A., Shailaja, K. *et al.* (2004). A novel microsatellite (STR) marker for forensic identification of big cats in India. *Forensic Science International*, **141**, 143–147.

Stiles, D. (2004) The ivory trade and elephant conservation. *Environmental Conservation*, **31**, 309–321.

Van Bemmel, A.C.V. (1968) Contribution to the knowledge of the geographical races of *Pongo pygmaeus* (Hoppius). *Bijdragen tot de Dierkunde*, **38**, 13–15.

Warren, K.S., Nijman, I.J., Lenstra, J.A. *et al.* (2000) Microsatellite DNA variation in Bornean orangutans (*Pongo pygmaeus*). *Journal of Medical Primatology*, **29**, 57–62.

Warren, K. S., Verschoor, E.J., Langenhuijzen, S. *et al.* (2001) Speciation and intrasubspecific variation of Bornean orangutans, *Pongo pygmaeus pygmaeus*. *Molecular Biology Evolution*, **18**, 472–480.

Wasser, S.K., Clark, W.J., Drori, O. *et al.* (2008) Combating the illegal trade in African elephant ivory with DNA forensics. *Conservation Biology*, **22**, 1065–1071.

Xu, X.F. and Arnason, U. (1996) The mitochondrial DNA molecule of Sumatran orangutan and a molecular proposal for two (Bornean and Sumatran) species of orangutan. *Journal of Molecular Evolution*, **43**, 431–437.

Xuan, T.P., Georgescu, S.E., Manea, M.A. *et al.* (2010) Genetic diversity and phylogenetic relationships of Romanian cattle breeds inferred from cytochome b gene partial sequences. *Romanian Biotechnological Letters*, **15**, 5154–5158.

Zhang, Y.W., Ryder, O.A. and Zhang, Y.P. (2001) Genetic divergence of orangutan subspecies (*Pongo pygmaeus*). *Journal of Molecular Evolution*, **52**, 516–526.

Zhi, L., Karesh, W.B., Janczewski, D.N. *et al.* (1996) Genomic differentiation among natural populations of orang-utan (*Pongo pygmaeus*). *Current Biology*, **6**, 1326–1336.

17

The Future of Wildlife Forensic Science

Edgard O. Espinoza, Jesica L. Espinoza, Pepper W. Trail, and Barry W. Baker

> *Those who have knowledge, don't predict. Those who predict, don't have knowledge.*
>
> Lao Tzu, 600 BC–531 BC, author of *Tao Te Ching* ("The Book of the Way")

Introduction

Broadly defined, forensic science is the application of science to criminal laws that are enforced by police agencies in a criminal justice system. While we work in the United States federal law enforcement system, our conversations with international partners and with CITES delegates (Convention on International Trade in Endangered Species of Wild Fauna and Flora) indicate that the material discussed below resonates with forensic scientists and law enforcement officers worldwide who are charged with protecting diminishing or endangered wildlife resources.

We have been asked to provide some thoughts on the future direction and needs of wildlife forensic science. Although predicting the future is fraught with pitfalls, the following is based on our over 50 years of cumulative experience in matters relating to forensic wildlife trade issues, and in the development of techniques needed to assist law enforcement in prosecuting wildlife cases. Though great advances have been made over the past few decades, the student of wildlife forensic science history will note that many of the issues discussed

Wildlife Forensics: Methods and Applications, First Edition. Edited by Jane E. Huffman and John R. Wallace.

here are similar to those discussed during the early formation of the discipline (Beattie *et al.*, 1977; Beattie and Giles, 1979).

This chapter is organized into three main sections:

1. Technical challenges to further wildlife forensic science.
2. Enhancing wildlife protection by integrating forensic science and the law.
3. The future of forensic scientists and the laboratories in which they work.

Technical Challenges

Table 17.1 summarizes the most frequently asked questions we receive related to evidence in wildlife crime cases. It is immediately apparent from this list that the scientific disciplines needed to answer each question are diverse and that the methods used for each question are technically challenging.

Table 17.1 Most frequently asked questions we receive related to forensic wildlife evidence in U.S. federal criminal investigations, arranged by our views on research priority.

Questions	Research priority	Frequency in casework	References
Where did this come from? (Geographic provenance of item)	High	Monthly	Kelly *et al.* (2008)
Identification of hybrids	High	Monthly	Haig *et al.* (2004)
Identification of subspecies	High	Monthly	Busack and Pandya (2001); Ramey *et al.* (2005, 2006)
When was it killed? (Pre- or post- the date of legal protection)	Medium	Monthly	O'Bannon (1994)
Captive vs. wild caught	Medium	Monthly	Kelly *et al.* (2008); Skaala *et al.* (2004)
Invasive and injurious species (Species identification and geographic provenance)	Medium	Yearly	Goodwin *et al.* (2010); Prentis *et al.* (2009)
What species did it come from?	Low	Daily	Yates *et al.* (2010)
What was the cause of death? (necropsy)	Low	Daily	Cooper and Cooper (2007)
Can you link the carcass to the suspect? (individualization analysis)	Low	Daily	Ogden *et al.* (2009)
How long has the animal been dead? (Time of death/post-mortem interval. Scale is from hours to years)	Low	Weekly	Cooper and Cooper (2007)
Real or fake? (of wildlife origin or imitation)	Low	Weekly	Espinoza *et al.* (2007)

Where did this come from? (Geolocation or provenance of origin of evidence items)

Determining the origin or geographic source of a carcass, or determining where wildlife evidence was collected in the wild is a challenge that needs further research. Because of the scope of the wildlife trade and the speed of modern transportation, it is generally not possible to infer geographic source either from the location of seizure, or from the natural taxonomic range of the species. In limited instances, morphological variability within a species may provide insight into an individual animal's origins. However, the two most common strategies for determining the geographic source of an evidence item are DNA-based techniques and isotopic techniques.

Geolocation: DNA-based techniques

Using DNA to determine the geographic source of an animal (e.g., elephant) or part of an animal (e.g., ivory tusk) is based on the premise that wildlife populations have identifiable genetic profiles based on their limited interbreeding with populations in other geographic areas. Wasser *et al.* (2004, 2007) have successfully used DNA profiling for sourcing ivory from African elephants covering the vast range of the African continent. Brown *et al.* (2009) used genetic techniques to document the effect of anthropogenic events leading to changes in the population distribution of black bears in California. Fain, Straughan and Taylor (2010) demonstrated that genetic markers are useful for determining the provenance of gray wolves from the Western Great Lakes region (Minnesota, Wisconsin, and Michigan). In all of these examples, the sample sizes are large and the conclusions are robust, but the obvious limitation is that the data cannot be extrapolated to different species. For example, if within five years the priority is to define the provenance of rhinoceros horns, then a new research effort is needed (i.e., funding, collection of samples, selection of appropriate loci, statistical modeling, etc.).

> **Future Need No. 1**
>
> Develop large DNA databases for taxa seen in trade so that geographic assignments or individualization can be made using genetic markers.

Geolocation: isotopic techniques

Another approach to determining geographic source of illegal wildlife contraband is to utilize isotope ratios that are specific to given geographic locations.

The strategy is based upon the fact that living organisms possess isotopic signatures that reflect the geographic location in which a particular species resides (Bowen *et al.*, 2005; West *et al.*, 2006). In some cases, an isotopic signature may even be indicative of an animal's natal origin (Wunder *et al.*, 2005; Wunder and Norris, 2008). Similarly, incorporation by organisms of trace elements from the environment can lead to geographic source identification of the organism once the appropriate elemental profiles have been established (Coetzee *et al.*, 2005).

Future Need No. 2

There is a need to create isotopic and/or elemental maps of the regions from where wildlife trade originates. Priorities for database development include the Amazon basin and Sub-Saharan Africa.

Identification of hybrids

As discussed below, the United States Endangered Species Act (ESA) does not protect hybrids, and thus suspects in wildlife crime investigations may claim that an animal they shot was a hybrid in order to evade prosecution. Genetic analysis is helpful in the identification of hybrids in the law enforcement context, as has been demonstrated for hybrids between wolves and dogs (Fain, *et al.*, 2010) and between Spotted and Barred Owls (Haig *et al.*, 2004). It is generally assumed that hybridization is maladaptive, and is an unusual phenomenon among free-living animals. But this may be changing, due in part to global climate change. Kelly, Whiteley and Tallmon (2010) recently reported 34 novel hybrids associated with the disappearance of the Arctic ice cap. The challenges associated with novel hybrids are immense, including: (1) do they have a value in the ecosystem?; (2) should they have legal protection?; and (3) can wildlife forensic science determine if an animal that expresses unusual phenotypes is a hybrid or not?

Future Need No. 3

Need to develop legally-accepted criteria to test whether novel-looking animals are hybrids. See also Future Need No. 11 for legal considerations.

Identification of subspecies

The ESA treats subspecies differently depending on the groups to which they belong. Subspecies of plants are not listed on the ESA, and therefore their identification is not required in the law enforcement context. However, subspecies of vertebrates and invertebrates are listed by name on the ESA, and thus wildlife forensic scientists are often asked to identify insect, reptile, bird, and mammal remains at the subspecies level. Subspecies are typically defined by the location in which they live. They often differ in only slight and subtle morphological characters, and may be indistinguishable based on DNA analysis. Since there are many instances where one or two subspecies are protected and others are not, it can be difficult to prove in court that the protected subspecies is the one the defendant was associated with. Savvy defendants may know this and use it as a defense.

In *U.S. v. One Handbag of Crocodilus Species*, 586 F.Supp. 128 (1994), a defendant imported 57 handbags composed of three main crocodilian subspecies, one of which was listed as endangered under the ESA at the time of the case. The defense argued that it was impossible to distinguish between the crocodilian subspecies in the finished condition they were in and presented testimony from an expert witness to support the argument. The government's expert testified that while there is no "fail safe" way to make the identification, the endangered subspecies commonly contains two identifiable characteristics and each unprotected subspecies only normally contain one. The court relied on the government's expert testimony and the defendant was ordered to forfeit the items. This case is an example of how close these cases can be. Morphological analysis depends on the form and condition of the wildlife evidence. In some instances, even if the entire animal is available for analysis, distinguishing subspecies can be extremely difficult.

Future Need No. 4

Develop detailed genetic databases allowing subspecies to be distinguished even with modified or partial remains. See also Future Need No. 12 for legal considerations.

When was it killed?

The laws that regulate the importation of threatened and endangered species have exceptions that allow for the importation of items from animals killed before the Act was instituted. Knowing if an animal was killed before or after a law was enacted is helpful in prosecutions.

Radioisotopes of carbon 14 (^{14}C) can be used on terrestrial mammals and birds to determine when an animal was killed. The theoretical foundation for this analysis is based on the fact that around 1964, atmospheric $^{14}CO_2$ became artificially elevated due to atmospheric testing of nuclear weapons from 1950–63. The levels of ^{14}C, which had been constant for the last 4000 years (Bowman, 1990) have not yet returned to historic levels seen before the weapons testing (Levin *et al.*, 1994; Manning and Melhuish, 1994). The decay curve of ^{14}C is useful for making inferences when a living animal last absorbed environmental ^{14}C. Birds, for example, which molt all of their feathers annually, are good examples where determining the level as ^{14}C accurately reflects the year of killing. Elephant ivory tusks are another good example where a ^{14}C analysis of the base (reflecting year of death) and tip (reflecting year of birth) allows year of death to be inferred with precision. Unfortunately, the incorporation of atmospheric $^{14}CO_2$ into marine environments is more complicated and to date, it is very difficult to determine if a marine mammal tusk (i.e., walrus), tooth (i.e., sperm and killer whale), or rug (i.e., polar bear) was killed before or after a particular date.

Future Need No. 5

Need for more basic research on the incorporation of atmospheric $^{14}CO_2$ into marine environments, to allow determination of year of death for marine mammal products. Alternatively, there is a need to change the laws that are unenforceable.

Captive bred vs. wild caught

The live-animal trade is an ever-increasing threat to wildlife populations. Captive-bred animals may be exempt from certain wildlife laws in some countries. Suspects frequently claim that live animals in their possession were captive-bred, and it may be difficult to disprove this with currently available methods. Analysis of stable isotopes is one promising avenue, particularly for animals that have only recently come out of the wild (e.g., birds that have not yet gone through a molt cycle) (Kelly *et al.*, 2008).

Future Need No. 6

More research needs to be done on the effectiveness of stable isotope analysis and other techniques for verifying whether live animals were taken out of the wild, or were bred and reared in captivity.

Injurious and invasive species

The U.S. Fish and Wildlife Service Office of Law Enforcement works to prevent the introduction of injurious and invasive species into the United States through the enforcement of the Lacey Act and its implementing regulations. The Lacey Act makes it illegal in the United States to import injurious wildlife or transport such wildlife between states without a permit. The ecological changes associated with global warming are facilitating the establishment of invasive species in areas where their presence is harmful to the ecosystem. This is leading to a dramatic increase in requests for forensic analysis related to invasive species.

The term "injurious wildlife" refers to a defined list of species identified in either the Lacey Act itself or in the related regulations. Species are placed on the list when they are determined to be injurious to human beings to the interests of agriculture, horticulture, forestry, or wildlife or to wildlife resources in the United States. Some of the most damaging invasive species, of course, are plants, including both noxious weeds and woody plants.

The biggest future challenge in this area for wildlife forensic scientists is how to identify the source of an injurious or invasive species. In addition, certain groups with many invasive species concerns, such as marine organisms and plants, pose significant identification challenges. In the legal and legislative arenas, there is a need to develop faster and more flexible responses to the multi-faceted threats posed by invasive and injurious species.

Future Need No. 7

Develop genetic databases from potential source populations of invasive organisms.

Future Need No. 8

Expand the pool of specialists available to identify invasive organisms and those qualified to work in the forensic context.

Identifying future trends

Finally, there is an urgent need for a better system to anticipate and identify emerging trends in the wildlife trade. This will require enhanced communication among forensic scientists, law enforcement officials, and field biologists. A recent article (Phelps *et al.*, 2010) highlighted this issue and proposed several approaches for funding enhanced data collection. In addition to these ideas, we propose that a mechanism be developed to upload the species identifications made by wildlife forensic scientists into CITES trade databases. In the United States, trade data are collected in a government database called LEMIS, which codes species information based on import declarations and/or the evaluation of wildlife inspectors at ports of entry. There is no system in place to amend these initial data with the conclusive identifications made by wildlife forensic scientists.

The work of wildlife forensic scientists has been vital in documenting emerging trade in bushmeat, shark fins, hornbill skulls, bear gall bladders, American ginseng, and many other wildlife products (Espinoza *et al.*, 1993; Trail, 2007; Chapman *et al.*, 2009). This contribution could be made even more effective through the development of more comprehensive and timely data-sharing.

Future Need No. 9

Develop a mechanism to input the conclusions of wildlife forensic scientists into CITES trade databases, and explore other mechanisms for the identification of emerging trends in the wildlife trade.

Enhancing Wildlife Protection by Integrating Forensic Science and the Law

In this section, we note several areas in which the laws established for the protection of wildlife confront the limitations of science; and conversely, situations in which cutting-edge science is not reflected in our current legal framework.

Taxonomy and the law

Biological taxonomy pervades the work of wildlife forensic scientists. The organisms that are protected by US and international wildlife laws are legally designated by their scientific names, that is, by their species or subspecies taxonomic classification. These designations are collected together to comprise the U.S. Endangered Species List, the lists of species protected under CITES Appendices I, II, and III, the Migratory Bird Treaty Act list, etc. Fish and Wildlife Service permits (including import, export, scientific collecting, and depredation permits) are issued for particular organisms, designated by taxonomic name. Enforcement officers must make decisions in the field regarding the legality of activities involving wildlife based on the taxonomic names of the species represented. Laboratory analysts are called upon to identify wildlife parts and products to species, using reference specimens, dichotomous keys, and other data, that all reflect taxonomic classification. In short, wildlife law enforcement is completely dependent on taxonomic information. To fulfill our mission, we require taxonomic information that is accurate, authoritative, and consistent.

Taxonomy and classification are ongoing scientific activities, and therefore taxonomy undergoes continual revision based on new data. Recent decades have seen an explosion of research on evolutionary relationships using DNA sequences and other molecular data, and these have led to many changes in taxonomy. In many instances, ESA or CITES-listed organisms have undergone taxonomic revision since their listing. A well-known example concerns the Preble's meadow jumping mouse, which was listed on the ESA in 1998 as a threatened subspecies (*Zapus hudsonius preblei*). Subsequent genetic and morphological research questioned whether this form is a discrete taxonomic entity, leading to an extended controversy over its eligibility for endangered species protection (Ramey *et al.*, 2005, 2006; Vignieri *et al.*, 2006).

Most taxonomic revisions (e.g., transfer from one genus to another) do not affect the listed status of a species. Nevertheless, such changes result in discordance between the classification of an organism under wildlife law and under current scientific taxonomy. This creates the potential for confusion on the part of both the public and law enforcement officials that may greatly hinder effective wildlife law enforcement. This can be particularly problematic in courtroom situations, where enforcement officers and forensic scientists may be called upon to explain taxonomic discrepancies, substantially weakening the case in the eyes of judge and jury.

Future Need No. 10

Wildlife forensic scientists must be familiar with both the legal and scientific realms, and are often the experts most qualified to interpret taxonomic questions in a legal context. Therefore, taxonomy should be incorporated into the training of wildlife forensic scientists, and mechanisms should be developed to allow forensic scientists to provide input when listing decisions are made.

The U.S. Endangered Species Act and the Limits of Science

Hybrids

Wildlife law enforcement has a need for more clarity on the legal status of hybrid organisms. The ESA does not specifically mention hybrids, which are thus considered to be unprotected. For example, a hybrid between a Northern Spotted Owl (ESA-listed) and Barred Owl (not ESA-listed) would have no protections under the ESA. On the other hand, CITES protects hybrid organisms at the level of the more-protected "parent" taxon. Thus a hybrid between a Gyrfalcon (CITES I) and a Prairie Falcon (CITES II) would be protected at the CITES I level.

This problem is not limited to hybridization that occurs in the wild, such as between Barred and Spotted Owls. Many hybrids are now being deliberately produced in captivity, for a variety of purposes. For example, falconers have long interbred falcon species to obtain desired combinations, such as the Peregrine's speed with the Gyrfalcon's size. The operators of hunting ranches in the United States, South Africa, and elsewhere are now routinely conducting interbreeding of big game species (e.g., sheep and antelope) to produce novel trophies.

To cite one concrete example, in *U.S. v. Kapp*, 419 F. 3d 666 (2005), the defendant was convicted by a jury of violating the ESA for the killing of, and trafficking in endangered tigers and leopards. On appeal, he claimed that the government failed to prove beyond a reasonable doubt that the tigers were not unprotected hybrids with lions ("ligers" or "tigons"). If the animal at issue turned out to be a hybrid, it would not have been afforded protection by the

ESA and the defendant would have had an effective argument. The morphology and DNA experts that testified in the case successfully proved the animal was a tiger and the conviction for ESA violations relating to tigers was upheld. In this case, the morphology of the animal was clear and the credibility of the expert was impeccable, but other hybrid cases may not always fare the same. The DNA expert identified the DNA as coming from tigers but conceded that current DNA identification methods could not definitively rule out the possibility that there could be some lion genes in the animal's paternal history. If the animal in this case were reduced to a form where morphology would not have been able to contribute, such as bone powder, the result might have been entirely different. This case is a cautionary tale about how defendants can build hurdles for the prosecution by simply mentioning the word "hybrid."

The U.S. Fish and Wildlife Service worked on hybrid policy years ago but the policy was never finalized and so the hybrid defense is still a viable strategy in some cases. This will continue to be a challenge in prosecuting cases as more and more hybrid forms develop in the future, both due to deliberate cross-breeding, and to range shifts associated with climate change. Higher instances of hybrids will impose a higher burden on scientists to perform extensive research to determine whether wildlife at issue in a case are hybrids or not. Currently this ability exists with only a limited number of hybrid species. This problem could be more easily solved if the ESA were amended to address hybrids and where they fall under the law.

Future Need No. 11

Expand legal protections to include hybrids, thus eliminating the need to assess hybrid status. See also Future Need No. 3 for technical considerations.

Subspecies

The ESA does two things to address the problem of subspecies identification difficulties: (1) the ESA is written to require only general intent; and (2) subpart E of the ESA provides protection for unlisted species that are similar in appearance to listed species.

The general intent aspect of the ESA will stop the defense of "I couldn't tell the protected subspecies apart from the unprotected subspecies and so thought I shot the unprotected subspecies." General intent requires only that the defendant shot at an animal, not that he recognized what he was shooting. *United States v. McKittrick*, 142 F.3d 1170 (9th Cir.1998), *cert. denied*, 525 U.S. 1072, 119 S.Ct. 806, 142 L.Ed.2d 667 (1999). "[B]ecause it would be nearly impossible to prove that the average hunter recognized the particular subspecies protected under the [ESA]..., the [g]overnment need prove only that the defendant acted with general intent when he shot the animal in question." (footnote omitted). *United States v. Billie*, 667 F.Supp. 1485, 1493 (S.D.Fla.1987).

Subpart E of the ESA provides protection for unlisted species that are similar in appearance to listed species. The Director of the Fish and Wildlife Service has authority to determine whether an unlisted species is so similar in appearance to a listed species that it also deserves protection as if it were listed. The criteria for this determination are: whether enforcement personnel would have substantial difficulty in attempting to differentiate between listed and unlisted species; whether the difficulty would pose an additional threat to listed species; and whether treating the unlisted species as listed would facilitate enforcement and further the policy of the ESA. The "similarity of appearance" clause must be in place before a case can be prosecuted based on the similar appearance status of a species. While this seems to offer an effective solution to the subspecies problem, there are few instances currently where similarity of appearance has been invoked to broaden ESA protections.

> **Future Need No. 12**
>
> Reassess the practice of listing vertebrate subspecies under the ESA. See also Future Need No. 4 for technical considerations.

The Future of Forensic Scientists and the Laboratories in which They Work

Forensic laboratory accreditation

From a wildlife forensic point to view, laboratory accreditation is more easily accomplished than scientists' certification. The existing accreditation bodies (i.e., ASCLD, ISO 17025, etc.) have clearly laid out the principles and expectations of what needs to be done to become an accredited forensic laboratory. The requirements are challenging for small labs that are poorly budgeted and understaffed, but it can be done.

> **Future Need No. 13**
>
> All forensic wildlife laboratories should be accredited by a recognized accrediting body.

Forensic scientist certification

Devising a certification program for wildlife forensic scientists themselves is a challenge that up to now has not been fully explored. The difficulties arise from:

(1) the breadth of scientific disciplines (e.g., ornithologists, herpetologists, population geneticists, economists to estimate resource damage assessment, wood anatomists, etc.); (2) the limited number of scientists who work full-time in wildlife forensic labs (in some disciplines, less than six scientists nationwide); and (3) the dynamic illegal wildlife trade that goes from one species to another, depending on market price and availability of diminishing endangered species. The challenges involved in the identification (class character analysis) of approximately 5,000 mammal species, 10,000 bird species, and 9,000 reptile species are daunting. The challenge to individualize all these taxa is, at this moment, insurmountable.

Another challenge associated with a wildlife forensic science certification is that there are unique forensic needs associated with different geographic areas of the country. Most of the human forensic laboratories in the United States deal with the allele frequencies of a single species: *Homo sapiens*. Because criminal prosecutions rely on the accuracy of "DNA fingerprinting," every state and many federal forensic labs have dedicated millions of dollars to developing large DNA databases that are the basis for statistical statements of identity.

In contrast, state wildlife forensic scientists are concerned with the taxa that are protected within their boundaries. Therefore a Great Basin forensic scientist may have a comprehensive DNA database for *Antilocapra americana*, an East Coast forensic scientist may have a comprehensive DNA database for *Odocoileus virginianus*, and a West Coast scientist may have a comprehensive DNA database for *Ursus americanus*. Therefore different labs have selected different species and loci for their respective databases, unlike our human-centric counterparts that have: (1) a single nationwide database; (2) the luxury of commercial kits using the same loci; and (3) access to commercial allelic ladders. We note that components of the certification process for human-based forensic scientists test their knowledge of the national DNA database.

A proposal for wildlife forensic scientist certification

In April of 2010, approximately 120 wildlife forensic scientists representing over 50 laboratories met at the inaugural triennial meeting of the Society for Wildlife Forensic Science (SWFS) (for a list of current laboratory members, see http://www.wildlifeforensicscience.org/). The mission of the SWFS is to develop wildlife forensic science into a comprehensive, integrated, and mature discipline. Some of the strategies to accomplish this mission are for the SWFS to promote the exchange of scientific and technical information, to encourage research in wildlife forensics, and to promote professional competence, uniform qualifications, certification, and ethical behavior among wildlife forensic scientists.

The SWFS has been a leader in the preparation, distribution and assessment of a wildlife proficiency genetics program that has been active since January of 2004. The SWFS has organized a group of wildlife forensic scientists and has developed a set of "Best Practices" to be adopted by all members' labs. The work product is similar to those produced in the United States by the Scientific Working Groups (SWGs) for other forensic disciplines.

Therefore, given (1) the uniqueness of wildlife forensic science; (2) the diversity of taxa involved; (3) the small number of practicing wildlife forensic scientists; and (4) the role of the SWFS in providing proficiency tests and the development of wildlife forensic best practices, we advocate that the SWFS take the lead in developing certification standards for wildlife forensic scientists.

Future Need No. 14

The Society for Wildlife Forensic Science, in consultation with it members, should develop a certification program for wildlife forensic scientists.

Conclusion

As scientific technology continues to advance, we view the future of wildlife forensic science with great optimism, but also with a sense of urgency, as wildlife resources throughout the world are impacted by habitat loss, over-exploitation, and climate change. In our view, the future of the discipline will center around three major areas. These include: (1) technical challenges in the further development of wildlife forensic science; (2) enhancing wildlife protection by integrating forensic science and the law; and (3) the future of forensic scientists and the laboratories in which they work. We reiterate here below our specific recommendations for developing wildlife forensic science into a comprehensive, integrated, and mature discipline.

1. **Future Need No. 1**: Develop large DNA databases for taxa seen in trade so that geographic assignments or individualization can be made using genetic markers.
2. **Future Need No. 2**: There is a need to create isotopic and/or elemental maps of the regions from where wildlife trade originates. Priorities for database development include the Amazon basin and Sub-Saharan Africa.
3. **Future Need No. 3:** Need to develop legally-accepted criteria to test whether novel-looking animals are hybrids. See also Future Need No. 11 for legal considerations.
4. **Future Need No. 4:** Develop detailed genetic databases allowing subspecies to be distinguished even with modified or partial remains. See also Future Need No. 12 for legal considerations.
5. **Future Need No. 5:** Need for more basic research on the incorporation of atmospheric $^{14}CO_2$ into marine environments, to allow determination of year of death for marine mammal products. Alternatively, there is a need to change the laws that are unenforceable.

6. **Future Need No. 6:** More research needs to be done on the effectiveness of stable isotope analysis and other techniques for verifying whether live animals were taken out of the wild, or were bred and reared in captivity.
7. **Future Need No. 7:** Develop genetic databases from potential source populations of invasive organisms.
8. **Future Need No. 8:** Expand the pool of specialists available to identify invasive organisms and those qualified to work in the forensic context.
9. **Future Need No. 9:** Develop a mechanism to input the conclusions of wildlife forensic scientists into CITES trade databases, and explore other mechanisms for the identification of emerging trends in the wildlife trade.
10. **Future Need No. 10:** Wildlife forensic scientists must be familiar with both the legal and scientific realms, and are often the experts most qualified to interpret taxonomic questions in a legal context. Therefore, taxonomy should be incorporated into the training of wildlife forensic scientists, and mechanisms should be developed to allow forensic scientists to provide input when listing decisions are made.
11. **Future Need No. 11:** Expand legal protections to include hybrids, thus eliminating the need to assess hybrid status. See also Future Need No. 3 for technical considerations.
12. **Future Need No. 12:** Reassess the practice of listing vertebrate subspecies under the ESA. See also Future Need No. 4 for technical considerations.
13. **Future Need No. 13:** All forensic wildlife laboratories should be accredited by a recognized accrediting body.
14. **Future Need No. 14:** The SWFS, in consultation with its members, should develop a certification program for wildlife forensic scientists.

Acknowledgments

The opinions, findings, and conclusions in this chapter are those of the authors and do not necessarily represent the views of the U.S. Fish and Wildlife Service. We thank Jane Huffman and John Wallace for inviting us to contribute this chapter and for the opportunity to provide our thoughts on the future of wildlife forensic science.

References

Beattie, K.H. and Giles, R.H. (1979) A survey of wildlife law enforcement research needs and current research. *Wildlife Society Bulletin*, 7, 185–188.

Beattie, K.H., Giles, R.H. and Cowles, C.J. (1977) Lack of research in wildlife law enforcement. *Wildlife Society Bulletin*, 5, 170–174.

Bowen, G.J., Wassenaar, L.I. and Hobson, K.A. (2005) Global application of stable hydrogen and oxygen isotopes to wildlife forensics. *Oecologia*, **143**, 337–348.

Bowman, S. (1990) *Interpreting the Past: Radiocarbon Dating*. Berkeley, CA: University of California Press.

Brown, S.K., Hull, J.M., Updike, D.R., Fain, S.R. and Ernest, H.B. (2009) Black bear population genetics in California: signatures of population structure, competitive release, and historical translocation. *Journal of Mammalogy*, **90**, 1066–1074.

Busack, S.D. and Pandya, S. (2001) Geographic variation in *Caiman crocodilus* and *Caiman yacare* (Crocodylia: Alligatoridae): systematic and legal implications. *Herpetologica*, **57**, 294–312.

Chapman, D.D., Pinhal, D. and Shivji, M.S. (2009) Tracking the fin trade: genetic stock identification in western Atlantic scalloped hammerhead sharks *Sphyrna lewini*. *Endangered Species Research*, **9**, 221–228.

Coetzee, P.P., Steffens, F.E., Eiselen, R.J., Augustyn, O.P., Balcaen, L. and Vanhaecke, F. (2005) Multi-element analysis of South African wines by ICP-MS and their classification according to geographical origin. *Journal of Agricultural and Food Chemistry*, **53**, 5060–5066.

Cooper, J.E. and Cooper M.E. (2007) *Introduction to Veterinary and Comparative Forensic Medicine*. Oxford: Blackwell Publishing.

Espinoza, E.O., Baker, B.W. and Berry, C.A. (2007) The analysis of sea turtle and bovid keratin artefacts using DRIFT spectroscopy and discriminant analysis. *Archaeometry* **49**, 685–698.

Espinoza, E.O., Shafer, J.A. and Hagey, L.R. (1993) International trade in bear gall bladders: forensic source inference. *Journal of Forensic Sciences*, **38**, 1363–1371.

Fain, S.R., Straughan, D.J. and Taylor, B.F. (2010) Genetic outcomes of wolf recovery in the western Great Lakes states. *Conservation Genetics*, **11**, 1747–1765.

Goodwin, D.H., Cohen, A.N. and Roopnarine, P.D. (2010) Forensics on the half shell: a sclerochronological investigation of a modern biological invasion in San Francisco Bay, United States. *Palaios*, **25**, 742–753.

Haig, S.M., Mullins, T.D., Forsman, E.D., Trail, P.W. and Wennerberg, L. (2004) Genetic identification of Spotted Owls, Barred Owls, and their hybrids: legal implications of hybrid identity. *Conservation Biology*, **18**, 1347–1357.

Kelly, A., Thompson, R. and Newton, J. (2008) Stable hydrogen isotope analysis as a method to identify illegally trapped songbirds. *Science & Justice*, **48**, 67–70.

Kelly,B.P., Whiteley, A., and Tallmon, D. (2010) The Arctic melting pot. *Nature*, **468**, 891.

Levin, I., Kromer, B., Schoch-Fischer, H., Bruns, M., Münnich, M., Berdau, D., Vogel, J.C. and Münnich, K.O. (1994) $\delta^{14}CO_2$ record from Vermont. In *Trends: A Compendium of Data on Global Change*. Oak Ridge, TN: Carbon Dioxide Information Analysis Center, Oak Ridge National Laboratory, U.S. Department of Energy.

Manning, M.R. and Melhuish, W.H. (1994) Atmospheric $\delta^{14}C$ record from Wellington. In *Trends: A Compendium of Data on Global Change*. Oak Ridge, TN: Carbon Dioxide Information Analysis Center, Oak Ridge National Laboratory, U.S. Department of Energy.

O'Bannon, J.K. (1994) Scientific dating and the law: establishing the age of old objects for legal purposes. *University of Missouri Kansas City Law Review*, **63**, 93–132.

Ogden, R., Dawnay, N. and McEwing, R. (2009) Wildlife DNA forensics: bridging the gap between conservation genetics and law enforcement. *Endangered Species Research*, **9**, 179–195.

Phelps, J., Webb, E.L., Bickford, D., Nijman, V. and Sodhi, N.S. (2010) Boosting CITES. *Science* **330**, 1752–1753.

Prentis, P.J., Sigg, D.P., Raghu, S., Dhileepan, K., Pavasovic, A. and Lowe, A.J. (2009) Understanding invasion history: genetic structure and diversity of two globally invasive plants and implications for their management. *Diversity and Distributions*, **15**, 822–830.

Ramey, R.R. II, Liu, H.-P., Epps, C.W., Carpenter, L.M. and Wehausen, J.D. (2005) Genetic relatedness of the Preble's meadow jumping mouse (*Zapus hudsonius preblei*) to nearby subspecies of *Z. hudsonius* as inferred from variation in cranial morphology, mitochondrial DNA and microsatellite DNA: implications for taxonomy and conservation. *Animal Conservation*, **8**, 329–346.

Ramey, R.R. II, Wehausen, J.D., Liu, H.-P., Epps, C.W. and Carpenter, L.M. (2006) Response to Vignieri *et al.* (2006): Should hypothesis testing or selective *post hoc* interpretation of results guide the allocation of conservation effort? *Animal Conservation*, **9**, 244–247.

Skaala, O., Hoyheim, B., Glover, K. and Dahle, G. (2004) Microsatellite analysis in domesticated and wild Atlantic salmon (*Salmo salar* L.): allelic diversity and identification of individuals. *Aquaculture*, **240**, 131–143.

Society for Wildlife Forensic Science. Available at: http://www.wildlifeforensicscience.org/.

Trail, P.W. (2007) African hornbills: keystone species threatened by habitat loss, hunting and international trade. *Ostrich*, **78**, 609–613.

Vignieri, S.N., Hallerman, E.M., Bergstrom, B.J., Hafner, D.J., Martin, A.P., Devers, P., Grobler, P. and Hitt, N. (2006) Mistaken view of taxonomic validity undermines conservation of an evolutionary distinct mouse: a response to Ramey *et al.* (2005). *Animal Conservation*, **9**, 237–243.

Wasser, S.K., Mailand, C., Booth, R., Mutayoba, B., Kisamo, E., Clark, B. and Stephens, M. (2007) Using DNA to track the origin of the largest ivory seizure since the 1989 trade ban. *Proceedings of the National Academy of Sciences*, **104**, 4228–4233.

Wasser, S.K., Shedlock, A.M., Comstock, K., Ostrander, E.A., Mutayoba, B. and Stephens, M. (2004) Assigning African elephant DNA to geographic region of origin: applications to the ivory trade. *Proceedings of the National Academy of Sciences*, **101**, 14847–14852.

West, J.B., Bowen, G.J., Cerling, T.E. and Ehleringer, J.R. (2006) Stable isotopes as one of nature's ecological recorders. *Trends in Ecology and Evolution*, **21**, 408–414.

Wunder, M.B., Kester, C.L., Knopf, F.L. and Rye, R.O. (2005) A test of geographic assignment using isotope tracers in feathers of known origin. *Oecologia*, **144**, 607–617.

Wunder, M.B. and Norris, D.R. (2008). Improved estimates of certainty in stable-isotope-based methods for tracking migratory animals. *Ecological Applications*, **18**, 549–559.

Yates, B.C., Espinoza, E.O. and Baker, B.W. (2010) Forensic species identification of elephant (Elephantidae) and giraffe (Giraffidae) tail hair using light microscopy. *Forensic Science, Medicine and Pathology*, **6**, 165–171.

Index

Wildlife Forensics: Methods and Applications, First Edition. Edited by Jane E. Huffman and John R. Wallace.